PHILOSOPHICAL
TRANSACTIONS OF
THE ROYAL SOCIETY

Volume I

TO THE
Royal Society.

It will not become me, to adde any Attributes to a Title, which has a Fulness of Lustre from his Majesties Denomination.

In these Rude Collections, which are onely the Gleanings of my private diversions in broken hours, it may appear, that many Minds and Hands are in many places industriously employed, under Your Countenance, and by Your Example, in the pursuit of those Excellent Ends, which belong to Your Heroical Undertakings.

Some of these are but the Intimations of large Compilements. And some Eminent Members of Your Society, have obliged the Learned World with Incomparable Volumes, which are not herein mention'd, because they were finisht, and in great Reputation abroad, before I entred upon this Taske. And no small Number are at present engaged for those weighty Productions, which require both Time and Assistance, for their due Maturity. So that no man can from these Glimpses of Light take any just Measure of Your Performances, or of Your Prosecutions; but every man may perhaps receive some benefit from these Parcels, which I guessed to be somewhat conformable to Your Design.

This is my Solicitude, That, as I ought not to be unfaithful to those Counsels you have committed to my Trust, so also that I may not altogether waste any minutes of the leasure you afford me. And thus have I made the best use of some of them, that I could devise; To spread abroad Encouragements, Inquiries, Directions, and Patterns, that may animate, and draw on Universal Assistances.

The Great God *prosper You in the Noble Engagement of Dispersing the true Lustre of his Glorious Works, and the Happy Inventions of obliging Men all over the World, to the General Benefit of Mankind: So wishes with real Affections,*

Your humble and obedient Servant
HENRY OLDENBURG.

{1}

PHILOSOPHICAL
TRANSACTIONS.

Munday, March 6. 166⁴/₅.

The Contents.

An Introduction to this Tract. An Accompt of the Improvement of Optick Glasses *at* Rome. *Of the Observation made in* England, *of a Spot in one of the Belts of the Planet* Jupiter. *Of the motion of the late* Comet *prædicted. The Heads of many New Observations and Experiments, in order to an Experimental* History of Cold; *together with some* Thermometrical *Discourses and Experiments. A Relation of a very odd Monstrous* Calf. *Of a peculiar* Lead-Ore *in* Germany, *very useful for Essays. Of an* Hungarian Bolus, *of the same effect with the* Bolus Armenus. *Of the New* American *Whale-fishing about the* Bermudas. *A Narative concerning the success of the* Pendulum-watches *at Sea for the* Longitudes; *and the Grant of a* Patent *thereupon. A Catalogue of the Philosophical Books publisht by* Monsieur de Fermat, *Counsellour at* Tholouse, *lately dead.*

The Introduction.

Whereas there is nothing more necessary for promoting the improvement of Philosophical Matters, than the communicating to such, as apply their Studies and Endeavours that way, such things as are discovered or put in practise by others, it is therefore thought fit to employ the *Press*, as the most proper way to gratifie those, whose engagement in such Studies, and delight in the advancement of Learning and profitable Discoveries, doth entitle them to the knowledge of what this Kingdom, or other parts of the World, do, from time to time, afford, as well {2} of the progress of the Studies, Labours, and attempts of the Curious and learned in things of this kind, as of their compleat Discoveries and performances: To the end, that such Productions being clearly and truly communicated, desires after solid and usefull knowledge may be further entertained, ingenious Endeavours and Undertakings cherished, and those, addicted to and conversant in such matters, may be invited and encouraged to search, try, and find out new things, impart their knowledge to one another, and contribute what they can to the Grand design of improving Natural knowledge, and perfecting all *Philosophical Arts*, and *Sciences*. All for the Glory of God, the Honour and Advantage of these Kingdoms, and the Universal Good of Mankind.

An Accompt of the improvement of Optick Glasses.

There came lately from *Paris* a Relation, concerning the Improvement of *Optick Glasses*, not long since attempted at *Rome* by Signor *Giuseppe Campani*, and by him discoursed of, in a Book, Entituled, *Ragguaglio di nuoue Osservationi*, lately printed in the said City, but not yet transmitted into these parts; wherein these following particulars, according to the Intelligence, which was sent hither, are contained.

The *First* regardeth the excellency of the long *Telescopes*, made by the said *Campani*, who pretends to have found a way to work great *Optick Glasses* with a Turne-tool, without any Mould: And whereas hitherto it hath been found by Experience, that *small* Glasses are in proportion better to see with, upon the Earth, than the *great* ones; that Author affirms, that his are equally good for the Earth, and for making Observations in the Heavens. Besides, he useth three Eye-Glasses for his great *Telescopes*, without finding any *Iris*, or such Rain-bow colours, as do usually appear in ordinary Glasses, and prove an impediment to Observations.

The *Second*, concerns the *Circle of Saturn*, in which he hath observed nothing, but what confirms Monsieur *Christian Huygens de Zulichem* his Systeme of that Planet, published by that worthy Gentleman in the year, 1659.{3}

The *Third*, respects *Jupiter*, wherein *Campani* affirms he hath observed by the goodness of his Glasses, certain *protuberancies* and *inequalities*, much greater than those that have been seen therein hitherto. He addeth, that he is now observing, whether those sallies in the said*Planet* do not change their scituation, which if they should be found to do, he judgeth, that*Jupiter* might then be said to turn upon his *Axe*; which, in his opinion, would serve much to confirm the opinion of *Copernicus*. Besides this, he affirms, he hath remarked in the *Belts* of*Jupiter*, the shaddows of his *satellites*, and followed them, and at length seen them emerge out of his Disk.

A Spot in one of the Belts of Jupiter.

The Ingenious Mr. *Hook* did, some moneths since, intimate to a friend of his, that he had, with an excellent twelve foot Telescope, observed, some days before, he than spoke of it, (*videl.* on the ninth of *May*, 1664, about 9 of the clock at night) a small Spot in the biggest of the 3 obscurer *Belts* of *Jupiter*, and that, observing it from time to time, he found, that within 2 hours after, the said Spot had moved from East to West, about half the length of the Diameter of *Jupiter*.

The Motion of the late Comet prædicted.

There was lately sent to one of the *Secretaries* of the *Royal Society* a Packet, containing some Copies of a Printed Paper, Entituled, The *Ephemerides* of the *Comet*, made by the same Person, that sent it, called *Monsieur Auzout*, a *French* Gentleman of no ordinary Merit and Learning, who desired, that a couple of them might be recommended to the said *Society*, and one to their *President*, and another to his Highness Prince *Rupert*, and the rest to some other Persons, nominated by him in a Letter that accompanied this present, and known abroad for their singular abilities and knowledge in Philosophical Matters. The end of the Communication of this Paper was, That, the motion of the *Comet*, that hath lately appeared, having been prædicted by the said *Monsieur* {4}*Auzout*, after he had seen it (as himself affirms) but 4 or 5 times: the *Virtuosi* of *England*, among others, might compare also their Observations with his *Ephemerides*, either to confirm the *Hypothesis*, upon which the *Author*had before hand calculated the way of this Star, or to undeceive him, if he be in a mistake. The said Author Dedicateth these his conceptions to the most Christian King, telling him, that he presents Him with a design, which never yet was undertaken by any *Astronomer*, all the World having been hitherto perswaded, that the motions of *Comets* were so irregular, that they could not be reduced to any Laws, and men having contented themselves, to observe exactly the places, through which they did pass; but no man, that he knows, having been so bold as to venture to foretel the places, through which they should pass, and where they should cease to appear: Whereas he exhibites here the *Ephemerides*, determining day by day, in what place of the Heavens this *Comet* shall be, at what hour it shall be in its *Meridian*, and at what hour it shall set; untill its too great remoteness, or the approach of the Sun, hide it from our eyes. Descending to particulars, he saith, that this Star, being disengaged from the beams of the Sun might have been observed, if his conjectures be good, ever since it hath been of 17 or 18 degrees *Southern Latitude*, and that about the middle of *November* last, and sooner, unless it have been too small: That however it hath been seen in *Holland* ever since the *2d.* of *December* last, at which time, according to his reckoning, the Diurnal motion of the *Comet* should already amount to 17 or 18 minutes. He finds, that this Star moveth *just enough* in the Plan of a *Great Circle*, which inclineth to the *Equinoctial* about 30 degrees, and to the *Ecliptick* about 49*d.* or 49½ cutting the *Equator* at about 45*d*½, and the *Ecliptick* at the 28*d* of *Aries*, or a little more. He saith *just enough*, because he thinks, there may perhaps be some *parallaxe*, which he wisheth could be determined.

Hence, (*so he goes on*) every one who pleaseth, may see, in tracing the *Comet* upon the *Globe*, through, or by which Stars it hath passed and shall pass; adding, that there will be neither cause to wonder, that having descended to about 6. deg. beneath the *Tropick* of *Capricorn*, he hath remounted afterwards, and shall go {5} on ascending so, as to pass the *Æquinoctial*, and perhaps proceed to 15. degrees *Northern Declination*, if it do not disappear before that time, by reason of its remoteness: Nor to believe, that there have been two *Comets*, upon its being seen again the 31. of *December*; since, according to him, it ought to have been so, if it continue to move in a *Great Circle*.

Having hereupon shewed, how the motion is to be traced upon the *Globe*, he finds, that, according to his Calculation, this *Comet* was to pass the *Tropick* of *Capricorn* about the 16 of *December*, and being entred into the Sign of *Virgo* on the 20. of the same month, and having been in *Quadrat* with the *Sun*, it should still descend, until the 26 of *December* in the morning, and then enter into *Leo*; that having entred, the 28. of the same month, into *Cancer*, and been, a little after that time, in its greatest Inclination to the *Ecliptick*, vid in the 28. degree of *Leo*, it was to repass the *Southern Tropick*, over against the *little Dogg*, on the 29. of *December* about 9 or 10 of the clock in the morning, after it had been opposite to the *Sun* 2. or 3. hours before; and that on the 29. of *December* in the evening it should be in *Gemini*; and at the very beginning of the New year, enter into *Taurus*.

After this, our Author finds, that this *Comet*, according to his account, should pass the *Æquator*, on the 4. of *January* before noon, and that about 5. or 6. of the clock in the evening of that day it was to come into the jaw of the *Whale*, and the 9. of the same, at 6. of the clock it should come close to the small Star of the *Whale*, which is in its way, a little below. At length he finds that it was to enter into *Aries* on the 12. of *January*, and to cut the *Ecliptick* on the 16. of the same month about noon, at which time it was to be again in *Quadrat* with the *Sun*, whence drawing a little to above the *Northern Line* of *Pisces*, it should in his opinion cease to appear a little beyond that place, without going as far as to the middle of *Aries*, if so be that its remoteness make it not disappear sooner.

He continueth, and saith, that this *Comet* shall not arrive to the place over against the *Line* of *Pisces* till the 10 of *February*, & that then its *Diurnal* motion shall not exceed 8 minutes, and not 5 minutes about the 20 of the same month: and that in the {6} beginning of *March*, if we see it so long, the said motion shall not exceed 4 minutes, and so shall be still diminishing; except the *Comet* become *Retrograde*, which, as very important, he would have well observed; as also, whether its motion will be about the end more or less swift, than he hath calculated it.

He subjoyneth, that the greatest way, which this Star could make in 24. hours, hath been 13.*d.* 25′; and in one houre, about 34′; and thinking it probable, that about the time, when it made so much way, it should be nearest to the *Earth*, he concludeth that its motion in 24. hours must be, in its least distance from the *Earth*, as about 3. to 14, or 1. to 4⅔, and that its motion in one hour was to be to the same least distance, as about 1. to 102¹/₇.

3

But that, which he judgeth most remarkable, is, that he found by his Calculation, that the said least distance should be on the 29. of *December*, when the *Comet* was opposite to the Sun; which he does not know whether it may not serve to decide the grand Question concerning the *Motion of the Earth*.

He taketh further notice, that the *Tayl* of the *Comet* was to turn *Westward*, with a point to the *North*, until the 29. of *December*, at which time it was to be opposite to the *Sun*, and that then the said *Tayl* was to look directly *North*; but that, after that time, the *Tayl* was to turn *Eastward*, and continue to do so, until it disappear; and that it shall draw a little towards the *North*, until the 8. or 10. of *February*, at which time the *Tayl* is to be parallel to the *Æquator*, as if the *Comet* be *yet* seen for some time after, the *Tayl* shall go a little lower towards the *South*, but grow smaller.

He finds by his *Hypothesis*, that on the 2. of *December*, which is the first observation, that he hath heard of, this Star was to be about 7. times more remote from the *Earth*, than when it was in its *Perigeum*; and that it will be again in an equall remoteness from the *Earth*, on the 27. of *January*, so that he is of opinion, that in case this *Comet* have not been seen before the 2. of *December*, it will not be seen any more after the 27. of *January*.

He wishes above all things, that it might be very exactly observed, at what Angle the way of the *Comet* cuts the *Æquator*, and, most of all, the *Ecliptick*, that so it may be seen, whether {7} there hath not been some *Parallaxe* in the *Circle* of his Motion; as also, that some observations could be had of its greatest descent beneath the *Tropick of Capricorn* in the more *Southern* parts, where he saith it would have been without *Refractions*; Moreover of the Time, when it hath been in *Quadrat* with the *Sun* about the 20 of *December*; and that also very exact Observation might be made of the time of its being again in *Quadrat* with the *Sun*, which, according to him, was to be *January* 16.

He wishes also, that some in *Madagascar* may have observed this Star; Seeing that it began to appear over the middle of that *Island*, and passed twice over their heads; he judgeth, that they have seen it before us. And he wisheth lastly, that there were some intelligent person in *Guiana* to observe it there, seeing that within a few daies, according to his reckoning, it will pass over their Heads, and will not remove from thence but 8 or 10 degrees Northward, where he saith, it will disappear; thinking it improbable, that it can still appear, after the *Sun* shall have passed it.

This Account beareth date of the 2. *January*, new stile, 1665. and the Author thereof addeth this Note, That, seeing it could not be printed nor distributed so soon as he desired, he hath had the opportunity to verifie it by some Observations, from which he affirms he hath found no sensible difference; or, if there be, that it proceeds only from thence, that the Stars have advanced, since his *Globe* was made. He concludeth, that if this continue, and the first Observations do likewise agree, or that the differences do arrive within the Times ghessed by him, that he hopes, he shall determine both the *Distance* and the *Magnitude* of this *Comet*; and that perhaps one may be enabled to decide the Question of the *Motion of the Earth*. In the interim, he assureth, that he hath not changed the least number in his Calculations, and that *Monsieur Huygens*, and several French Gentlemen, to whom he saith, he hath given them long since, can bear him witness that he hath done so; as also many other friends of his, who saw upon his *Globe*, several daies before, the way of the *Comet* from day to day.

Thus for the *Parisian* Account of the Comet, which is here inserted at large, that the intelligent and curious in *England* may {8} compare their Observations therewith, either to verifie these *Prædictions*, or to shew wherein they differ; which is (as was also hinted above) the design of this *Philosophical Prophet* in dispersing his Conceptions, who declareth himself ready, in case he be mistaken in his reckoning, to learn another *Hypothesis*, to explicate these admirable appearances by.

An Experimental History of Cold.

There is in the Press, a New *Treatise*, entituled, *New Observations and Experiments in order to an Experimental History of Cold*, begun by that Noble Philosopher, Mr. *Robert Boyle*, and in great part already Printed; He did lately very obligingly present several Copies of so much as was Printed, to the *Royal Society*, with a desire that some of the Members thereof might be engaged to peruse the Book, and select out of it for trial, the hints of such Experiments, as the *Author* there wisheth might be either yet made or prosecuted. The Heads thereof are,

1. Experiments touching Bodies capable of Freezing others.

2. Experiments and Observations touching Bodies Disposed to be Frozen.

3. Experiments touching Bodies, Indisposed to be Frozen.

4. Experiments and Observations touching the Degrees of Cold in several Bodies.

5. Experiments touching the Tendency of Cold Upwards or Downwards.

6. Experiments and Observations touching the Preservation and Destruction of (Eggs, Apples, and other) Bodies by Cold.

7. Experiments touching the Expansion of Water and Aqueous Liquors by Freezing.

8. Experiments touching the Contraction of Liquors by Cold.

9. Experiments in Consort, touching the Bubbles, from which the Levity of Ice is supposed to proceed.

10. Experiments about the Measure of the Expansion and the Contraction of Liquors by Cold.

11. Experiments touching the Expansive Force of Freezing Water.

12. Experiments touching a New way of estimating the {9}Expansive force of Congelation, and of highly compressing Air without Engines.

13. Experiments and Observations touching the Sphere of Activity of Cold.

14. Experiments touching differing *Mediums*, through which Cold may be diffused.

15. Experiments and Observations touching Ice.

16. Experiments and Observations touching the duration of Ice and Snow, and the destroying of them by the Air, and several Liquors.

17. Considerations and Experiments touching the *Primum Frigidum*.

18. Experiments and Observations touching the Coldness and Temperature of the Air.

19. Of the strange Effects of Cold.

20. Experiments touching the weight of Bodies frozen and unfrozen.

21. Promiscuous Experiments and Observations concerning Cold.

This Treatise will be dispatched within a very short time, and would have been so, ere this, if the extremity of the late Frost had not stopt the Press. It will be accompanied with some Discourses of the same *Author*, concerning *New Thermometrical Experiments and Thoughts*, as also, with an Exercitation about the *Doctrine of the Antiperistasis*. In the former whereof is *first* proposed this *Paradox*, That not only our Senses, but common Weather-glasses, may mis-inform us about Cold. *Next*, there are contained in this part, New Observations about the deficiencies of Weather-glasses, together with some considerations touching the New or*Hermetrical* Thermometers. *Lastly*, they deliver another *Paradox*, touching the cause of the Condensation of the Air, and Ascent of water by cold in common Weather-glasses. The latter piece of this part contains an Examen of *Antiperistasis*, as it is wont to be *taught* and*proved;* Of all which there will, perhaps, a fuller account be given by the Next.{10}

An Account of a very odd Monstrous Calf.

By the same Noble person was lately communicated to the *Royal Society* an account of a very Odd Monstrous Birth, produced at *Limmington* in *Hampshire*, where a Butcher, having caused a Cow (which cast her Calf the year before) to be covered, that she might the sooner be fatted, killed her when fat, and opening the Womb, which he found heavy to admiration, saw in it a Calf, which had begun to have hair, whose hinder Leggs had no Joynts, and whose Tongue was, *Cerberus*-like, triple, to each side of his Mouth one, and one in the midst: Between the Fore-leggs and the Hinder-leggs was a great Stone, on which the Calf rid: the *Sternum*, or that part of the Breast, where the Ribs lye, was also perfect Stone; and the Stone, on which it rid, weighed twenty pounds and a half; the outside of the Stone was of Grenish colour, but some small parts being broken off, it appeared a perfect Free-stone. The Stone, according to the Letter of Mr. *David Thomas*, who sent this Account to Mr. *Boyle*, is with Doctor *Haughteyn* of *Salisbury*, to whom he also referreth for further Information.

Of a peculiar Lead-Ore of Germany, and the Use thereof.

There was, not long since, sent hither out of *Germany* from an inquisitive Physician, a List of several *Minerals* and *Earths* of that Country, and of *Hungary*, together with a *Specimen* of each of them: among which there was a kind of *Lead-Ore* which is more considerable than all the rest, because of its singular use for *Essays* upon the *Coppell*, seeing that there is not any other *Mettal* mixed with it. 'Tis found in the *Upper Palatinate*, at a place called *Freyung*, and there are two sorts of it, whereof one is a kind of Crystalline Stone, and almost all good Lead; the other not so rich, and more farinaceous. By the information, coming along with it, they are fetcht, not from under the ground, but, the Mines of that place having lain long neglected, by reason of the Wars of *Germany* and the increase of Waters, the people, living{11}there-about take it from what these Forefathers had thrown away, and had lain long in the open Air. The use above mentioned being considerable, the person, who sent it, hath been intreated, to inform what quantities may be had of it, if there should be occasion to send for some.

Of an Hungarian Bolus, of the same Effect with the Bolus Armenus.

The same person gave notice also, that, besides the *Bolus Armenus*, and the *Terra Silesiaca*, there is an Earth to be found in *Hungary* about the River *Tockay*, thence called *Bolus Tockaviensis*, having as good effects in *Physick*, as either of the former two, and commended by experience in those parts, as much as it is by *Sennertus* out of *Crato*, for its goodness.

Of the New American Whale-fishing about the Bermudas.

Here follows a Relation, somewhat more diverting, than the precedent Accounts, which is about the new *Whale fishing* in the *West-Indies* about the *Bermudas*, as it was delivered by an understanding and hardy Sea-man, who affirmed he had been at the killing work himself. His account, as far as remembred, was this; that though hitherto all Attempts of mastering the Whales of those Seas had been unsuccesful, by reason of the extraordinary fierceness and swiftness of these monstrous Animals; yet the enterprise being lately renewed, and such persons chosen and sent thither for the work, as were resolved not to be baffled by a Sea-monster, they did prosper so far in this undertaking, that, having been out at Sea, near the said Isle of *Bermudas*, seventeen times, and fastned their Weapons a dozen times, they killed in these expeditions 2 old Female-Whales, and 3 Cubs, whereof one of the old ones, from the head to the extremity of the Tayl, was 88. Foot in length, by measure; its Tayl being 23. Foot broad, the swimming Finn 26. Foot long, and the Gills three Foot long: having great bends underneath from the Nose to the Navil; upon her after-part, a Finn on the back; being within{12}paved (this was the plain Sea-man's phrase) with fat, like the Cawl of a Hog.

The other old one, he said, was some 60. Foot long. Of the Cubs, one was 33. the other two, much about 25 or 26. Foot long.

The shape of the Fish, he said, was very sharp behind, like the ridge of a house; the head pretty bluff, and full of bumps on both sides; the back perfectly black, and the belly white.

Their celerity and force he affirmed to be wonderful, insomuch that one of those Creatures, which struck himself, towed the boat wherein he was, after him, for the space of six or seven Leagues, in ¾ of an hours time. Being wounded, he saith, they make a hideous roaring, at which, all of that kind that are within hearing, come towards that place, where the Animal is, yet without striking, or doing any harm to the wary.

He added, that they struck one of a prodigious bigness, and by guess of above 100 foot long. He is of opinion, that this Fish comes nearest to that sort of Whales, which they call the *Jubartes*; they are without teeth, and longer than the *Greenland*-Whales, but not so thick.

He said further, that they fed much upon Grass, growing at the bottom of the Sea; which, he affirmed, was seen by cutting up the great Bag of Maw, wherein he had found in one of them about two or three Hogsheads of a greenish grassy matter.

As to the quantity and nature of the Oyl which they yield, he thought, that the largest sort of these Whales might afford seven or eight Tuns if well husbanded, although they had lost much this first time, for want of a good Cooper; having brought home but eleven Tuns. The Cubbs, by his relation, do yield but little, and that is but a kind of a Jelly. That which the old ones render, doth candy like Porks Grease, yet burneth very well. He observed, that the Oyl of the Blubber is as clear and fair as any Whey: but that which is boyled out of the Lean, interlarded, becomes as hard as Tallow, spattering in the burning and that which is made of the Cawl, resembleth Hoggs grease.

One, but scarce credible, quality of this Oyl, he affirms to be, that though it be boiling, yet one may run ones hand into it without scalding; to which he adds, that it hath a very healing{13}Vertue for cuttings, lameness, &c., the part affected being anointed therewith. One thing more he related, not to be omitted, which is, that having told, that the time of catching these Fishes was from the beginning of *March*, to the end of *May*, after which time they appeared no more in that part of the Sea: he did, when asked, whither they then retired, give this Answer, That it was thought, they went into the Weed-beds of the Gulf of *Florida*, it having been observed, that upon their Fins and Tails they have store of Clams or Barnacles, upon which, he said, Rock-weed or Sea-tangle did grow a hand long; many of them having been taken of them, of the bigness of great Oyster-shels, and hung upon the Governour of *Bermudas* his Pales.

A Narrative concerning the success of Pendulum-Watches at Sea for the Longitudes.

The Relation lately made by Major *Holmes*, concerning the success of the *Pendulum-Watches* at Sea (two whereof were committed to his Care and Observation in his last voyage to *Guiny* by some of our Eminent *Virtuosi*, and Grand Promoters of Navigation) is as followeth;

The said *Major* having left that Coast, and being come to the Isle of St. *Thomas* under the *Line* accompanied with four Vessels, having there adjusted his Watches, put to Sea, and sailed Westward, seven or eight hundred Leagues, without changing his course; after which, finding the Wind favourable, he steered towards the Coast of *Africk*, North-North-East. But having sailed upon that *Line* a matter of two or three hundred Leagues, the Masters of the other Ships, under his Conduct, apprehending that they should want Water, before they could reach that Coast, did propose to him to steer their Course to the *Barbadoes*, to supply themselves with Water there. Whereupon the said Major, having called the Master and Pilots together, and caused them to produce their Journals and Calculations, it was found, that those Pilots did differ in their reckonings from that of the Major, one of them eighty Leagues, another about an hundred, and the third, more; but the Major judging by his *Pendulum-Watches*, that they were only some thirty Leagues distant from {14}the Isle of *Fuego*, which is one of the Isles of *Cape Verde*, and that they might reach it next day, and having a great confidence in the said Watches, resolved to steer their Course thither, and having given order so to do, they got the very next day about Noon a sight of the said Isle of *Fuego*, finding themselves to sail directly upon it, and so arrived at it that Afternoon, as he had said. These Watches having been first Invented by the Excellent Monsieur *Christian Hugens* of *Zulichem*, and fitted to go at Sea, by the Right Honourable, the Earl of *Kincardin*, both Fellows of the *Royal Society*, are now brought by a New addition to a wonderful perfection. The said Monsieur *Hugens*, having been informed of the success of the Experiment, made by *Major Holmes*, wrought to a friend at *Paris* a Letter to this effect;

Major *Holmes* at his return, hath made a relation concerning the usefulness of *Pendulums*, which surpasseth my expectation: I did not imagine that the Watches of this first Structure would succeed so well, and I had reserved my main hopes for the New ones. But seeing that those have already served so succesfully, and that the other are yet more just and exact, I have the more reason to believe, that the Invention of *Longitudes* will come to its perfection. In the mean time I shall tell you, that the *States* did receive my Proposition, when I desired of them a Patent for these new Watches, and the recompense set a-part for the invention in case of success; and that without any difficulty they have granted my request, commanding me to bring one of these Watches into their Assembly, to explicate unto them the Invention, and the application thereof to the *Longitudes*; which I have done to their contentment. I have this week published, that the said Watches shall be exposed to sale, together with an Information necessary to use them at Sea: and thus I have broken the Ice. The same Objection, that hath been made in your parts against the exactness of these *Pendulums*, hath also been made here; to wit, that though they should agree together, they might fail both of them, by reason that the Air at one time might be thicker, than at another. But I have answered, that this difference, if there be any, will not be at all perceived in the *Penduls*, seeing that the continuall Observations, made in Winter from day to day, until Summer, have shewed me that {15} they have alwaies agreed with the Sun. As to the Printing of the *Figure* of my New Watch, I shall defer that yet a while: but it shall in time appear with all the Demonstrations thereof, together with a *Treatise* of *Pendulums*, written by me some daies since, which is of a very subtile Speculation.

The Character, lately published beyond the Seas, of an Eminent person, not long since dead at Tholouse, where he was a Councellor of Parliament.

It is the deservedly famous *Mounsieur de Fermat*, who was, (saith the Author of the Letter) one of the most Excellent Men of this Age, a *Genius* so universal, and of so vast an extent, that if very knowing and learned Men had not given testimony of his extraordinary merit, what with truth can be said of him, would hardly be believed. He entertained a constant correspondence with many of the most Illustrious Mathematicians of *Europe*, and did excel in all the parts of Mathematical Science: a Testimony whereof he hath left behind him in the following Books.

A Method for the Quadrature of *Parabola's* of all degrees.

A Book *De Maximis & Minimis*, which serveth not only for the determination of Problems of *Plains* and *Solids*, but also for the invention of *Tangents* and *Curve Lines*, and of the *Centres* of Gravity in Solids; and likewise for Numerical Questions.

An Introduction to the Doctrine of *Plains* and *Solids*, which is an *Analytical* Treatise, concerning the solution of *Plains* and *Solids*, which has been seen (as the Advertiser affirms) before Monsieur *Des Cartes* had publish'd any thing upon this Subject.

A Treatise *De Contactibus Sphæricis*, where he hath demonstrated in *Solids*, what Mr. *Viet*, Master of Requests, had but demonstrated in *Plains*.

Another Treatise, wherein he establisheth and demonstrateth the two Books of *Apollonius Pergæus*, of *Plains*.

And a General Method for the dimension of *Curve Lines*, &c. Besides, having a perfect knowledge in Antiquity, he was consulted from all parts upon the difficulties that did emerg therein: he hath explained abundance of obscure places, that are {16} found in the Antients. There have been lately printed some of his Observations upon *Athenæus*; and he that hath interpreted *Benedetto Castelli*, of the Measure of running waters, hath thence inserted in his Work a very handsome one upon an Epistle of *Synesius*, which was so difficult, that the Jesuit *Petavius*, who hath commented upon this Author, acknowledges, that he could not understand it.

He hath also made many Observations upon *Theon of Smyrne*, and upon other Antient Authors: but most part of them are not found but scattered in his Epistles, because he did not write much upon these kinds of Subjects, but to satisfie the curiosity of his friends.

All these Mathematical Works, and all these curious searches in Antiquity, did not hinder this great *Virtuoso* from discharging the duties of his place with much assiduity, and with so much ability, that he hath had the reputation of one of the greatest *Civilians* of his Age.

But that, which is most of all surprizing to many, is, that with all that strength of understanding, which was requisite to make good these rare qualities, lately mentioned, he had so polite and delicate parts, that he composed *Latin*, *French*, and *Spanish* Verses with the same elegancy, as if he had lived in the time of *Augustus*, and passed the greatest part of his life at the Courts of *France* and *Spain*.

More particulars will perhaps be mention'd of the Works of this Rare person, when all things, that he hath publish'd, shall be recovered, and when liberty shall be obtained of his Worthy Son, to impart unto the World the rest of his Writings, hitherto unpublished.

LONDON,

Printed with Licence, By *John Martyn*, and *James Allestry*, Printers to the *Royal-Society*.
{17}

Num. 2.

PHILOSOPHICAL
TRANSACTIONS.

Munday, April 3. 1665.

The Contents.

Extract of a Letter written from Rome, *concerning the late* Comet, *and a* New one. *Extract of another Letter from* Paris, *containing some Reflections on the precedent*Roman *Letter. An Observation concerning some particulars, further considerable in the* Monster, *that was Mention'd in the first Papers of these* Philosophical Transactions. *Extract of a Letter written from* Venice, *concerning the Mines of*Mercury *in Friuly. Some Observations, made in the ordering of* Silk-worms. *An Account of Mr.* Hooks Micrographia, *or the Physiological descriptions of* Minute Bodies, *made by* Magnifying Glasses.

Extract of a Letter, lately written from Rome, *touching the late Comet, and a New one.*

I Cannot enough wonder at the strange agreement of the thoughts of that acute French Gentleman, Monsieur *Auzout*, in the *Hypothesis* of the Comets motion, with mine; and particularly, at that of the *Tables*. I have with the same method, whereby I find the motion of this Comet, easily found the Principle of that Author's *Ephemerides*, which he then thought not fit to declare; and 'tis this, that this Comet moves about the *Great Dog*, in so great a Circle, that that portion, which is {18}described, is exceeding small in respect of the whole circumference thereof, and hardly distinguishable by us from a streight line.

Concerning the New Comet you mention, I saw it on the 11. of *February*, about the 24. deg. of *Aries*, with a Northern latitude of 24. deg. 40. min. The cloudy weather hath not yet permitted me to see it in *Andromeda*, as others affirm to have done.

Extract of a Letter, written from Paris, *containing some Reflections on part of the precedent* Roman Letter.

As to the *Hypothesis* of *Georg. Domenico Cassini*, touching the motion of the *Comet* about the *Great Dog* in a Circle, whose Centre is in a streight line drawn from the Earth through the said Star, I believe it will shortly be publish'd in print, as a thought I lighted upon in discoursing with one of my Friends, who did maintain, that it turned about a Centre, because that its *Perigee* had been over against the *Great Dog*, as I had noted in my *Ephemerides*. This particular I did long since declare to many of my acquaintance, whereof some or other will certainly do me that right, as to let the world know it by the Press. I have added an Observation, which I find not, that Signior *Cassini* hath made, *viz.* that there was ground to think, that the *Comet* of 1652. was the same with the present, seeing that besides the parity of the swiftness of its motion, the *Perigee* thereof was also over against the *Great Dog*, if the Observations extant thereof, deceive not. But, to make it out, what ground I had for these thoughts, I said, that if they were true, the Comet must needs acomplish its revolution from 10. to 12. years, or thereabout. But, seeing it appears not by History, that a Comet hath been seen at those determinate distances of time, nor that over against the *Perigee* of all the other Comets, whereof particular observations are recorded, are alwaies found Stars of the first Magnitude, or such others, as are very notable, besides other reasons, that might be alledged, I shall not pursue this speculation; but rather {19}suggest what I have taken notice of in my reflexions upon former Comets, which is, that more of them enter inter our Systeme by the sign of *Libra* and about *Spica virginis*, than by all the other parts of the Heavens. For, both the present Comet, and many others registred in History, have entred that way, and consequently passed out of it by the sign *Aries*, by which also many have entred.

9

I did found my *Hypothesis* upon three Observations only, *viz.* those of the 22, 26, and 31. of *December.* Nor have I done, as some have fancied of me, who having been able to observe the Comet, the 27, 28, 29, 30, and 31. of *December,* and to see the diminution of its motion, have judged, that I had only determined that diminution for the time to come, conform to the augmentation thereof in time passed until the 29. of *December.* For *January* 1. (on which day I composed my *Ephemerides*) I knew not (nor any person here) that the motion of the Comet did diminish; but on the contrary, most men believed, it was not the same Comet. But Signior *Cassini* knows very well, that that was not necessary, seeing that two portions of a *Tangent* being given, and the *Angles* answering thereunto, 'tis easie to find the position and magnitude of its Circle. The reason, which I think the true one, of the diminution of its Motion in Longitude, and of its Retrogradation, by me conjectured in my *Ephemerides,* I began to be assured of, *Febr.* 10. For until the sixth, the Comet had alwaies advanced, as Signior *Cassini* also hath very well noted: but after that day, I found that it returned in augmenting alwaies its Latitude. And I have constantly observed it, until *March* 8. between many Stars, which must be the same with these mentioned by *Cassini,* whereof the number was so great, that I think, I saw of them *March* 6. with one *Aperture* of my Glass, more than 40. or 50. and especially, above the head of *Aries*; but I did not particularly note the scituation of more than 12. or 15; amongst which I have observed the position of the Comet since *January* 28. every day, when the weather did permit, *viz. January* 29. *February* 3, 6, 10, 17, 19, 24, 26, 27. and *March* 6, {20}7, 8. I left it on *March* 8. at the 18. of the Horn of *Aries,* almost in the same latitude: and I am apt to believe, it will be Eclipsed, which I wish I may be able to observe this evening, if it be not already passed.

If Signior *Cassini* hath observed it on those daies that I have, he will be glad to find the conformity of our Observations. I shall only add, that on *February* 3. we were surprized, to see the Comet again much brighter than ordinary, and with a considerable Train. Some did believe, that it approach'd again to us. But having beheld it with a *Telescope,* I soon said, that it was joyned with two small Stars, whereof one was pretty bright, which I had already seen, on *February* 28. and 29. And this conjunction gave the *Comet* that brightness, as it happens to most of the Stars of the fifth and sixth magnitude, where 2. or 3. or more are conjoyned, which perhaps would shew but faintly single, though by reason of their proximity to one another, they appear but one Star. Hence it was, that I assured my friends here, that the following daies we should no more see it so bright, because I knew, that there were none such small bright Stars in the way, which by my former observations I conjectured it was to move.

An Observation imparted to the Noble Mr. Boyle, by Mr. David Thomas, touching some particulars further considerable in the Monster mentioned in the first Papers of these Philosophical Transactions.

Upon the strictest inquiry, I find by one, that saw the Monstrous Calf and stone, within four hours after it was cut out of the Cows belly, that the Breast of the Calf was not stony (as I wrote) but that the skin of the Breast and between the Legs and of the Neck (which parts lay on the smaller end of the stone) was very much thicker, than on any other part, and that the Feet of the Calf were so parted as to be like the Claws of a Dog. The stone I have since seen; it is bigger at one end {21} than the other; of no plain *Superficies,* but full of little cavities. The stone, when broken, is full of small peble stones of an Ovall figure: its colour is gray like free-stone, but intermixt with veins of yellow and black. A part of it I have begg'd of Dr.*Haughten* for you, which I have sent to *Oxford,* whither a more exact account will be conveyed by the same person.

Extract of a Letter, lately written from Venice by the Learned Doctor Walter Pope, to the Reverend Dean of Rippon, Doctor John Wilkins, concerning the Mines of Mercury in Friuli; and a way of producing Wind by the fall of Water.

The mines of *Mercury* in *Friuli,* a Territory belonging to the *Venetians,* are about a days Journey and a half distant from *Goritia* Northwards, at a place call'd *Idria,* scituated in a Valley of the *Julian Alps.* They have been, as I am inform'd, these 160. years in the possession of the Emperor, and all the Inhabitants speak the *Sclavonian* Tongue. In going thither, we travell'd several hours in the best Wood I ever saw before or since, being very full of *Firrs*, *Oakes*, and *Beeches*, of an extraordinary thickness, straitness, and height. The Town is built, as usually Towns in the *Alps* are, all of wood, the Church only excepted, and another House wherein the Overseer liveth. When I was there, in *August* last, the Valley, and the Mountains too, out of which the *Mercury* was dug, were of as pleasant a verdure, as if it had been in the midst of Spring, which they there attribute to the moistness of the *Mercury*; how truly, I dispute not. That Mine, which we went into, the best and greatest of them all, was dedicated to Saint *Barbara*, as the other Mines are to other Saints, the depth of it was 125. paces, every pace of that Country being, as they inform'd us, more than 5 of our Feet. There are two ways down to it; the shortest perpendicular way is that, whereby they bring up the Mineral in great Buckets, and {22}by which oftentimes some of the workmen come up and down. The other, which is the usual way, is at the beginning not difficult, the descent not being much; the greatest trouble is, that in several places you cannot stand upright: but this holds not long, before you come to descend in earnest by perpendicular Ladders, where the weight of on's body is found very sensible. At the end of each Ladder, there are boards a-cross, where we may breath a little. The Ladders, as we said, are perpendicular, but being imagined produced, do not make one Ladder, but several parallel ones. Being at the bottom, we saw no more than we saw before, only the place, whence the Mineral came. All the way down, and the bottom, where there are several lanes cut out in the Mountain, is lined and propt with great pieces of Firr-trees, as thick as they can be set. They dig the Mineral with Pick-axes, following the veins: 'tis for the most part hard as a stone, but more weighty; of a Liver-colour, or that of *Crocus Metallorum*. I hope shortly to shew you some of it. There is also some soft Earth, in which you plainly see the *Mercury* in little particles. Besides this, there are oftentimes found in the Mines round stones like Flints, of several bignesses, very like those Globes of Hair, which I have often seen in *England*, taken out of Oxes bellies. There are also several *Marcasites* and stones, which seem to have specks of Gold in them, but upon tryal they say, they find none in them. These round stones are some of them very ponderous, and well impregnated with *Mercury*; others light, having little or none in them. The manner of getting the *Mercury* is this: They take of the Earth, brought up in Buckets, and put it into a Sive, whose bottom is made of wires at so great a distance, that you may put your finger betwixt them: 'tis carried to a stream of running water, and wash'd as long as any thing will pass through the Sive. That Earth which passeth not, is laid aside upon another heap: that which passeth, reserved in the hole, G. in Fig. 1. and taken up again by the second Man, and so on, to about ten or twelve sives proportionably less. It often happens in the first hole, where the second Man takes up his {23}Earth, that there is *Mercury* at the bottom; but towards the farther end, where the Intervals of the wires are less, 'tis found in very great proportion. The Earth laid aside is pounded, and the same operation repeated. The fine small Earth, that remains after this, and out of which they can wash no more *Mercury*, is put into Iron retorts and stopt, because it should not fall into the Receivers, to which they are luted. The fire forces the *Mercury* into the Receivers: the Officer unluted several of them to shew us; I observed in all of them, that he first poured out perfect *Mercury*, and after that came a black dust, which being wetted with water discover'd it self to be *Mercury*, as the other was. They take the *Caput mortuum* and pound it, and renew the operation as long as they can get any *Mercury* out of it.

This is the way of producing the *Mercury*, they call *Ordinary*, which exceeds that, which is got by washing, in a very great proportion, as you will perceive by the account annext. All the *Mercury* got without the use of Fire, whether by washing, or found in the Mines (for in the digging, some little particles get together, so that in some places you might take up two or three spoonfuls of pure *Mercury*) is call'd by them *Virgin Mercury*, and esteem'd above the rest. I inquir'd of the Officer what vertue that had more, than the other; he told me that making an *Amalgama* of Gold and *Virgin Mercury*, and putting it to the fire, that *Mercury* would carry away all the Gold with it, which common *Mercury* would not do.

The Engins, employed in these Mines, are admirable; the Wheels, the greatest that ever I saw in my life; one would think as great as the matter would bear: all moved by the dead force of the water, brought thither in no chargeable Aqueduct from a Mountain, 3

Miles distant: the water pumpt from the bottom of the Mine by 52 pumps, 26 on a side, is contrived to move other wheels, for several other purposes.

The Labourers work for a *Julio* a day, which is not above 6 or 7 pence, and indure not long; for, although none stay {24}underground above 6 hours; all of them in time (some later, some sooner) become *paralitick*, and dye *hectick*.

We saw there a man, who had not been in the Mines for above half a year before, so full of *Mercury*, that putting a piece of *Brass* in his mouth, or rubbing it in his fingers, it immediately became white like Silver: I mean he did the same effect, as if he had rubb'd *Mercury* upon it, and so paralitick, that he could not with both his hands carry a Glass, half full of Wine, to his mouth without spilling it, though he loved it too well to throw it away.

I have been since informed, that here in *Venice*, those that work on the back-side of Looking-glasses, are also very subject to the *Palsey*. I did not observe, that they had black Teeth; it may be therefore, that we accuse *Mercury* injustly for spoiling the Teeth, when given in *Venereal* diseases. I confess, I did not think of it upon the place; but, black Teeth being so very rare in this Country, I think I could not but have markt it, had all theirs been so.

They use exceeding great quantity of Wood, in making and repairing the Engins, and in the Furnaces (whereof there are 16. each of them carrying 24. Retorts;) but principally in the Mines, which need continual reparation, the Fir-trees lasting but a small time under ground. They convey their Wood thus: About four miles from the Mines, on the sides of two mountains, they cut down the Trees, and draw them into the interjacent Valley, higher in the same Valley, so that the Trees, according to the descent of the water lye betwixt it and *Idria*: with vast charges and quantities of Wood they made a Lock or Dam, that suffers not any water to pass; they expect afterwards till there be water enough to float these Trees to *Idria*; for, if there be not a spring, (as generally there is,) Rain, or the melting of the Snow, in a short time, afford so much water, as is ready to run over the Dam, and which (the Flood-gates being open'd) carries all the Trees impetuously to *Idria*, where the Bridge is built very strong, and at very oblique Angles to the stream, on purpose to stop them, and throw them on shore neer the Mines.{25}

Those Mines cost the *Emperour* heretofore 70000. or 80000. *Florens* yearly, and yielded less *Mercury* than at present, although it costs him but 28000. *Florens* now. You may see what his Imperial Majesty gets by the following account, of what *Mercury* the Mines of *Idria* have produced these last three years.

	1661.	*l.*		1662.	*l.*		1663.	*l.*
Ord			Ord		:	Ord		:
inary*Mercur*	9848		inary*Mercur*	2506		inary*Mercur*	4411	
y	1		*y*	6		*y*	9	
Virg		'	Virg		'	Virg		
in*Mercury*	194		in*Mercury*	612		in*Mercury*	1862	
	0467			3467	:		5598	
	5			8			1	

There are alwaies at work 280 persons, according to the relation I received from a very civil person, who informed me also of all the other particulars above mentioned, whose name is *Achatio Kappenjagger*; his Office, *Contra-scrivano per sua Maestà Cesarea in Idria del Mercurio*.

To give some light to this Narrative, take this Diagramme: *F.* is the water, *C. B.* a vessel, into which it runs. *DG. EH. FI.* are streams perpetually issuing from that vessel; *D. E. F.* three sives, the distance of whose wires at bottom lessen proportionally. *G.* the place, wherein the Earth, that pass'd through the sive *D.* is retained; from whence 'tis taken by the second man; and what passes through the sive *E.* is retained in *H.* and so of the rest. *K. L. M.* wast water, which is so much impregnated with *Mercury*, that it cureth Itches and sordid Ulcers. See Fig. 1.

I will trespass a little more upon you, in describing the contrivance of blowing the Fire in the *Brassworks* of *Tivoli* neer *Rome* (it being new to me) where the Water blows the Fire, not by moving the Bellows, (which is common) but by affording the Wind. See Fig. II. Where *A.* is the {26}River, *B.* the Fall of it, *C.* the Tub into which it falls, *LG.* a Pipe, *G.* the orifice of the Pipe, or Nose of the Bellows, *GK.* the Hearth, *E.* a hole in the Pipe, *F.* a stopper to that hole,*D.* a place under ground, by which the water runs away. Stopping the hole *E*, there is a perpetual strong wind, issuing forth at *G*: and *G.* being stopt, the wind comes out so vehemently at *E*, that it will, I believe, make a Ball play, like that at *Frescati.*

An Extract of a Letter, containing some Observations, made in the ordering of Silk-worms, communicated by that known Vertuoso, Mr. Dudley Palmer, from the ingenuous Mr. Edward Digges.

I herewith offer to your *Society* a small parcel of my *Virginian* Silk. What I have observed in the ordering of Silk-worms, contrary to the received opinion, is:

1. That I have kept leaves 24. hours after they are gathered, and flung water upon them to keep them from withering; yet when (without wiping the leaves) I fed the worms, I observed, they did as well as those fresh gathered.

2. I never observed, that the smell of *Tobacco*, or smels that are rank, did any waies annoy the worm.

3. Our country of *Virginia* is very much subject to Thunders: and it hath thundered exceedingly when I have had worms of all sorts, some newly hatched; some half way in their feeding; others spinning their Silk; yet I found none of them concern'd in the Thunder, but kept to their business, as if there had been no such thing.

4. I have made many bottoms of the Brooms (wherein hundreds of worms spun) of *Holly*; and the prickles were so far from hurting them, that even from those prickles they first began to make their bottoms.

I did hope with this to have given you assurance, that by retarding the hatching of seed, two crops of silk or more {27} might be made in a Summer: but my servants have been remiss in what was ordered, I must crave your patience till next year.

An account of Micrographia, or the Physiological Descriptions of Minute Bodies, made by Magnifying Glasses.

The Ingenious and knowing Author of this *Treatise*, Mr. *Robert Hook*, considering with himself, of what importance a faithful *History of Nature* is to the establishing of a solid Systeme of *Natural Philosophy*, and what advantage *Experimental* and *Mechanical*knowledge hath over the Philosophy of *discourse* and *disputation*, and making it, upon that account, his constant business to bring into that vast Treasury what portion he can, hath lately published a Specimen of his abilities in this kind of study, which certainly is very welcome to the Learned and Inquisitive world, both for the *New discoveries* in *Nature*, and the *New Inventions* of *Art.*

As to the *former*, the Attentive Reader of this Book will find, that there being hardly any thing so small, as by the help of *Microscopes*, to escape our enquiry, a new visible world is discovered by this means, and the Earth shews quite a new thing to us, so that in every *little particle* of its matter, we may now behold almost as great a variety of creatures, as we were able before to reckon up in the whole *Universe* it self. Here our Author maketh it not improbable, but that, by these helps the subtilty of the composition of Bodies, the structure of their parts, the various texture of their matter, the instruments and manner of their inward motions, and all the other appearances of things, may be more fully discovered; whence may emerge many admirable advantages towards the enlargement of the *Active* and *Mechanick*part of knowledge, because we may perhaps be enabled to discern the secret {28}workings of*Nature*, almost in the same manner, as we do those that are the productions of *Art*, and are managed by *Wheels*, and *Engines*, and *Springs*, that were devised by Humane wit. To this end, he hath made a very curious *Survey* of all kinds of bodies, beginning with the *Point of a Needle*, and proceeding to the *Microscopical* view of the *Edges* of *Rasors, Fine Lawn, Tabby, Watered Silks, Glass-canes, Glass-drops, Fiery Sparks, Fantastical Colours, Metalline Colours, the Figures of Sand, Gravel in Urine, Diamonds in Flints, Frozen Figures, the Kettering Stone, Charcoal, Wood and other Bodies petrified, the Pores of Cork, and of other substances, Vegetables growing on blighted Leaves, Blew mould and Mushromes, Sponges, and other Fibrous Bodies, Sea-weed, the Surfaces of some Leaves, the* *stinging points of a Nettle, Cowage, the Beard of a wild Oate, the seed of the Corn-violet, as also of Tyme, Poppy and Purslane.* He continues to describe *Hair, the scales of a Soal, the sting of a Bee, Feathers* in general, and in particular those of *Peacocks; the feet of Flies; and other Insects; the Wings and Head of a Fly; the Teeth of a Snail; the Eggs of Silk-worms; the Blue Fly; a water Insect; the Tufted Gnat; a White Moth; the Shepheards-spider; the Hunting Spider, the Ant; the wandring Mite; the Crab-like insect, the Book-worm, the Flea, the Louse, Mites, Vine mites.* He concludeth with taking occasion to discourse of two or three very considerable subjects, viz. *The inflexion of the Rays of Lights in the Air; the Fixt stars; the Moon.*

In representing these particulars to the Readers view, the Author hath not only given proof of his singular skil in delineating all sorts of Bodies (he having drawn all the *Schemes* of these 60 *Microscopical* objects with his own hand) and of his extraordinary care of having them so curiously engraven by the Masters of that Art; but he hath also suggested in the several reflexions, made upon these Objects, such conjectures, as are likely to excite and quicken the Philosophical heads to very noble contemplations. Here are found inquiries concerning the *Propagation of Light* through {29} differing mediums; concerning *Gravity*, concerning the *Roundness* of Fruits, stones, and divers artificial bodies; concerning *Springiness* and *Tenacity*; concerning the *Original* of *Fountains*; concerning the *dissolution of Bodies into Liquors*; concerning *Filtration*, and the ascent of Juices in Vegetables, and the use of their *Pores*. Here an attempt is made of solving the strange *Phænomena* of *Glass-drops*; experiments are alleged to prove the *Expansion* of *Glass* by heat, and the *Contraction* of *heated-Glass* upon cooling; *Des Cartes* his *Hypothesis of Colours* is examined: the *cause of Colours*, most likely to the Author, is explained: Reasons are produced, that *Reflection* is not necessary to produce *colours*, nor a *double refraction*: some considerable *Hypotheses* are *offered*, for the explication of Light by Motion; for the producing of all colours by Refraction; for reducing all sorts of colours to two only, *Yellow* and *Blew*; for making the *Air*, a dissolvent of all *Combustible Bodies*: and for the explicating of all the regular figures of *Salt*, where he alleges many notable instances of the *Mathematicks* of *Nature*, as having even in those things which we account vile, rude & course, shewed abundance of curiosity and excellent *Geometry* and *Mechanism*. And here he opens a large field for inquiries, and proposeth Models for prosecuting them, 1. By making a full collection of all the differing kinds of *Geometricall* figur'd bodies; 2. By getting with them an exact History of their places where they are generated or found: 3. By making store of Tryals in Dissolutions and Coagulations of several Crystallizing Salts: 4. By making trials on metalls, Minerals and Stones, by dissolving them in severall *Menstruums*, and Crystallizing them, to see what Figures will arise from those several compositums: 5. By compounding & coagulating several Salts together into the same mass, to observe the Figure of that product: 6. By inquiring the closeness or rarity of the texture of those bodys by examining their gravity, and their refraction, &c. 7. By examining what operations the fire hath upon several kinds of Salts, what changes it causes in their figures, Textures, or {30} Vertues. 8. By examining their manner of dissolution, or acting upon those bodies dissoluble in them and the Texture of those bodies before and after the process. 9. By considering, by what and how many means, such and such figures, actions and effects could be produced, and which of them might be the most likely, &c.

He goes on to offer his thoughts about the Pores of bodies, and a *kind* of *Valves* in wood; about spontaneous generation arising from the Putrefaction of bodies; about the nature of the Vegetation of mold, mushromes, moss, spunges; to the last of which he scarce finds any Body like it in texture. He adds, from the naturall contrivance, that is found in the leaf of a Nettle, how the stinging pain is created, and thence takes occasion to discourse of the poysoning of Darts. He subjoyns a curious description of the shape, *Mechanism* and use of the *sting* of a *Bee*; and shews the admirable Providence of Nature in the contrivance and fabrick of *Feathers* for Flying. He delivers those particulars about the Figure, parts and use of the head, feet, and wings of a Fly, that are not common. He observes the various wayes of the generations of Insects, and discourses handsomely of the means, by which they seem to act so prudently. He taketh notice of the *Mechanical* reason of the *Spider's* Fabrick, and maketh pretty Observations on the hunting Spider, and other Spiders and their Webs. And what he notes of a Flea, Louse, Mites, and Vinegar-worms, cannot but exceedingly please the curious Reader.

Having dispatched these Matters, the Author offers his Thoughts for the explicating of many *Phænomena* of the Air, from the *Inflexion*, or from a *Multiplicate Refraction* of the rays of Light within the Body of the *Atmosphere*, and not from a *Refraction* caused by any terminating *superficies* of the Air above, nor from any such exactly defin'd *superficies* within the body of the *Atmosphere*; which conclusion he grounds upon this, that a *medium*, whose parts are unequally *dense*, and mov'd by various motions and transpositions as to one another, will produce all these {31} visible effects upon the rays of Light, without any other *coefficient* cause: and then, that there is in the Air or *Atmosphere, such* a variety in the constituent parts of it, both as to their *density* and *rarity*, and as to their divers mutations and positions one to another.

He concludeth with two *Celestial Observations*; whereof the *one* imports, what multitudes of Stars are discoverable by the *Telescope*, and the variety of their magnitudes; intimating with all, that the longer the Glasses are, and the bigger apertures they will indure, the more fit they are for these discoveries: the *other* affords a description of a *Vale* in the *Moon*, compared with that of *Hevelius* and *Ricciolo*; where the Reader will find several curious and pleasant Annotations, about the Pits of the *Moon*, and the Hills and Coverings of the same; as also about the variations in the *Moon*, and its *gravitating* principle, together with the use, that may be made of this Instance of a gravity in the *Moon*.

As to the *Inventions of Art*, described in this Book, the curious Reader will there find these following:

1. A *Baroscope*, or an Instrument to shew all the Minute Variations in the *Pressure of the Air*; by which he affirms, that he finds, that before and during the time of rainy weather, the Pressure of the Air is less; and in dry weather, but especially when an *Easterly* Wind (which having past over vast Tracts of Land, is heavy with earthy particles) blows, it is much more, though these changes be varied according to very odd Laws.

2. A *Hygroscope*, or an Instrument, whereby the *Watery steams*, volatile in the Air, are discerned, which the Nose it self is not able to find. Which is by him fully described in the Observation touching the *Beard of a wild Oate*, by the means whereof this Instrument is contrived.

3. An Instrument for *graduating Thermometers*, to make them *Standards* of *Heat* and *Cold*.

4. A *New Engine* for *Grinding Optick Glasses*, by means of which he hopes, that any Spherical Glasses, of what length {32} soever, may be speedily made: which seems to him most easie, because, if it succeeds, with one and the same Tool may be ground an *Object Glass* of any length or breadth requisite, and that with very little or no trouble in fitting the *Engine*, and without much skill in the *Grinder*. He thinks it very exact, because to the very last stroke the Glass does regulate and rectifie the *Tool* to its exact Figure; and the longer or more the *Tool* and *Glass* are wrought together, the more exact will both of them be of the desired Figure. He affirms further, that the motions of the Glass and Tool do so cross each other, that there is not one point of eithers surface, but hath thousands of cross motions thwarting it, so that there can be no kind of *Rings* or *Gutters* made, either in the *Tool* or *Glass*.

5. A *New Instrument*, by which the *Refraction* of all kinds of Liquors may be exactly measured, thereby to give the Curious an opportunity of making Trials of that kind, to establish the *Laws* of *Refraction*, to wit, whether the *Sines of the Angles of Refraction are respectively proportionable to the Sines of the Angles of Incidence:* This Instrument being very proper to examine very accurately, and with little trouble, and in small quantities, the *Refraction* of any Liquor, not only for *one* inclination, but for *all*; whereby he is enabled to make accurate *Tables*. By the same also he affirms to have found it true, that what *proportion* the *Sine* of the Angle of the one *inclination* has to the *Sine* of its Angle of *Refraction*, correspondent to it, the same proportion have all the other *Sines* of Inclination to their respective *Sines* of *Refractions*.

Lastly, this Author despairs not that there may be found many Mechanical Inventions, to improve our Senses of *Hearing, Smelling, Tasting, Touching*, as well as we have improved that of *Seeing* by *Optick Glasses*.

London, Printed with Licence for *John Martyn*, and *James Allestry*, Printers to the *Royal Society*.

{33}

PHILOSOPHICAL
TRANSACTIONS.

Munday, May 8. 1665.

The Contents.

Some Observations and Experiments upon May-dew. *The Motion of the* Second Comet *predicted, by the same person, who predicted that of the former. A Relation of the Advice, given by a* French *Gentleman, touching the Conjunction of the* Ocean *and the* Mediterranean. *Of the way of killing* Ratle-snakes, *used in* Virginia. *A Relation of Persons kill'd with Subterraneous* Damps. *Of the* Mineral *of* Liege, *yielding both* Brimstone, *and* Vitriol, *and the way of extracting them out of it, used at* Liege. *An Account of Mr.* Boyle's *Experimental History of* Cold.

Some Observations and Experiments upon May-Dew.

That ingenious and inquisitive Gentleman, Master *Thomas Henshaw,* having had occasion to make use of a great quantity of *May-dew,* did, by several casual Essayes on that Subject, make the following Observations and Tryals, and present them to the *Royal Society.* {34}

That *Dew* newly gathered and filtred through a clean Linnen cloth, though it be not very clear, is of a yellowish Colour, somewhat approaching to that of Urine.

That having endevoured to putrefy it by putting several proportions into Glass bodies with blind heads, and setting them in several heats, as of dung, and gentle baths, he quite failed of his intention: for heat, though never so gentle, did rather clarify, and preserve it sweet, though continued for two moneths together, then cause any putrefaction or separation of parts.

That exposing of it to the Sun for a whole Summer in Glasses, that hold about two Gallons, with narrow mouths, that might be stopp'd with Cork, the only considerable alteration, he observed to be produced in it, was, that Store of green stuff (such as is seen in Summer in ditches and standing waters) floated on the top, and in some places, grew to the sides of the Glass.

That putting four or five Gallons of it into a half Tub, as they call it, of Wood, and straining a Canvas over it, to keep out Dust and Insects, and letting it stand in some shady room for three weeks or a month, it did of itself putrefy and stink exceedingly, and let fall to the bottom a black sediment like Mudd.

That, coming often to see, what Alterations appeared in the putrefaction, He observed, that at the beginning, within twenty four hours, a slimy film floated on the top of the water, which after a while falling to the bottom, there came another such film in its place.

That if *Dew* were put into a long narrow Vessel of Glass, such as formerly were used for Receivers in distilling of *Aqua Fortis,* the slime would rise to that height, that He could take it off with a Spoon; and when he had put a pretty quantity of it into a drinking Glass, and that it had stood all night, and the water dreined from it, if He had turned it out of his hand, it would stand upright in figure of the Glass, in substance like boyled white Starch, though something more transparent, if his memory *(saith he)* fail him not.

That having once gotten a pretty quantity of this gelly, and put it into a Glass body and Blind-head, He set it into a gentle {35} Bath with an intention to have putrefied it, but after a few days He found, the head had not been well luted on, and that some moisture exhaling, the gelly was grown almost dry, and a large *Mushrom* grown out of it within the Glass. It was of a loose watrish contexture, such an one, as he had seen growing out of rotten wood.

That having several Tubs with good quantity of *Dew* in them, set to putrefy in the manner abovesaid, and comming to pour out of one of them to make use of it, He found in the water a great bunch, bigger than his fist, of those Insects commonly called *Hog-lice* or *Millepedes*, tangled together by their long tailes, one of which came out of every one of their bodies, about the bigness of a Horsehair: The Insects did all live and move after they were taken out.

That emptying another Tub, whereon the Sun, it seems, had used sometimes to shine, and finding, upon the straining it through a clean linnen cloth, two or three spoonfulls of green stuff, though not so thick nor so green as that above mentioned, found in the Glasses*purposely* exposed to the Sun, He put this green stuff in a Glass, and tyed a paper over it, and coming some dayes after to view it, He found the Glass almost filled with an innumerable Company of small Flyes, almost all wings, such as are usually seen in great Swarms in the Aire in Summer Evenings.

That setting about a Gallon of this *Dew* (which, he saith, if he misremember not, had been first putrefied and strained) in an open Jarre-Glass with a wide mouth, and leaving it for many weeks standing in a South-window, on which the Sun lay very much, but the Casements were kept close shut; after some time coming to take account of his *Dew*, He found it very full of little Insects with great Heads and small tapering Bodies, somewhat resembling Tadpoles, but very much less. These, on his approach to the Glass, would sink down to the bottom, as it were to hide themselves, and upon his retreat wrigle themselves up to the top of the water again. Leaving it thus for some time longer, He afterwards found the room very full of Gnats, though the Door and Windows were kept shut. He adds, that He did not at first suspect, that those Gnats had any {36}relation to the *Dew*, but after finding the Gnats to be multiplied and the little watry Animals to be much lessened in quantity, and finding great numbers of their empty skins floating on the face of his *Dew*, He thought, he had just reason to perswade himself, the Gnats were by a second Birth produced of those little Animals.

That vapouring away great quantities of his putrefied *Dew* in Glass Basons, and other Earthen glased Vessels, He did at last obtain, as he remembers, above two pound of *Grayish Earth*, which when he had washed with more of the same *Dew* out of all his Basons into one, and vapoured to siccity, lay in leaves one above another, not unlike to some kind of brown Paper, but very friable.

That taking this Earth out, and after he had well ground it on a Marble, and given it a smart Fire, in a coated Retort of Glass, it soon melted and became a Cake in the bottom, when it was cold, and looked as if it had been Salt and Brimstone in a certain proportion melted together; but, as he remembers, was not at all inflamable. This ground again on a Marble, *he saith*, did turn Spring water of a reddish purple Colour.

That by often calcining and filtring this Earth, He did at last extract about two ounces of a fine small *white Salt*, which, looked on through a good *Microscope*, seemed to have Sides and Angles in the same number and figure, as *Rochpeeter*.

The Motion of the **Second** *Comet predicted, by the same Gentleman, who predicted that of the* **former.**

Monsieur *Auzout*, the same Person, that not long since communicated to the World his*Ephemerides* touching the course of the former *Comet*, and recommended several Copies of them to the *Royal Society*, to compare their Observations with his Account, and thereby, either to verifie his Predictions, or to shew, wherein they differ, hath lately sent another*Ephemerides* concerning the Motion of the Second *Comet*, to the same end, that invited him to send the other.{37}

In that Tract he observes, first in *General*, that this second *Comet* is contrary to the precedent, almost in all particulars: seeing that the *former* moved very swift, *this*, pretty slow; *that* against the Order of the signs from East to West, *this*, following them, from West to East: *that*, from South to North, *this*, from North to South, as far as it hath been hitherto, that we hear off, observed: *that*, on the side opposite to the Sun, *this*, on the same side: *that*, having been in its *Perigee* at the time of its Opposition, *this*, having been there, out of the time of its Conjunction: where he taketh also notice, that this *Comet* differs in brightness from the other, as well in its Body, which is far more vivid and distinct, as in its *Train*, whose splendor is much greater, since it may be seen even with great *Telescopes*, which were useless in the former, by reason of its dimness. After this he descends to particulars, and informs us, that he began to observe this Comet *April* the second, and continued for some days following, and that as soon as he had made three or four Observations, he resolved to try again an *Ephemerides*; but that, having no instruments exact enough, and the Comet being in a place, destitute of Stars, and subject to Refractions, he feared to venture too much upon Observations so neer one another, since in such matters a perfect exactness is necessary, and wished to see some precedent Observations to direct him: which having obtained, he thereby verified what he had begun, and resolved to carry on his intended *Ephemerides*, especially being urged by his Friends, and engaged by his former undertaking, that so it might not be thought a meer hazard, that made him hit in the former; as also, that he might try, whether his Method would succeed as well in slower, as in swifter Comets, and in those, that are neer the Sun; as in such as are opposite thereunto, to the end, that men might be advertised of the *determination* of its use, if it could not serve but in certain particular Cases.

He relateth therefore, that he had finished this New *Ephemerides April* the sixth, and put it presently to the Press; in doing of which, he hopes, he hath not disobliged the Publick: seeing that, though we should loose the sight of this Star within a few days, by reason of its approach to the Sun, yet having found, {38} that it is always to rise before the Sun, and that we may again see it better, when it shall rise betimes, towards the end of *May*, and in the beginning of *June*, if the cleerness of the Day-break hinder us not; he thought it worth the while to try, whether the truth of this *Ephemerides* could be proved.

He affirms then, that the *Line* described by this Star resembles hitherto a *Great Circle*, as it is found in all other Comets in the midst of their Course. He finds the said Circle inclined to the *Ecliptick* about 26. *d.* 30'. and the *Nodes*, where it cuts it, towards the beginning of *Gemini* and *Sagittary*; that it declines from the *Equator* about 26. *d* and cuts it towards the 11. *d.* and consequently, that its greatest *Latitude* hath been towards *Pisces*, where it must have been *March* 24. and its greatest *Declination*, towards the 25 *d.* of the *Equator*, where it was to have been *April* 11.

He puts it in its *Perigee March* 27. about three of the Clock in the Afternoon, when it was about the 15 degrees of *Pisces*, a little more *Westerly* then *Marshab*, or the *Wing* of *Pegasus*, and that it was to be in *Conjunction* with the *Sun*, *April* 9. Where yet he noteth, that according to another Calculation, the *Perigee* was *March* 27. more towards Night, so that the Comet advances a little more towards the *East*, and retards towards the *West*; which not being very sensible in the first days, differs more about the end, and in the beginning; which he leaves to Observation.

He calculateth, that the greatest Motion it could make in one day, hath been 4. *d.* and 8'. or 9'; in one hour, about 10'. and 25''. so that its *Diurnal Motion* is to its last distance from the Earth a little more than as 1. to 14. and its *Hourly Motion*, as 1. to 330.

He wonders, that it hath not been seen sooner; the first Observations that he hath seen, but made by others, being of *March* 17. Whereas he finds, that it might have been seen since *January*, at least in the Months of *February* and *March*, when it rose at 2 of the Clock and before: because it is very likely, that, considering its bigness and brightness, when it was towards its *Perigee*, it was visible, since that towards the end of *February* it was not three times as much remote from the Earth, than when it was in its *Perigee*, and that towards the end of *January* it was not five times as much. {39}

In the interim, *saith he*, the other *Comet* could be seen with the naked eye until *January* 31. when it was more than ten times further remote, than in its *Perigee*, although it was not by far so bright, nor its streamer shining as this hath appeared.

He wishes, that all the changes that shall fall out in this *Comet*, might be exactly observ'd; because of its not being swift, and the Motion of the Earth very sensible, unless the *Comet* be extreamly remote, we should find much more light from this, than the former Star, about the Grand Question, whether the *Earth* moves or not; this Author having all along entertained himself with the hopes, that the Motion of *Comets* would evince, whether the *Earth* did move or not; and this very *Comet* seemed to him to have by design appeared for that end, if it had had more *Latitude*, and that consequently we might have seen it before Day break. He wishes also, that, if possible, it may be accurately observed, whether it will not a little decline from its great Circle towards the *South*; Judging, that some important truth may be thence deduced, as well as if its motion retarded more, than the place of its *Perigee* (which will be more exactly known when all the passed Observations shall have been obtained) and its greatest Motion do require.

He fears only, that it being then to rise at Break of Day, exact Observations cannot be made of it: but he would, at least have it sought with *Telescopes*, his *Ephemerides* directing whereabout it is to be.

April 10. it was to be over against the point of the *Triangle*, and from thence more *Southerly* by more than two degrees; and *April* 11. over against the bright Star of *Aries*, *April* 17. over against the Stars of the *Fly*, a little more *Southerly*, and *May* 4 it is to be over against the *Pleiades*, and about the fourth or fifth of the same Month, it is to be once more in *Conjunction* with the *Sun*; after which time, the *Sun* will move from it *Eastward*, and leave it towards the *West*; which will enable us to see it again at a better hour, provided the cleerness of the Day-break be no impediment to us. He addeth, that this Star must have been the third time in *Conjunction* with the *Sun*, about the time when it first began to appear: and foresees, that from all these particulars many considerable consequences may be deduced.{40}

It will cut the *Ecliptick* about the end of *July*, new Style, a little more *Eastwards* than the *Eye* of *Taurus*; at which time there will be no seeing of it, except it be with a *Telescope*.

It will be towards the *End* of *April*, new style, twice as far distant as it was in *Perigee*, thrice as far, *May* the fourth, four times, *May* the eighteenth, and five times, *June* the first, *&c.*

He would not have Men surprised, that there have been two *Comets* within so short a time; seeing, *saith he*, there were four, at least three, in the Year 1618. and in other Years there have been two and more at the same time. What he adds about their signification, we leave to *Astrologers* to dispute it with him. He concludeth with asking pardon, if he have committed mistakes, which he hopeth he shall obtain the sooner, because of the small time he hath had for these calculations; and he wishes that he could have made all the Observations himself, seeing that it is easie to fail, when one must trust to the Observations of others, whereof we know not the exactness: where he instanceth, that according to his Observations, the way of the *Comet* should go neerer the Ecliptick than he hath marked it, even without having any great regard to the Refractions: but since he would subject himself to others, he hath made it pass a little higher, which, he saith, was almost insensibly so, in those few days that he was observing and writing, but that this may perhaps become sensible hereafter; which if it be so, he affirms that it will cut the *Ecliptick* and *Equator* sooner, than he hath marked it, *&c.* However, he thinks it convenient, to have given aforehand a common Notion of what will become of a *Comet*, to prepare men for all the Changes that may fall out concerning it: which he affirms he hath endeavoured to do; the rest being easie to correct, as soon as any good Observations, somewhat distant, have been obtained, considering, that there need but two very exact ones, a little distant when the Star is not swift, to trace its Way; although there must be at least three, to find out all the rest. But, then would he have it considered, that although his Method should be very exact, if there be not at hand Instruments big enough, and Globes good enough to trust to, nothing can be done perfectly in these kind of Predictions.{41}

A Relation of the advice given by Monsieur Petit, *Intendant of the Fortifications of* Normandy, *touching the Conjunction of the* Ocean *and* Mediterranean.

This Intelligent Gentleman, Monsieur *Petit*, having been consulted with, touching the Conjunction of the *Ocean* and *Mediterranean*, delivers first the Proposition, and then giveth his thoughts upon it.

The Proposition is, That there being about two Leagues below *Castres* in *Languedoc* a Rivolet, called *Sor*, passing to *Revel*, there may by the means thereof be made a Communication of the two Seas, by joyning the Waters of this Rivolet by a Channel (to be kept full all the year long) with those of St. *Papoul*, and others, which fall into *Fresqueil*(another small River) that runs into the *Aude* below *Carcassone*, and go together to*Narbonne*, scituated upon the *Mediterranean*.

Having given the Proposition, he adds some particulars, to illustrate the same, before he declares his judgment upon it. For he relateth, that there is but one way, after the division of the Waters, to pass to the *Mediterranean*, which is by a Rivolet, called *Fresqueil*, that is conjoyn'd with the *Aude*: But, to pass to the *Ocean*, there are three; One, by *Riege*, entring into the *Caronne* above *Tholouse*; the other, by *Lers*, passing on the side, and below the same Town; and the third, by *Sor*, falling into the River *Agoust* under *Castres*, afterwards into the *Tarne*, and thence to *Montauban*, and lastly into the *Garonne*. And that, to compass this design, all these Rivers and Rivolets are first to be made Navigable unto their *Sluces*; that of *Aude* and *Fresqueil* for the *Mediterranean*, and one of the others, such as shall be chosen, for the *Ocean*. He addeth, that, as to the several Ways passing to the *Ocean*, all of them commended as proper and convenient, and the three Countries concerned therein, speaking every one for their advantage: Those of *Castres* and {42}*Montauban*, are for the River*Agoust*; those of *Tholouse*, for *Riege*; and the rest, for *Lers*.

Now concerning his Opinion upon this Proposition, he thinks, that all that hath been represented touching this matter, can signifie very little, seeing that the main thing is wanting, which is the assurance, and certain and positive mensuration of the height and quantity of the Waters, necessary to fall into both the Channels of the *Aude* and *Caronne*: that there must be plenty of that, to furnish at all times and always the highest and first*sluces*, since what once issues thence, doth never enter again into them; and after some Boats are passed, if there should not be a sufficient supply for those that come after; either to go up, or to go down, all would stand dry, and Merchants and their commodities would stay long enough expecting the supply of Rains, to their great detriment. He concludeth therefore, that no knowing and discreet Person is able, in matters of this nature, to give a positive answer, without having before him a large and exact Topographical Map of those places, and of the sources of all the Rivolets, that are to supply the Water to the Head of the pretended Channel, together with a full account of the survey and mensuration of all the places, through which it is to pass; of the Nature of the Ground, whether it be stony, sandy, rocky,*&c.* of the exact level of all the places, where it is to be made, and of the several risings and depressions thereof, to be assured that the Water may be conveyed to the greatest rising, and to the highest *Sluce*; and lastly, of the quantity, that may be had at high, middle, and low Water, to have enough for all times; that all these things being first made out, 'tis then time enough to judge of the possibility of the thing, and to calculate the charges necessary for Execution.

This Artist having thus prudently waved this Proposition, diverts himself with reflecting upon several others of the like nature, among which he insists chiefly upon two, whereof one is that so much celebrated in *Egypt*; the other, of *Germany*. And he is of Opinion, that the most important of all is that, of conjoyning the *Red sea* by the *Nile* with the *Mediterranean*, which he looks upon as the most excellent conveniency to go into the *East Indies* without doubling the *Cape of Good Hope*; and yet it {43}could not be executed by those great Kings of*Egypt*, that raised so many stupendious *Pyramids*; although in his Opinion the reasons alleged by *Historians* to justifie them for having abandoned that undertaking are of no validity, and that the *Red Sea* cannot be, as they feared, higher than the *Nile*, and therefore not indanger the inundation of *Egypt*.

The other Proposition was made to *Charles Magna, Anno* 793. for joyning the *Euxine* Sea and the *Ocean* together, by a Channel, which was begun for that end, and designed to be 2000. paces long and 100. paces broad, betwixt the River *Altmull*, falling into the *Danube*above *Ratisbone*, and the River *Rott*, passing at *Nurenberg*, and thence running into the*Main*, and so into the *Rhine*. But yet this also proved abortive, though there was great appearance of success at first.

Of the *Way of killing* Ratle-Snakes.

There being not long since occasion given at a meeting of the *Royal Society* to discourse of*Ratle Snakes*, that worthy and inquisitive Gentleman, Captain *Silas Taylor*, related the manner, how they were killed in *Virginia*, which he afterwards was pleased to give in writing, attested by two credible persons in whose presence it was done; which is, as follows.

The Wild *Penny-royal* or *Ditany* of *Virginia*, groweth streight up about one foot high, with the leaves like *Penny-royal*, with little blue tufts at the joyning of the branches to the Plant, the colour of the Leaves being a reddish green, but the Water distilled, of the colour of Brandy, of a fair Yellow: the Leaves of it bruised are very hot biting upon the Tongue: and of these, so bruised, they took some, and having tyed them in the cleft of a long stick, they held them to the Nose of the *Ratle-Snake*, who by turning and wriggling laboured as much as she could to avoid it: but she was killed with it, in less than half an hours time, and, as was supposed, by the scent thereof; which was done *Anno* 1657. in the Month of *July*, at which season, they repute those creatures to be in the greatest vigour for their poison.{44}

A Relation of Persons killed with subterraneous Damps.

This Relation was likewise made to the *Royal Society*, by that Eminent *Virtuoso* Sir R. *Moray*, who was pleased, upon their desire, to give it them in writing; as followeth.

In a Coal-pit, belonging to the Lord *Sinclair* in *Scotland*, where the Coal is some 18 or 20 foot thick, and antiently wasted to a great depth: The Colliers, some Weeks agoe, having wrought as deep as they could, and being to remove into new Rooms (as they call them) did, by taking off, as they retired, part of the Coal that was left as Pillars to support the Roof and Earth over it, so much weaken them, that within a short space, after they were gone out of the Pitt, the Pillars falling, the Earth above them filled up the whole Space, where the Colliers had lately wrought, with its ruins. The Colliers being here-by out of work, some of them adventured to work upon old remains of Walls, so near the old wastes, that striking through the slender partition of the Coal-wall, that seperated between them and the place, where they used to work, they quickly perceived their Errour, and fearing to be stifled by the bad Air, that they knew, possessed these old wastes, in regard not onely of the Damps, which such wastes do usually afford, but because there having for many years been a Fire in those wastes, that filled them with stifling fumes and vapors, retired immediately and saved themselves from the eruptions of the Damp. But next day some seven or eight of them came no sooner so farr down the staires, that led them to the place where they had been the day before, as they intended, but upon their stepping into the place, where the Air was infected, they fell down dead, as if they had been shott: And there being amongst them one, whose Wife was informed he was stifled in that place, she went down so far without inconvenience, that seeing her Husband near her, ventured to go to him, but being choaked by the Damp, as soon as she came near him, she fell down dead by him.{45}

This Story of Sir R. *Moray* affirmed to have received from the *Earl* of *Weymes*, Brother in Law to the Lord *Sinclair*, as it was written to him from *Scotland*.

Of the **Mineral** of **Liege**, *yeilding both* **Brimstone** *and* **Vitriol**, *and the way of extracting them out of it, used at* **Liege**.

The Account of this *Mineral*, and of the way of extracting both *Brimstone* and *Vitriol* out of it, was procured from *Liege*, by the lately mentioned Sir *Robert Moray* and by him communicated to the *Royal Society*, as follows.

The *Mineral*, out of which *Brimstone* and *Vitriol* are extracted, is one and the same, not much unlike Lead ore, having also oft times much Lead mingled with it, which is seperated from it by picking it out of the rest. The Mines resemble our *English* Coal Mines dugg according to the depth of the *Mineral*, 15, 20, or more fathoms, as the Vein leads the Workmen, or the subterranean waters will give them leave, which in Summer so overflow the Mines, that the upper waters, by reason of the drought, not sufficing to make the Pumps goe, the Work ceases.

To make *Brimstone*, they break the Stone or Ore into small pieces, which they put into Crucibles made of Earth, five foot long, square and Pyramid-wise. The Entry is near a foot square. These Crucibles are laid sloaping, eight undermost, and seven above them, as it were betwixt them, that the Fire may come at them all, each having its particular Furnace or Oven. The *Brimstone* being dissolved by the violence of the heat, drops out at the small end of the Crucible, and falls into a Leaden-Trough or Receptacle, common to all the said

Crucibles, through which there runs a continual Rivolet of cold water, conveyed thither by Pipes for the cooling of the dissolved Sulphur, which is ordinarily four hours in melting. This done, the Ashes are drawn out by a crooked Iron, and being put into an Iron Wheel barrow, are carried out of the Hutt, and {46}being laid in a heap, are covered with other exiled or drained Ashes, the better to keep them warm; which is reiterated, as long as they make *Brimstone*.

To make *Coperas* or *Vitriol*, they take a quantity of the said Ashes, and throwing them into a square planked pit in the Earth, some four foot deep, and eight foot square, they cover the same with ordinary water, and let it lye twenty four hours, or until an Egg will swim upon the liquor, which is a sign, that it is strong enough. When they will boyl this, they let it run through Pipes into the Kettles, adding to it half as much Mother-water, which is that water, that remains after boyling of the hardned *Coperas*. The Kettles are made of Lead, 4½ foot high, 6 foot long, and 3 foot broad, standing upon thick Iron Barrs or Grates. In these the Liquor is boyled with a strong Coal-fire, twenty four hours or more, according to the strength or weakness of the Lee or Water. When it is come to a just consistence, the fire is taken away, and the boyled liquor suffered to cool somewhat, and then it is tapp'd out of the said Kettles, through holes beneath in the sides of them, and conveyed through wooden Conduits into several Receptacles, three foot deep and four foot long (made and ranged not unlike our Tan-pits) where it remains fourteen or fifteen dayes, or so long till the *Coperas*separate it self from the water, and becomes icy and hard. The remaining water is the above-mentioned Mother-water; and the elixed or drained Ashes are the Dregs, or *Caput mortuum*, which the Lee, whereof the *Vitriol* is made, leaves behind it in the planked Pits.

A further Account of Mr. Boyle*'s Experimental* History *of* Cold.

In the first Papers of these *Philosophical Transactions*, some promise was made of a *fuller*account, to be given by the next, of the *Experimental History of Cold*, composed by the Honourable Mr. *Robert Boyle*; it being then supposed, that this *History* would have been altogether printed off at the time of publishing the {47}*Second* Papers of these *Transactions*; but the Press, employed upon this Treatise, having been retarded somewhat longer than was ghessed, the said promise could not be performed before this time: wherein it now concerns the inquiring World to take notice, that this subject, as it hath hitherto bin almost totally neglected, so it is now, by this Excellent Author, in such a manner handled, and improved by near *Two* hundred choice *Experiments* and *Observations*, that certainly the *Curious* and*Intelligent* Reader will in the perusal thereof find cause to admire both the Fertility of a Subject, seemingly so barren, and the Author's Abilities of improving the same to so high a Degree.

But to take a short view of some of the particulars of this *History*, and thereby to give occasion to *Philosophical* men, to take this Subject more into their consideration, than hitherto hath been done; the Ingenious Readers will here see,

1, That not only all sorts of *Acid* and *Alcalizate* Salts, and Spirits, even Spirit of Wine, but also Sugar, and Sugar of Lead mixed with Snow, are capable of freezing other Bodies, and upon what account they are so.

2, That among the Substances capable of being frozen, there are not only all gross sorts of Saline Bodies, but such also as are freed from their grosser parts, not excepting Spirit of Urine, the *Lixivium* of Pot-ashes, nor Oyl of Tartar, *per deliquium*, it self.

3, That many very spiritous liquors, freed from their aqueous parts, cannot be brought to freeze, neither naturally, nor artificially: And here is occasionally mentioned a way of keeping *Moats* unpassable in very cold Countries, recorded by *Olaus Magnus*.

4, What are the ways proper to estimate the greater or lesser Coldness of Bodies; and by what means we can measure the intensness of Cold produced by Art, beyond that, which Nature needs to employ for the freezing of Water; as also, in what proportion water of a moderate degree of Coldness will {48}be made to *shrink* by Snow and Salt, before it begin by Congelation to *expand* it self; and then, how to measure by the differing Weight and Density of the same portion of Water, what change was produced in it, betwixt the hottest time of Summer, and first glaciating degree of Cold, and then the highest, which our Author could produce by *Art*: Where an Inquiry is annex'd, whether the making of these kind of

Tryals with the waters of the particular Rivers and Seas, men are to sail on, may afford any useful estimate, whether or not, and how much, ships may on those waters be safely loaden more in Winter, than in Summer. To which is added the way of making exact Discoveries of the differing degrees of Coldness in differing Regions, by such Thermometers, as are not subject to the alterations of the *Atmosphere's* gravitation, nor to be frozen.

5. Whether, in Cold, the diffusion from Cold Bodies be made more strongly downwards, contrary to that of Hot Bodies: Where is delivered a way of freezing Liquors without danger of breaking the Vessel, by making them begin to freeze at the bottom, not the top.

6. Whether that Tradition be true, that if frozen Apples or Eggs be thaw'd neer the Fire, they will be thereby spoil'd, but if immersed in cold water, the Internal Cold will be drawn out, as is supposed, by the External Cold; and the frozen Bodies will be harmlesly thawed? *Item,* Whether Iron, or other Metals, Glass, Stone, Cheese, *&c.* expos'd to the freezing Air, or kept in Snow, or Salt, upon the immersing them in Water will produce any Ice? *Item,* What use may be made of what happens in the different waies of thawing Eggs and Apples, by applying the Observation to other Bodies, and even to Men, dangerously nipp'd by excessive Cold. Where is added not only a memorable Relation, how the whole Body of a Man was succesfully thawed and cased all over with Ice, by being handled, as frozen Eggs and Apples are; but also the Luciferousness of such Experiments, as these: and likewise, what the effects of Cold may be, as to the Conservation or Destruction of the Textures of Bodies: and in particular, how Meat and Drink {49}may be kept good, in very Cold Countries, by keeping it under Water, without glaciation? as also, how in extreme Cold Countries, the Bodies of Dead Men and other Animals may be preserved very many years entire and unputrified? And yet, how such Bodies, when unfrozen, will appear quite vitiated by the excessive Cold? Where it is further inquired into, whether some Plants, and other Medicinal things, that have specifique Vertues, will loose them by being throughly congealed and (several wayes) thawed? And also, whether frozen and thawed Harts-horn will yield the same quantity and strength of Salt and saline Spirit, as when unfrozen? *Item,* Whether the *Electrical* faculty of *Amber,* and the *Attractive* or *Directive* Virtue of *Loadstones* will be either impaired, or any wayes altered by intense Cold? This Head is concluded by some considerable remarks touching the operation of Cold upon Bones, Steel, Brass, Wood, Bricks.

7, What Bodies are expanded by being frozen, and how that expansion is evinced? And whether it is caused by the intrusion of Air? As also, whether, what is contained in icy bubbles, is true and Springy Air, or not.

8, What Bodies they are, that are contracted by Cold; and how that Contraction is evinced? Where 'tis inquired, whether *Chymical Oyles* will, by Congelation, be like expressed Oyls, contracted, or, like aqueous Liquors, expanded?

9, What are the wayes of *Measuring* the *Quantity* of the Expansion and Contraction of Liquors by Cold? And how the Author's account of this matter agrees with what Navigators into cold Climats, mention from experience, touching pieces of Ice as high as the Masts of their Ships, and yet the Depth of these pieces seems not at all answerable to what it may be supposed to be.

10, How strong the Expansion of freezing water is? Where are enumerated the several sorts of Vessels, which being filled {50}with water, and exposed to the cold Air, do burst; and where also the weight is expressed, that will be removed by the expansive force of Freezing? Whereunto an Inquiry is subjoyned, whence this prodigious force, observed in water, expanded by Glaciation, should proceed? And whether this *Phænomenon* may be solved, either by the *Cartesian,* or *Epicurean* Hypothesis?

11, What is the *Sphere of Activity* of Cold, or the Space, to whose extremities every way the Action of a cold Body is able to reach: where the difficulty of determining these limits, together with the causes thereof, being with much circumspection mentioned, it is observed, that the *Sphere of Activity* of Cold is exceeding narrow, not only in comparison of that of Heat in Fire, but in comparison of, as it were, the *Atmosphere* of many odorous Bodies; and even in comparison of the *Sphere of Activity* of the more vigorous Loadstones, insomuch, that the Author hath doubted, whether the Sense could discern a Cold Body, otherwise then by immediate Contract. Where several Experiments are delivered for the examining of this matter, together with a curious relation of the way used in *Persia*, though a very hot Climate, to furnish their *Conservatories* with solid pieces of Ice of a considerable thickness: To which is added an Observation, how far in Earth and Water the Frost will pierce downwards, and upon what accounts the deepness of the Frost may vary. After which, the care is inculcated, that must be had, in examining, whether Cold may be diffused through all *Mediums* indefinitely, not to make the Trials with *Mediums* of two great thickness: where it is made to appear, that Cold is able to operate through Metalline Vessels, which is confirmed by a very pretty Experiment of making *Icy Cups* to drink in, whereof the way is accurately set down. Then are related the Trials, whether, or how, Cold will be diffused through a *Medium*, that *some* would think a *Vacuum*, and which to *others* would seem much less disposed to assist the diffusion of Cold, than Common Air it self. After which follows a curious Experiment, shewing whether a Cold Body can operate through {51}a *Medium* actually hot, and having its heat continually renewed by a fountain of heat.

12, How to estimate the solidity of the Body of Ice, or how strong is the mutual adhesion of its parts? and whether differing Degrees of Cold may not vary the Degree of the compactness of Ice. And our Author having proceeded as far as he was able towards the bringing the strength of Ice to some Estimate by several experiments, he communicateth the information, he could get about this matter among the Descriptions that are given us of cold Regions: and then he relateth out of Sea-mens *Journals*, their Observations touching the insipidness of resolved Ice made of Sea-water; and the prodigious bigness of it, extending even to the height of two hundred and forty Foot above water, and the length of above eight Leagues. To which he adds some promiscuous, but very notable Observations concerning Ice, not so readily reducible to the foregoing Heads: *videlicet*, Of the blew colour of Rocky pieces of Ice; and the horrid noise made by the breaking of Ice, like that of Thunder and Earthquakes, together with a Consideration of the cause, whence those loud Ruptures may proceed.

13, How Ice and Snow may be made to last long; and what Liquor dissolves Ice sooner than others, and in what proportion of quickness the Solutions in the several Liquors are made, where occasion is offered to the Author, to examine, whether Motion will impart a heat to Ice? After which he relates an Experiment of *Heating* a *Cold* Liquor with Ice, made by himself in the presence of a great and Learned Nobleman, and his Lady, who found the Glass wherein the Liquor was, so hot that they could not endure to hold it in their Hands. Next it is examined, whether the effects of Cold do continually depend upon the actual presence and influence of the manifest Efficient causes, as the Light of the Air depends upon the Sun or Fire, or other Luminous Bodies. To this is annexed an Account of the *Italian* way of making *Conservatories* of Ice and Snow, as the Author had received it from that Ingenious and Polite Gentleman, Master *J. Evelyn*.{52}

But want of time prohibiting the accomplishment of the intended account of this Rich Piece: what remains, must be referred to the next Occasion. It shall only be intimated for a Conclusion, that the *Author* hath annexed to this *Treatise*, an Examen of Master *Hob*'s Doctrine touching *Cold*; wherein the *Grand* Cause of *Cold* and its Effects is assigned to *Wind*, in so much that 'tis affirmed, that almost any Ventilation and stirring of the Air doth refrigerate.

LONDON,

Printed with Licence, By *John Martyn*, and *James Allestry*, Printers to the *Royal-Society*, 1665

{53}

PHILOSOPHICAL
TRANSACTIONS.

Munday, June 5. 1665.

The Contents.

A Relation of some extraordinary Tydes in the West-Isles of Scotland, *as it was communicated by Sr.* Robert Moray.

In that Tract of *Isles*, on the West of *Scotland*, called by the Inhabitants, the *Long-Island*, as being about 100. miles long from *North* to *South*, there is a multitude of small Islands, situated in a *Fretum*, or *Frith*, that passes between the Island of *Eust*, and the *Herris*; amongst which, there is one called *Berneray*, some three miles long, and {54} more than a mile broad, the length running from *East* to *West*, as the *Frith* lyes. At the *East* end of this *Island*, where I stayed some 16. or 17. dayes, I *observed* a very strange Reciprocation of the Flux and Re-flux of the Sea, and *heard* of another, no less remarkable.

Upon the *West* side of the *Long Island*, the Tides, which came from the *South-west*, run along the Coast, *Northward*; so that during the ordinary course of the Tides, the Flood runs *East* in the *Frith*, where *Berneray* lyes, and the Ebb *West*. And thus the Sea ebbs and flows orderly, some 4. days before the *full Moon*, and *change*, and as long after (the ordinary Spring-tides rising some 14. or 15. foot upright, and all the rest proportionably, as in other places). But afterwards, some 4. days before the *Quarter-moons*, and as long after, there is constantly a great and singular *variation*. For *then*, (a *Southerly* Moon making there the full Sea) the course of the Tide being *Eastward*, when it begins to flow, which is about 9½ of the Clock, not onely continues so till about 3½ in the afternoon, that it be high water, but, after it begins to ebb, the Current runs on still *Eastward*, during the whole Ebb; so that it runs *Eastward* 12 hours together, that is, all day long, from about 9½ in the morning, til about 9½ at night. But then, when the night-Tide begins to flow, the Current turns, and runs *Westward* all night, during both Floud & Ebb, for some 12. hours more, as it did *Eastward* the day before. And thus the Reciprocations continue, one Floud and Ebb, running 12 hours *Eastward*, and another twelve hours *Westward*, till 4. days before the *New* and *Full* Moon; and then they resume their ordinary regular course as before, running *East*, during the six hours of Floud, and *West*, during the six of Ebb. And this I observed curiously, during my abode upon the place, which was in the Moneth of *August*, as I remember.

But the Gentleman, to whom the *Island* belongs at present, and divers of his Brothers and Friends, knowing and discreet persons, and expert in all such parts of Sea-matters, as other *Islanders* commonly are, though I shrewdly suspected their skill in Tides, when I had not yet seen what they told me, and I have now related of these irregular Courses of the Tides, did most confidently assure me, and so did every body I spake with {55} about it, that there is yet another irregularity in the Tides, which never fails, and is no less extraordinary, than what I have been mentioning: which is, That, whereas between the *Vernal* and *Autumnal Equinoxes*, that is, for six Moneths together, the Course of irregular Tides about the Quartermoons, is, to run all day, that is, twelve hours, as from about 9½ to 9½, 10¼ to 10¼ *&c. Eastward*, and all night, that is, twelve hours more, *Westward*: during the other six Moneths, from the *Autumnal* to the *Vernal Equinox*, the Current runs all day *Westward*, and all Night *Eastward*.

Of this, though I had not the opportunity to be an Eye-witness, as of the other, yet I do not at all doubt, having received so credible Information of it.

To penetrate into the *Causes* of these strange Reciprocations of the Tides, would require exact descriptions of the Situation, Shape, and Extent of every piece of the adjacent Coasts of *Eust* and *Herris*; the Rocks, Sands, Shelves, Promontorys, Bays, Lakes, Depths, and other Circumstances which I cannot now set down with any certainty, or accurateness; seeing, they are to be found in no *Map*, neither had I any opportunity to survey them; nor do they now occur to my Memory, as they did some years ago, when upon occasion I ventured to make a *Map* of this whole *Frith* of *Berneray*, which not having copied, I cannot adventure to beat it out again.

Monsieur Auzout's *Judgment touching the Apertures of* Object-Glasses, *and their* Proportions, *in respect of the several* Lengths *of* Telescopes.

This Author, observing in a small *French Tract* lately written by him to a Countryman of his, Monsieur *L' Abbe Charles,* That great *Optick Glasses* have almost never as great an *Aperture* as the small ones, in proportion to what they Magnifie, and that therefore they must be more dim; takes occasion to inform {56} the *Reader,* that he hath found, that the *Apertures,* which *Optick-Glasses* can bear with distinctness, are in about a *subduplicate proportion* to their *Lengths;* whereof he tells us he intends to give the reason and demonstration in his *Diopticks,* which he is now writing, and intends to finish, as soon as his Health will permit. In the mean time, he presents the *Reader* with a *Table* of such *Apertures,* which is here exhibited to the Consideration of the Ingenious, there being of this *French* Book but one Copy, that is known, in *England.*

A *TABLE* of the *Apertures* of *Object-Glasses.*
The *Points put to some of these Numbers denote Fractions.*

Lengths of Glasses. Feet, Inches.	F or excellent ones. Inch, Lines.	F or good ones. Inch, Lines.	F or ordinary ones. Inch, Lines.	Lengths of Glasses. Feet, Inches.	F or excellent ones. Inch, Lines.	F or good ones. Inch, Lines.	F or ordinary ones. Inch, Lines.
	.			5		0	.
	.			0			
	.			5		.	0
	.			0			
			.	5		0	.
	1	0		0			.
		1		5			.
			0	0			.
	.		1	5			0
				0		0	
				5			.
				0		1	
	.			0			.

				0 0			0
	0			2 0			
	1.			5 0			1
0			0	0 0			
2				5 0	0		.
4			.	0 0	1	0	
6			1.	5 0	2	. 0	
8	0			0 0	3	1	
0			.				

Considerations of Monsieur Auzout *upon* Mr. Hook's *New Instrument for Grinding of* Optick-Glasses.

In the above-mentioned *French* Tract, there are, besides several other particulars, to be represented in due place, contained some *Considerations* of Monsieur *Auzout* upon Mr.*Hook*'s New *Engine* for grinding *Optick-Glasses.* Where he premises in *General* his thoughts touching the working of *Great* Optick-Glasses, and that by the help of a *Turn lathe*; affirming first of all, that not only the *Engin* is to be considered for giveing the *Figure*, but the *Matter* also, which ought to be brought to greater perfection, than it hath been hitherto. For, he finds it not so easie (as least, *where he is*) to procure *Great* pieces of Glass without *Veins*, and other faults, nor to get such, as are thick enough without *Blebbs*; which, if they be not, they will yield to the pressure and weight, either when they are fitted to the *Cement*, or wrought.

Secondly, He finds it difficult to work these *Great* Glasses of the *same* thickness, which yet is very necessary, because, that the least difference in *Figures* so little *convex*, can put the *Center* out of the *Midle*, 2 or 3 *Inches*; and if they be wrought in *Moulds*, the length of time, which is required to wear and to smooth them, may spoil the best *Mould*, before they be finished. Besides, that the strength of Man is so limited, that he is unable to work Glasses beyond a certain bigness, so as to finish and polish them all over so well, as *small* Glasses; whereas yet, the bigger they are, the more compleat they ought to be: And if any weight or Engine be used to supply strength, there is then danger of an unequal pressure, and of wearing away the Engine; In the mean time, the preciseness and delicateness is {58} greater than can easily be imagined. Wherefore he could never, having some experience of this preciseness, conceive, that a *Turn-lathe*, wherein must be two different, and in some manner contrary motions, can move with that exactness and steddiness, that is required, especially, for any considerable length of time.

Having premised this, he discourses upon Mr. *Hook* his *Turne*, intimating first of all, that he was impatient to know what kind of *Turne* this was, imagining, that it had been tried, and had succeeded, as coming from a Society that professeth, they publish nothing but what hath been maturely examin'd. But that he was much surprised when he saw the *Micrography* of Mr. *Hook*, and found there, that his *Engine* was published upon a *meer Theory*, without having made any Experiment, though that might have been made with little charge and great speed; expence of Money and Time being the onely thing, that can excuse those who in matter of *Engines* impart their inventions to the publick, without having tried them, to excite others to make trial thereof.

Whereupon he proposes some difficulties, to give the *Inventor* occasion to find a way to remove them. He affirms therefore, that though it be true in the *Theory*, that a *Circle*, whose *Plain* is inclined to the *Axis* of the *Sphere* by an *Angle*, whereof half the *Diameter* is the *Sine*, and which touches the *Sphere* in its *Pole*, will touch in all its parts a *spherical Surface*, that shall turn upon that *Axe*. But that it is true also, that that must be but a *Mathematical Circle*, and without *Breadth*, and which precisely touches the Body in its middle: Whereas in the practice, a *Circle* capable to keep Sand and Putty, must be of some *breadth*, and he knows not whether we can find such a dexterity of keeping so much of it, and for so long a time, as needs, upon the Brim of a *Ring* that is half an Inch broad. He adds, that it is very difficult to contrive, that the middle of the Glass do always precisely answer to the Brim of this *Ring*, seeing that the position of the Glass does always change a little in respect of the *Ring*, in proportion as 'tis worn, and as it must be pressed because of its inclination. He believes it also very hard, to give to the *Axis* or to the *Mandril*, which holds the Glass, that little {59}*Inclination*, that would be necessary for great Glasses, and to make the two *Mandrils* to have one and the same *Plain*, as is necessary. And, having done all this, he persuades himself, that it is exceedingly difficult, if not impossible, for two contrary motions, where so many pieces are, to rest for a long time steddy and firm, as is requisite for the not swarving from it a hair's thickness, since less than that can change all.

He goes on, and, seeing that this *Inventor* speaks of Glasses of a thousand, & ten thousand foot, which he supposed not impossible to be made by this *Engine*, discourses of what is necessary for the making Glasses of such bignesses; which he believes this *Inventor* may perhaps not have thought of. Wherefore he affirms, that if the *Table*, made by himself for the *Apertures* of Glasses (which is that, that is above delivered) be continued unto a thousand feet, by taking always the *Subduplicate proportion* of *Lengths*, it will be found, that for pretty good ones, the *Aperture* must be of 15. Inches; for good ones, more than 18. and for such as are excellent, more than 21. Inches: whence it may be judged, what piece of Glass, and of what thickness it must be, to endure the working. But he proceeds to speak of the *Inclination*, which the *Mandril* must have upon the *Plain* of the *Ring*, when the *Ring* should have 10. or 12 Inches; and finds, that it would make but 6 or 7. minutes of inclination, and that a Glass would have less *Convexity*, and consequently, less difference from a Glass perfectly plain, than the 7. or 8. part of a Line. And then he leaveth it to be judged, whether a Glass of such a Length being found, we ought to hope, that a *Turn* can be firm enough to keep such a piece of Glass in the same Inclination, so that a *Mandril* do not recede some Minutes from it: and, though even the Glass could be fastned perfectly perpendicular to the *Mandril*, that those two *Mandrils* could be put in one and the same Plain, & that that little Inclination, which is requisite, could be given, and the *Mandril* be continued to be pressed in that same *Inclination*, according as the Glass is worn. All which particulars, he conceives to be very hard in the practice; not to mention, that the weight of the Glass, that should be inclined to the *Horizon*, as 'tis represented by Mr. *Hook*, would make it slide upon the *Cement*, and so {60}change the *Center*; and that the Glass is not pressed at the same time by the *Ring* but in one part on the side, *vid.* about a fourth; and that the parts of the Glass are not equally worn away, *&c.* What then, *saith he*, would becom of a Glass of 10000 feet, which, according to the said Table, would have more than four feet, or four feet and nine inches, or five feet, seven inches *Aperture*, and of which the *Ring*, though it were two feet nine inches, would have but one minut of *Inclination*, and the Glass of 5 feet *Aperture* would have but 4 minuts, and the curvity of it would be less than the eight part of a Line.

But, *saith he*, let us consider, only a Glass of 300 foot, to see, what is to be hoped of that, and to know at least the difficulty, to be met with in making a Glass only of that Length. A Glass then of 300 foot, according to his Table, must have more than 8 inches *Aperture*, which maketh but 16 minuts of its *Circle*, and it should have more than 11 inches, if it be an excellent one. If Mr. *Hook* (adds he) did use but his *Ring* of 6 inches, which he would use from twelve to an hundred foot Glass, the *Inclination*, which the *Axis*, or *Mandril*, that bears his Glass, should have, should be but 16 minuts, and the *Curvity* of the Glass would be less than the eighth part of a Line, and if he should use a bigger, the *Inclination* would be proportionable.

Whence it may be judged (continues he) that we are yet very far from seeing *Animals &c.* in the *Moon*, as Monsieur *Des Cartes* gave hope, and Mr. *Hook* despairs not of. For, he believes by what he knows of *Telescopes*, that we are not to look for any above 300 or 400 foot at most; and he fears, that neither *Matter* nor *Art* will go even so far.

When therefore (*saith he*) a Glass of 300 foot should bear an Eye-glass of 6 inches (which would appear wonderful) it would magnifie but 600. times in *Diameter*, that is, 360000 times in *Surface*: but suppose, that such could be made, as would magnifie a 1000 times in *Diameter*, and 1000000. of times in *Surface*, admitting there were but 60000 leagues from the *Earth* to the *Moon*, and that the smalness of the *Aperture* of the Glasses (which yet would diminish the Light more than 36 times) and the obstacle of the Air were not considered, we should not {61} see the *Moon*, but as if we were a 100, or at least, 60. leagues distant from her without a Glass. He here wishes, that those, that promise to make us see *Animals* and *Plants* in the Moon, had thought on what our naked Eyes can make us discern of such Objects, only at 10 or 12 leagues distance.

But this he would not have understood as a discouragement from searching with all care and earnestness after the means of making long *Telescopes*, or of facilitating the working thereof; but only as an Advertisement to those, who light upon the *Theory* of any *Engine*, not to expose it presently as possible and useful, before they have tried it, or if it have succeeded in small, not to endeavour to persuade, that it will also succeed in great.

As it may happen (*saith he*) that the Engin of Mr. *Hook* may, by using all necessary precautions, succeed in the making of *Eye-Glasses*, or *small* Optick-Glasses, but not in making *great* ones; as we see, that an instrument composed of two Rulers, wherewith are traced Portions of Circles, succeeds well enough in *small*, but when there is no more than half a Line, a quarter of a Line, or less convexity, it will be no longer just at all, as he tells us to have made the proof of it in Circles drawn by the means of one of these Instruments, made by one of the best Workmen in his time, who, whilst he lived, esteemed them above price, although they be not just; as others and my self (*saith he*) have by tryal found, when we endeavoured to make *Moulds* by their means, & as those, who by the like Instrument laboured to trace portions of Circles of 80 or 100 foot, *&c. Diameter*, can attest.

But, notwithstanding all this, he hath thought upon two or three things, which he thinks may remedy some inconveniencies of Mr. *Hook* his *Turn*. The *first* is, to invert the Glass, and to put it under the *Ring*, that so not only the Glass may be placed more *Horizontally*, and not slide upon the *Cement*, but that the *Sand* also, and the *Putty* may stay upon the Glass.

The *other* is, that there must be two *Poppetheads*, into which the *Mandril* must pass, where the *Ring* is to be fastned; and the *Mandril* must be perfectly *Cylindrical*, that so it may advance upon the Glass as it wears away by the means of its weight, or by the means of a spring, pressing it, without wrigling from one place to another, as it would presently happen in the fashion, {62} as the *Turn* is composed. For, when the Glasses do wear, especially when they are very *convex*, it cannot be otherwise, but the *Mandril* will play and wrigle, before the *Scrue* be made firm.

But he doubts, whether all can be remedied, which he leavs to the industry of Mr. *Hook*, considering what he saith in the *Preface* of his *Micrography*, touching a Method, he knows, of finding out as much in *Mechanicks*, as can be found in *Geometry* by *Algebra*.

Besides this, he taketh notice, that most of those that medle with *Optick-Glasses*, give them not as much *Aperture*, nor charge them so deep as they ought. And he instances in the *Telescope*, which His *Majesty* of *Great Britain* presented the *Duke* of *Orleans* with, *videl.* that it did bear but 2 inches, and 9 lines *French*, for its greatest *Aperture*, though there be 5 or 6 lesser *Apertures*, of which it seems (*saith he*) the Artificer would have those, that use it, serve themselves more ordinarily, than of the greatest; which conveys but almost half as many Rays as it should do, according to his Calculation, which is, as 9 to 16; Whereas, according to his *Table of Apertures*, an excellent 35 foot *Telescope* should bear 4 inches *Aperture* in proportion to *excellent* small ones. He notes also, that the Eye-glass of the said *Telescope*, composed of 2 Glasses, hath no more effect, when it is most charged, than a Glass of 4½ inches; which makes it magnifie not a 100 times. And he finds by Mr. *Hook*, that he esteems a *Telescope* made in *London* of 60 feet, (which amount to about 57 feet of *France*, the foot of *France* being to that of *England* as about 15 to 16) because it can bear at least 3 *English* inches *Aperture*, and that there are few of 30 feet, that can bear more than 2 inches, (which is but 22½ Lines *French*) although he (M. *Auzout*) gives no less *Aperture* than so, to a 15 foot-*Telescope*, and his of 21 feet hath ordinarily 2 Inches, 4 Lines, or 2 inches, 6 Lines *Aperture*.

This Discourse he Concludeth with exhorting those, that work *Optick-Glasses*, to endeavor to make them such, that they may bear great *Apertures* and deep Eye-glasses; seeing it is not the length that gives esteem to *Telescopes*; but on the contrary renders them less estimable, by reason of the trouble {63} accompanying them, if they perform no more, than shorter ones. Where, by the by, he takes notice, that he knows not yet, what *Aperture* Signor *Campani* gives to his Glasses, seeing he hath as yet signified nothing of it; but that the small one, sent by him to Cardinal *Antonio*, hath no more *Aperture*, than ordinary ones ought to have.

He promises withall, that he will explicate this way in his *Treatise of the usefulness of Telescopes*, where he intends to assign the Bigness of the *Diameter* of all the *Planets*, and their proportion to that of the *Sun*; as also, that of the *Stars*, which he esteems yet much less, than all those have done, that have written of it hitherto; not believing, that the *Great Dog*, which appears to be the fairest Star of the *Firmament*, hath 2 *Seconds* in Diameter, nor that those, which are counted of the sixth Magnitude, have 20 *thirds*; nor thinking, that all the Stars, that are in the *Firmament*, do enlighten the Earth as much as a Luminous Body of 20 *seconds* in Diameter would do, or, because there is but one half of them at the same time above our *Horizon*, as a Body of 14 *seconds* in Diameter; and as the 18432th part of the *Sun* would enlighten us, or as the *Sun* would do, if we were 14 times more distant from it, than *Saturn*, and 137 times further, than the Earth: Which, *he saith*, would not be credible, if he did not endeavor to evince it both by *Experience* and *Reason*. And he doubts not, but that *Venus*, although she sends us no Light but what is reflected, does sometimes enlighten the *Earth* more, than all the Stars together. Yet he would not have us imagine, from what he hath spoken of the smallness of the Stars, that *Telescopes* do not magnifie them by reason of their great distance, as they do *Planets*; for this he judgeth a Vulgar Error, to be renounced. *Telescopes* magnifie the *Stars* (*saith he*) as much in proportion, as they do all other Bodies, seeing that the demonstration of their magnifying is made even upon *Parallel* rays, which do suppose an infinite distance, though the Stars have none such: And if the *Telescopes* did not magnifie the Stars, how could they make us see some of the *fiftieth*, and it may be some of the *hundreth*, and *twohundreth* Magnitude, as they do, and as they would shew yet much lesser ones, if they did magnifie more? {64}

M^r. Hook's *Answer to Monsieur* Auzout's *Considerations, in a Letter to the Publisher of these* Transactions.

SIR,

Together with my most hearty thanks for the favour you were pleased to do me, in sending me an *Epitome* of what had been by the ingenious Monsieur *Auzout* animadverted on a description, I had made of an *Engine* for *grinding spherical Glasses*, I thought my self obliged, both for your satisfaction, and my own Vindication, to return you my present thoughts upon those Objections. The chief of which seems to be against the very *Proposition* it self: For it appears, that the *Objector* is somewhat unsatisfied, that I should propound a thing in *Theory*, without having first tried the *Practicableness* of it. But first, I could wish that this worthy Person had rectified my mistakes, not by speculation, but by experiments. Next, I have this to answer, that (though I did not tell the *Reader* so much, to the end that he might have the more freedom to examine and judg of the contrivance, yet) it was not meer*Theory* I propounded, but somewhat of *History* and *matter of Fact*: For, I had made trials, as many as my leisure would permit, not without some good success; but not having time and opportunity enough to prosecute them, I thought it would not be unacceptable to such, as enjoyed both, to have a description of a way altogether *New*, and *Geometrically* true, and seemingly, not unpracticable, whereof they might make use, or not, as they should see reason. But nothing surprised me so much, as, that he is pleased (after he had declared it a fault, to write this *Theory*, without having reduced it to practice) to lay it, as he seems to do, in one place of his book, *p.* 22 upon the *Royal Society*. Truly, *Sir*, I should think my self most injurious to that *Noble Company*, had I not endeavoured, even in the beginning of my Book, to prevent such a misconstruction. And therefore I cannot but make this interpretation of what Monsieur *Auzout* saith in this particular, that either he had not so {65}much of the Language wherein I have written, as to understand all what was said by me, or, that he had not read my *Dedication* to the *Royal Society*, which if he had done, he would have found, how careful I was, that that *Illustrious Society* should not be prejudiced by my *Errors*, that could be so little advantaged by my *Actions*. And indeed, for any man to look upon the matters published by their Order or Licence, as if they were *Their* Sense, and had *Their*Approbation, as *certain* and *true*, 'tis extremely wide of their intentions, seeing they, in giving way to, or encouraging such publications, aim chiefly at this, that *ingenious conceptions*, and important *philosophical matter of Fact* may be communicated to the learned and enquiring World, thereby to excite the minds of men to the examination and improvement thereof. But, to return; As to his *Objections* against the *Matter*, I do find that they are no more against mine, than any other way of *Grinding Glasses*; nor is it more than I have taken notice of my self in this Passage of the same *Paragraph*, of which sort are also those difficulties he raises about *Long Glasses*, which are commonly known to such, as are conversant in making them *It would be convenient also* (these are my words) *and not very chargeable, to have four or five several Tools: One*, &c. *And, if curiosity shall ever proceed so farr, one for all lengths, between 1000. and 10000. foot long; for indeed, the* Principle *is such, that supposing the* Mandrils *well made, and of a good length, and supposing great care*be used in working and polishing them, I see no reason, but that a Glass of 1000. nay, 10000. foot long may be made, as well as one of 10. For, the reason is the same, supposing the* Mandrils and Tools be made sufficiently strong, so that they cannot bend; and supposing also that the Glass out of which they are wrought, be capable of so great a regularity in its parts, as to its Refraction. But next, I must say that his *Objections* to me, seem not so considerable, as perhaps he imagines them. For, as to the possibility of getting Plates of Glass thick and broad enough without veins, I think *that* not now so difficult here in*England*, where I believe is made as good, if not much better Glass for *Optical Experiments*, than ever I saw come from *Venice*. Next, though it were better, that the thickest part of a long *Object-Glass* were exactly in the middle, yet I can assure Monsieur *Auzout*, that it may be a very {66}good one, when it is an Inch or two out of it. And I have a good one by me at present, of 36. foot, that will bare an *Aperture*, if *Saturn* or the *Moon* in the *twilight*, be look'd on with it, of 3½ Inches over, and yet the thickest part of the Glass is a great way out of the middle. And I must take the liberty to doubt, whether ever my *Animadversor* saw a long Glass, that was otherwise; as he might presently satisfie himself by a way I could shew him (if he did not know it) whereby the difference of the thickness of the sides might be found to the hundreth part of a Line.

As to the exceeding exactness of the *Figure* of Long *Object-Glasses*, 'tis not doubted, but that it is a matter difficult enough to be attained any way: but yet, I think, much easier by*Engine*, than by *Hand*; and of all *Engines*, I conceive, none more plain and simple, than that of a *Mandril*. And for making *spherical Glasses* by an *Engine*, I am apt to think, there hardly can be any way more plain, and more exact, than that which I have described; wherein there is no other motion, than that of two such *Mandrils*, which may be made of sufficient strength, length, and exactness, to perform abundantly much more, than I can believe possible to be done otherwise than by chance, by a man's hands or strength unassisted by an*Engine*, the motion and strength being much more certain and regular. I know very well, that in making a 60. foot Glass by the strength of the hand, in the common way, not one of ten that are wrought, will happen to be good, as I have been assured by Mr. *Reeves*; who, I am apt to think, was the first that made any good of that length. For the *Figure* of the *Tool* in that way is presently vitiated by the working of the Glass, and without much *gaging* will not do any thing considerable. Besides, the strength of a man's hands, applied to it for the working and polishing of it, is very unequal, and the motions made, are very irregular; but in the way, I have ventured to propose, by *Mandrils*, the longer the *Glass* and *Tool* are wrought together, the more exact they seem to be and if all things be ordered, as they should be, the very polishing of the Glass, does seem most of all rectifie the *Figure*.

As to what he objects, that the Tool does only touch the Glass in a *Mathematical Circle*; that is true, perhaps, at first, but before the Glass is wrought down to its true *Figure*, the *Edge* of the *Tool* {67}will be worn or grownd away, so as that a Ring of an inch broad may be made to touch the *Spherical Surface* of the Glass; nay, if it be necessary (without much trouble, especially in the grinding of longer Glasses) the whole *Concave Surface* of the *Tool* may be made to touch a Glass. Besides, that as to the keeping a quantity of the same sand and Powders of several finesses, according as the glass wears, the same is possible to be don, as with the same Sand wrought finer by working in the Ordinary way.

The giving the *Inclination* to the *Mandrils*, is not at all difficult; though perhaps to determine the length exactly which the Glass so made shall draw, is not so easie: But 'tis no matter, what length the Glass be off, so it be made good, whether 60 or 80 foot, or the like. Nor is it so very difficult, to lay them both in the same *Plain*. And to keep them *steddy*, when once fix'd, is most easie.

As to the Calculation of the propriety of a Glass of a thousand foot, perhaps for that particular Length, I had not, nor have as yet calculated, that the Convexity of one of eighteen inches broad, will not be above a seventh part of a Line. But it does not thence follow, that I had not considered the difficulties, that would be in making of it. For, I must tell him, that I can make a *Plano convex* Glass though its convexity be a smaler sphere than is usual for such a length to be an *Object-Glass* of about 150 foot in Length, nay of 300 foot, and either longer or shorter, *without* at all *altering the convexity*. So that, if he will by any Contrivance he hath, give me a *Plano-convex* Glass of 20, or 40 foot *Diameter*, without *Veins*, and truly wrought of that *Figure*, I will presently make a *Telescope* with it, that with a single Ey-glass shall draw a thousand foot: Which *Invention*, I shall shortly discover, there being, I think, nothing more easie and certain. And if a *Plano-convex* Glass can be made of any *Sphere*between twenty and fourty foot *radius*, so as that both the *Convex* and *Plain* side of the Glass be exactly polish'd of a true *Figure*, I will shortly shew, how therewith may be made a*Telescope* of any Length, supposing the Glass free from all kind of *Veins*, or inequality of*Refraction*.

As for the sliding of the Glass upon the *Cement*, I see no reason at all for it, at least in the*Cement*, I make use of, having never observed any such accident in hard *Cement*.{68}

And for the Bearing of the *Ring* against one side of the Glass only at a time, I cannot see, why *that* should produce any inequality, since all the sides of the Glass have successively the same pressure.

His ratiocination concerning a Glass of 300 foot, is much the same with the former, about the difficulty of working a true surface of a convenient figure; which how considerable both*that* and his Conclusion thereupon (*videl. That we are not to expect Glasses of above 300 or 400 foot long at most, and that neither* Matter *nor* Art *will go so far*) is, may be judged from what I have newly told you of making any *Object-Glass* of any Length.

And for his good wishes, that those, who promise to make him see *Plants* or *Animals* in the*Moon* (of which I know not any, that has done so, though perhaps there may be some, notwithstanding his Objections, that do not yet think it impossible to be done) had considered, what a Man is able to see with his *bare* Eye at 60 Leagues distance: I cannot but return him my wishes, that he would consider the difference between seeing a thing through the *Gross* and *Vaporous* Air neer the Earth, and through the Air over our heads: Which, if he observe the Moon in the *Horizon*, and neer the *Zenith* with a *Telescope*, he will experimentally find; and, having done so, he will perhaps not be so dissident in this matter.

Concerning his Advertisement to such, as publish *Theories*, I find not, that he hath made use of it in his own case. For, in his *Theory* about *Apertures* he seems to be very positive, not at all doubting to rely upon it, *vid.* that the *Apertures* must be *thus* and *thus* in *great* Glasses, because he had found them *so* or *so* in some *small* ones.

For his Proposal of amendments of some inconveniencies in this way, I return him my thanks; but as to his first I believe, that the matter may be conteined as wel in the *Concave*Tool, as on the *convex* Glass. And as to that of 2 *Poppet-heads* I do not well understand it, if differing from mine; and the keeping of the Tool upon the Glass with a spring or weight, must quickly spoyl the whole; since, if either of the *Mandrils* will easily yield backwards, the *regularity* of *all* will be spoiled: and as to the wrigling and playing of the *Mandril*, I do not at all apprehend it.{69}

His *Theory* of *Apertures*, though he seems to think it very authentick, yet to me it seems not so cleer. For, the same Glass will endure greater or lesser *Apertures*, according to the lesser or greater Light of the *Object*: If it be for the looking on the *Sun* or *Venus*, or for seeing the*Diameters* of the *Fix'd Stars*, then smaller *Apertures* do better; if for the *Moon* in the*daylight*, or on *Saturn*, or *Jupiter*, or *Mars*, then the largest. Thus I have often made use of a 12 foot-Glass to look on *Saturn* with an *Aperture* of almost 3 inches, and with a single Eye-glass of 2 inches *double convex*: but, when with the same Glass I looked on the *Sun* or*Venus*, I used both a smaller *Aperture*, and shallower *Charge*. And though M. *Auzout* seems to find fault with the *English* Glass of 36 foot, that had an *Aperture* of but 2¾ inches *French*; as also, with a 60 foot *Tube*, used but with an *Aperture* of 3 inches; yet I do not find, that he hath seen Glasses of that length, that would bear greater *Apertures*, and 'tis not impossible, but his *Theory* of *Apertures* may fail in longer Glasses.

Of a means to illuminate an Object in what proportion one pleaseth; and of the Distances requisite to burn Bodies by the Sun.

One of the means used by M. *Auzout* to enlighten an Object, in what proportion one pleaseth, is by some great *Object-Glass*, by him called a *Planetary* one, because that by it he shews the difference of Light, which all the *Planets* receive from the *Sun*, by making use of several*Apertures*, proportionate to their distance from the *Sun*, provided that for every 9 foot draught, or thereabout, one inch of *Aperture* be given for the *Earth*. Doing this, one sees (*saith he*) that the Light which *Mercury* receives, is far enough from being able to burn Bodies, and yet that the same Light is great enough in *Saturn* to see cleer there, seeing that (to him) it appears greater in *Saturn*, than it doth upon our *Earth*, when it is overcast with Clouds: Which (he adds) would scarce be believed, if by means of this Glass it did not sensibly appear so; Whereof he promises to discourse more fully in his {70}*Treatise of the usefulness of great Optick-Glasses*, where he also intends to deliver several Experiments, by him made, 1. Touching the quantity of Light, which a Body, that is 10, 15 and 20 times, *&c.*remoter than *Saturn*, would yet receive from the *Sun*. 2. Touching the quantity of Light, by which the *Earth* is illuminated even in the *Eclipses* of the *Sun*, in proportion of their bigness. 3. Touching the quantity of Light, which is necessary to burn Bodies: he having found, that not abating the Light, which is reflected by the Surfaces of the Glass (whereof he confesseth, he doth not yet exactly know the quantity) there would be necessary about 50 times as much Light, as we have here, for the burning of *Black* Bodies; and neer 9 times more for the burning of *White* Bodies, than for the burning of *Black* ones: and so observing the immediate proportions between these two, for burning bodies of *other* Colors. Whence (he tells us) he hath drawn some consequences, touching the distance, at which we may hope, to burn Bodies here, by the means of *great Glasses* and great *Looking-glasses*. So that (*saith he*) we must yet be seven times neerer the *Sun*, than we are, to be in danger of being burned by it. Where he mentions, that having given *Instructions* to certain persons, gon to travel in *Hot Countries*, he hath among other particulars recommended to them, to try by means of great*Burning-glasses*, with how much less *Aperture* they will burn *there*, than *here*, to know from thence, whether there by more Light *there* than *here*, and how much; since this perhaps may be the only means of trying it, supposing, the same matters be used: although the difference of the Air already heated, both in *hot Countries*, and in the *Planets*, that are neerer than we, may alter, if not the quantity of Light, at least that of the Heat, found there.

A further Account, touching Signor Campani's Book and Performances about Optick-glasses.

In the above-mentioned *French* Tract there is also conteined M. *Auzout's* Opinion of what he had found New in the *Treatise* of Signor *Campani*, which was spoken of in the first *Papers* of these *Transactions*, concerning both the Effect of the *Telescopes*, contrived after a peculiar way by the said *Campani* at *Rome*, and {71} his New Observations of *Saturn* and *Jupiter*, made by means thereof.

First therefore, after that M *Auzout* had raised some scruple against the Contrivance of Signor *Campani* for making *Great Optick-Glasses* without *Moulds*, by the means of a *Turn-lath*, he examines the *Observations*, made with such *Glasses.* Where, having commended *Campani's* sincerity in relating what he thought to have seen in *Saturn*, without accomodating it to M. *Hugens's Hypothesis*, he affirms, that supposing, there be a *Ring* about *Saturn*, Signor *Campani* could not see in all those different times, that he observed it, *the same Appearances*, which he notes to have *actually* seen. For, having seen it sometimes in *Trine Aspect* with the *Sun*, and *Oriental*, sometimes, in the same *Aspect*, but *Occidental*, sometimes in *Sextil Aspect*, and *Occidental*, at another time, again in *Trine*, and *Oriental*, this Author cannot conceive, how *Saturn* could in all these different times have no difference in its *Phasis*, or keep always the same *Shadow*; seeing that, according to the *Hypothesis* of the *Ring*, when it was *Oriental*, it must cast the *Shadow* upon the *left* side of the *Ring* beneath, without casting any on the *right* side: and when it was *Occidental*, it could not but cast it on the *right* side beneath, and nothing of it on the other.

Concerning the *Shadow above*, which *Campani* affirms to be made by the *Ring* upon the Body of *Saturn*, M. *Auzout* judges, that there could be no such *Phænomenon*, by reason of its *Northern Latitude* at the times, wherein the *Observations* were made, *vid.* in *April* 1663; in the midst of *August*, and the beginning of *October*, next following, and in *April* 1664, except it were in *October*, and the *Shadow* strong enough to become *visible*.

But as to the *Shadow below*, he agrees with *Campani*, that it does appear, yet not as he notes it, seeing that it must be sometimes on the one side, sometimes on the other; and towards the *Quadrat* with the *Sun* it must appear biggest, as *indeed* he affirms to have seen it himself *this* year, insomuch that sometimes it seemed to him, that it covered the whole *Ring*, and that the *Shadow*, joyning with the obscure space between both, did interrupt the circumference of the *Ring*; but beholding it at other times in a cleer Sky, and when there was no Trepidation of the Air, {72} he thought, that he saw also the Light continued from without, although very slender. But he acknowledges, that he could never yet *precisely* determine, by how much the largeness of the *Ring* was bigger than the *Diameter* of *Saturn's* Body. As for the proportion of the Length to the Breadth, he affirms, to have alwaies estimated it to be two and a half, or very neer so; and to have found in his *Observations*, that in *January* last, one time, the length of *Saturn* was 12 *Lines*, and the breadth 5. Another time, the length was 12. *Lines*, and the breadth 4. and this by a peculiar method of his own. But yet he acknowleges also, that sometimes he hath estimated it as 7. to 3. and at other times as 13. to 5. and that if there do not happen a change in the magnitude of the *Ring* (as it is not likely there does) that must needs proceed from the Constitution of the air, or of the Glass's having more or less *Aperture*, or from the difficulty of making an exact estimate of their proportions. However it is not much wide (saith he) of two and a half, although *Campani* make the length of the *Ring* but double to its breadth.

Monsieur *Auzout* believes, that he was one of the first that have well observed this shadow of *Saturn's* Body upon its *Rings* which he affirms happened two years since; when, observing in *July*, for the first time, with a *Telescope* of 21. and then another of 27. foot, he perceived, that the *Angle* of the obscure space on the *right side* beneath, was bigger and wider, than the three other *Angles*, and that some interruption appear'd *there*, between the *Ring*, and the *Body of Saturn*; of which he saith to have given notice from that time to all his friends, and in particular, as soon as conveniently he could, to Monsieur *Hugens*.

He confesseth, that he hath not had the opportunity of observing *Saturn* in his *Oriental Quadrat*; yet he doubts not, but that the *shadow* appears on the *Left-side*, considering, that the *Existence* of the *Ring* can be no longer doubted of, after so many *Observations* of the *shadow* cast by *Saturn's* Body upon it, according as it must happen, following that *Hypothesis*; there being no reason, why it should cast the said *shadow* on one side, and not on the other.

Concerning the Observation of *Jupiter* and its *satellites*, the famous *Astronomer* of *Bononia*, *Cassinus*, having {73}published, that on the 30. day of *July*, 1664. at 2½ of the clock in the morning, he had observ'd, with *Campani*'s Glasses, that there passed through the broad obscure *Belt* of *Jupiter* two obscurer *spots*, by him esteemed to be the *shadows* of the *Satellites*, moving between *Jupiter* & the *Sun*, and eclipsing him, and emerging from the Occidental Brim thereof: This *Authour* did first conceive, that they were not *shadows*, but some *Sallies*, or *Prominencies* in that *Belt*; which he was induced to believe, because he perceived not, that that *Prominency*, which he there saw, was so black, nor so round as *Cassini* had represented his *spots*; wherefore, seeing it but little differing in colour, from the *Belt*, and so not judging it round, because it did stand only about half its diameter out of the *Belt*, he persuaded himself, that it was rather a *Sally*, or *Prominency* of the *Belt*, than a round *shadow*, as that of a *Satellite* of *Jupiter* must have bin. But having been since informed of *all* the *Observations* made by *Cassini* and *Campani*, with the *New* Glasses, and seen his *Figure*, he candidly and publickly wisheth, that he had not spoken of that *Sally*, or *Prominency*; advowing that he can doubt no longer, but that it was the *shadow* of the *Satellit* between *Jupiter* and the *Sun*, having seen the other emerge, as soon as with a 20. foot Glass he made the Observation, and having not perceiv'd these *shadows* with a 12. foot Glass: But although he grants that they did ghess better than he, yet he doth it with this *proviso*, *vid.* in case they made *that* Observation on of *July* 30. not with their 36. but 12. or 17. foot *Telescope*. If it be wondred at, that Monsieur *Auzout* did not see this *shadow* move, he allegeth his indisposition for making *long Observations*, and addeth, that it may be much more wondred at, that neither *Campani* nor himself did see upon the obscure *Belt* the Bodies of the *Satellites*, as parts more Luminous than the *Belt*. For (saith he) although the *Latitude* was *Meridional*, it being no more than of 9. or 10. minutes, the Body of the *Satellites* should, thinks he, pass between *us* and the *Belt*, especially according to *Campani*, who maketh the *Belt* so large, and puts the *shadows* farr enough within the same. This maketh him conclude, that either they have not observed well enough, or that the motion of the *Satellites* doth not exactly follow the *Belts*, and is inclin'd unto them. Whereupon he resolves, that when he shall know that they are to pass between *Jupiter* and *us*, and to be over against the *Belt*, that {74}then he will observe, whether he can see them appear upon the *Belt*, as upon a darker ground, especially, the *third* of them, which is sensibly greater, and more Luminous, than the rest. He hopeth also, that in time, the *shadow* of *Saturns Moon* will be seen upon *Saturn*, although we are yet some years to stay for it, and to prepare also for better Glasses.

From this rare Observation, he inferrs the *Proportion* of the *Diameter* of the *Satellites* to that of *Jupiter*; and judgeth, that no longer doubt can be made of the turning of these 4. *Satellites*, or *Moons* about *Jupiter*, as our *Moon* turns about the *Earth*, and after the same way as the rest of the Celestial Bodies of our *Systeme* do move: whence also a strong conjecture may be made, that *Saturns* Moon turns likewise about *Saturn*.

Hence he also taketh occasion to intimate, that we need not scruple to conclude, that if these two *Planets* have *Moons* wheeling about them, as our *Earth* hath one that moves about it, the conformity of these *Moons* with our *Moon*, does prove the conformity of our *Earth* with those *Planets*, which carrying away their *Moons* with themselves, do turn about the *Sun*, and very probably make their *Moons* turn about them in turning themselves about their *Axis*; and also, that there is no cause to invent perplex'd and incredible *Hypotheses*, for the receding from this *Analogie* since (saith he) if this be truth, the Prohibitions of publishing this doctrine, which formerly were caused by the offence of Novelty, will be laid aside, as one of the most zealous Doctors of the contrary Opinion hath given cause to hope, witness *Eustachius de Divinis*, in his *Tract* against Monsieur *Hugen*'s *Systeme* of *Saturn*, *p.* 49. where we are inform'd, that that learned Jesuit, *P. Fabry*, Penitentiary of *S Peter* in *Rome*, speaks to this purpose:

Ex vestris,   *It hath been more than once asked of your Chieftains, whether they had*
iisque Coryphæis   *a Demonstration for asserting the motion of the Earth? They durst never yet*

non semel quæsitum est, utrum aliquam haberent demonstrationem pro *Terræ motu*adstruendo. Nunquam ausi sunt id asserere Nul igitur obstat quin loca illa in sensu literali Ecclesia intelligat, & intelligenda esse declaret, quamdiu nulla demonstratione contrarium evincitur; quæ si forte aliquando a vobis excogitetur (quod vix crediderim) in hoc casu nullo modo dubitabit Ecclesia declarare, loca illa in sensu figurato & improprio intelligenda esse, ut illud Poetæ, *Terræque Urbesque recedunt*.

affirm they had; wherefore nothing hinders, but that the Church may understand those Scripture-places, that speak of this matter, in a literal *sence, and declare they should be so understood, as long as the contrary is not evinced by any demonstration;* {75}*which, if perhaps it should be found out by you (which I can hardly believe it wil) in this case the Church will not at all scruple to declare, that these places are to be understood in a figurative and improper sence, according to that of the Poet,*Terræque Urbesque recedunt.

Whence this Author concludes, that the said *Jesuite* assuring us that the *inquisition* hath not*absolutely* declared, that those Scripture-places are to be understood *literally*, seeing that the*Church* may make a contrary declaration, no man ought to scruple to follow the *Hypothesis*of the *Earths motion*, but only forbear to maintain it in *publick*, till the prohibition be called in. But to return to the matter in hand, this Author, upon all these observations and relations of *Cassini* and *Campani*, doth find no reason to doubt any more of the excellency of the Glass used by them, above his; except this difference may be imputed to that of the *Air*, or of the *Eys*. But yet he is rather inclined to ascribe it to the goodness of their Glasses, and that the rather, because, he would not be thought to have the vanity of magnifying his own; of which, yet he intimates by the by, that he caused one to be wrought, of 150 *Parisian* feet; which though it proved none of the best, yet he despairs not to make good ones of *that*, and of far greater Length.

Signor Campani's *Answer: and Monsieur* Auzout's *Animadversions thereon.*

The other part of this *French Tract*, conteining *Campani*'s Answer, and Mr. *Auzout* his*Reflections* thereon, begins with the pretended *Shadows* of the *Ring* upon *Saturn*, and of*Saturn* upon the *Ring*. Concerning which, the said *Campani* declareth, that he never believed them to be *shadows*, made by the *Ring* upon the *Disk* of *Saturn*, or by the body of *Saturn*upon the *Ring*, but the *Rimms* of these bodies, which being *unequally* Luminous, did shew these appearances. In which Explication, forasmuch as it represents, that the said *Campani*meant to note only the *Inequality of the Light*, which, *he saith*, his Glasses did

36

discover, Mr. *Auzout* does {76} so far acquiesce, that he only wishes, that his own Glasses would shew him those differences. Next to the Objection, made by Monsieur *Auzout*, against Signor *Campani*, touching the Proportion of the Length of the *Ring* to its breadth, *Campani* replyeth, that the Glasses of Monsieur *Auzout*, shew not all the particulars, that his do, and therefore are unfit for determining the true Figure and breadth of the apparent *Ellipsis* of the *Ring*. To which M. *Auzout* rejoyns, that he is displeased at his being destitute of better Glasses, but that it will be very hard for the future to convince *Campani* touching the *Proportion* of the *Ring*, seing that the breadth of the *Ellipsis* is always diminishing, although, if the declination of the *Ring* remains always the same, one can at all times know, which may have been its greatest breadth. But he assures, that the breadth of the *Ring* is not the half of its length, and that it doth not spread out so much beyond *Saturn's* Body, as he hath alleged. And withal desirs to know, what can be answered by Sig. *Campani* to M. *Hugens*, who being persuaded, that the Declination of the *Ring* is not above 23 deg. 30' having seen the *Ring* to spread out above the Body of *Saturn*, concludes, in a Letter to M. *Auzout*, that the length of the *Ring* is more than treble the *Diameter* of *Saturn's* body, which, according to *Campani*, is only as about 67 to 31. Which difference yet dos not appear to M. *Auzout* to be so great; but that M. *Hugens* perhaps will impute it to the Optical reason, which he (*Auzout*) hath alleged of the Advance of the light upon the obscure space; although he is of Opinion, he should not have concluded so great a Length, if he had not seen the Breadth spread out more, than he hath done: for (*saith he*) if the Length of the *Ring* be to the body of *Saturn*, 2½ to 1. and the *Inclination* be 23 deg. 30' the *Ring* will be just as large, as the body, without spreading out; but if the *Ring* be bigger, it will a little spread out; and if it were treble, it must needs spread out the half of its breadth, which hath not so appeared to him.

Further, to M. *Auzout's* change of Opinion, and believing, that the *Advance* or *Sally*, seen by him in *Jupiter*, was the *Shadow* of one of his Moons, *Campani* declares, that he would not have him guilty of that change: Whereupon M. *Auzout* wonders, why *Campani* then hath not marked it in his *Figure*; and would {77} gladly know, whether that *Sally* be more easie to discover, than the *Shadows* of the *Satellites*, which *Campani* believs, *Auzout* hath not seen; and whether he be assured, that those obscure parts, which he there distinguishes, do not change: for if they should not change, then *Jupiter* would not turn about his *Axis*, which yet, he saith, it doth, according to the *Observation* made by Mr. *Hook*, *May* 9 1664. inserted in the first papers of these *Transactions*. The full Discovery of which particular also he makes to be a part of *Cassini's* and *Campani's* work, seeing that they so distinctly see the inequalities in the *Belts*, and see also sometimes other *Spots* besides the *Shadows* of the *Satellites*: where he exhorts all the Curious, that have the conveniency of observing, to endeavor the discovery of a matter of that importance, which would prove one of the greatest *Analogies* for the *Earth's Motion*.

An Account of Mr. Richard Lower's *newly published* Vindication *of Doctor* Willis's Diatriba *de* Febribus.

The Title of this Curious piece, is *Diatribæ Thomæ Willisii Med. Doct. & Profess. Oxon. De Febribus Vindicatio, Authore Richardo Lower, &c.* In it are occasionally discussed many considerable Medical and Anatomical inquiries, as, Whether a Fever does consist in an Effervescence of Blood? And if so, of what kind? Whether there be a *Nervous* and *Nutritious* Juice? Whether the office of sanguification belongs to the Blood it self, existing *before* those *Viscera* (at least) that are commonly esteemed to be the Organs of sanguification? How *Nutrition* is performed, and the nourishing substance assimilated? Whether the Blood affords both the Matter for the structure of the Body, and such parts also, as are fit for the nourishment of the same? Whether the Pulse of the Heart ceasing, there remains yet a certain Motion in the blood, arguing, that *Pulse* and *Life* do ultimately rest in the *Blood*? Whether the Umbilical Vessels convey the blood of the Mother to the Child, or whether the *Fœtus* be for the most part form'd and {78} acted by the circulating blood, before the existence of the Umbilical Vessels, or before the connecting of the *Fœtus* with the *Uterus*? A new Experiment to prove that the *Chyle* is not transmuted into *Blood* by the *Liver*. A discourse of the Nature of the *Blood*, and what difference there is between the *Venal* and *Arterial* blood, and for what Uses both the one and the other are particularly designed. Where it is considered, what *Life* is, and whence the *Soul* of *Brutes*, and its subsistence, and operations do depend. It is also inquired into, what the uses of the *Lungs* are in *hot* Animals? And many other such material disquisitions are to be found in this small, but very Ingenious and Learned Treatise.

A Note touching a Relation, inserted in the last Transactions.

In the Experiment of killing *Ratle-Snakes*, mentioned in the last of the precedent Papers (wherein, by a mistake, these words, *The way*, were put for *A way*, or *An Experiment*) it should have been added, that the Gentleman there mention'd, did affirm, that, in those places, where the Wild *Penny-Royal* or *Dittany* grows, no *Ratle-Snakes* are observed to come.

Errata.

Pag. 59. line 11. read, *bignesses*, l. 20. r. *endure*, for, resist. l. 30. r. *those*, for, these. l. 31. r.*Plain*, for, place.

LONDON,

Printed with Licence, By *John Martyn*, and *James Allestry*, Printers to the *Royal-Society*, at the *Bell* in St. *Pauls Church-Yard*. 1665.

{79}

PHILOSOPHICAL
TRANSACTIONS.

Munday, July 3. 1665.

The Contents.

An Account, how Adits *and* Mines *are wrought at* Liege *without* Air-shafts, *communicated by Sir* Robert Moray. *A way to break* easily *and* speedily *the hardest*Rocks; *imparted by the same* Person, *as he received it from Monsieur* Du Son *the Inventor. Observables upon a* Monstrous Head. *Observables in the Body of the Earl of*Belcarres, *sent out of* Scotland. *A Relation of the designed Progress to be made in the*Breeding of Silk-worms, *and the* Making *of* Silk, *in* France. *Enquiries touching*Agriculture, *for* Arable *and* Meadows.

An Account, how Adits *&* Mines *are wrought at* Liege *without* Air-shafts, *communicated by Sir* Robert Moray.

It is well known to those conversant in *Mines*, that there is nothing of greater inconvenience in the working or *driving*, as they call it, of *Mines* or *Adits* under ground, for carrying away of Water, or such *Minerals* as the *Mine* affords, than the *Damp, want*, and *impurity of Air*,that {80}occur, when such *Adits* are wrought or driven inward upon a *Level*, or near it, 20, 30, or 40. fathom, more or less. Aswel because of the expence of money, as of time also, in the*Ordinary* way of preventing or remedying those inconveniences; which is, by letting down*shafts* from the *day* (as *Miners* speak) to meet with the *Adit*; by which means the Air hath liberty to play through the whole work, and so takes away bad vapours and furnishes good Air for Respiration. The Expence of which *shafts*, in regard of their vast depth, hardness of the Rock, drawing of water, *&c.* doth sometimes equal, yea exceed the *ordinary* charge of the whole *Adit*.

Amongst the *Expedients* that have been devised to remedy this, there is one practised in the*Coal-mines*, near the Town of *Liege* (or *Luyck*) that seems preferable to all others for Efficacy, Ease, and Cheapness: the description whereof followeth.

At the mouth or entry of the *Adit* there is a structure raised of *Brick*, like a *Chimney*, some 28. or 30. foot high in all: at the bottom, two opposite sides are (or may be) some 5½ foot broad; and the other two, 5. foot: the wall 1½ *Brick* thick. At the lower part of it, is a hole, some 9. or 10. inches square, for taking out of the Ashes, which when it is done, this

38

Ash-hole is immediately stopt so close, as Air cannot possibly get in at any part of it. Then, some 3. foot above ground or more, there is on that side, that is next to the *Adit* or Pit, a square hole of 8. or 9. inches every way, by which the Air enters to make the Fire burn: Into this hole there is fixed a square *Tube* or *Pipe* of Wood, whereof the Joints and Chinks are so stopt with Parchment pasted or glewed upon them, that the Air can no where get in to the Pipe but at the end: And this Pipe is still lengthened, as the *Adit* or Pit advanceth, by fitting the new Pipes so, as one end is alwaies thrust into the other, and the Joints and Chinks still carefully cemented and stopt as before. So the Pipe or Tube being still carried on, as near as is necessary, to the wall or place, where fresh Air is requisite; the Fire within the Chimney doth still attract {81}(so to speak) Air through the Tube, without which it cannot burn, which yet it will do, as is obvious to conceive (all Illustrations and Philosophical Explications being here superfluous,) and so, while the Air is drawn by the fire from the farthest or most inward part of the *Mine* or *Adit*, fresh Air must needs come in from without to supply the place of the other, which by its motion doth carry away with it all the ill vapors, that breath out of the ground; by which meanes the whole *Adit* will be alwaies filled with fresh Air, so that men will there breath as surely as abroad, and not only Candles burn, but Fire, when upon occasion there is use for it for breaking of the Rock.

Now that there may be no want of such fresh Air, the Fire must alwaies be kept burning in the Chimney, or at least as frequently as is necessary: For which purpose there must be two of the Iron Grates or Chimneys, that when any accident befals the one, the other may be ready to be in its place, the Coals being first well kindled in it: but when the fire is neer spent, the Chimney or Grate being haled up to the dore, is to be supplied with fresh fuel.

The Figure of the Fabrick, Chimney, and all the parts thereof being hereunto annexed, the rest will be easily understood.

Figure 1.

A. The *Hole* for taking out the Ashes.

B. The *Square-hole*, into which the Tube or Pipe for conveying the Air is to be fixed.

C. The *Border* or *Ledge* of *Brick* or *Iron*, upon which the *Iron-grate* or *Cradle*, that holds the burning Coals, is to rest, the one being exactly fitted for the other.

D. The *Hole* where the *Cradle* is set.

E. The woodden *Tube*, through which the Air is conveyed towards the *Cradle*.

F. The *Dore*, by which the *Grate* and *Cradle* is let in, which is {82}to be set 8. or 10. foot higher than the Hole D. and the *Shutter* made of Iron, or Wood that will not shrink, that it may shut very close, this*Dore* being made large enough to receive the*Cradle* with ease.

G. The *Grate* or *Cradle*, which is narrower below than above, that the Ashes may the more easily fall, and the Air excite the Fire; the bottom being barred as the sides.

H. The *Border* or *Ledge* of the *Cradle*, that rests upon the *Ledge* C.

I. Four *Chains* of *Iron* fastned to the four corners of the *Cradle*, for taking of it up, and letting of it down.

K. The *Chain* of *Iron*, to which the other are fastned.

L. The *Pulley* of *Iron* or *Brass*, through which the *Chain* passeth.

M. A *Hook*, on which the end of the *Chain* is fastned by a *Ring*, the *Hook* fixed being placed in the side of the Dore.

N. A *Barr* of *Iron* in the Walls, to which the *Pulley* is fastned.

The higher the *Shaft* of the Chimney is, the Fire draws the Air the better. And this Invention may be made use of in the *Pits* or *Shafts*, that are *Perpendicular*, or any wise inclining towards it, when there is want of fresh Air at the bottom thereof, or any molestation by unwholsom Fumes or Vapors:

A way to break easily and speedily *the hardest* Rocks*, communicated by the same Person, as he received it from Monsieur* Du Son, *the Inventor.*

Though the invention of breaking with ease, and dispatch, hard Rocks, may be useful on several occasions, the benefit is incomparably great, that may thereby accrue to those, who have *Adits* or Passages to cut through hard *Rocks*, for making passage for Water to run out by, in *Mines* of *Lead*, *Tin*, or any other whatsoever; these *Adits* appearing to be the surest, cheapest, and most advantagious way imaginable, for draining of the same.{83}

That which is here to be described, was invented by one of the most Excellent*Mechanicks* in the World, *Monsieur du Son*, who lately put it in practice himself in *Germany*, at the desire of the *Elector* of *Mentz*. The manner is, as followeth.

The *Mine* or *Adit* is to be made seven or eight foot high, which though it seem to make more work downwards, yet will be found necessary for making the better dispatch by rendring the Invention more effectual.

There is a *Tool* or *Iron* well steeled at the end, which cuts the Rock, (of the shape shewed by *Fig.* 2. here annexed,) 20. or 22. Inches long or more, and some 2½ Inches *Diameter* at the steeled end, the rest being somewhat more slender. The steeled end is so shaped, as makes it most apt to pierce the Rock, the Angles at that end being still to be made the more obtuse, the harder the Rock is. This *Tool* is to be first held by the hand, in the place, where the Hole, to be made for the use, which shall here be shewed, is to be placed; that is, in the middle between the sides of the Rock, that is to be cut, but as near the bottom as may be. The *Tool* being placed, is to be struck upon with an Hammer, the heavier the better, either suspended by a Shaft turning upon a Pin, or otherwise, so as one man may manage the Hammer, while another holds the Tool or Piercer. If it be hung in a *Frame*, or other convenient way, he that manageth it hath no more to do, but to pull it up at first as high as he can, and let it fall again by its own weight, the motion being so directed, as to be sure to hit the Piercer right. After the stroke of the Hammer, he that holds the Piercer, is to turn it a little on its point; so that the Edges or Angles at the point may all strike upon a new place; and so it must still be shifted after every stroke, by which means small Chipps will at every stroke be broken off, which must from time to time be taken out, as need requires. And thus the work must be continued, till the*Hole* be 18. or 20. Inches deep, the deeper the better. This *Hole* being made as deep as is required, and kept as streight and smooth in the sides, as is possible, there is then a kind of double *Wedge* to be made, and {84} fitted exactly for it; the shape whereof is to be seen in the annexed 3. Figure.

This double *Wedge*, being 12. or 13. Inches long, each piece of it, and so made, as being placed in their due position they may make up a *Cylinder*, but*Diagonal*-wise. The two flat sides that are contiguous, are to be greased or oyled, that the one may slip the more easily upon the other; and one of them, which is to be uppermost, having at the great end a hollow *Crease* cut into it round about, for fastening a *Cartridge*, full of *Gunpowder*, to it with a thred, the round end of the *Wedge* being pared as much as the thickness of the Paper or Pastboard, that holds the Powder, needs to make the outside thereof *even*with the rest of the *Wedge*. This *Wedge* must have an Hole drilled through the longest side of it, to be filled with *priming Powder*, for firing of the Powder in the *Cartridge*; which needs have no more, than half a pound of Powder, though upon occasion a greater quantity may be used, as shall be found requisite.

Then this *Wedge*, being first thrust into the Hole with the *Cartridge*, the round side, whether the Priming-hole is, being uppermost, the other *Wedge* is to be thrust in, home to the due position, care being taken, that they fit the Hole in the Rock as exactly as may be. Then the end of the lower *Wedge* being about an Inch longer, than that of the upper outwardly, and flatned, priming Powder is to be laid upon it; and a piece of burning *Match* or *Thread* dipt in *Brimstone* or other such prepared combustible Matter, fastned to it, that may burn so long before it fire the Powder, as he, that orders it, may have time enough to retire quite out the Pit or *Adit*, having first placed a piece of Wood or Iron so, as one end thereof, being set against the end of the lower Wedge, and the other against the side-wall, so as it cannot slip. Which being done, and the Man retired, when the Powder comes to take fire, it will first drive out the uppermost Wedge, as far as it will go, but the slaunting figure of it being so made, as the farther it goes backward, the thicker it grows, till at the last it can go no farther, then the {85} fire tears the Rock to get forth, and so cracks and breaks it all about, that at one time a vast deal of it will either be quite blown out, or so crackt and broken, as will make it easie to be remov'd: And according to the effect of one such *Cartridge*, more may be afterwards made use of, as hath been said.

Observables upon a Monstrous Head.

This was the Head of a *Colt*, represented in the annexed *Figure* 4. first viewed by Mr. *Boyle*, who went into the Stable where the *Colt* lay, and got the Head hastily and rudely cut off, the *Body* thereof appearing to his Eye compleately formed, without any *Monstrosity* to be taken notice of in it. Afterwards he caused it to be put into a Vessel, and covered with *Spirit of Wine* thereby chiefly intending, to give good example, together with a proof, that by the help of the said *Spirit*, (which he hath recommended for such Properties in one of his *Essays* of the *Usefulness* of *Natural Philosophy*) the parts of *Animals*, and even *Monsters*, may in *Summer* it self be preserved long enough to afford *Anatomists* the opportunities of examining them.

The Head being opened, and examined, it was found.

First, That it had no sign of any *Nose* in the usual place, nor had it any, in any other place of the Head, unless the double Bag CC, that grew out of the midst of the forehead, were some rudiment of it.

Next, That the *two Eyes* were united into one *Double Eye*, which was placed just in the middle of the Brow, the Nose being wanting, which should have separated them, whereby the two Eye-holes in the Scull were united into one very large round hole, into the midst of which, from the Brain, entred one pretty large *Optik Nerve*, at the end of which grew a great *Double Eye*; that is, that *Membrane*, called *Sclerotis*, which contained both, was one and the same, but seemed to have a *Seam*, {86} by which they were joined, to go quite round it, and the fore or pellucid part was distinctly separated into two *Cornea*'s by a white *Seam* that divided them. Each *Cornea* seemed to have its *Iris*, (or Rain-bow-like Circle) and Apertures or Pupils distinct; and upon opening the *Cornea*, there was found within it two *Balls*, or *Crystalline Humours*, very well shaped; but the other parts of it could not be so well distinguished, because the eye had been much bruised by the handling, and the inner parts confused and dislocated. It had four Eye-browes, placed in the manner exprest in Figure 4. by *a a, b b; a a* representing the *lower*, and *b b*, the *upper* Eye-lids.

Lastly, That just above the Eyes, as it were in the midst of the Forehead, was a very deep depression, and out of the midst of that grew a kind of double *Purse* or *Bagg*, C C, containing little or nothing in it; but to some it seemed to be a production of the matter designed for the Nose, but diverted by this Monstrous Conception; perhaps the *Processus mammillares* joyned into one, and covered with a thin hairy skin.

Observables in the Body of the Earl *of* Balcarres.

These following Observations, were a while since sent out of *Scotland* by an ingenious person, an Eye-witness, to Sir *Robert Moray*.

1. That the Belly of this Nobleman being opened, the *Omentum* or *Net* was found lean and small: his *Liver* very big; the *Spleen* big also, filled with a black and thick humour. His *Stomack* and *Entralls* all empty, of a Saffron-colour, distended with wind only. The *Bladder* of *Gall* swelled with a black humour: The *Kidneys* filled with a kind of *grumous blood*.

2. That in the *Thorax* or *Chest*, the *Lobes* of the *Lungs* were all entire, but of a bad colour; on the left side somewhat black and blue, and on the right, whitish; with a yellowish knob under one of the *Lobes*. {87}

3. That the *Pericardium* or the *Case* of the *Heart* being opened, there appeared none of that water, in which the *Heart* uses to swim; and the external Surface of it, from the *Base* to the *Tipp*, was not smooth, but very rough. It being cut asunder, a quantity of white and inspissate liquour run out, and beneath the *Base*, between the right and left Ventricle, *two stones* were found, whereof the one was as bigg as an *Almond*, the other, *two* Inches long and *one* broad, having three *Auricles* or crisped *Angles*. And in the Orifice of the right Ventricle, there was a fleshy fattish Matter.

4. That the whole Body was bloudless, thin, and emaciated, of a black and bluish Colour.

5. The *Scull* being opened, both the *Cerebrum* and *Cerebellum* were bigg in proportion to the Body; and out of it run much more Bloud, than was seen in both the other Regions together.

Of the designed Progress to be made in the Breeding of Silkworms, *and the*Making *of* Silk, *in* France.

The *French* King *Henry the Fourth*, having made a general Establishment all over *France*, of planting and propagating of *Mulberry-trees*, and *Breeding of Silkworms*, in order to set up and entertain a *Silk-trade* there; and having prospered so well in that Design, that in many parts of his Dominions great store of such Trees were raised, and Multitudes of Silk-works propagated, to the great benefit of the *French* people, forasmuch as it was a considerable beginning to avoid the transport of several Millions abroad for buying of Silks, and withall an excellent means of well-imploying abundance of poor Orphans and Widows, and many old, lame, and other indigent and helpless people; The present *French King*, hath lately revived and seconded that Undertaking by giving express order that it should be promoted by all possible means, and particularly in the *Metropolis* of that Kingdom, and round about it; and that for that end the whole way concerning that Work and {88}Trade should be fully and punctually communicated in Print; which hath also been executed by one *Monsieur Isnard*, in a Treatise published at *Paris*, in *French*, Intituled, *Instructions for the Planting of White Mulberryes, the Breeding of Silkworms, and the Ordering of Silk in* Paris, *and the circumjacent Places*, In which Book, the Method being represented, which that Great Prince*Henry* IV used in establishing the said Work and Trade, together with the success thereof, and the advantages thence derived to his Subjects, the *Author*, from his own *Experience*, and long *Practice*, delivers (and seems to do it candidly) all what belongs in this business in four main heads. *First*, he teaches the Means of sowing, planting, and raising *White Mulberryes*(as the Foundation of Silkworks) shewing how many several wayes *that* may be done.*Secondly*, The Breeding of *Silkworms*, the choosing of good Eggs, and their hatching, as also the Feeding of the *Worms*, and preserving them from sickness, and Curing them of it, together with the way of making them spin to best advantage. *Thirdly*, The manner of winding their Silk from their Bottoms, adding the *Scheme* of   the *Instrument* serving   for   that   purpose. *Fourthly*,   The   way of *keeping Silkworms* Eggs for the ensuing year.

Through the whole Book are scattered many not inconsiderable particulars, though perhaps known to most. The *White Mulberry Tree*, as it is in other qualities preferable to the *Black*, so this *Author* esteems it the best, not only for the durableness of the wood, and its large extent of usefulness in Carpentry and Joyners work; but also for the fitness of its leaves (besides their principal use for the food of *Silkworms*) to fatten Sheep, Goats, Cowes, and Hoggs, only by boyling and mingling them with Bran. The Berryes themselves he commends as very excellent to fatten Poultry, and to make them lay Eggs plentifully. In the*Changes*, *Working*, and *Generation* of this *Insect*, he is very curious to observe many things. Their *Metamorphoses*, as is known, are four, whereof the form of the one hath no conformity with any of the rest. The first from an Egge (of the bigness of a Mustard-seed, and of a darkish Gray Colour, when good) to a *Worm* or *Caterpillar*, but of a domestick, noble, and profitable kind, *Black*, when it first comes {89}forth, but growing *white* at last; having 24. feet, 8. on each side of the body, and 4. besides, close to each side of the head. During this form, they undergo constantly 4. Sicknesses, in which they cast their Skins, each sickness lasting about 4. days, wherein they feed not at all; but grow clearer, shorter, and thicker. The second from a *Worm* to an *Aurelia* or *Chrysalis*, having the shape of a small Plum, whereunto it is transformed after its spinning time is past; in which state it lies shut up, in hot Countries, for 14. or 15. dayes; in more temperate ones, 18. or 20. without any Food or Air, known to us. During which time this *Insect* leaves two Coats, both that of a *Worm*, whence 'tis changed into an *Aurelia*, and that of an *Aurelia*, whence it becomes a *Papilio* or *Butterfly*, in the*Theca* or *Case*. The third is, from an *Aurelia* to a *Butterfly*, coming out of the *Theca* with a head, leggs, and horns; for which passage it makes way by a whitish water, it casts upon the Silk, which moistning, and thereby in a manner putrefying it, the new creature thrusts out its head through the sharp end of the *Case*, by a Hole as big as its self. There is found no Excrement in the *Case*, but the two Skins only, just now mentioned.

Before they begin to spin, and about the latter end of their feeding, they must, saith the *Author*, be often changed, and have Air enough, by opening the Windows of the Room, they are in, if it be not too ill Weather; else, saith he, the Silk that is in their Belly, will cause so extraordinary a heat in them, that it burns their gutts, and sometimes bursts them; and the same (being a substance that resembleth Gum or Burgundy Pitch) will putrefy and turn into a yellowish matter.

He maketh the best marks of their maturity for spinning to be, when they begin to quit their white Colour, & their green and yellow Circles, and grow of the Colour of Flesh, especially upon the tail; having a kind of *consistent* softness shewing that they have something substantial in their Stomachs.

As for their *Working*, he gives this account of it, that the first day they make only a *Webb*; the second, they form in this *Webb* their *Cases*, and cover themselves all over with Silk; the third day, they are no longer seen, and the dayes following they thicken their *Cases*, alwayes by one *end* or *thread*, which they {90}never break off, themselves. This, he affirms, they put out with so much quickness, and draw it so subtle and so long, that without an *Hyperbole*, the *end* or *thread* of every *Case* may have two Leagues in length. He advertiseth, that they must be by no means interrupted in their work, to the end, that all the Silk, they have in their bellyes, may come out.

Some eight dayes after they have finished their Work, as many of the best *Cases*, as are to serve for *seed*, *viz.* the first done the hardest, the reddest and best coloured, must be chosen, and put a-part; and all diligence is to be used to winde off the silk with as much speed, as may be, especially if the *Worms* have nimbly dispatched their work.

Here he spends a good part of his Book, in giving very particular Instructions, concerning the way of winding off the silk, setting also down the form of the Oven and Instruments necessary for that work, which is the painfullest and nicest of all the rest.

Touching their *Generation*, he prescribeth that there be chosen as many male as female *Cases* (which are discerned by this, that the males are more pointed at both ends of the *Cases*, and the females more obtuse on the ends, and bigger-bellyed) and that care be had, that no *Cases* be taken, but such wherein the *Worms* are heard rolling; which done, and they being come forth in the form of *Butterflies*, having four wings, six feet, two horns, and two very black eyes, and put in a convenient place, the males fluttering with their wings, will joyn and couple with the females, after that these have first purged themselves of a kind of reddish humour by the fundament: in which posture they are to be left from Morning (which is the ordinary time of their coming forth) till evening, and then the females are to be gently pulled away, whereupon they will lay their eggs, having first let fall by the Fundament another humour, esteemed to proceed from the seed of the males; but the males are then thrown away as useless. He advertiseth, that if they be coupled longer than 9. or 10. hours, (which they will be, and that sometimes for 24. hours together, if they be let alone) either the female will receive very great hurt by it, or much seed will remain in her belly. {91}

The seed at first coming out is very white, but within a day it becoms greenish, then red, at last by little and little gray, which colour it retains alwaies, the most coloured of an obscure gray, being the best; those grains which never quit their whiteness, having no fecundity in them.

Each female emits ordinarily some 300 grains, more or less, some of them not being able to render them all, and dying with them in their belly. One ounce of seed will require an hundred pair of *Cases*, of as many Males as Females.

Care must be taken, that no Rats, Mice, Ants, or other Vermin, nor any Hens, or Birds, come near the Seed, they being very greedy to eat them.

This is the substance of what is contained in this *French* Author, published at *Paris* on purpose to promote the *Making* of *Silk* there, as well as it is practised already in other parts of that Kingdom; which is represented here, to the end, that from this occasion the design, which the English Nation once did entertain of the *increasing of Mulberry trees*, and the *Breeding of Silk-worms*, for the *Making of Silk* within themselves, may be renewed, and *that* encouragement given by King *James* of Glorious memory for that purpose (witness that*Letter* which he directed to the Lords Lievtenants of the several shires of *England*) and seconded by his *Most Excellent Majesty*, that now is, be made use of, for the honour of*England* and *Virginia*, and the increase of wealth to the people thereof; especially since there is cause of hope, that a *double Silk harvest* may be made in *one* Summer in *Virginia*, without hindring in the least the *Tobacco*-Trade of that Countrey.

Enquiries concerning Agriculture.

Whereas the *Royal Society*, in prosecuting the *Improvements of Natural knowledge*, have it in design, to collect *Histories of Nature and Arts*, and for that purpose have already, according to the several Inclinations and Studies of their Members, divided themselves into divers *Committees*, to execute the said design: Those Gentlemen, which do constitute the*Committee* for considering of *Agriculture*, and the *History* and *Improvement* thereof, have begun their work with drawing up certain {92}Heads of *Enquiries*, to be distributed to persons*Experienced in Husbandry* all over *England*, *Scotland*, and *Ireland*, for the procuring a*faithful* and *solid* information of the *knowledge* and *practice* already obtained and used in these Kingdoms; whereby, besides the aid which by this means will be given to the general End of collecting the aforementioned *History*, every place will be advantaged by the helps, that are found in any, and occasion ministred to consider, what improvements may be further made in this whole matter. Now to the End, that those *Enquiries* may be the more universally known, and those who are skilful in Husbandry, publickly invited to impart their knowledge herein, for the *common* benefit of their Countrey, it hath been thought fit to publish the *effect* of them in Print, and withal to desire that what such persons shall think good from their own *Knowledge* and *Experience* to communicate hereupon, they would be pleased to send it to the Printers of the *Royal Society*, to be delivered to either of the*Secretaries* of same. The Enquiries follow.

1. For *Arable*.

1. The several kinds of the soyls of *England*, being supposed to be, either Sandy, Gravelly, Stony, Clayie, Chalky, Light mould, Heathy, Marish, Boggy, Fenny, or Cold weeping Ground; information is desired, what kind of soyls your Country doth most abound with, and how each of them is prepared, when employed for *Arable*?

2. What *peculiar* preparations are made use of to these Soyls for each kind of Grain; with what kind of Manure they are prepared; when, how, & in what quantity the Manure is laid on?

3. At what seasons and how often they are ploughed; what kind of Ploughs are used for several sorts of Ground?

4. How long the several Grounds are let lie fallow?

5. How, and for what productions, *Heathy* Grounds may be improved? And who they are (if there be any in your Country) that have reduced *Heaths* into profitable Lands?

6. What ground *Marle* hath over head? How deep generally it lieth from the surface? What is the depth of the *Marle* it self? What the colour of it? Upon what grounds it is used? {93}What time of the year it is to be laid on? How many loads to an Acre? What Grains *Marled* Land will bear, and how many years together? How such *Marled* Land is to be used afterwards,*&c*?

7. The kinds of Grain or Seed, usual in *England*, being supposed to be either Wheat, Miscelane, Rye, Barley, Oats, Pease, Beans, Fitches, Buck-wheat, Hemp, Flax, Rape; We desire to know, what sorts of Grains are sown in your Country, and how each of these is prepared for Sowing? Whether by *steeping*, and in what kind of Liquor? Or by mixing it, and with what?

8. There being many sorts of Wheat, as the White or Red Lammas, the bearded Kentish Wheat, the gray Wheat, the red or gray Pollard, the Ducks-bill Wheat, the red-eared-bearded Wheat, *&c*. And so of Oats, as the common Black, Blue, Naked, Bearded in *North-wales*. and the like of Barley, Pease, Beans, *&c*. The Enquiry is, which of these grow in your Country, and in what Soyl; and which of them thrive best there; and whether each of them require a peculiar Tillage; and how they differ in goodness?

9. What are the chief particulars observable in the choice of Seed-Corn, and all kinds of Grain; and what kinds of Grain are most proper to succeed one another?

10. What Quantity of each kind is sown upon the Statute-Acre? And in what season of the Moon and year 'tis sowed?

11. With what instruments they do Harrow, Clod and Rowl, and at what seasons?

12. How much an Acre of good Corn, well ordered, generally useth to yield, in very good, in less good, & in the worst years?

13. Some of the common Accidents and Diseases befalling Corn in the growth of it, being Meldew, Blasting, Smut; what are conceived to be the Causes thereof, & what the Remedies?

14. There being other Annoyances, the growing Corn is exposed to, as Weeds, Worms, Flies, Birds, Mice, Moles, &c. how they are remedied?

15. Upon what occasions they use to cut the young Corn in the Blade, or to seed it; and what are the benefits thereof?

16. What are the seasons and waies of Reaping and Ordering each sort of Grain, before it be carried off the Ground?{94}

17. What are the several waies of preserving Grain in the Straw, within and without doors, from all kind of Annoyance, as Mice, Heating, Rain, &c.?

18. What are the waies of separating the several sorts of Grain from the Straw, and of dressing them?

19. What are the waies of preserving any stores of separated Grain, from the Annoyances they are obnoxious to?

2. For *Meadows.*

1. How the above mentioned sorts of Soyl are prepared, when they are used for Pasture or Meadow?

2. The common Annoyances of these Pasture or Meadow Grounds being supposed to be, either Weeds, Moss, Sour-grass, Heath, Fern, Bushes, Bryars, Brambles, Broom, Rushes, Sedges, Gorse or Furzes: what are the Remedies thereof?

3. What are the best waies of Drayning Marshes, Boggs, Fenns, &c?

4. What are the several kinds of Grass, and which are counted the best?

5. What are the chief circumstances observable in the Cutting of Grass; and what in the making and preserving of Hay?

6. What kind of Grass is fittest to be preserved for Winter feeding? And what Grass is best for Sheep, for Cows, Oxen, Horses, Goats, &c.

Advertisement.

The Reader *is hereby advertised, that by reason of the present Contagion in* London, *which may unhappily cause an interruption aswel of* Correspondencies, *as of* Publick Meetings, *the Printing of these* Philosophical Transactions *may possibly for a while be intermitted; though endeavours shall be used to continue them, if it may be.*

LONDON,

Printed with Licence, by *John Martyn*, and *James Allestry*, Printers to the *Royal Society*, at the *Bell* in St. *Pauls Church-Yard*. 1665.

{95}

PHILOSOPHICAL
TRANSACTIONS.

Monday, *November* 6. 1665.

The Contents.

An Account of a not ordinary Burning Concave, *lately made at* Lyons, *and compared with several others made formerly. Of Monsieur* Hevelius *his promise of communicating to the World his Invention of making* Optick Glasses*; and of the hopes, given by Monsieur* Christian Hugens *of* Zulichem, *to perform something of the like nature; as also of the Expectations, conceived of* *some Persons in* England, *to improve*Telescopes. *An intimation of a way of making more lively Counterfeits of Nature in*Wax, *then are extant in* Painting; *and of a new kind of* Maps *in a low* Relievo, *or*Sculpture, *both practised in* France. *Some* Anatomical *Observations of Milk found in Veins instead of Blood; and of Grass found in the Wind-pipes of some Animals. Of a place in* England, *where, without Petrifying Water, Wood is turned into Stone. Of the nature of a certain Stone, found in the* Indies *in the head of a* Serpent. *Of the way, used in the* Mogol's *Dominions, to make* Salt-petre. *An Account of* Hevelius *his* Prodromus Cometicus, *and of some Animadversions made upon it by a* French *Philosopher; as also of the Jesuit* Kircher's Mundus Subterraneus.

An Account of a not ordinary Burning Concave, *lately made at* Lyons, *and compared with several others made formerly.*

An opportunity being presented to revive the publishing of these Papers, which for some Moneths hath been {96}discontinued by reason of the great Mortality in *London*, where they were begun to be Printed; it hath been thought fit to embrace the same, and to make use thereof for the gratifying of the Curious, that have been pleased to think well of such Communications: To re-enter whereupon, there offers it self, first of all a Relation of an uncommon *Burning-glass*, not long since made in *France*, in the City of *Lyons*, by one called Monsieur *de Vilette*, as it was sent to the Publisher of these Tracts, in two Letters, whereof the one was in *Latine*, the other in French, to this effect.

Concerning the Efficacy of Monsieur *de Villete* his Burning Glass, all what the *P. Bertet*hath written of it, is true. We have seen the effects of it repeated over and over again, in the Morning, at Noon, and in the Afternoon, alwaies performing very powerfully; burning or melting any Matter, very few excepted. The *Figure* of it is round, being thirty Inches, and somewhat better in *Diameter*. On one side it hath a Frame of a Circle of Steel, to the end that it may keep its just Measure: 'Tis easie to remove it from place to place, though it be above an hundred weight, and 'tis easily put in all sorts of postures. The *burning Point* is distant from the Centre of the Glass, about three Feet. The *Focus* is about half a *Louys d'or* large. One may pass ones hand through it, if it be done nimbly; for if it stay there the time of a second Minute, there is danger of receiving much hurt.

Green wood takes fire in it, in an instant, as do also many other Bodies.

	S
	econds
A small peice of *Pot-Iron* was melted, and ready to drop down, in	4
	0.
A *Silver Peice* of 15 *Pence* was pierced, in	2
	4.
A *gross Nail* (called *le Claude paisan*) was melted, in	3
	0.
The end of a *Sword-blade* of *Olinde*, was burn'd, in	4
	3.
A *Brass Counter* was pierced, in	0
	6.
A piece of *red Copper* was melted ready to drop down, in	4
	2.
{97}A peice of a *Chamber Quarry-stone* was vitrified, and put into a Glass-drop, in	4
	5.
Steel, whereof Watch-makers make their springs, was found melted, in	0
	9.
A *Mineral-Stone*, such as is used in Harquebusses *à rovët*, was calcin'd and vitrified, in	1 . *ust.*
A peice of *Morter* was vitrified, in	5
	2.

In short, there is hardly any Body, which is not destroyed by this Fire. If one would melt it by it any great quantity of Mettal, that would require much time, the Action of

Burning not being perform'd but within the bigness of the *Focus*, so that ordinarily none but small pieces are exposed to it. One Mounsieur *de Alibert* buys it, paying for it Fifteen hundred Livers.

Since this Information, there were, upon occasion given from thence, upon the same subject, further communicated from *Paris* the following Particulars.

I see by two of the Letters, that you incline to believe, the Glasses of *Maginus* and *Septalius*do approach to that of *Lyons*: But I can assure you, they come very far short of it. You may consult *Maginus* his Book, where he describes his; and there are some persons here that have seen one of his best, which had but about twenty Inches Diameter; so that this of *Lyons* must perform at least twice as much. As to *Septalius*, we expect the Relations of it from Intelligent and Impartial men. It cannot well be compared to that of *Lyons*: but in bigness; and in this case, if it have five *Palms* (as you say) that would be about 3½ feet *French*, and so it were a Foot bigger, which would make it half as much greater in surface: But as to the Effects, seeing it burns so far off, they cannot be very violent. And I have heard one say, that had seen it, that it did not set Wood on Fire but after the time of saying a *Miserere*. You may judge of the difference of the Effects, since that of *Lyons* gathers its Beams together within the space of seven or eight *Lines*, {98}and that of *Septalius* must scatter them in the compass of three Inches. Some here do intend to make of them yea and bigger ones; but we must stay till they be done, *&c.*

Of *Monsieur* Hevelius's *Promise of imparting to the World his Invention of making* Optick Glasses; *and of the hopes given by Monsieur* Hugens *of*Zulichem, *to perform something of the like nature; as also of the Expectations, conceived of some Ingenious Persons in* England *to improve*Telescopes.

That eminent Astronomer of *Dantzick*, Monsieur *Hevelius*, writes to his Correspondent in*London*, as followeth:

What hath been done in the grinding of Optick-glasses in your parts, and how those beginnings, mentioned by you formerly, do continue and succeed, I very much covet to hear, 'Tis now above Ten Years, since I my self invented a peculiar way of grinding such Glasses, and reduced it also into practice; by which 'tis easie, without any considerable danger of failing, to make and polish Optick-glasses of any *Conick* Section, and that (which is most notable) in any dish of any Section of a *Sphere*: which Invention I have as yet discovered to none, my purpose being, for the Improvement of Natural Knowledge, to describe the whole method thereof in my *Celestial Machine*, and to propose it to the Examination and Judgment of the *Royal Society*; not doubting at all, but they will find the way true and practicable, my self having already made several Glasses by it, which many Learned Men have seen and tryed.

Monsieur *Hugens*, inquiring also in a Letter, newly written by him to a Friend of his in*England*, of the success of the attempts made by an ingenious *English* Man for perfecting such Glasses, and urging the prosecution of the same, {99}so as to shew by the effects the practicableness of the Invention, mentions thereupon, That he intends very shortly to try something in that kind, of the success whereof he declares to have good hopes.

Monsieur *du Son*, that excellent Mechanician, doth also at this very present employ himself in *London*, to bring *Telescopes* to perfection, by grinding Glasses of a *Parabolical* Figure, by the means whereof he hopes to enable the Curious to discover more by a Tube of one Foot long, or thereabouts, furnished with Glasses thus figured, then can be done by any other Tubes of very many times more that length: The success hereof will ('tis thought) shortly appear.

*An Advertisement of a way of making more lively Counterfeits of Nature in*Wax, *then are extant in* Painting: *And of a new kind of* Maps *in a low*Relievo. *Both practised in* France.

This was communicated by the Ingenious Mr. *John Evelyn*, to whom it was sent from *Paris*is a Letter, as followeth.

Here is in our Neighbourhood a *French-man*, who makes more lively Counterfeits of Nature in *Wax*, then ever I yet saw in *Painting*, haveing an extraordinary address in modelling the Figures, and mixing the Colours and Shadows; making the Eyes so lively, that they kill all things of this Art I ever beheld; He pretends to make a visit into *England* with some of his Peices.

I have also seen a new kind of *Maps* in low *Relievo*, or Sculpture; For example the Isle of *Antibe*, upon a square of about eight Foot, made of Boards, with a Frame like a Picture: There is represented the Sea, with Ships and other Vessels Artificially made, with their *Canons* and Tackle of Wood fixed upon the surface, after a new and most admirable manner. The Rocks about the Island exactly form'd, {100}as they are upon the Natural Place; and the Island it self, with all its Inequalities, and Hills and Dales; the Town, the Forts, the little Houses, Platform, and Canons mounted; and even the Gardens and Platforms of Trees, with their green leaves standing upright, at if they were growing in their Natural Colours: in *fine*, Men, Beasts, and whatever you may imagine to have any protuberancy above the level of the Sea. This new, delightful, and most instructive form of *Map*, or *Wooden Country*, you are to look upon either *Horizontally*, or *side-long*, and it affords equally a very pleasant object.

Some Anatomical *Observations of Milk found in Veins, instead of Blood; and of Grass, found in the Wind-pipes of some* Animals.

A curious Person wrote not long since from *Paris*, that there they had, in the house of a Physitian, newly open'd a Mans Vein, wherein they found *Milk*, instead of *Blood*. This being imparted to Mr. *Boyle* at *Oxford*, his Answer was, That the like Observation about *White Blood*, had been made by a Learned Physitian of his acquaintance, and the thing being by him look'd upon as remarkable, he was desirous to have it very circumstantially from the said Physitian himself, before he would say more of it. The next Moneth may bring us in this Account.

The other Particular, mention'd in the Title of this Head, came in a Letter sent also by Mr. *Boyle*, in these words:

I shall acquaint you, That Two very Ingenious Men, Dr. *Clark*, and Dr. *Lower*, were pleased to give me an account of a pretty odd kind of Observation: One of them assuring me, That he had several times, in the *Lungs* of *Sheep*, found considerable quantity of Grass in the very Branches of the *Aspera Arteria*: And the other relating to me, That a few Weeks since, he, and a couple of {101}Physitians, were invited to look upon an Ox, that had for two or three daies almost continually held his Neck streight up, and was dead of a Disease, the owner could not conjecture at; whereupon the parts belonging to the Neck and Throat, being open'd, they found, to their wounder, the *Aspera Arteria* in its very Trunk all stuff'd with Grass as if it had been thrust there by main force: which gives us a just cause of marvelling and inquiring, both how such a quantity of Grass should get in there; and how, being there, such an Animal could live with it so long.

Of a place in England, *where, without petrifying Water, Wood is turned into Stone.*

The same Searcher of Nature, that was alledged in the immediately precedent Observations, did impart also the following, in another Letter from *Oxford*, where he saith,

I was a while since visited by a Gentleman, who tells me, That he met with a place in these parts of *England*, where, though there be no petrifying Spring (for that I particularly asked) Wood is turned into Stone in the *Sandy Earth* it self, after a better manner then by any Water I have yet seen: For I had the Curiosity to go to look upon peices of Wood, he brought thence, and hope for the opportunity of making some tryals to examine the matter a little further, then I have yet been able to do. *Thus far that Letter.*

Since which time, He was pleased to give this further Information of the same matter, with a *Mantissa* of some other Particulars, belonging to this Subject, in these Words.

I was lately making some Tryals with the Petrifyed Wood I told you off, which I find to be a very odde substance, wonderfully hard and fixed. If I had opportunity to Re-print the *History of Fluidity* and *Firmness*, I could add divers things about *Stones*, that perhaps would not be disliked; and I hope, if God vouchsafe me a little leisure, {102}to insert several of them in fit places of that *History*, against the next Edition. Here is a certain Stone, that is thought to be Petrifyed Bone, being in shap'd like a Bone, with the Marrow taken out; but with a fit *Menstruum*, I found that I could easily dissolve it, like other soft Stones: and possibly it may prove as fit as *Osteocolla*, for the same Medicinal uses.

Of the nature of a certain Stone, found in the **Indies**, in the head of a **Serpent**.

There was, some while ago, sent by Sir *Philiberto Vernatti*, from *Java major*, where he resides, to Sir *Robert Moray*, for the Repository of the *Royal Society*, a certain Stone, affirmed by the presenter to be found in the Head of a *Snake*, which laid upon any Wound, made by any venomous Creature, is said to stick to it, and to draw away all Poyson: and then, being put in Milk, to void its Poyson therein, and to make the Milk turn blew; in which manner it must be used, till the Wound be cleansed.

The like Relations having been made, by several others, of such a Stone, and some also in this City affirming, to have made the Experiment with success, it was thought worth while, to inquire further into the truth of this Matter: since which time, nothing hath been met with but an Information, delivered by that Ingenious *Parisian*, Monsieur *Thevenot*, in his second *Tome*, of the *Relations of divers considerable Voyages*, whereof he lately presented some Exemplars to his Friends in *England*. The Book being in French, and not common, 'tis conceived it will not be amiss to insert here the said Information, which is to this effect:

In the *East Indies* and in the Kingdom of *Quamsy* in *China*, there is found a Stone in the Head of a certain *Serpent* (which they call by a name signifying *Hairy Serpents*) which heals the bitings of the same Serpent, that else would kill in 24 hours. This Stone is round, white in the middle and about the {103} edges blew or greenish. Being applyed to the Wound, it adheres to it of it self, and falls not off, but after it hath sucked the Poyson, then they wash it in Milk, wherein 'tis left awhile, till it return to its natural condition. It is a rare Stone, for if it be put the second time upon the Wound, and stick to it, 'tis a sign it had not suck'd all the Venome during its first application, but if it stick not, 'tis a mark that all the Poyson was drawn out at first. So far our *French* Author: wherein appears no considerable difference from the written Relation before mentioned.

Of the way, used in the **Mogol's Dominions**, to make **Saltpetre**.

This is delivered in the same Book of Monsieur *Thevenot*, and the manner of it having been inquired after, by several curious Persons, to compare it with that which is used in *Europe*, 'tis presum'd, they will not be displeased to find it inserted here in *English*, which is as followeth:

Saltpetre is found in many places of the *East-Indies*, but cheifly about *Agra*, and in the Villages, that heretofore have been numerously inhabited, but are now deserted. They draw it out of three sorts of Earth, black, yellow, and white: the best is that which is drawn out of the black, for it is free from *common* Salt. They work it in this manner: They make two Pits, flat at the bottom, like those wherein common Salt is made; one of them having much more compass than the other, they fill *that* with Earth, upon which they let run Water, and by the feet of People they tread it, and reduce it to the consistency of a Pap, and so they let it stand for two daies, that the Water may extract all the Salt that is in the Earth: Then they pass this Water into another Pit, in which it christallizes into *Saltpetre*, They let it boil once or twice in a Caldron, according as they will have it whiter and purer. Whilest it is over the Fire, they scum it continually, and fill it out into great Earthen Pots, which {104} hold each 25 or 30 pounds, and these they expose to clear Nights; and if there be any impurity remaining, it will fall to the bottom: Afterwards they break the Pots, and dry the Salt in the Sun. One might make vast quantities of Saltpetre in these parts; but the Country people feeling that *We* buy of it, and that the *English* begin to do the same, they now sell us a *Maon* of 6 pounds for two *Rupias* and a half, which we had formerly for half that price.

An account of **Hevelius** his **Prodromus Cometicus**, together with some Animadversions made upon it by a **French Philosopher**.

This excellent *Dantiscan* Astronomer, *Hevelius*, in his *Prodromus* (by him so call'd, because it is as a Harbinger to his *Cometography*, which hath already so far passed the Press, that of twelve Books there are but three remaining to be Printed) gives an account of the Observations he hath made of the *First* of the two late Comets; reserving those he hath made of the *second*, for that great Treatise, where he also intends to deliver the Matter of this *first* more particularly, and more fully than he hath done here.

In this Account he represents the Rise, Place, Course, Swiftness, Faces and Train of this Comet, interweaving his Conceptions both about the Region of Comets in general (whether in the *Air*, or the *Æther*?) and the Causes of their Generation: In the search of which latter, he intimates to have received much assistance from his *Telescope*.

He observes this Comet not before *Decemb.* 4/14, (though he conceives it might have been seen since *Novemb.* 23 *st. n.*) & he saw it no longer then *Feb.* 3/13: though several others have seen it both sooner, and later: and though himself continued to look out for it till *March* 7. *st. n.* but fruitlesly, whereof he thinks the reason to have been its too great distance and tenuity.

{105}

He finds, its apparent Motion was not made in a *Just* great Circle, but deviated considerably from it; and conceives, that every Comet falls to this deviation, when this apparent Motion grows slow, and the Star becomes Stationary (which, as he saith, it doth in respect of the *Ecliptick*, not its own *Orbite*,) Here he observes, That from *Decemb.* 8/18, to *Decem.* 30. *Jan.* 9. its course was almost a great Circle: but that *then* it began to deflect from that Circle towards the *North*; so that afterwards, with a very notable and conspicuous Curvity, it directed its course towards *Primam Arietis*. Of which deflection, he ventures to assign the cause from the Cometical Matter, the various position and the distance of the Comet from the Earth and the Sun, the annual Motion of the Earth, and the impressed Motion, and the inclination of the *discus* of the Cometical Body.

He is pretty positive, that without the *annual Motion* of the *Earth*, no rational Account can be given of any Comet, but that all is involved with perplexities, and deform'd by absurdities.

He inquires, since all Comets have the peculiar *Ingenite* Motion, what kind of Line it is, they describe by that Motion of their own? whether circular, or streight, or curve, or partly streight and partly curve? And if curve, whether regular or irregular? if regular, whether Elliptick, or Parabolar, or Hyperbolical? He answers, That this Motion is *Conical*; and judgeth, that by the *Conick* path all the *Phænomena* of Comets can, without any inconveniency, be ready solved; even of that, which (by History) in fifty daies, passed through more then the 12 Signs in the *Zodiack*: And of that, which in two daies ran through eight Signs: and of another, which in 48 daies posted through all the Signs, *contra seriem*. Which how it can be explicated upon the supposition of the Earths standing still, and upon the denying of the annual Motion thereof, he understands not at all. {106}

He refers to his *Cometography* these Disquisitions: whether all Comets (in their innate Motion) move equal *spaces* in equal *Times*? which is the swiftest, and which the slowest Motion they are capable of? what the cause of this acceleration and retardation of their true Motion?

He puts it out of doubt, that they are in the *Sky* it self, producing reasons for it that are very considerable, and alledging amongst others, That the *Parallaxes* doe clearly evince it, which he finds far less in Comets, then in the *Moon*, yea then sometimes in the *Sun* it self. Where he also represents, That he hath deduced the *Horizontal Parallax* of this very Comet from one onely Observation, made *Feb.* 4. *st. n.* by which he found, That then it was distant from the Earth 5000 Semidiameters of the same, or 4300000 *German* miles. From this distance from the earth, he deduces, That on that Day when it was so remote from the Earth, its true *Diameter* was 2560 *German* miles, which is three times bigger then the Diameter of the Earth, and almost six times bigger then that of the Moon, whose Diameter, according to his *Theory*, is 442 *German* miles.

He finds the *Matter* of Comets to be in the *Æther* it self, making the *Æther* and the *Air* to differ only in purity, and esteeming, That the *Planets* do emit their Exhalations, and have their *Atmospheres* like unto our Earth. Where he affirms, That the Sun alone may cast out so much Matter at any time in one year, as that thence shall be produced not one or two Comets, equallizing the Moon in Diamiter, but very many; which if so, what contribution may not be expected from the other Planets?

Of this Cometical Matter, he thinks, That first it is by little and little gathered together, then coagulated and condensed, and thereby reduced to a less Diameter; but then, after a while it resolves again, and grows dilute and pale, and at last is dissipated. And accordingly he affirms, That he hath observed the Head of this Comet at first more confused, thin and pale, afterwards clearer and clearer.{107}

He conceives, That all Comets do respect the *Sun* as their *King* and *Centre*, as *Planets* do, making them a kind of *Spurious Planets*, that emulate the *true* ones in their Motion almost in all things.

The *Train*, he makes nothing else but the Beams of the Sun, falling on the head of the Comet, and passing through the same, refracted and reflected. And amongst his *Observations* and *Schemes* of this Comet, there occurs one, wherein the Tail is *curve*, so seen by him *Decemb.* $^{11}/_{21}$. He assigns the causes why the Trains do so much vary, and shews also, on what depends their length.

Whether the *same* Comet returns again, as the Spots in the Sun? and, whether in the time of great *Conjunctions* they are more easily generated? and whether they can be certainly foretold? with several other Inquiries, he refers for to his *great Book*.

As to *Prognostications*, he somewhat complains, That men do more inquire what Comets *signifie*, then what they *are*, or how they are generated and moved; professing himself to be of the mind of those that would have Comets rather *admired* then *feared*; there appearing indeed no cogent reason, why the Author of Nature may not intend them rather as Monitors of his *Glory* and *Greatness*, then of his *Anger* or *Displeasure*; especially seeing that some very diligent Men (among whom is *Gemma Frisius*) take notice of as great a number of *good* as *bad* Events, consequent to Comets. *Seneca* also relating, That that Comet which appeared in his time, was so happy, that it did *Cometis detrahere infamiam*, it cleared the credit of Comets, and made People have good thoughts of them.

Having given some Account of what may be look'd for in this *Prodromus*, it follows, That some also should be rendred of the *Animadversions* mention'd to have been made upon the same. This was done by that *Parisian* Philosopher Monsieur *Auzout*, in a Letter of his to his Country-man Monsieur *Petit*; in which he strongly conceives, That this {108} *Prodromus* contains some mistakes, of which he chiefly singles out one, as most considerable, in *Hevelius*'s Observation of *Feb.* $^{8}/_{18}$, and declares thereupon, That he, and several very intilligent Astronomers of *France* and *Italy* concurring with him therein, (whereas M. *Hevelius* to him seems to stand single, as to this particular) found by their Observations, That this Comet could not, on that day of *February*, be there where M. *Hevelius* placeth it, *viz.* In *Prima Arietis*; unless it be said, That it visited that Star of *Aries* on the 18, and returned thence the 19th, into its ordinary course; in which, according to his, and his several Correspondents Observations the Comet on *Feb.* 17. was distant from that *first Star* of *Aries* at least 1 degree and 17 minutes; and on *February* 19. (he having missed, as well as his other Friends, the Observation on *Febr.* 18) was advanced in its way 12 or 13 minutes, but yet distant from the said Star *some minutes* above a *whole degree*, and consequently far from having then passed it. After which time M. *Auzout* affirms to have seen it as well as several others, for many daies, and that until *March* $^{7}/_{17}$, observing, That about *Feb.* 26. or 27, when the Comet was nearest to the often-mentioned *first* of *Aries*, it approached not nearer thereunto, then the distance of 50. minutes.

This important Difference between two very Learned, and very deserving Persons, being come to the knowledge of some of the ablest *Philosophers* & *Astronomers* of *England*, hath been by them thought worthy their Examination: and they being at this very present employed in the discussion thereof, by comparing what hath been done and published by the Dissenters, and by confronting with them their own Domestick Observations, are very likely to discern where the mistake lies; and having discern'd it, will certainly be found hightly impartial and ingenuous in giving their sense of the same.{109}

Of the Mundus Subterraneus *of* Athanasius Kircher.

This long expected *Subterraneous World*, is now come to light, dedicated (at least the *Exemplar*, that hath been perused by the *Publisher* of these *Papers*, who hears, That other *Copies* bear Dedication to other *Great Princes*) both to the present Pope, as being esteemed by the author to have a part of his *Apostolical Kingdom* there; and to the *Roman Emperor* now Regent, who indeed in his Kingdom of *Hungary*, and in several Provinces of *Germany*, hath very many and very considerable things, worthy to be observed, under *Ground*.

To give the Curious a taste of the *Contents* of this *Volume*, and thereby to excite them to a farther search into the recesses of Nature, for the composure of a good *Natural History*; they may first take notice, That the Author, having given an account in the *Preface*, what encouragement he received, for writing this Book, from the opportunity of Travelling with the *Cardinal* of *Hassia* into *Sicily* (in which Voyage, he saith, He met with, as it were, an *Epitome* of what may be observable in the Subterraneous parts of the Earth; and in particular, with an Earth-quake of 14 daies duration, very instructive to him concerning several great Secrets of Nature:) having I say, thus Prefaced, he divided his Work into 12 *Books*, wherein he affirms not only to have explicated the Divine Structure of the under-ground World, and the wondrous distribution of the Work-houses of Nature, and her Majesty and Riches therein; but also to have opened the Causes of her Effects and Productions; whence, by the Marriage of Nature and Art, a happy Issue may follow for the use and benefit of Humane Life.

In the *First* Book, he considers the nature of the Centre of the Earth, where he delivers several *Paradoxes* touching the same, and Discourses of the Motion of heavy Bodies, of Pendulems, of Projectils. {110}

In the *second* he treats of the Fabrick of the *Terrestrial Globe*, of the Influences it receives from the Cœlestial Bodies, especially the *Sun* and *Moon*, of both which *Luminaries* he gives a *Scheme*; of the proportion of the Earth to the Sun and Moon; of the external conformation of the Earth, its Mountains, and their concatenations, decrease and increase, together with the strange transformation thereof. Further, of the Waters encompassing the Earth, and their various Communications by hidden Passages; as also the heighth of Mountains, and of the depth of Seas; the dimension of the *Sicilian Straights*; the Magnetical Constitution of the Earth, its Heterogeneous Nature, Interior Frame, Laboratories, Caves, Channels, *&c.*

In the *third*: Of the Nature of the Ocean, and the diversity of its Motions; of its general Motion from the *East* to *West*, Currents; Reciprocations, Gulfs, Whirle-pools, Saltness, *&c.*

In the *fourth*: Of the Nature of the Subterraneous *Fire*, its necessity, diffusiveness, food, prodigious Effects through ignivomous Mountains; as also of the Nature of *Air*, and *Winds*, their power and variety; of the general Wind, how and whence generated; of Periodical and Anniversary Winds, and their Causes; as also of the production of Artificial Winds, for refreshment and other advantages. To which he subjoyns a Discourse, tending to prove, That all Meteors owe their Nativity to the Fiers of the Subterraneous World.

In the *fifth*: Of the Original of Springs, Rivers, Lakes; various differences and qualities of Waters, and the marks where they are to be met with under Ground; of Waters *Medical*, hot Baths, and their Differences, Causes, Virtues; together with the Wonderful Qualities and Proprieties of some Springs, as to their Colour, Taste, Smell, Weight, Salubrity, Flux and reflux, Petrifying power, *&c.*

In the *sixth*: Of the *Earth* it self, and the great variety contained in the Womb thereof; of the manifold Productions {111} made therein, by the virtue of Salt and its Auxiliaries, the differences whereof are largly discoursed of, together with the way of extracting the same. In particular of *Saltpetre*, its Generation, Nature, Virtues; of the way of making *Gunpowder*, and the various uses thereof, as also the Nature, Qualities, Preparation, Medicinal and other uses of *Alume* and *Vitriol*.

In the *Seventh*: Of some *Fossils*, as Sand, Gravel, Earths, and their various Differences, Qualities, uses Economical, Chymical, Medical: together with the strange varieties & changes happening in the Earth, and their causes; as also the requisits to *Agriculture*.

In the *eight*: First, of *Stones*, their Origine, Concretion, difference of Colours; and in particular, of *Gems* and their variety, causes of generation, transparency in some and colours in others; as also of their various Figures and Pictures by Nature framed both in common and precious Stones, with their Causes. Secondly, of the Transformation of Juices, Salts,

Plants, yea of Beasts and Men turn'd into Stone: together with the generation of Bony Substances under ground, by many esteemed to be the Bones of *Gyants*; and of *Horny* Substances, taken for *Unicorns* horns: as also of *Fossile wood* and *Coals*, Thirdly, of *Bituminous Flowers, lapis Asbestos, Amber*, and its *Electrical* virtue; together with the way how Insects, little Fishes, and Plants are Intombed therein. Fourthly; of Subterraneous *Animals*, Moles, Mice, Birds, Dragons; where is also treated, of those Animals that are found in the midst of Stones.

In the *ninth*; First, of Poysons, their primeval Origine from Minerals, and their accidental Generation in Vegetable and Animal Bodies, together with their differences; where 'tis discoursed, not only how Poysons may be bred in Men, but also, how the Poyfons of some Animals do infect and kill Men; and, where the Venom of Vipers lodges, and how mad *Dogs* and *Tarantula's* so communicate their Poyson, as that it exserts not its noxiousness, till after some {112} time: Where also occasion is taken to discourse on the Original of Diseases, and cure of Poysonous ones. Secondly, of the wonderful Nature of *Sulphur, Antimony, Quick-silver*, their origine and qualities; together with the productions of *Corals* and *Pearls*.

In the *tenth*: First of *Metallurgy*, and the way how that unctuous Body, out of which mettals are produced, is elaborated by Nature, and what therein are *Sulphur, Salt*, and *Mercury*; besides, what it is that renders Mettals fluid in the Fire, but not Stones and Vegetables, *&c.* Secondly, of the Requisits to a perfect knowledge of the *Metallick Art*, and of the Qualities of the *Mine-master*; then of the Diseases of Mine-men, and their Cure, and the waies of purging the Mines of the Airs malignity; as also of *Metallognomy*, or the signs of latent Mettals, and by what Art they may be discovered. Thirdly, several Accounts sent to the Author, upon his Inquiries by the Mine-masters themselves, or other cheif Over-seers of the Mine-works, touching the variety, nature and properties of Minerals, and the many Accidents happening in Mines, particularly the *Hungarian* ones at *Schemnitz*, and those of *Tyrol*. Fourthly, of several both *Hydraulick* and *Wind-Engines*, to free the Mines from Water and noxious damps. Fiftly, Of the way of working Mettals, Gold, Silver, Copper, Iron, and particularly of the method used at *Potosi* in *Peru*, of extracting the Silver out of the Mineral: to which is added, a Discourse of *Salt-pits*, and the way of making Salt.

In the *eleventh*, First, of *Alchimy*, its Original and Antiquity, the Vessels and Instruments belonging thereunto. Secondly, of the *Philosophers Stone*, what is meant by it, and whether by means thereof true Gold can be produced? And in general, whether there be any such thing, as a true and real Transmutation of one Mettal into another? Where are delivered the several Processes of the reputed *Adepti, Raymund Lulle, Azoth, Arnold de Villanova, Paracelsus, Sendivogius, &c.* but all exploded as fals and deceitful. Thirdly, {113} of the decisions in Law concerning Chimical Gold, true or fals. Fourthly, what the celebrated *Philosophers Stone* was among the Ancients, and what they understood by the same?

In the *twelfth*: First, Of the *Seminal Principle* of all things, its origine, nature and property; of the way how Nature proceeds in the Generation of *Minerals, Vegetables, Animals*; of Spontaneous Generation; of *Zeophyts, Insects* of all sorts, and particularly of the Worms bred in Men; together with the causes why Nature would produce such swarms of infinite sorts of Insects. Secondly, of the variety and differences of *Vegetables*, of the requisits to know the *virtues* of *Plants*, and of the several waies of *Engrafting*. Thirdly, of the *Art of Distilling*, whereby Nature is imitated, as doing all her under-ground works, in the Opinion of this Author, by *Distillation*. Fourthly, of the *Laboratories of various Arts*, in which, according to Natures pattern, used in her Subterraneous Operations, strange things may be performed: where treating of *Chymical Secrets*, the truth of the Preparation of *Aurum potabile* is discussed, and the *Magisteries* of Gold, Silver, Iron, Tin, Copper and Lead, examined: to which is subjoyned an *Appendix*, furnishing such Rules, whereby Students in *Chymistry* may be directed in their work, and true Operations distinguished from fals ones. Fiftly, Of *Metallostaticks*, where by the mixture of Mettals and Minerals may be certainly known; together with a way of weighing the Proportions of *moist* and *dry*, existent in every Compound, as well Vegetable and Animal, as Mineral. Sixthly, of *Glass-making*, where is treated of the Nature of *Glass*; of the Artificial Production of all sorts of Precious Stones, partly from the Authors own Experiments, partly from the Communication of his Friends, and the Collection of the best

Writers upon that subject. Seventhly, of *Fire-works*, where the Invention and Preparation of Gunpowder is largely discoursed of, and the waies of making *Squibs, Fires burning in Water*, {114}and many others, used in Publick Festivities, are described. Eighthly, of some *Mechanical Arts*, as that of *Gold-smiths, Black smiths, Copper smiths, Wyre-drawers*, in the last whereof he resolves this *Problem*; a certain weight of Mettal, and the bigness of the hole, through which the Wyre is to be drawn, being given, to find into what length so much Mettal can be spun out.

Thus you have a view of this whole *Volume*; to which it may perhaps not be amiss to adde, for a Conclusion, some of those Particulars which are esteemed by the Authour to out-shine the rest, and are here and there inter-woven as such. For example, in the *First Part*.

The use of *Pindules*, for knowing by their means the *state* of ones *Health*, from the different beatings of the *Pulse, p.* 51.

The *Chain* of *Mountains*, so drawn over the Earth, that they make, as it were, an *Axis*, passing from *Pole* to *Pole*; and several transverse *ductus*, so cutting that *Axis*, as to make, in a manner, an *Equator* and *Tropicks* of Mountains: by which concatenation he imagines, That the several parts of the Earth are bound together for more firmness, *p.* 69.

A Relation of a strange *Diver*, by his continual converse in Water, so degenerated from himself, That he was grown more like an *Amphibium*, than a man, who, by the command of a *Sicilian* King, went down to the bottom of *Charibdis*, and brought a remarkable account of the condition of that place, *p.* 98.

A Description of the Origine of the *Nile*, as this Author found it in a certain *MS.* of one of his own *Society*, called *Peter Pais*, whom he affirms to have been an Eye-witness, and to have visited the Head of the *Emperor of Æthiopia* himself *Anno* 1618. which *Manuscript*, he saith, was brought to *Rome*, out of *Africa*, by their *Procurator* of *India* and *Æthiopia, p.* 72.{115}

The *Communication* of the *Seas* with one another by Subterraneous Passages, *viz.* of the *Caspian*, with the *Pont Euxin* and the *Persian Gulf*; of the *Mare Mortuum*, with the *Mare Rubrum*, and of this latter with the *Mediterranean*; as also of *Scylla* with *Charybdis, p.* 85. 101.

The Subterraneous *Store-houses* (in all the four parts of the Earth) of *Water*, and *Fire*, and *Air*; together with their important Uses, *p.* 111.

An account of the state of the Earth about the *Poles*, how the Waters are continually swallowed up by the *Northern*, and running along through the Bowels of the Earth, do regurgitate at the *Southern Pole, p.* 159.

A description of Mount *Vesuvius* and *Ætna*, both visited by the Author himself, *Anno* 1638. their Dimensions, Communication, Incendiums, Paths of Fiery Torrents cast out by them, *&c.* as also of the *Vulcans* in *Iceland* and *Groenland*, and their Correspondence and Effects. *p.* 180.

An Account of that famous and strange *Whirl-pool* upon the Coasts of *Norway*: commonly call'd *The Maelstrom*; which the Author fancies to have Communication, by a Subterraneous Channel, with another such *Whirl-pool* in the *Bodnick Bay*; by which commerce, according to him, the Waters, when, upon their accumulation and crowding together in one of these places, they are swallowed up by the Gulf there, carrying along with them whatsoever is in the way and lodging it in a certain receptacle at the bottom thereof, are conveyed through the same under-ground Channel to the other Gulf; where again, upon the like flux and retumescence of Waters, they are absorbed, and through the same Channel do reciprocally run to the former Gulf, and meeting in their impetuous Passage with the things formerly sunk down into the Repository, carry them aloft, with themselves; and cast them up again on the Coast of *Norway, p.* 146.

A Relation of strange *Earth-quakes, p.* 220

{116}

An Enumeration of all the celebrated *Medical Water, and hot Baths*, in all parts of the world, *p.* 236. *et seq.*

In the *Second* Part, some of his special Observations, are, How *Stones* are *coloured* and *figured* under ground, *p.* 13. 24, 25.

Natures skill in *Painting* of *Stones, p.* 22.

A whole Natural *Alphabet* represented upon *Stones*, and all sorts of *Geometrical* Figures, naturally Imprinted upon them, *p.* 23.

The cause of the variety of Colours in *Prismes*, and the Authors severe Judgment concerning those, that hold them to be meerly *Phantastical, pag.* 15, 16, 17. Where he also delivers an Experiment, by him counted wonderful, exhibiting all sorts of Colours by the means of*Mercury*, coagulated by the vapour of Lead, and put in a Brass spoon upon burning Coals.

The cause of the curious Colours in *Birds, p.* 17.

The way of Nature in the Generation of *Diamonds, p.* 21.

A way of preparing such a Liquor, that shall sink into, & colour the whole Body of Marble, so that a Picture made on the surface thereof, shall, the stone being cut through, appear also in the inmost part of the same, *p.* 43.

A Story of a whole Village in *Africa* turned into Stone, with all the people thereof, *p.* 50.

An Experiment, representing the Generation of the *Stone* in the *Bladder, p.* 52.

An *Asbestin* Paper, that shall last perpetually, *p.* 74.

Several Relations of numerous Societies of People living under ground, and their *Oeconomy*; whereof a strange one is alledged to have been found in *England*, attested by an *English*Author, *p.* 97, 98, 99.

A Relation of a Man that bred a Serpent in his Stomach, which came from him of the length of one Foot and a half, affirmed by the Author to have been seen by himself, *p.* 126.

Of whole Forrests of Coral at the bottom of the *Red Sea, p.* 159.{117}

The vanity of *Virga Divinatoria, p.* 181.

A peculiar way of washing out very small *Dust-gold, p.* 198.

Of some extraordinary big pieces of perfect *Natural* Gold and Silver, *p.* 203.

Of a very rare Mineral, sent to the Author out of the *Hungarian* Mines, which had pure Silver branching out into Filaments, and some splendid yellow parts, which was pure Gold, and some dark parts, which was Silver mixed with Gold, 189.

Salt the *Basis* of all Natural Productions, and the admirable variety of Salts, *p.* 299.

Strange Figures of *Plants, p.* 348.

The way of producing *Plants; p.* 414.

In how much time a Swallow can fly about the World, *p.* 411, *&c.*

This may suffice, to give occasion to the Searchers of Nature, to examine this Book, and the Observations and Experiments contained therein, together with the Ratiocinations raised thereupon, and to make severer and more minute Inquiries and Discussions of all.

A farther account of an Observation above-mentioned, about White Blood.

Since the Printing of the former Sheet, there is this farther account from the same hand.

Mr. *Boyle*,

I have at length, according to your desire, received from the Ingenious Dr. *Lower*, an account in writing of the Observation about *Chyle* found in the Blood; which though you may think strange, agrees well with some Experiments of his and mine, not now to be mentioned. The Relation, though short, comprizing the main Particulats of what he had more fully told me in Discourse, I shall give it you with little or no variation from his own words.{118}

A Maid, after eating a good Break-fast, about seven in the Morning, was let Blood about eleven the same day in her Foot; the first Blood was receiv'd in a Porringer, and within a little while it turn'd very white; the last Blood was received in a Sawcer, which turn'd white immediately, like the white of a Custard. Within five or six hours after, he (the Physitian) chanced to see both, and that in the Porringer was half Blood and half Chyle, swimming upon it like a Serum as white as Milk, and that in the Sawcer all Chyle without the least appearance of a drop of Blood; and when he heated them distinctly over a gentle fire, they both harden'd: As the white of an Egge when 'tis heated, or just as the *Serum* of Blood doth with heating, but far more white. This Maid was then in good health, and only let Blood because she never had her Courses, yet of a very florid clear Complexion.

Note.

The Reader *of these Papers is desired, that in those of* Numb. 4. pag. <u>60</u>. lin. 10. *he would be pleased to read* eight, *instead of* hundred*: this latter word having been put in by a great over-sight, and without this Correction, injuring that Author, whose Considerations are there related. This Advertisement should have been given in* Number 5. *but was omitted for haste.*

Imprimatur *Rob. Say, Vice-Cancel.* Oxon.
Oxford, Printed by *Leonard Lichfield:* for *Richard Davis.* 1665.

{119}

PHILOSOPHICAL
TRANSACTIONS.

Monday, *Decemb.* 4. 1665.

The Contents.

Monsieur de Sons *progress in working* Parabolar *Glasses. Some speculations of Monsieur* Auzout *concerning the changes, likely to be discovered in the Moon. The instance of the same Person to Mr.* Hook, *for communicating his Contrivance of making with Glasses of a few feet Diameter,* Telescopes *drawing several hundred feet; together with his Offer of recompensing that secret with another, which teaches, How to measure with a* Telescope *the Distances of Objects upon the Earth. The Experiment of* Kircher, *of preparing a Liquor, that shall sink into, and colour the whole Body of Marble, delivered at length. An Intimation of a Way found in* Europe, *to make good* China-Dishes. *An Account of an odd Spring in* Westphalia, *together with an Information touching* Salt-Springs*; and a way of straining* Salt-water. *Of the Rise and Attempts of a way to conveigh Liquors immediately into the Mass of Blood.*

Of Monsieur de Sons *Progress in working* Parabolar *Glasses.*

Since what was mentioned in the immediately precedent *Tract,* touching Monsieur *de Son's* noble attempt of grinding Glasses of a *Parabolical* Figure, the *Publisher* of these *Papers* hath himself seen two *Eye-glasses* of that shape, about one inch & a half deep, and one inch and a quarter broad, wrought by this Eminent *Artist* with a rare Steel-instrument of his own contrivance and workmanship, and by himself also polished to admiration. And certainly it will be wondred at by those, {120} who shall see these Glasses, how they could be truly wrought to such a Figure, with such a Cavity; & yet more, when they shall hear the Author undertake to excavate other such *Eye-Glasses* to above two inches, and *Object-glasses* of five inches *Diameter.* He hath likewise already begun his *Object-glasses* for the mentioned two *Ocular* ones, of the same Figure of about two inches *Diameter,* which are to be left all open, yet without causing any colours. Of all which 'tis hoped, that shortly a fuller and more particular accompt will be given.

Monsieur Auzout's *Speculations of the Changes, likely to be discovered in the* Earth *and* Moon, *by their respective Inhabitants.*

This Inquisitive *Philosopher* in a letter of his, lately written to his correspondent in *London,* takes occasion to discourse of his considerations concerning those Changes, mentioned in the *Title,* as followes;

I have (saith he) sometimes thought upon the *Changes,* which 'tis likely, the supposed Inhabitants of the *Moon* might discover in our *Earth,* to see, whither reciprocally I could observe any such in the *Moon.* For example, methinks, that the *Earth* would to the people of the *Moon* appear to have a different face in the several seasons of the year; and to have another appearance in *Winter,* when there is almost nothing green in a very great part of the *Earth;* when there are Countries all covered with snow, others, all covered with water, others, all obscured with Clouds, and that for many weeks together: *Another* in *Spring,* when the Forrests and Fields are green. *Another* in *Summer,* when whole Fields are yellow &c. Me thinks, I say, that *these* changes are considerable enough in the force of the reflexions of

56

Light to be observed, since we see so many differences of Lights in the *Moon*. We have*Rivers* considerable enough to be seen, and they enter far enough {121}into the Land, and have a bredth capable to be observed. There are *Fluxes* in certain places, that reach into large Countries, enough to make there some apparent change; & in some of our Seas there float sometimes such bulky masses of Ice, that are far greater, than the Objects, which we are assured, we can see in the *Moon*. Again, we cut down whole Forrests, and drain Marishes, of an extent large enough to cause a notable alteration: And men have made such works, as have produced Changes great enough to be perceived. In many places also are *Vulcans*, that seem big enough to be distinguish't, especially in the shadow: And when Fire lights upon Forrests of great extent, or upon Towns, it can hardly be doubted, but these Luminous Objects would appear either in an Ecclipse of the Earth, or when such parts of the Earth are not illuminated by the Sun. But yet, I know no man, who hath observed such things in the*Moon*; and one may be rationally assured that no *Vulcans* are there, or that none of them burn at this time. This it is (*so he goes on*) which all Curious men, that have good*Telescopes*, ought well to attend; and I doubt not; but, if we had a very particular *Map* of the*Moon*, as I had designed to make one with a *Topography*, as it were, of all the considerable places therein, that We or our Posterity would find some changes in Her. And if the *Mapps*of the *Moon* of *Hevelius*, *Divini*, and *Riccioli* are exact, I can say, that I have seen there some places considerable enough, where *they* put *parts that are clear*, whereas *I* there see *dark ones*. 'Tis true that if there be *Seas* in the *Moon*, it can hardly fall out otherwise, than it doth upon our *Earth*, where *Alluvium's* are made in some places, and the Sea gains upon the Land in others. *I say*, if those Spots we see in the *Moon*, are Seas, as most believe them to be; whereas I have many reasons, that make me doubt, whether they be so; of which I shall speak elsewhere. And I have sometimes thought, whether it might not be, that all the Seas of the *Moon*, if there must be Seas, were on the side of the other *Hemisphere*, and that for this cause it might be that the *Moon* turns not upon its *Axis*, as our *Earth*, {122}wherein the Lands and Seas are, as it were, ballanced: That thence also may proceed the non-appearance of any Clouds raised there, or of any Vapors considerable enough to be seen, as there are raised upon this Earth; and that this absence of Vapors is perhaps the cause, that no *Crepuscle* is there, as it seems there is none, my selfe at least not having hitherto been able to discerne any mark thereof: For, me thinks, it is not to be doubted, but that the reputed Citizens of the*Moon* might see our *Crepuscle*, since we see, that the same is without comparison stronger, than the *Light* afforded us by the *Moon*, even when she is *full*; for, a little after Sun-set, when we receive no more than the *first* Light of the *Sun*, the sky is far clearer, than it is in the fairest night of the *full Moon*. Mean while, since we see in *the Moon*, when she is increasing or decreasing, the Light she receives from the Earth, we cannot doubt, but that the People of the *Moon* should likewise see in the *Earth* that Light, wherewith the *Moon* illuminates it, with perhaps the difference, there is betwixt their bigness. Much rather therefore should they see the Light of the *Crepuscle*, being, as we have said, incomparably greater. In the mean time we see not any faint Light beyond the *Section* of the Light, which is every where almost equaly strong, and we there distinguish nothing at all, not so much that cleerest part, which is called *Aristarchus*, or *Porphyrites*, as I have often tryed; although one may there see the Light, which the *Earth* sends thither, which is sometimes so strong, that in the *Moon's*decrease I have often *distinctly* seen *all* the parts of the *Moon*, that were *not enlightned* by the *Sun*, together with the difference of the clear parts, and the Spots, so far as to be able to discern them all. The *Shaddows* also of all the *Cavities* of the *Moon* seem to be stronger, than they would be, if there were a *Second* Light. For, although a far off, the shaddows of our Bodies, environed with Light, seem to Us almost dark; yet they doe not so appear so much, as the Shaddows of the *Moon* doe; and those that are upon the *Edge* of the *Section*,{123} should not appear in the like manner. But, I will determine nothing of any of these things. When I shall hereafter have made more frequent Observations of the Moon with my *great Telescopes*, in convenient time, I shall then perhaps learn more of it, than I know at present, at least it will excite the *Curious* to endeavor to make the like Observations; and it may be, others, that I have not thought of.

The Instance of the same Person to Mr. Hook, for communicating his Contrivance of making, with a Glass of a Sphere of 20 or 40 foot diameter, a Telescope drawing several hundred foot; and his offer of recompensing that Secret with another, teaching To measure with a Telescope the Distances of Objects upon the Earth.

In *Numb.* 4. Of these *Papers*, pag. <u>67</u>. Mr. *Hook* had intimated, that he would shortly discover a way of his, with a *Plane-convex* Glasse of a Sphære of 20. or 40. feet *Diameter*, without *Veines*, and truly wrought of that *Figure*, to make a *Telescope*, that with a single *Eye-glass* should draw 300, 400, yea 1000 feet, *without* at all *altering the Convexity*: Monsieur *Auzout* returns this consideration, and offer upon it, which follows:

To perform (*saith he*) with a *lesser Object-glass* the effect of a *great Telescope*, we must find out a way to make such an *Object-glass* to receive as many Rayes as one will, without their being sensibly distant from one another; to the end, that by applying to it a *stronger Eye-glass*, there may be still Beams enough to see the Object, and to obliterate the small specks and imperfections of the *Eye-glass*. And if Mr. *Hook* hath this Invention, I esteem it one of the greatest, that can be found in the matter of *Telescopes*. If he please to impart it to us, we shall be obliged to him; and {124}I wish, I had a secret in *Opticks* to encourage him to that communication. If I did believe, that this would be esteemed one, To measure with a *great Telescope* the *distance of Objects* upon the *Earth*, which I have found long since, and proposed to some by way of Paradox; *Locorum distantias ex unica statione, absque ullo Instrumento Mathematico, metiri*; I doe here promise to discover it to him, with the necessary Tables, as soon as He shall have imparted his to me; which I will use, as he shall order me. For, although the *Practise* doe not altogether answer the *Theory* of my Invention, because that the length of the *Telescopes* admits of some Latitude; yet one comes near enough, and perhaps as Just, as by most of the wayes, ordinarily used with Instruments. That, which I am proposing, I doubt not but M. *Hook* will soon understand, and see the determination of all Cases possible. I shall only say, that if we look upon the sole *Theory*, we make use of an ordinary *Telescope*, whereof the *Eye-glass* is to be *Convexe*: for, by putting the Glasses at a little greater distance, than they are, proportionably to the distance for which it is to serve, and by adding to it a *new Eye-glass*, the Object will be seen distinct, though obscure; and if the *Eye-glass* be *Convexe*, the Object will appear erect. They may be done two manner of wayes; either by leaving the *Telescope* in its ordinary situation, the *Object-glass* before the *Eye-glass*, or by inverting it, and putting *this* before *that*. But if any will make use of two *Object-glasses*, whereof the *Focus's* are known, the distance of them will be known. If it be supposed, that the *Focus* of the *first* be B. and *that* of the *second* C, and the distance given, B + 2D, and that D *minus* C, be *equal* to F; for, this distance will be *equal* to B + C + F - rF^2 - C^2. And if you have the *Focus* of the *first Object-glass*, equal to B, the distance, where you will put the *second* Glass equal to B + C + D, the *focus* of the 2d Glasse will be found equal to $^{CD}/_{C+D}$. And if you will that the Object shall be magnified as much with these two Glasses, as it would be with a single one, whereof the *Focus* {125}should be of the distance given, having the *Focus* of the *Object-glass* given equal to B, and the distance to B + D; the distance between the first and the second Glass will be equal to $^{2B^2 + 2BD}/_{2B + D}$, whence subducting B (the *Focus* of the *Object-glass* given) there remains $^{BD}/_{2B + D}$; and if this sum be supposed equal to C, we shall easily know, by the preceding Rule, the *Focus* of the *second* Glass.

So far M. *Auzout*, who, I trust, will receive due satisfaction to his desire, as soon as the happy end of the present Contagion shall give a beginning and life again to the Studies and Actions of our retired *Philosophers*.

I shall onely here adde, That the Secret he mentions [*Of measuring the distance of Places by a Telescope (fitted for that purpose) and from one Station*] is a thing already known (if I am not mis-informed) to some Members of our Society; who have been a good while since considering of it, and have contrived ways for the doing of it: Whether the same with those of Mr. *Auzout*, I know not. Nor have I (at the distance that I am now from them) opportunity of particular Information.

58

An Experiment of a way of preparing a Liquor, that shall sink into, and colour the whole Body of **Marble**, *causing a* **Picture**, *drawn on a surface, to appear also in the* inmost *parts of the Stone.*

This *Experiment*, having been hinted at in the next foregoing *Papers*, out of the *Mundus Subterraneus* of *Athanasius Kircher*, and several Curious Persons, who either have not the leisure to read Voluminous Authors, or are not readily skilled in that Learned Tongue wherein the said Book is written, being very desirous to have it transferred hither, it was thought fit to comply with their desire herein.

The Author therefore of the *Mundus*, &c, having seen {126} some stones reputed to be *natural* that had most lively Pictures, not only upon them, but passing *thorow* their whole substance, and thereupon finding an *Artist*, skilful to perform such rare workmanship, did not only pronounce such stones to be *artificial*, but when that *Artist* was unwilling to communicate unto him his Secret, did joyn his study and endeavors with those of one *Albertus Gunter* a *Saxon*, to find it out themselves: wherein having succeeded, it seems, they made the Experiments which this Industrious and communicative *Jesuit* delivers in this manner:

The Colours, saith he, are thus prepared; I take of *Aqua fortis* and *Aqua Regis*, two ounces *ana*; of *Sal Armoniack* one ounce; of the best *Spirit of Wine*, two drachms; as much *Gold* as can be had for nine *Julio*'s (a *Julio* being about six pence English) of pure *Silver*, two drachmes. These things being provided, let the Silver, when calcined, be put into a Vial; and having powred upon it the two drachmes of *Aqua fortis*, let it evaporate, and you shall have a Water yielding first a *blew* Colour, and afterwards a *black*. Likewise put the Gold, when calcin'd, into a Vial, and having powred the *Aqua Regis* upon it, set it by to evaporate: then put the *Spirit of Wine* upon the *Sal Armoniack*, leaving it also till it be evaporated; and you will have a Golden coloured Water, which will afford you divers Colours. And, after this manner, you may extract many *Tinctures* of Colours out of other Mettals. This done, you may, by the means of these two Waters, paint what Picture you please upon white Marble, of the *softer* kind, renewing the Figure every day for several days with some fresh superadded Liquor, and you shall find in time, that the Picture hath penetrated the *whole* solidity of the Stone, so that cutting it into as many parts as you will, it will always represent unto you the same Figure on both sides.

So far he, which how far it answers expectation, is referred to the Tryal of Ingenious Artists. In the mean time there are not wanting Experienced Men that scruple the Effect, but {127} yet are far from pronouncing any thing positively against it, so that they doe not discourage any that have conveniencies, from trying.

But whether the way there mentioned will succeed, or not, according to expectation: Sure it is that a Stone-cutter in *Oxford*, Mr. *Bird*, hath many years since found out a way of doing the same thing, in effect, that is here mentioned; and hath practised it for many years. That is, he is able so to apply a colour to the outside of polished Marble, as that it shall sink a considerable depth into the body of the stone; and there represent like figures or images as those are on the outside; (deeper or shallower according as he continues the application, a longer, or lesser while.) Of which kind there be divers pieces to be seen in *Oxford*, *London*, and elsewhere. And some of them being shewed to his Majesty, soon after his happy restauration, they were broken in his presence, and found to answer expectation. And others may be dayly seen, by any who is curious, or desirous to see it.

An Intimation of a *Way, found in* **Europe** *to make* **China-dishes.**

Notice was lately given by an inquisitive *Parisian* to a friend of his in *London*, that by an Acquaintance he had been informed, that Signor *Septalio*, a Canon in *Millan*, had the Secret of making as good *Porcelane* as is made in *China* it self, and transparent; adding that he had seen him make some.

This as it deserves, so it will be further inquired after, if God permit.

An Account of an odd **Spring** in **Westphalia**, *together with an Information touching* **Salt-Springs** *and the straining of salt-water.*

An observing Gentleman did lately write out of *Germany*, that in *Westphalia* in the Diocess of *Paderborn*, is a Spring, which looses it self twice in 24 houres; coming always, after 6 houres, back again with a great noise, and so forcibly, as {128} to drive 3 Mills not far from its source. The Inhabitants call it the *Bolderborn*, as if you should say, the *Boysterous Spring*.

The same Person, having mentioned the many *Salt-Springs* in *Germany*, as those at *Lunenburg*, at *Hall* in *Saxony*, at *Saltzwedel* in *Brandenburger Mark*, in *Tyrol*, &c. observes, that no Salt-water, which contains any Metal with it, can well be sodden to Salt in a Vessel of the same Metal, which it self contains, except *Vitriol* in Copper Vessels.

He adds, that, to separate Salt from Salt-water, without Fire, if you take a Vessel of Wax, hollow within, and every where tight; and plunge it into the Sea, or into other Salt-water, there will be made such a separation, that the vessel shall be full of sweet water, the Salt staying behind: but, though this water have no saltish taste, yet, *he saith*, there will be found a Salt in the Essay, which is the Spirit of Salt, subtile enough with the water to penetrate the Wax.

An Account of the Rise and Attempts, of a Way to conveigh Liquors immediately into the Mass of Blood.

Whereas there have lately appeared in publick some *Books*, printed beyond the Seas, treating of the Way of *Injecting liquors into Veines*; in which Books the *Original* of the *Invention* seems to be adscribed to others, besides him, to whom it really belongs; It will surely not be thought amiss, if something be said, whereby the true *Inventor's* right may beyond exception be asserted & preserved; To which end, there will need no more, than barely to represent the *Time* when, and the *Place* where, & among whom it was first started and put to tryal. To joyn all these circumstances together, 'Tis notorious, that at least six years since (a good while before it was heard off, that any one did pretend to have so much as thought of it) the Learned and Ingenious Dr. *Christopher Wren* did propose in the *University* of *Oxford* (where he now is the Worthy Savilian Professor of *Astronomy*, and where very many Curious Persons are ready to {129} attest this relation) to that Noble Benefactor to Experimental Philosophy, Mr. *Robert Boyle*, Dr. *Wilkins*, and other deserving Persons, That he thought, he could easily contrive a Way to conveigh any liquid thing immediately into the Mass of Blood; *videl*: By making Ligatures on the Veines, and then opening them on the side of the Ligature towards the Heart, and by putting into them slender Syringes or Quills, fastened to Bladders (in the manner of Clyster-pipes) containing the matter to be injected; performing that Operation upon pretty big and lean doggs, that the Vessels might be large enough and easily accessible.

This Proposition being made, M. *Boyle* soon gave order for an *Apparatus*, to put it to Experiment; wherein at several times, upon several Doggs, *Opium* & the Infusion of *Crocus Metallorum* were injected into that part of the hind-legs of those Animals, whence the larger Vessels, that carry the Blood, are most easy to be taken hold of: whereof the success was, that the *Opium*, being soon circulated into the Brain, did within a short time stupify, though not kill the Dog; but a large Dose of the *Crocus Metallorum*, made another Dog vomit up Life and all: All which is more amply and circumstantially delivered by Mr. *Boyle* in his Excellent Book of the *Usefulness of Experimental Philosophy*, Part 2. Essay 2. pag. 53. 54. 55. Where 'tis also mention'd, that the fame of this Invention and of the succeeding Tryals being spread, and particularly coming to the knowledge of a foreign *Ambassadour*, that was Curious, and then resided in *London*, it was by him tryed with some *Crocus Metallorum*, upon a Malefactor, that was an inferiour Servant of his; with this success, that the Fellow, as soon as ever the Injection began to be made, did, either really or craftily, fall into a swoon; whereby, being unwilling to prosecute so hazardous an Experiment, they desisted, without seeing any other effect of it, save that it was told the Ambassadour, that it wrought once downwards with him: Since which time, it hath been frequently practised both in *Oxford* & *London*; as well before the *Royal Society*, as elsewhere. And particularly that Learned {130} Physitian, Dr. *Timothy Clerk*, hath made it part of his business, to pursue those Experiments with much industry, great accurateness, and considerable observations thereon; which above two years since, were by him produced and read before the *Royal Society*, who thereupon desired him, as one of their Members, to compleat, what he had proposed to himself upon that subject, and then to publish the same: the Effect whereof 'tis hoped, will now shortly appear, and not prove unwelcome to the Curious.

Some whereof, though they may conceive, that liquors thus injected into Veines without preparation and digestion, will make odde, commotions in the Blood, disturb Nature, and cause strange Symptoms in the Body, yet they have other thoughts on Liquors, that are prepared of such things, as have passed the Digestion of the Stomach; for example, of Spirit of Urine, of Harts-horne, of Blood &c. And they hope likewise, that besides the *Medical*Uses, that may be made of this *Invention*, it may also serve for *Anatomical* purposes, by filling, after this way, the vessels of an Animal as full, as they can hold, and by exceedingly distending them, discover *New* Vessels, &c: But not now to enlarge upon the Uses, the Reader may securely take this Narrative, as the naked real Matter of Fact, whereby 'tis as clear, as Noon day (both from the Time, and irrefragable Testimony of very many considerable Persons in that University, who can jointly attest it; as well as from that particular unquestionable one of Mr. *Boyle* and his worthy Company, who were the first Eye-witnesses of the Tryals made,) that to *Oxford*, and in it, to Dr. *Christopher Wren*, this Invention is due; and consequently, that all others, who discourse or write of it, doe either derive it from Him, or are fallen upon the same Devise several years after Him.

Published with License.
Oxford, Printed by *A: & L: Lichfield*, for *Ric: Davis*. 1665.

{131}

Num. 8.

PHILOSOPHICAL
TRANSACTIONS.

Munday, *Januar.* 8. 166^5/$_6$.

The Contents.

An Account of the Tryals, made in Italy *of* Campani's *new* Optick Glasses. *A further relation of the Whale-fishing about the* Bermudas, *and upon the Coast of* New England, *and* New Netherland. *Of a remarkable Spring of* Paderborn *in* Germany. *Of some other uncommon Springs at* Basel *and in* Alsatia. *Of the richest Salt-springs in*Germany. *Some Observations of Strange Swarms of* Insects, *and the mischiefs done by them: as also of the Brooding of Snakes and Vipers. Observations of odd Constitutions of humane Bodies. Of a way, used in* Italy, *of preserving Ice and Snow by* Chaffe. *Directions for Sea-men bound for far Voyages, drawn up by Master* Rook, *late*Geometry *Professour of* Gresham Colledge. *Some Observations of* Jupiter; *Eclipsed by one of his* Satellites: *and of his Conversion about his* Axis. *Of some Philosophical and Curious Books, that are shortly to come abroad.*

An Account of the Tryalls, made in Italy of **Campani's new** Optick Glasses.

An Inquisitive *Parisian* writes to his Correspondent in *London*, as follows;

We received lately news from *Rome*, from a very Curious Person of our acquaintance, importing, that *Campani* hath had the advantage of *Divini*. The Great Duke of *Toskany*, and Prince *Leopold*, his Brother, upon Tryal, made of both their Glasses, have found those of*Campani* excel the other, and with them they have been able, easily to distinguish people {132}at 4 Leagues distance: Of which I intend you more particulars hereafter.

Among them are expected the *Length* of these *Telescopes*, and the Largeness of the *Aperture*of their *Object-glasses*. In the mean time, the *Parabolical-glasses*, formerly mentioned to be in hand here at *London*, are finishing with all possible care and industry.

A Further Relation of the Whale-fishing *about the* Bermudas, *and on the* Coast of **New-England** and **New-Netherland.**

The same Person, that communicated the particulars about the new Whale-fishing near the*Bermudas*, mentioned in the first of these *Tracts*, gives this further Information; That there have been since taken by order of the *Bermudas* Company, sixteen of those Whales, the

Oyle whereof, to the quantity of 50 or 60 Tuns arrived in *Ireland* at *Limrick*, some few months agoe.

He adds, that about two years since, there stranded upon the Coast of *New-England* a dead Whale, of that sort, which they call *Trumpo*, having Teeth resembling those of a Mill, and its mouth at a good distance from, and under the Nose or Trunk, and several boxes or partitions in the Nose, like those of the Tailes in Lobsters; and that that being open'd there run out of it a thin oily substance, which would candy in time; after which, the remainder, being a thick fatty substance, was taken out of the same part, with a scoope. And this substance he affirmed to be the *Sperma Ceti*; adding further, that the *Blubber*, as they call it, it self, of the same sort of Whales, when stewed, yields on the top a creamy substance, which taken off, and thrown upon white wine, lets fall a dirty heterogeneous sediment, but what remains aloft, affords a *Sperma-Ceti*-like matter.{133}

He concluded his relation with observing, that these whales were to be met with, between the Coast of *New-England*, and *New-Netherland*, where they might be caught eight or nine months in the year, whereas those about the *Bermudas* are to be found there only in the Months of *February*, *March* and *April*.

Concerning the death of the Whale, which hath been related to have stranded upon *New-England*, it is not very improbable, but, (that Fish having also more than one Enemy, whereof a small Fish called the *Thresher* is one, who, by Mr. *Terry's* Relation in his *East-Indian* Voyage, with his nimbleness vexes him as much, as a Bee does a great Beast on the land; and a certain horny Fish another, who runs its horn into the Whal's belly) it may have been kill'd by the latter of these two; which kind of Fish is known, sometimes to run its horn into Ships (perhaps taking them for Whales) and there snapping it asunder; as hapned not long since to an English Vessel in the *West-Indian* Seas; the broken piece of that Horn being by the Master of that ship presented to the King, and now kept in His Majesties Repository: the like whereof befel a *French* Vessel, sailing towards the *East-Indies*, according to the Relation, made by Monsieur *Thevenot* in his second *Tome* of *Curious Voyages*.

Of a remarkable Spring, about Paderborn *in* Germany.

An inquiring Gentleman of those parts writes to his Friend in *London*, as follows;

In this Diocess of *Paderborn*, about 2 leagues from that Town, is a treble Spring call'd*Methorn*, which has three streams, two wherof are not above one foot and a half distant from one another, and yet of so differing qualities, that whereas one of them is limpid, blewish, lukewarm, bubling, and holding Sal-armoniack, Ochra, Iron, Vitriol, {134}Allum, Sulphur, Niter, Orpiment, used against Epilepsie, bad Spleens, and the Wormes; the other is Ice-cold, turbid and whitish, much stronger in tast, and heavier than the former, holding much Orpiment, Salt, Iron, Niter, and some Sal-Armoniack, Allum and Vitriol; Of this all Birds, observed to drink of it, doe dye; which I have also privately experimented by taking some of it home, and giving it to Hens, after I had given them Oates, Barly and Bread-crums; For, soon after they had drunk of it, they became giddy, reeled, and tumbled upon their backs, with convulsion-fitts, and so dyed with a great extention of their leggs. Giving them common-salt immediatly after they had drunk; they dyed not so soon; giving them vineger, they dyed not at all, but seven or eight days after were troubled with the *Pipp*. Those that dyed, being open'd, their Lungs were found quite shrivelled together. Yet some men, that are troubled with Worms, taking a litle quantity of it, and diluting it in common water, have been observed by this means to kill the Worms in their bellies, so that a great number of worms come from them; whereupon though they are sick, yet they dye not. As to the third stream, that lyes lower than the other two, about 20 paces distant from them, it is of a greenish colour, very clear, and of a sowre sweet tast, pleasing enough. It hath about a middle weight between the other two; whence wee guess, that it is mixed of them both, meeting there together: to confirm which, we have mixed equal quantities, of those two, with an addition of a litle common well-water, and have found that they, being stirred together and permitted to setle, made just a water of the same colour and tast of this third stream.

Of some other not-common Springs at Basel *and in* Alsatia.

A Curious Person writes from those Places in manner following;{135}

At *Basel* the Spring, running in the *Gerbergasse* (or *Tanners-street*) from St. *Leonard's* Hill, is of a Blewish colour, and somewhat troubled, holding Copper, Bitumen, and Antimony, about 3 parts of the first, one of the second, and two of the last, as has been examined by skilful Persons. Our Tanners do water their Skins in it; and being a well-tasted and wholesome Water, it is both much drunk, and used to Bath in. It mingles with another Spring water, call'd the *Birsick*, and with it, between the *Salt-tower* and the *Rhine-gate* runs into the *Rhine*.

In the same Town (which abounds with Spring-waters) there are two, among the rest, called *Bandulph's-well*, and *Brun Zum Brunnen*, that are more observable then the other; the former of them having a *Camphory* and drying Quality, and used against Hydropical Distempers; the latter containing some Sulphur, Saltpeter and Gold, and being an excellent Water to drink, much used in the principal Tavern of the City, where the chief of the Town do resort, and near which it runs.

In *Alsatia* in the Valley, called *Leberthal*, near *Geesbach* (an ancient Mine-work) there runs out of a *Cavern* a foul, fattish, oily Liquor, which, though the Country-men of that place employ to the vile use of greasing their Wheels, instead of ordinary Wheel-grease; yet doth it afford an excellent Balsom, by taking a quantity of it, and putting it in an Earthen Pot well luted, that no steam may exhale; and then with a gentle Fire at first, but a stronger afterwards, boyling it for three hours together; in which space it will boyl in a fourth part, and an Earthen Matter, like Pitch, will settle it self at the bottom: but on the top thereof, when cold, there will swim a fatty Substance, like Lyne-Oyl, limped and somewhat yellowish, which is to be decanted from the thick Sediment, and then gently distilled in an Alembick in *Arena*, by which means, there will come over two differing Liquors, one Phlegmatick, the other Oily, {136}which latter swimming on the Phlegm, is to be severed from it. The Phlegm is used as an excellent Resister and Curer of all the Putrefactions of the Lungs and Liver, and it heals all foul Wounds and Ulcers. The Oily part, being diluted with double its quantity of distilled Vineger, and brought three times over the Helm, yields a rare Balsom, against all inward and outward Corruptions, stinking Ulcers, hereditary Scurfs and Scabs: 'Tis also much used against Apoplexies, Palsies, Consumptions, Giddinesses, and Head-aches. Inwardly they take it with Succory-water against all corruptions of the Lungs. It is a kind of *Petroleum*, and contains no other Mineral Juice, but that of *Sulphur*, which seems to be thus distilled by *Nature* under ground; the distillation of an Oyl out of *Sulphur* by Art, being not so easie to perform.

Of the richest Salt-Springs in Germany.

An Account having been desired of those two chief *Salt-Springs* in *Germany*, at *Hall* and *Lunenburg*, it was lately transmitted thus:

The *Salt-Springs* at *Hall* in *Saxony* are four, called *Gutiaar*, the *Dutch-Spring*, the *Mettritz*, and the *Hackel-dorn*; whereof the three first hold near the same proportion of Salt; the last hold less, but yields the purest Salt. The three first hold about seven parts of Salt, three of Marcasit, and fourteen of water: They are, besides their Oeconomical use, employed Medicinally to Bath in, and to draw a Spirit out of it, exhibited with good success against Venom, and the putrefaction of the Lungs, Liver, Reins, and the Spleen.

The *Salt Water* at *Lunenburgh*, being more greenish then white, and not very transparent, is about the same nature and hold with that of *Hall*. It hath a mixture of Lead with it, whence also it will not be sod in Leaden Pans, and if it held no Lead at all, it would not be so good, that Metal being judged to *purifie* the Water: whence also the Salt of {137} *Lunenburg* is preferred before all others, that are made of Salt Springs.

Some Observations of swarms of strange Insects, and the Mischiefs done by them.

A great Observer, who hath lived long in *New England*, did upon occasion, relate to a Friend of his in *London*, where he lately was, That some few Years since there was such a swarm of a certain sort of Insects in that *English* Colony, that for the space of of 200 Miles they poyson'd and destroyed all the Trees of that Country; there being found innumerable little holes in the ground, out of which those Insects broke forth in the form of *Maggots*, which turned into *Flyes* that had a kind of taile or sting, which they struck into the Tree, and thereby envenomed and killed it.

The like Plague is said to happen frequently in the Country of the *Cosacks* or *Ukrani*, where in dry Summers they are infested with such swarms of *Locusts*, driven thither by an *East*, or *South-East* Wind, that they darken the Air in the fairest weather, and devour all the Corn of that Country; laying their Eggs in *Autumn*, and then dying; but the Eggs, of which every one layeth two or three hundred, hatching the next Spring, produce again such a number of Locusts, that then they do far more mischief than afore, unless Rains do fall, which kill both Eggs and the Insects themselves, or unless a strong *North* or *North-West* Wind arise, which drives them into the *Euxin* Sea: The Hogs of that Country loving these Eggs, devour also great quantities of them, and thereby help to purge the Land of them; which is often so molested by this Vermine, that they enter into their Houses and Beds, fall upon their Tables and into their Meat, insomuch that they can hardly eat without taking down some of them; in the Night when they repose themselves upon the ground, they cover it three, or four Inches thick, and if a Wheel pass {138} over them, they emit a stench hardly to be endured: All which, and much more may be fully seen in the *French* Description of the Countries of *Poland*, made by *Monsieur de Beauplan*, and by *Monsieur Thevenot*, in his Relation of the *Cosacks*, contained in the First part of his *Curious Voyages*.

An Observation touching the Bodies of Snakes and Vipers.

Several have taken notice, that there is a difference between the brooding of Snakes and Vipers, those laying their Eggs in Dung-hills, by whose warmth they are hatched; but these (Vipers) brooding their Eggs within their Bellies, and bringing forth live Vipers. To which may be added, That some affirm to have seen Snakes lye upon their Eggs, as Hens sit upon theirs.

Some Observations of odde Constitutions of Bodies.

A very curious Person, studying Physick at *Leyden*, to whom had been imparted those Relations about a Milky Substance in Veins, heretofore alledged in *Numb*. 6. returns, by way of gratitude, the following Observations.

There was (saith he) not many Years since, in this Country a Student, who being much addicted to the study of *Astronomy*, and spending very many Nights in Star-gazing, had, by the Nocturnal wet and cold temper of the Air, in such a manner obstructed the pores of his skin, that little or nothing exhaled from his Body; which appeared hence, because that the shirt, he had worn five or six weeks, was then as white as if he had worn it but one day. In the mean while he gathered a subcutaneous Water, of which yet he was afterwards well cured.

We have also (*saith the same*) seen here a young Maid, of about thirteen Years of age, which from the time that she was but six Years old, and began to be about her Mother in {139} the Kitchin, would, as often as she was bid to bring her Salt, or could else come at it, fill her Pockets therewith, and eat it, as other children doe Sugar: whence she was so dried up, and grown so stiff, that she could not stirre her limbs, and was thereby starved to death.

That Learned and Observing Doctor *John Beal*, upon the perusal of the forementioned *Numb*. 6. was pleased to communicate this Note:

To your Observation, of Milk in Veines, I can add a *Phænomenon* of some resemblance to it, which I received above 20 years agoe from *Thomas Day*, an Apothecary in *Cambridg*; *vid*. That himself let a man bloud in the arme, by order of Doctor *Eade*, a Physitian there. The mans bloud was white as Milk, as it run out of his arme, it had a little dilute redness, but immediately, as it fell into the Vessel, it was presently white; and it continued like drops of Milk on the pavement, where ever it fell. The conjecture which the said Physitian had of the cause of this appearance, was, that the Patient had much fed on Fish; affirming withall, that he had soon been a Leper, if not prevented by Physick.

A way of preserving Ice and Snow by Chaffe.

The Ingenious Mr. *William Ball* did communicate the relation hereof, as he had received it from his Brother, now residing at *Livorne*, as follows;

The Snow, or Ice-houses are here commonly built on the side of a steep hill, being only a deep hole in the ground, by which meanes, they easily make a passage out from the bottom of it, to carry away all the water, which, if it should remain stagnating therein, would melt the Ice and Snow: but they thatch it with straw, in the shape of a Saucepan-cover, that the rain may not come at it. The sides (supposing it dry) they line not with any thing, as is done in St. *Jeames*'s Park, by reason of the moistness of the ground. This Pit they fill {140} full of Snow or Ice (taking care that the Ice be made of the purest water, because they put it into their wine) over-spreading first the bottom very well with *Chaffe;* by which I mean not any part of the straw, but what remains upon the winnowing of the Corn; and I think, they here use Barley-chaffe. This done, they further, as they put in the Ice, or the Snow, (which latter they ram down,) line it thick by the sides with such Chaffe, and afterwards cover it well with the same; and in half a years lying so, 'tis found not to want above an eight part of what it weighed, when first put in. When ever they take it out into the Aire, they wrap it in this Chaffe, and it keeps to admiration. The use of it in *England* would not be so much for cooling of drinks, as 'tis here generally used; but for cooling of fruits, sweetmeats &c. *So far this Author.*

The other usual way both in *Italy* and other Countries, to conserve Snow and Ice with *Straw* or *Reed,* is set down so punctually by Mr. *Boyle* in his *Experimental History of Cold,* pag. 408. 409. that nothing is to be added. It seems *Pliny* could not pass by these *Conservatories,* and the cooling of drinks with Ice, without passing this severe, though elegant and witty, Animadversion upon them: *Hi Nives, illi glaciem potant, pænásque montium in voluptatem gulæ vertunt: Servatur algor æstibus, excogitatúrque ut alienis mensibus nix algeat,* lib. 19. cap. 4. But the *Epigrammatist* sports with it thus;

> *Non potare nivem, sed aquam potare rigentem*
> *De nive, commenta est ingeniosa sitis.* Martial. 14. Ep. 117.

Directions for Sea-men, bound for far Voyages.

It being the Design of the R. *Society,* for the better attaining the End of their Institution, to study *Nature* rather than *Books,* and from the Observations, made of the *Phænomena* and Effects she presents, to compose such a {141} History of Her, as may hereafter serve to build a Solid and Useful Philosophy upon; They have from time to time given order to several of their Members to draw up both *Inquiries* of things Observable in forrain Countries, and *Directions* for the Particulars, they desire chiefly to be informed about. And considering with themselves, how much they may increase their *Philosophical* stock by the advantage, which *England* injoyes of making Voyages into all parts of the World, they formerly appointed that Eminent Mathematician and Philosopher Master *Rooke,* one of their Fellowes, and *Geometry* Professor of *Gresham Colledge* (now deceased to the great detriment of the Common-wealth of Learning) to think upon and set down some *Directions* for *Sea-men* going into the *East* & *West-Indies,* the better to capacitate them for making such observations abroad, as may be pertinent and suitable for their purpose; of which the said Sea-men should be desired to keep an exact *Diary,* delivering at their return a fair Copy thereof to the *Lord High Admiral* of *England,* his Royal Highness the *Duke* of *York,* and another to *Trinity-house* to be perused by the R. *Society.* Which *Catalogue* of *Directions* having been drawn up accordingly by the said Mr. *Rook,* and by him presented to those, who appointed him to expedite such an one, it was thought not to be unseasonable at this time to make it publique, the more conveniently to furnish Navigators with Copies thereof. They are such, as follow;

1. To observe the Declination of the *Compass,* or its Variation from the *Meridian* of the place, frequently; marking withal, the *Latitude* and *Longitude* of the place, wherever such Observation is made, as exactly as may be, and setting down the *Method,* by which they made them.

2. To carry *Dipping Needles* with them, and observe the Inclination of the Needle in like manner.

3. To remark carefully the Ebbings and Flowings of the Sea, in as many places as they can, together with all the Accidents, {142} Ordinary and Extraordinary, of the Tides; as, their precise time of Ebbing and Flowing in Rivers, at *Promontories* or *Capes*; which way their Current runs, what Perpendicular distance there is between the highest Tide and lowest Ebb, during the Spring-Tides and Neap-Tides; what day of the *Moons* age, and at times of the year, the highest and lowest Tides fall out: And all other considerable Accidents, they can observe in the Tides, cheifly neer Ports, and about Ilands, as in St. *Helena*'s Iland, and the three Rivers there, at the *Bermodas* &c.

4. To make Plotts and Draughts of prospect of Coasts, Promontories, Islands and Ports, marking the Bearings and Distances, as neer as they can.

5. To sound and marke the Depths of Coasts and Ports, and such other places nere the shoar, as they shall think fit.

6. To take notice of the Nature of the Ground at the bottom of the Sea, in all Soundings, whether it be Clay, Sand, Rock, *&c.*

7. To keep a Register of all changes of Wind and Weather at all houres, by night and by day, shewing the point the Wind blows from, whether strong or weak: The Rains, Hail, Snow and the like, the precise times of their beginnings and continuance, especiall *Hurricans* and *Spouts*; but above all to take exact care to observe the *Trade-Winds*, about what degree of *Latitude* and *Longitude* they first begin, *where* and *when* they cease, or change, or grow stronger or weaker, and how much; as near and exact as may be.

8. To observe and record all Extraordinary *Meteors*, Lightnings, Thunders, *Ignes fatui*, Comets, &c. marking still the places and times of their appearing, continuance. &c.

9. To carry with them good Scales, and Glasse-Violls of a pint or so, with very narrow mouths, which are to be fill'd with Sea-water in different degrees of *Latitude*, as often as {143} they please, and the weight of the Vial full of water taken exactly at every time, and recorded, marking withall the degree of *Latitude*, and the day of the Month: And that as well of water near the Top; as at a greater Depth.

Some Observations concerning **Jupiter.** Of the shadow of one of his Satellites seen, by a Telescope passing over the Body of **Jupiter.**

I have received an Account from very good hands, That on the 26th of *September* last, at half hour after seven of the Clock, was seen, both in *Holland* and in *France* (by curious Observers, with very good Telescopes) the shadow of one of the *Satellites* of *Jupiter*, passing over his Body. One of those small Stars moving about his Body (which are therefore called his *Satellites*) coming between the Sun and it, made a small Eclipse, appearing in the Face of *Jupiter* as a little round black Spot. The Particulars of those Observations, when they shall come to our Hands, we may (if need be) make them publik: Which Observations, as they are in themselves very remarkable, and argue the Excellency of the Glasses by which they were discovered; So are we, in part, beholding to Monsieur *Cassini* for them, who giving notice before hand of such Appearances to be expected, gave occasion to those Curious Observers to look for them.

Of a permanent Spot in **Jupiter:** by which is manifested the conversion of **Jupiter** about his own Axis.

Besides that Transient Shadow last mentioned, there hath been observed, by Monsieur *Cassini*, a permanent Spot in the Disque of *Jupiter*; by the help whereof, he hath been able to observe, not onely that *Jupiter* turns about upon his own Axis, but also the Time of such conversion; which he {144} estimates to be, 9 hours and 56 minutes.

For as *Kepler* did before conjecture, from the motion of the Primitive Planets about the Sun as their Center, that the Sun moved about its own Axis, but could not prove it, till by *Galileo* and *Shiner* the Spots in the Sun were discovered; so it hath been thought reasonable, from the Secundary Planets moving about *Jupiter*, that *Jupiter* is also moved about his Axis; yet, till now, it hath not been evinced by Observation, That it doth so move; much less, in what Period of Time. And the like reason there is to judge so of *Saturn*, because of the Secundary Planet discovered by Monsieur *Hugens de Zulichem* to move about it; (though such motion be not yet evinced from Observation:) as well as that of the *Earth*, from its Attendant the *Moon*.

Whether the same may be also concluded of the other Planets, *Mars*, *Venus*, and *Mercury*, (about whom have not yet been observed any Secondary Planets to move,) is not so evident. Yet there may be somewhat of like probability in those. Not onely, because it is possible they may have Secundary Planets about them, though not yet discovered; (For, we know, it was long after those of *Jupiter*, before that about *Saturn* was discovered; and who knows, what after times may discover about the rest?) But because the Primary Planets being all in like manner inlightned by the Sun, and (in all likely hood) moved by it; it is likely that they be moved by the same Laws and Methods; and therefore, turn'd about their own Axis, as it is manifest that some of them are.

But, as for the Secundary Planets, as well those about *Jupiter*, as that about *Saturn*; it is most likely that they have no such Rotation upon their Axis. Not so much because, by reason of their smalness, no such thing hath been yet observed, (or, indeed, could be, though it were true;) But because they being Analogical to our *Moon*, it is most likely that they are moved in like manner. Now, though it be {145}true, that there is some kind of *Libration* of the Moon's body, so that we have not precisely just the same part of it looking towards us; (as is evident by *Hevelius* observations, and others;) yet is there no Revolution upon its Axis; the same part of it, with very little alteration, always respecting us, as is to be seen in *Hevelius* his Tratise *de Motu Lunæ Libratorio*, and indeed, by all those who have written particularly of the spots on the Moon; and is universally known to all that have with any curiosity viewed it with Telescopes.

Of some Philosophical and curious Books, that are shortly to come abroad.

1. Of the *Origine* of *Forms* and *Qualities*, deduced from *Mechanical* Principles; by the Honorable *Robert Boyle* Esq.

2. *Hydrostatical Paradoxes*, by the same. Both in *English*.

3. A Tract of the *Origine* of the *Nile*, by Monsieur *Isaac Vossius*, opposed to that of Monsieur *de la Chambre*, who is maintaining, That *Niter* is the principal cause of the Inundation of that River.

4. A Dissertation of *Vipers*, by *Signor Redi*, an *Italian*.

5. A Discourse of the *Anatomy* of a *Lyon*, by the same.

6. Another, *De Figuris Salium*, by the same.

7. A Narration of the Establishment of the *Lyncei*, an *Italian* Academy, and of their Design and Statutes: the Prince *Cesi* being the Head of them, who did also intend to establish such Philosophical Societies in all parts of the World, and particularly in *Africa* and *America*, to be by that means well informed of what considerable productions of Nature were to be found in those parts. The Author yet *Anonymus*.

8. To these I shall add, a Book newly Printed in *Oxford* (and not yet dispersed) being, *A Catalogue of Fixed Stars* with their *Longitudes*, *Latitudes*, and *Magnitudes*, according to the *Observations* of *Uleg-Beig* (a King, and famous Astronomer, who was *Great-Grand-child* to the famous {146}*Tamerlane*, and one of his Successors in some of his Kingdoms) made at *Samarcand*, his cheief seat, (for the year of the Hegira 841, for the year of Christ 1427), who not finding the *Tables* of *Ptolemy* to agree sufficiently with the Heavens, did with great diligence, and expense, make observations anew; as *Tycho Brahe* hath since done. It is a small part of a larger *Astronomical Treatise* of his, whereof there be divers *Persian* Manuscript Copies in *Oxford*. Out of which this is Translated and Published, both in *Persian* and *Latine*, by Mr. *Thomas Hyde*, now Library Keeper to the *Bodleyan* Library in *Oxford*: (with Commentaries of his annexed:) Like as another part of it hath formerly been by Mr. *John Graves*. And it were a desirable work that the whole were Translated, that we might be the better acquainted with what was the Eastern Astronomy at that time.

Published with License.
Oxford, Printed by *A: & L: Lichfield*, for *Ric: Davis*. 1666.

{147}

PHILOSOPHICAL
TRANSACTIONS.

Munday, Feb. 12. 166⁵/₆.

The Contents.

An Apendix *to the* Directions *for Seamen, bound for far voyages. Of the judgment of some of the* English *Astronomers, touching the difference between two learned men, about an Observation made of the first of the two late* Comets. *Of a* Correspondency, *to be procured, for the finding out of the* True *distance of the* Sun *and* Moon *from the Earth. Of an Observation not long since made in* England *of* Saturn. *An Account of some* Mercurial *Observations, made with a* Barometer, *and their Results. Some Observations of* Vipers, *made by an Italian* Philosopher.

An **Appendix** *to the* **Directions** *for* ***Seamen, bound for far Voyages.***

Whereas it may be of good use, both *Naval* and *Philosophical*, to know, both how to sound depths of the sea *without a Line*, and to fetch up water from any depth of the same; the following waies have been contrived by Mr. *Hook* to perform both; (which should have been added to the lately printed *Directions for Seamen*, if then it could have been conveniently done.){148}

First, for the sounding of depths without a Cord, consider *Figure* 1, and accordingly take a Globe of *Firr*, or *Maple*, or other light Wood, as A: let it be well secured by Vernish, Pitch, or otherwise, from imbibing water; then take a piece of Lead or Stone, D, considerably heavier then will sink the Globe: let there be a long Wire-staple B, in the Ball A, and a springing Wire C, with a bended end F, and into the said staple, press in with your fingers the springing Wire on the bended end: and on it hang the weight D, by its ring E, and so let Globe and all sink gently into the water, in the posture represented in the first *Figure*, to the bottom, where the weight D touching first, is thereby stopt; but the Ball, being by the*Impetus*, it acquired in descending, carried downwards a little after the weight is stopt, suffers the springing wire to fly back, and thereby sets it self at liberty to reascend. And, by observing the time of the Ball's stay under water (which may be done by a Watch, having minuts and seconds, or by a good Minut-glass, or best of all, by a Pendulum vibrating seconds) you will by this way, with the help of some *Tables*, come to know any depth of the sea.

Note, that care must be had of proportioning the weight and shape of the Lead, to the bulk, weight, and figure of the Globe, after such a manner, as upon experience shall be found most convenient.

In some of the Tryals already made with this Instrument, the Globe being of Maple-wood, well covered with Pitch to hinder soaking in, was 5¹³/₁₆ inches in diameter, and weighed 2½ pounds: the Lead of 4½ pounds weight, was of a *Conical* figure, 11. inches long, with the sharper end downwards, 1⁹/₁₆ inches at the top, and ¹/₁₆ at the bottom in diameter. And in those Experiments, made in the *Thames*, in the depth of 19. foot water, there passed between the Immersion and Emersion of the Globe, 6. seconds of an hour; and in the depth of 10. foot water, there passed 3½ seconds or thereabout: From many of which kind of Experiments it will likely not be hard to finde {149}out a method to calculate, what depth is to be concluded from any other time of the like Globes stay under water.

In the same Tryals, made with this Instrument in the said River of*Thames*, it has been found, that there is no difference in time, between the submersions of the Ball at the greatest depth, when it rose two Wherries length from the place where it was let fall (being carried by the Current of the *Tide*) and when it rose within a yard or so of the same place where it was let down.

The *other* Instrument, for Fetching up water from the depth of the sea, is (as appears by *Figure* 2.) a square woodden *Bucket* C, whose bottoms *EE*, are so contrived, that as the weight A, sinks the Iron B, (to which the Bucket C, is fastned by two handles DD, on the ends of which are the moveable bottoms or Valves EE,) and thereby draws down the Bucket, the resistance of the water keeps up the Bucket in the posture C; whereby the water hath, all the while it is descending, a clear passage through; whereas, as soon as the Bucket is pulled upwards by the Line F, the resistance of the water to that motion beats the Bucket downward, and keeps it in the posture G, whereby the Included water is preserved from getting out, and the Ambient water kept from getting in.

By the advantage of which Vessel, it may be known, whether sea water be Salter at and towards the bottom, then at or near the top: Likewise, whether in some places of the sea, any sweet water is to be found at the bottom; the *Affirmative* whereof is to be met with in the *East Indian* Voyages of the industrious *John Hugh Van Linsckoten*, who page 16 of that Book, as 'tis *Englished*, records, that in the *Persian Gulph*, about the Island *Barem*, or *Baharem*, they fetch up with certain Vessels (which he describes not) water out of the sea, from under the salt-water, four or five fathom deep, as sweet, as any Fountain water. {150}

Of the Judgement of some of the English *Astronomers, touching the difference between two learned men, about an Observation made of the First of the two late* Comets.

By Telescopical *Stars are understood such, as are not seen, but by the help of a Telescope.*

Whereas notice has been taken in *Num.* 6. of these *Transactions*, that there was some difference between those two deservedly celebrated Philosophers, *Monsieur Hevelius* and *Monsieur Auzout*, concerning an Observation, made by the former of them, on the $^8/_{18}$ of *February* 1665. & that thereupon some Eminent *English* Astronomers, considering the importance of the dispute, had undertaken the examination thereof; it will, 'tis conceived, not be unacceptable to such, as saw those Papers, to be informed, what has been done and discerned by them in that matter. They having therefore compared the Printed Writings of the two Dissenters, and withall consulted the observations made with *Telescopes* at home, by some of the most intelligent Astronomers amongst them, who have attentively observed the Position of that *Comet* to the *Telescopical* stars, that lay in its way; Do thereupon Joyntly conclude, that, whatever that Appearance was, which was seen near the *First Star* of *Aries*, by *Monsieur Hevelius* (the truth of whose relation concerning the same, they do in no wise question) the said *Comet* did not come neer that *Star* in the left *Ear* of *Aries*, where the said M. *Hevelius* supposes it to have passed, but took its course neer the *Bright Star* in its *Left Horn*, according to *Bayers* Tables. And since that the Observations of judicious both *French, Italian, & Dutch* Astronomers (as many of them, as are come to the knowledge of the *English*) do in the main fully agree with theirs, they do not at all doubt, but that, there being such an unanimous {151} consent in what has been just now declared, & the Controversie being about *Matter of fact*, wherein Authority, Number, and Reputation must cast the Ballance, Mons. *Hevelius*, who is as well known for his Ingenuity, as Learning, will joyn and acquiesce in that sentiment.

Of a correspondency, to be procured, for the Finding out the True *distance of the* Sun *and* Moon *from the Earth, by the* Paralax, *observed under (or neer) the same* Meridian.

Seeing that the knowledge of this distance may prove of important Use, for the Perfecting of Astronomy, and for the better establishing the doctrine of *Refractions*, it is in the thoughts of some very curious Persons in *England*, for the finding out the same, to settle a Correspondency with some others abroad, that are understanding in Astronomical matters, and live in places farr distant in *Latitude*, and under (or near) the same *Meridian*.

To perform which, the following Method is proposed to be observed; *viz.* That at certain times agreed on by two Observatours, making use of *Telescopes*, large, good and well fitted for this purpose, by a measuring rod, placed within the Eye glass at a convenient distance, that it may be distinctly seen, and serve for measuring small distances by minuts and seconds (which is easie enough in large *Telescopes*) that, I say, each of such observers, thus furnish't shall observe the visible way of the *Moon* among the *Fixt Stars*, (by taking her exact distance from any *Fixt Starr*, that lyes in or very near her way, together with the exact time of her so appearing) and the then apparent Diameter of her Disk; continuing these Observations every time for two or three hours; that so, {152}if possible, two exact observations of her *Apparent* place among the *Fixt Stars* being made, at two places thus distant in *Latitude*, and as near as may be under the same *Meridian*, by these Observators concurring at the same time, her true and exact distance may be hence collected, not onely for that time, but at all other times, by any single Observator's viewing her with a *Telescope*, and measuring exactly her *Apparent*Diameter. It were likewise desirable, that as often as there happens any considerable *Eclipse*of the *Sun*, that this also might be observed by them, noting therein the exact measure of the greatest Obscuration compared with the then *Apparent* Diameter of his Disk. For by this means, after the distance of the *Moon* hath been exactly found, the distance of the *Sun* will easily be deduced.

As for the time, fittest for making Observations of the *Moon*, that will be, when she is about a Quarter or somewhat less illuminated, because then her light is not so bright, but that with a good *Telescope* she may be observ'd to pass close by, and sometimes over several *Fixt Stars*; which is about four or five days before or after her Change: Or else at any other time, when the *Moon* passes near or over some of the bigger sort of *Fixt Stars*, such as of the first or second *Magnitude*; which may be easily calculated and foreseen: Or best of all, when there is any *Totall Eclipse* of the *Moon*; for then the smallest *Telescopical Stars* may be seen close adjoyning to the very body of the *Moon*. Of all which particulars the two Correspondents are to agree, as soon as he, that is to joyn abroad, shall be found out; whereupon they are mutually to communicate to each other, what they shall have thus observed in each place.

Of an Observation, not long since made in England, *of* Saturn.

This Observation was made by Mr. *William Ball*,{153}accompanied by his brother, Dr. *Ball*, *October* 13. 1665. at six of the Clock, at *Mainhead* near *Exeter* in *Devonshire*, with a very good *Telescope* near 38 foot long, and a double Eye-glass, as the observer himself takes notice, adding, that he never saw that *Planet* more distinct. The observation is represented by *Figure* 3. concerning which, the Author saith in his letter to a friend, as follows; This appear'd to me the present figure of *Saturn*, somewhat otherwise, than I expected, thinking it would have been decreasing, but I found it full as ever, and a little hollow above and below. Whereupon the Person, to whom notice was sent hereof, examining this shape, hath by Letters desired the worthy Author of the*Systeme of this Planet*, that he would now attentively consider the present *Figure* of his*Anses* or *Ring*, to see whether the appearance be to him, as in this *Figure*, and consequently whether he there meets with nothing, that may make him think, that it is not *one* body of a Circular Figure, that embraces his *Diske*, but *two*.

And to the end that other Curious men, in other places might be engaged, to joyn their Observations with him, to see, whether they can find the like appearance to that, represented here, especially such Notches or Hollownesses, as at A and B, it was thought fit to insert here the newly related Account.

A Relation of some Mercurial *Observations, and their Results.*

Modern *Philosophers*, to avoyd Circumlocutions, call that Instrument, wherein a Cylinder of Quicksilver, of between 28. and 31. Inches in Altitude, is kept suspended after the manner of the *Torricellian* Experiment, a *Barometer* or *Baroscope*, first made publick by that Noble Searcher of Nature, Mr. *Boyle*, and imployed by Him and others, to detect all the minut variations in the Pressure and weight of the Air. For the more {154}curious and nice distinguishing of which small changes, Mr. *Hook* in the *Preface* to his *Micrography*, has described such an Instrument with a *Wheel*, contrived by himself, and, by these two last years trials of it, constantly found most exact for that purpose: which being so accurate, and not difficult to be made, it were desirable, that those who have a Genius and opportunities of making Observations of this kind, would furnish themselves with such of these Instruments, as were exactly made and adjusted according to the Method, delivered in the newly mentioned place.

To say something of the Observations, made by this Instrument, and withal to excite studious *Naturalists* to a sedulous prosecution of the same, the *Reader* may *first* take notice, that the lately named Mr. *Boyle* hath (as himself not long since did intimate to the Author of these *Tracts*) already made divers Observations of this kind in the year 1659. and 1660. before any others were publick, or by him so much as heard of; though he has hitherto forborn to divulge them, because of some other Papers (in whose Company they were to appear) which being hindred by other studies and employments, he hath not as yet finished.

Next, that, besides several others, who, since have had the curiosity of making such observations, the Worthy and Inquisitive Dr. *John Beal*, is doing his part with much assiduity (of which he hath by several Letters acquainted his Friends in *London*) both by observing himself, and by procuring many Correspondents in several places in *England* for the same purpose; judging it of great importance, that Observations of this kind be made in parts somewhat distant from one another, that so from many of those, accurately made and then compared, it may be discovered, whether the Aire gravitates more in the parts of the Earth lying more *East* or *West, North* or *South*? whether on such as lie neerer to the *Sea*, or further up into the *Mainland*? in hotter or colder weather? whether in {155} high Winds or Calms? whether in wet weather or dry? whether most when a North, or when a South, when an East or a West wind blows? and whether it keeps the same seasons of Changes? and whether the seasons and changes of the Air and Weather can be thereby discover'd, and the now hidden causes of many other *Phænomena* detected?

The said *Doctor* is so much pleased with the discovery already made by the help of this Instrument, that he thinks it to be one of the most wonderful that ever was in the World, if we speak of strangeness, and just wonder, and of Philosophical importance, separate from the interest of lucre. For (*saith he in one of his Letters*) who could ever expect, that we men should find an Art, to weigh all the Air that hangs over our heads, in all the changes of it, and, as it were, to weigh, and to distinguish by weight, the Winds and the Clouds? Or, who did believe, that by palpable evidence we should be able to prove, the *serenest* Air to be most heavy, and the *thickest* Air, and when darkest Clouds hang neerest to us, ready to dissolve, or dropping, *then* to be lightest. And though (*so he goes on*) we cannot yet reach to all the Uses and Applications of it, yet we should be entertain'd for a while, by the truly Honourable Mr. *Boyle*, as the leading person herein, upon the delight and wonder. The *Magnet* was known many hundreds of years before it was applied to find out *New Worlds*. To me (*saith he*) tis a wonderful delight, that I have alwaies in my Study before my eye such a *Curious Ballance*.

Having thus in *General* expressed his thoughts about this Invention, and the singular pleasure, he takes in the Observations made therewith, he descends to particulars, and in several Letters communicates them to his Correspondent, as follows:

The Exclusion of all *Air is here necessary, because Air being subject to the operation of Heat and Cold, if any of it remain in the* Barometer, *it will cause it to vary from shewing the true Pressure of the Air.*

1. My *Wheel-barometer* I could never fill so exactly with *Mercury* as to exclude *all* Air; and therefore I trust more {156} to a *Mercurial* Cane, and take all my Notes from it. This Cane is but 35. Inches long, of a very slender Cavity, and thick Glass. This may easily be conveyed to any place, for Trials. The Vessel for the stagnating *Mercury*, into which the said Cane is immersed, is about two *Inches* wide. The *Mercury* so well fill'd, that for some daies it would not subside, but hung to the top of the Glass-cane. I keep it in a Closet pretty close, 9. foot high, 8. foot broad, 15. foot long; neer a Window. This I note, because possibly the closeness of the room may hinder, that it gives not the full of all Changes, as it might in a more passable Air.

2. In all my Observations from *May* 28. 1664 to this present (*December* 9. 1665.) the Quicksilver never ascended but very little above 30¼ Inches.

3. It ascended very seldom so high (*videl.* to 30¼ Inches) chiefly *Decemb.* 13. 1664. the weather being fickle-fair, Evening.

4. I find by my *Calender* of *June* 22. 1664. at 5. in the Morning, in a time of long setled fair weather, that the *Mercury* had ascended about half an Inch higher then 30: but I fear some mistake, because I then took no impression of *wonder* at it; yet for 3. or 4. daies, at that time it continued high, in well-setled, fair and warm weather; most part above 30. Inches. So

71

that I may note, the *Mercury* to rise as high in the hottest *Summer*, as in the coldest *Winter*-weather.

Perhaps this is from some included Air.

5. Yet surely I have noted it ascend a little higher for the Coldness of the Weather; and very frequently, both in {157}Winter and Summer to be higher in the cold Mornings and Evenings, then in the warmer Mid-day.

6. Generally in setled and fair weather both of Winter and Summer, the *Mercury* is higher, than a little *before* or *after*, or *in* Rainy weather.

7. Again, generally it descended lower after Rain, than it was before Rain.

It seems these were Easterly *winds.*

8. Generally also it falls in great winds; and somewhat it seem'd to sink, when I open'd a wide door to it, to let in stormy winds; yet I have found it to continue very high, in a long stormy wind of 3. or 4. daies.

9. Again, generally it is higher in an *East* and *North*-wind. (*Cæteris paribus*) than in a *South* and *West*-wind.

10. I tryed several times, by strong fumes and thick smoaks to alter the Air in my Closet; but I cannot affirm, that the *Mercury* yielded any more, then might be expected from some increase of heat. Such as have exact *Wheel-Barometers*, may try whether Odors or Fumes do alleviate the Air.

11. In this Closet I have not in all this time found the extreamest changes of the Quicksilver to amount to more, than to $2\frac{3}{4}$, or to $2\frac{7}{8}$. inches, at most.

12. Very often I have found great changes in the Air, without any perceptible change in the *Barometer*; as in the dewy nights, when the moisture descends in a great quantity, and the thickness sometimes seems to hide the Stars from us: In the days foregoing, and following, the Vapors have been {158}drawn up so *Invisibly*, that the Air and Sky seem'd very clear all day long. This I account a great change between ascending and descending Dews and Vapors (which import Levity and Weight,) and between thick Air and clear Air: which changes do sometimes continue in the Alternative course of day and night, for a week or fortnight together; and yet the *Baroscope* holding the same.

13. Sometimes (I say not often) the *Baroscope* yields not to other very great changes of the Air. As lately (*December* 18.) an extraordinary bright and clear day; and the next following quite darkened, some Rain and Snow falling; but the *Mercury* the same: so in high winds and calms the same.

14. I do conceive, that such as converse much *Sub dio*, and walk much abroad, may find many particulars much more exactly, then I, who have no leisure for it, can undertake. To instance in one of many, *December* 16. last, was a clear cold day, very sharp and strong *East* wind, the *Mercury* very near 30. inches high, about three in the afternoon, I saw a large black cloud, drawing near us from the *East* and *South-East*, with the *East-wind*. The *Mercury* changed not that day nor the day following; the Stars and most of the sky were very bright and clear till Nine of the Clock; and then suddenly all the sky was darkned, yet no change of weather happened; *December* 17. the frost held, and 'twas a clear day, till about two of the clock in the afternoon; and then many thick clouds appear'd low in the *West*; yet no change of the weather here; the Wind, Frost, and Quick-silver, the same, *December* 18. the *Mercury* fell almost ¼ of an inch, and the sky and Air so clear and bright and cold with an *East-wind*, that I wondred what could cause the *Mercury* to descend. I Expected, it should have ascended, as usually it does in such clear skys. Casually I sent my servant abroad, and he discovered the remote Hills, about 20. miles off, cover'd with {159}snow, This seem'd to manifest, that the Air, being discharged of the clouds by snow, became lighter.

15. I have seldom seen the change to be very great, at any one time. For, though I do not now take a deliberate view of my Notes, yet I wonder'd once to see, that in one day it subsided about ¾ of an inch.

16. Of late I have altered my Method upon the *Barometer*, observing it, as it is before my Eyes, all day long, and much of the night, being watchful for the moments of every particular change, to examine, what cause in the Air and Heavens may appear for such

changes. And now my wonder is, to see, how slow it is, it holding most between the nine and twentieth and thirtieth inch of late.

17. I must now (*January* 13. 166⁵/₆) tell you, that the *Mercury* stands at this time (as it did also yesterday) a quarter above 30. inches; yet both days very dark and cloudy, sometimes very thick and misty Air; which seldom falls out. For, for the most part, I see it higher in clearest setled weather, than in such cloudy and misty Foggs. This thick Air and darkness hath lasted above a week; lately more Cold, and *East* and *North-East* wind.

*This seems to be wished, because the motion of the*Mercury *may be more free in a wider Cane.*

Thus far the Notes of this Observing *Divine;* of which Mr. *Boyle,* to whom they were also communicated, entertains these thoughts, that they seem to him very faithfully made, and do for the main, agree well enough with his observations, as far as he remembers, not having them, it seems, at that time, when he wrote this, at hand; and though it be wished by him, that the Observer's Glass-Cane had been somewhat bigger; yet his diligence in fitting it so carefully, or rather so skilfully, as is above-mentioned, is much by him commended.{160}

Some Observations of Vipers.

A curious *Italian*, called *Francesco Redi*, having lately had an opportunity, by the great number of Vipers, brought to the *Grand Duke* of *Toscany* for the composing of *Theriac* or*Treacle*, to examine what is vulgarly delivered and believed concerning the Poyson of those Creatures, hath, (according to the account, given of it in the French *Journal des Scavans*, printed *January* 4. 166⁵/₆) performed his undertaking with much exactness, and published in an Italian tract, not yet come into *England*, these Observations.

1. He hath observed, that the poyson of Vipers is neither in their *Teeth*, nor in their *Tayle*, nor in their *Gall*: but in the two *Vesicles* or *Bladders*, which cover their teeth, and which coming to be compressed, when the Vipers bite, do emit a certain yellowish Liquor, that runs along the teeth and poysons the wound. Whereof he gives this proof, that he hath rub'd the wounds of many Animals with the *Gall* of Vipers, and pricked them with their *Teeth*, and yet no considerable ill accident follow'd upon it, but that as often as he rubbed the wounds with the said yellow Liquor, not one of them escaped.

2. Whereas commonly it hath hitherto been believed, that the poyson of Vipers being swallowed, was present death; this *Author*, after many reiterated Experiments, is said to have observed, that in Vipers there is neither Humour, nor Excrement, nor any part, not the *Gall* it self, that, being taken into the Body, kills. And he assures, that he hath seen men eat, and hath often made Bruit Animals swallow all that is esteem'd most poysonous in a Viper, yet without the least mischief to them. Whence he shews, that it needs not so much to be wondred at, that certain *Empiricks* swallow the juyce of the {161}most venomous Animals without receiving any harm thereby; adding, that, which is ascribed to the vertue of their *Antidote*, ought to be attributed to the nature of those kinds of Poysons, which are no poysons, when they are swallow'd, (for which Doctrine he also alledges *Celsus*) but onely when they are put into wounds. Which also has been noted by *Lucan*, who introduces *Cato* thus speaking;

Noxia serpentum est admisto sanguine pestis,
Morsu *virus habent, & fatum* dente *minantur;*
Pocula *morte carent.*

And what also some Authors have affirm'd, *videl.* That it is mortal, to eat of the Flesh of creatures killed by Vipers; or to drink of the Wine wherein Vipers have been drowned; or to suck the wounds that have been made by them, is by this Authour observed to be wide of truth. For he assures, that many persons have eaten Pullets and Pigeons, bitten by Vipers, without finding any alteration from it in their health. On the contrary, he declares, That it is a soveraign Remedy against the biting of Vipers, to suck the wound; alledging an Experiment, made upon a Dog, which he caused to be bitten by a Viper at the nose, who by licking his own wound saved his life. Which he confirms by the example of those people, celebrated in*History* by the name of *Marsi* and *Psilli*, whose Employment it was, to heal those, that had been bitten by Serpents, by sucking their wounds.

3. He adds, that although *Galen* and many modern *Physitians* do affirm, that there is nothing, which causeth so much thirst, as Vipers-flesh, yet he hath experimented the

contrary and knows divers persons, who did eat the flesh of Vipers at all their meals, and yet did assure him, they never were less dry, then when they observed that kind of Diet.

4. As for the Salt of Vipers, whereof some *Chymists* have {162} so great esteem, he saith, that it hath no *Purging* vertue at all in it; adding that even of *All Salts*, none hath more vertue than another, as he pretends to have shew'd in an other *Book* of his, *De natura salium*, which also hath not been yet transmitted into these parts.

5. He denies, what *Aristotle* assures, and what *Galen* saith to have often tryed, that the *Spittle* of a *Fasting* person kills Vipers; and he laughs at many other particulars, that have been delivered concerning the *Antipathy* of Vipers unto certain things; and their manner of Conception and Generation, and several other properties, commonly ascribed to them; which the alledged French Author affirms to be refuted by so many experiments made by this *Italian* Philosopher, that it seems to him, there is no place left for doubting, after so authentick a testimony.

Advertisement.

The *Reader* of these *Transactions* is desired to correct these *Errata* in *Number* 8. *viz.* page.132. line penult. read *Wine* for *Lime*; and page 133. line 10. read *Thresher* for *Trepher*, as some *Copies* have it; and page 136. line ult. read *purifie* for *putrifie*.

LONDON,

Printed for *John Martyn* and *James Allestree*, Printers to the Royal Society. 1666.
{163}

PHILOSOPHICAL
TRANSACTIONS.

Munday, March 12. 166⁵/₆.

The Contents.

Observations continued upon the Barometer, or rather Ballance of the Air.

These *Transactions* being intended, *not only* to be (by parcels) brief Records of the Emergent Works and Productions in the Universe; Of the Mysteries of Nature of later discoveries; And, of the growth of Useful Inventions and Arts; *but* also, and chiefly, to sollicite in all parts mutuall Ayds and Collegiate endeavours for the farther advancement thereof: We shall begin this *Second* year of our Publications in this kind (in which, for 3-moneths the Printing-presses were interrrupted by the publick Calamity) with a few more particular Observations upon the *Ballance of the Air*, as they are most happily invented and directed by Mr. *Boyle*; and deserve to be prosecuted with care and diligence in all places.

But it is to be premised, that the Worthy person, who was alledged as the Author of the Observations, delivered of this kind in the last of these *Tracts* (Dr. *Beale*) gives notice, That {164} he did not pretend to exactness, but only to excite the carefulness of others in the several distant places, and chiefly such, as can have the assistance of a *Wheel-ballance* perfectly filled: without both which aids he hopes not to obtain all the benefits and mysteries of this Invention.

This being thus briefly intimated, the Account of the Observations themselves, as they were extracted out of a late Letter of the same Person, are, as followes:

1. As I have fitted and filled the *Single Cane*, I can say in the general, That I have not yet found any such infallible Prognostick of these changes of weather, which do follow a long serenity, or setled weather. And perchance in brighter Climats it may be constantly infallible. In these *Northern Islands*, the Clouds are so short, and narrow, and by fickle changes are sometimes emptied upon us, sometimes so neer, as may make so little variation in the weight of the whole Atmosphere of Air, as may sometimes deceive us, or smother and hide from us the Hygroscopes *are Instruments, to discover the degrees of Moisture and Drought of the Air.*causes of fixedness, or of changes. I wish I could see a good*Calendar* or *Journal* taken in taken in *Tangier*, and in some of our*Northern* and most *Southern* parts of *America.* I have store of*Hygroscopes* of divers kinds; and I do remark them, and the sweatings of Marble, and as many other famed Prognosticks, as I can hear off; but can find nothing so neerly indicative of the change of weather, as this*Ballance.* Those others are often changed by Dews, which do not at all alter the *Ballance,* nor alter the state of the weather: And the open Weather-glass is known to signifie nothing at certainty, having a double obedience to two Masters, sometimes to the *Weight of the Air,* sometimes to *Heat,* as the service is commanded.

2. And in further confirmation of this Note, I may adde to the former, That in *January* last 165⁵/₆, from the *fourth,* and more especially from the *seventh* day, for many daies it continued very dark, so that all men expected daily great rain; yet the *Mercury* held very high, neer to the greatest height; And though in those daies sometimes thick mists arose, and some small rain fell, yet the *Quick-silver* held at a great height: which did indicate to me, there could *then* be no great change of weather. As the small rain fell, it yeilded somewhat, not much; and that does more {165}confirm the indication. And more lately, in very dark daies, I had the same confidence upon the same ground, and I was not disappointed.

3. Again, if the *Mercury* ascends to a good height after the fall of rain (as sometimes, but less often it does) then I look for a setled serenity; but if it proceeds after rain in a descending motion, then I expect a continuance of broken and showry weather. But in all, as I only say,*For the most part,* so I dare not positively declare it an affirmative result, but do refer it to the remarks of others. And this may explicate the Notes 6. and 14 of *Num.* 9. into more clearness.

4. That we find the Weather and our Bodies more chill, cold, and drooping, when the*Mercury* is lowest, and the Air lightest, besides other causes, I guess, That as Air is to us the breath of life, as water is to Fishes; so, when we are deprived of the usual measure of this our food, 'tis the same to us, as when the water is drawn ebb from Fishes. But I would much rather be instructed by others, then offer much in this kind.

5. The lowest descent of the *Mercury* in all the time, since I have observed it, was *Octob.* 26. 1665. in the Evening, when it was very near at 27½ Inches. Which I find thus circumstanced with the weather in my notes.

Oct. 25. Morning; *Mercury* at 28½ Inch. Great storms and much rain.

Oct. 26. Morning; *Merc.* at 28. winds quiet, thick dark clouds.

Oct. 26. Evening; *Merc.* at 27½. That day, and some daies following, the weather was variable, frequent rain, and as you see, the *Mercury* lower, than usual.

6. Over the place, where this *Mercurial Cane* stands, I have set a *Wind vane,* with purpose of exactness, of a Streamer in Brass so large, and pointing to a Board indented in the Margin, that I can at a sure Level upon the *Vane,* take every of the 32. points of the Wind, half points, and quarter points, at good distance. Otherwise we may find our guesses much deceived, as the best guessers, upon trial, do acknowledge. And this exactness may become the *Wheel-ballance,* which shews the minutest variations almost beyond imagination. And thus any servant, at the approach of a thick Cloud, or other *Meteor,* higher or lower, or at the rising of a storm or fresh wind in the night, or day, may bring a report of the Weight of the Air, as certainly and almost as {166}easily, as of the Sun from the *Dial* in a Sunshine. It were good to have an *Index* of Winds, that discover'd as well their Ascent and Descent, as their Side-coastings.

A Relation concerning the late **Earthquake** *neer* **Oxford***; together with some Observations of the sealed Weatherglass, and the Barometer both upon that***Phænomenon***, and in* **General.**

75

This Relation was communicated by the excellently learned Dr. *Wallis*, as follows:

On the 19. of *January* 1665. *Stylo Angliæ* (or *Jan*. 29. 1666. *stylo novo*) at divers places neer*Oxford*, was observed a small *Earthquake* (as at *Blechington, Stanton-St. Johns, Bril*, &c.) towards evening. In *Oxford* it self, I doe not hear, that it was observ'd to be an Earthquake; yet I remember about that time (whether precisely then or not; I cannot say) I took notice of some kind of odde shaking or heaving I observed in my study, but did impute it to the going of Carts or Coaches, supposed to be not far off; though yet I did take notice of it, as a little differing from what is usual on such occasions; (and wondered the more, that I did not hear any:) But not knowing, what else to refer it to, I thought no more of it. And the like account I have had from some others in *Oxford*, who yet did not think of an Earth-quake; it being a rare thing with us. Hearing afterwards of an Earthquake observed by others; I looked on my Notes concerning my *Thermoscope* and *Baroscope*, to see if any alteration considerable had then happened.

My *Thermoscope* consists of a round large Glass, containing about half a pint or more; from whence issues a long Cylindrical neck of Glass, about two foot and a half in length, and less than a quarter of an inch diameter; which neck was *hermetically* sealed at the top, to exclude communication with the External Air; but before the sealing of it, the whole Glass was filled with *Spirit of Wine* (tinged with *Cochineel*, to make it the more discernable to the Eye) so warmed, that it filled the whole content of the Glass; but afterwards, as it cooled, did so subside, as to leave a void space in the upper part of the Neck. Which Instrument, so prepared, doth by the rising or falling of the tinged liquor in the neck (consequent upon the expanding or contracting of the whole liquor contained in it and the Ball below) give a very nice account of the Temperature of the Air, {167} as to *Heat* or *Cold*: Even so nice, as that my being or not being in my Study I find to vary its hight sometimes almost a quarter of an inch.

My *Baroscope*, I call another Instrument for estimating the *Weight* or *Pressure* of the Incumbent Air, consisting of a long *Glass-tube* of about 4. foot in length, and about a quarter of an inch Bore: which tube (*hermetically* sealed at the one end) being filled with Quicksilver (according to the *Torricellian* Experiment) is inverted, so as to have the open end of it immersed in Stagnant Quicksilver, contained in a larger Glass under it, exposed to the pressure of the outward Air: Out of which open end (after such immersion) the Quicksilver in the Tube being suffered to run out, as much as it will, into the Stagnant Quicksilver, in which that mouth or open end is immersed, there is wont to remain (as is commonly known to those acquainted with this Experiment) a Cylinder of Quicksilver suspended in the Tube, about 28, 29, or 30. inches high; measuring from the surface of the Stagnant Quicksilver perpendicularly; (but more or less, within such limits, according as the Weight or Pressure of the Air incumbent on the External Stagnant Quicksilver exposed to it, is greater or less:) leaving the upper part of the Tube void. (Both which Instruments being the contrivance of the Honourable *Robert Boyle*, they are by him more particularly described in his *Physico-Mechanical Experiments touching the Air, Exper*. 17. and 18. and in his*Thermometrical Discourses*, premised to his *History of Cold*.)

Now, according to both these Instruments, having kept a daily *Register* of Observations for more than a whole year (saving when I have been for some short time absent from home) I find my Notes for that day to be these.

January. Day. Hour.	*Thermoscope.* inches.	*Baroscope.* inches.	1665/6.	
19.	14¹	2	Har	C
8. Morn.	/16.	9½.	d frost.	lose.
4.	14⅜	2	Har	C
Even.	.	9¼.	d frost.	loudy.
9.	14	2	Rai	W
Even.	¾.	9¾.	n.	ind
20.	15	2	Sun	W
8. Morn.	¼.	8¾.	shine.	ind.

So that, there being in the morning (*January* 19.) a hard frost (which began the day before about 4. of the Clock in the {168}afternoon (*Jan.* 18.) and continued (with us) till about 5. of the Clock in the afternoon of that day, *Jan* 19. with some fierceness) and the weather, *Jan.* 19. being in the morning, close; and cloudy all the day, with little of Sun-shine; the Liquor in the*Thermoscope* was very little raised, by 4. of the Clock afternoon, that is, but $^5/_{16}$ of an inch (which, had the Sun shone, would, it's likely, have been near an Inch:) and after that time (or somewhat before) had there been no considerable change of weather, it would upon the Sun's setting have fallen (and probably so it did, till about 5. of the Clock, though I took no Observation in the interim.) But, contrary to what would have been expected, it was at 9. of the Clock at night, higher by ⅛ of an inch, than it had been at 4. occasioned by the change of weather, the Frost suddenly breaking, with us, between 5. and 6. of the Clock; about which time also it began to rain, and continued raining that Evening and good part of the Night. And the next morning I found the Liquor yet higher by half an inch, *vid.* 15¼ inches: (by reason of the Air that night being so much warmer, than it had been the day before;) whereas commonly it is considerably lower in the morning, than over night.

As to the *Baroscope*, for the Weight or Pressure of the Air; I find, that for the 11, 12, 13, 14, 15, 16, and 17. dayes, the *Mercury* in the Tube, was (by the ballancing Pressure of the incumbent Air on the stagnant Quicksilver, exposed to it) kept up to the height of near 30. Inches above the surface of the External Quicksilver, (though with some little variation, as 30, 29$^{15}/_{16}$, 29⅞, 29$^{13}/_{16}$ but never so low, all that time, as 29¾;) which is the greatest height I have know it at, (for I do not find that I have ever, till then, observed it to be, in my Glasses, full 30. Inches, though it have been very near it:) the Weather having been almost continually Foggy, or very thick Mists, all that time. *January* 18. it came down to 29¾. in the forenoon; and afternoon, to 29$^{11}/_{16}$. about the time the frost began: And *Jan.* 19. it was, at 8. in the morning, come down to 29½; at 4. in the afternoon, to 29¼. But at 9. in the evening (when the Earth quake had intervened) it was risen half an inch, *vid.* to 29¾. And, by the next morning, fallen again a whole inch, *vid.* to 28¾; which fall I attribute (at least in part) to the rain that fell in the night.

This being what I observed out of my *Register* of these Instruments, (which, if I had then thought of an Earthquake, I {169}should have more nicely watched) what I have further gathered from Reports, is to this purpose.

I hear, it was observed at *Blechington*, above 5. miles to the *North* of *Oxford*, and so along by *Bostol*, *Horton*, *Stanton-St. Johns*, and so towards *Whately*, which is about 4. miles*Eastward* from *Oxford*. Not at all these places at the same time, but moving forward from*Blechington* towards *Whately*. For it was at *Stanton* about 6. of the Clock or later (as I understand from Mr. *Boyle*, who was there at that time;) but had been at *Blechington* a good while sooner. And I am told, that it was taken notice of by Doctor *Holder* (a Member of our*Society*) who was then at *Blechington*, to be observed by those in the further part of the Garden, some very discernable time before it was observed by those in the House; creeping forward from the one place to the other. What other places in the Country it was observed at, I have not been informed: but at *Oxford* (which, it seems, was about the skirts of it) it was so small, as would have been hardly noted at all, had not the notice, taken of it abroad, informed us of it.

Upon this Occasion, it will not be unseasonable to give some General accounts of what I have in my *Thermoscope* and *Baroscope* observed.

My *Thermoscope*, being fitted somewhat at adventures, I have found at the lowest to be somewhat more than 12. inches high, in the fiercest time of the long Frost in the beginning of the last year 1665. and about 27. Inches high, at the highest, in the hottest time of the last Summer: (which I mention, that it may appear at what temperature in proportion, the Air was at the time above-mentioned.) But I must add withall, that this standing so, as never to be exposed to the Sun, but in a room, that has a window only to the North, it would have been raised much higher than 27. inches, if it were put in the hot Sun-shine in Summer; this, as it is placed, giving therefore an account onely of the Temperature of the Air in *general*, not of the immediate heat of the Sun-shine.

This Instrument, thus situated, when it is about 15. inches, or lower, is for the most part hard frost; but seldom a frost, if higher than 16. Yet this I have often observed, that the Air by the *Thermoscope* has appeared considerably colder (and the liquor lower) at sometimes when there is no Frost, than at some other times, when the Frost hath been considerably hard.{170}

In my *Baroscope*, I have never found the Quicksilver higher than 30. inches, nor lower than 28. (at least, scarce discernably, not $^1/_{16}$ of an inch higher than *that*, or lower than *this*,) which I mention, not only to shew the limits, within which I have observed mine to keep,*vid.* full 2 inches, but likewise as an Estimate of the Clearness of the Quicksilver from Air. For, though my Quicksilver were with good care cleansed from the Air; yet I find that which Mr. *Boyle* useth, much better: for, comparing his with mine at the same times, and both in *Oxford*, at no great distance; I find his Quicksilver to stand alwaies somewhat higher than mine (sometimes neer a quarter of an Inch;) which I know now how to give a more probable account off, than that my Quicksilver is either heavier than his; or else, that his is better cleansed from Air, (unless, possibly, the difference of the Bore, or other circumstances of the Tube, may cause the alteration; mine being a taller Tube, and a bigger Bore, than his.) And upon like reason, as his stands higher than mine; so another less cleansed from Air, may at the same time be considerably lower, and consequently under 28. Inches at the lowest.

In *thick foggy* weather, I find my Quicksilver to rise; which I adscribe to the heaviness of the Vapours in the Air. And I have never found it higher, than in the foggy weather above-mentioned.

In *Sunshiny* weather it riseth also (and commonly the clearer, the more;) which, I think, may be imputed *partly* to the Vapors raised by the Sun, and making the Air heavier; and *partly* to the Heat, increasing the Elastick or Springy power of the Air. Which latter I the rather add, because I have sometimes observed in Sunshiny weather, when there have come Clouds for some considerable time (suppose an hour or two) the Quicksilver has fallen; and then, upon the Suns breaking out again, it has risen as before.

In *Rainy* weather, it useth to fall (of which the reason is obvious, because the Air is lightned, by so much as falls:) In *Snowy* weather, likewise, but not so much as in *Rain*. And sometimes I have observed it, upon a *Hoar-frost*, falling in the night.

* The Author of these Observations intends hereafter more particularly to observe, from what points *those Winds blow, that make the Quicksilver thus subside.*

For *Windy* weather, I find it *generally* to fall; and that more universally, and more discernably, than upon Rain: (which I attribute to the Winds moving the Air *collaterally*, and thereby not suffering it to press so much *directly* downwards: the like of {171}which we see in swimming, &c.) And I have never found it lower than in high Winds.*

I have divers times, upon discerning my Quicksilver to fall without any visible cause at home, looked abroad; and found (by the appearance of broken Clouds, or otherwise) that it had rained not far off, though not with us: Whereupon, the Air being then lightened, our heavier Air (where it rained not) may have, in part, discharged it self on that lighter.

A more particular Account of those Observations about Jupiter, *that were mentioned in* Numb. 8.

Since the publishing of *Numb.* 8. of these *Transactions*, where, among other particulars, some short Observations were set down touching both the *shadow* of one of *Jupiter's Satellits*, passing over his Body, and that *Permanent Spot*, which manifests the Conversion of that Planet about his own *Axis*; there is come to hand an *Extract* of that Letter, which was written from *Rome*, about those Discoveries, containing an ample and particular Relation of them, as they were made by the Learned *Cassini*, Professor of *Astronomy* in the University of *Bononia*. That *Extract*, as it is found in the *French Journal des Scavans* of Febr. 22. 1666. we thus *English*.

Monsieur *Cassini*, after he had discovered (by the means of those Excellent Glasses of 50.*palmes*, or 35. *feet*, made by M. *Campani*) the *Shadows*, cast by the 4 Moons or *Satellits* of *Jupiter* upon his Diske, when they happen to be between the Sun and Him; after he had also distinguished their Bodies *upon* the Diske of *Jupiter*; made the last year some Prædictions for the Months of *August* and *September*, noting the dayes and hours, when the

Bodies of the said *satellits* and their *Shadows* should appear upon *Jupiter*, to the end that the Curious might be convinced of this matter by their own Observations.

Some of these Prædictions have been verified not only at *Rome*, and in other places of *Italy*, but also at *Paris* by M. *Auzout*, the most Celebrated and the most Exact of our *Astronomers*; and in *Holland*, by M. *Hugens*. And we can now doubt no longer, of the rotation of the *Satellits* about *Jupiter*, as the Moon turns about the Earth; nor believe, that *Jupiter* or his *Attendants* have any other Light, than that, which they receive from the Sun; as some did {172} assure before these Observations. There remained to find by Experience, whether *Jupiter* did turn about his *Axis*, as many believe, that the *Earth* turns about her's. And although most *Astronomers* had conjectur'd, it did so, either by this Analogy, or by other Congruities, yet it was much wish'd, that we might be assured thereof by Observations. And this it is, for which we are obliged to M. *Cassini*, who, having by the advantage of the same Glasses discover'd several changes, as well in the three obscure *Belts*, commonly seen in *Jupiter*, as in the rest of his *Diske*, and having also observed Spots in the midst of that *Planet*, and sometimes *Brightnesses*, such as have bin formerly seen in the *Sun*, hath at length discover'd a *Permanent Spot* in the *Northern* part of the most *Southern* Belt; by the means whereof, he hath concluded, that *Jupiter* turns about his *Axis* in 9. hours, 56. minutes, and makes 29. whole circumvolutions in 12 dayes 4. minutes of ours, and 360 in 149. dayes. For he has found, that this *Spot* was not caused by the Shadow of any *Satellit*, as well by reason of its Situation, as because it appeared, when there could be no Shadow. Besides, that its motion differed from that of the Shadows, which is almost equal, as well towards the Edges as towards the Middle of *Jupiter*. Whereas, on the contrary, this *Spot* hath all the accidents, that must happen to a thing, which is upon the surface of a round Body moving; for example, to move much more slowly towards the Edges, than towards the Middle, and to pass over that part, which is in the middle of the Diske, equal to the half of the *Diameter*, in the sixth part of the time, it takes to make the whole revolution: he having seen this half pass'd over, in 99 or 100 minutes just, as it must happen, supposing the whole circumrotation is made in 9. hours 56. minutes.

He hath not yet been able to determine the Situation of the *Axis*, upon which this motion is made, because the *Belts*, according to which it is made, have for some years appeared streight, though in the precedent years, other *Astronomers* have seen them a little crooked: Which sheweth, that the *Axis* of the diurnal motion of *Jupiter* is a little inclined to the plain of the *Ecliptick*. But in time we may discover, what certainty there is in this matter.

These Tables *are not yet sent over, but, 'tis hoped, will be, ere long.*

After this excellent Discovery, he hath calculated many *Tables*, whereof he gives the Explication and Use in the Letters by him addressed to the Abbot *Falconieri*. By the means of them, one may know, *when* this *Spot* may be seen by us. For, having first {173} considered it in relation to the *Sun*, in respect whereof, its motion is regular, he considers the same in relation to the *Earth*, where *We* observe it; and shews by the means of his *Tables*, what is to be added or subtracted, to know, at what time the said *Spot* is to come into the middle of *Jupiter's* Diske, according as he is Oriental or Occidental. He hath also considered it in relation to an unmovable point, which he has supposed to be the first point of *Aries*, because we thither refer here upon Earth the beginning of all the Celestial motions, and *there* is the *Primum mobile*, that one would imagine, if we were in *Jupiter*, as we do here imagine Ours of 24. hours.

The Discovery is one of the best, that have been yet made in the Heavens; and those, that hold the Motion of the earth, find in it a full Analogy. For, *Jupiter* turning about the Sun, does nevertheless turn about his *Axis*; and although he be much bigger than the Earth, he does nevertheless turn much more swiftly than it, since he makes more than two Turns, and a third part, for its one; and carries with him 4. Moons, as the Earth does one.

This Observation ought to excite all Curious persons to endeavour the perfecting of *Optick Glasses*, to the end that it may be discovered, whether the other *Planets*, as *Mars*, *Venus* and *Mercury*, about whom no Moon hath as yet been discovered, do yet turn about their *Axes*, and in how much time they do so; especially *Mars*, in whom some *Spot* is discover'd, and *Venus*, wherein M. *Burattini* hath signified from *Poland*, he has observ'd Inequalities, as in the Moon.

79

It will be worth while, to watch for the seeing of *Jupiter* again this Spring, that this happy Observation may be confirmed in divers places, and endeavours used to make new ones.

An Account of some Books, lately published.

I. *Hydrostatical Paradoxes, made out by New Experiments (for the most part Physical, and Easie) by the Honourable Robert Boyle.* This Treatise, promised in *Numb.* 8. of these Papers, is now come forth: And was occasioned by the perusal of the Learned Monsieur *Paschall's*Tract, *Of the Æquilibrium of Liquors*, and of the *Weight of the Air.* Of which two Subjects, the *latter* having been more clearly made out in *England* by Experiments, which could not be made by Monsieur *Paschal* and others, that wanted the advantage of such Engines and Instruments, as have here been frequently made use {174}off; Our Noble Author insists most upon giving us his thoughts of the former, *videl.* the *Æquilibrium of Liquors.* Which Discourse consisting partly of *Conclusions*, and partly of *Experiments*, the *former* seem to Him to be almost all of them consonant to the Principles and Laws of the *Hydrostaticks*; but as for the*latter*, the Experimental proofs, offered by M. *Paschall* for his Opinions, are by our Author esteemed such, that he confesses, he hath no mind to make use of them: for which he alledges more reasons than one; which, doubtless, will appear very satisfactory to Intelligent*Readers.*

Wherefore, instead of the those *Paschalian* Experiments, there is in this *Treatise* deliver'd a far more Expeditious way, to make out, *not only* most of the *Conclusions*, agreed on these two Authors, *but* others also, that M *Paschall* mentions not: and that with so much more ease and clearness, that persons, but ordinarily versed in the common principles of *Hydrostaticks*, may readily apprehend, what is deliver'd, if they will but bring with them a due Attention, and Minds disposed to prefer Reason and Experience to Vulgar opinions and Authors.

It not being our *Authors* present Task, to deliver a Body of *Hydrostaticks*, but only some*Paradoxes*, which he conceives to be proveable by his New way of making them out, he delivers them in as many distinct Propositions; after each of which, he endeavours, in a Proof, or an Explication, to show, both that it is true, and why it ought to be so.

The *Paradoxes* themselves (after a premised *Postulatum*) are these:

1. That in Water, and other Fluids, the Lower parts are pressed by the Upper.

2. That a lighter Fluid may gravitate or weigh upon a heavier.

3. That, if a Body, contiguous to the Water, be altogether, or in part, lower than the highest level of the said Water, the lower part of the Body will be pressed upward by the Water, that touches it beneath.

4. That in the Ascension of Water in Pumps, &c. there needs nothing to raise the Water, but a Competent weight of an External Fluid.

5. That the pressure of an External Fluid is able to keep an Heterogeneous Liquor suspended at the same height in several Pipes, though these Pipes be of very different Diameters.

{175}

6. If a Body be placed under Water, with its uppermost Surface parallel to the Horizon; how much Water soever there may be on this or that side above the Body, the direct pressure susteined by the Body (for we now consider not the Lateral nor the Recoyling pressure, to which the Body may be exposed, if quite environed with Water) is no more, than that of a Column of water, having Horizontal Superficies of the Body for its Basis, and the Perpendicular depth of the Water for its height.

And so likewise,

If the Water, that leans upon the Body, be contained in Pipes open at both ends, the pressure of the Water is to be estimated by the weight of a pillar of Water, whose Basis is equal to the lower Orifice of the Pipe (which we suppose to be parallel to the Horizon) and its height equal to a perpendicular, reaching thence to the top of the Water; though the Pipe be much inclined towards the Horizon, or though it be irregularly shap'd, and much broader in some parts, than the said Orifice.

7. That a Body, immersed in a Fluid, sustains a Lateral pressure from the Fluid; and that increased, as the depth of the immersed Body, beneath the Surface of the Fluid, increaseth.

8. That Water may be made as well to depress a Body lighter than it self, as to buoy it up.

9. That, whatever is said of Positive Levity, a parcel of Oyl lighter than Water, may be kept in Water without ascending in it.

10. That the cause of the Ascension of Water in Syphons, and of its flowing through them, may be explicated without having a recourse to Nature's abhorrency of a *Vacuum*.

11. That a Solid Body, as ponderous as any yet known, though near the Top of the water it will sink by its own weight; yet if it be placed at a greater depth, than that of twenty times its own thickness; it will not sink, if its descent be not assisted by the weight of the incumbent Water.

These are the *Paradoxes*, evinced by our Authour with much evidence and exactness, and very likely to invite Ingenious men to cultivate and to make further disquisitions in so excellent a part of Philosophy, as are the *Hydrostaticks*; and Art deserving great *Elogiums*, not only, upon the account of the *Theorems* and *Problems*, which are most of them pure and handsome productions of Reason, very delightful and divers of them surprising, and besides, much conducing to the clear explication and {176}thorow-understanding of many both familiar and abstruse *Phænomena* of Nature; but also, upon the score of its *Practical* use, since the Propositions, it teaches, may be of great importance to Navigation, and to those that inquire into the Magnitudes and Gravities of Bodies, as also to them, that deal in Salt-works: Besides, that the *Hydrostaticks* may be made divers waies serviceable to *Chymists*, as the Author intimates, and intends to make manifest, upon several occasions, in his yet unpublisht part of the *Usefulness of Natural and Experimental Philosophy.*

These Propositions are shut up by two important *Appendixes*, whereof the *one* contains an Answer to seven Objections by a late learned Writer, to evince, that the upper parts of water press not upon the lower; the *other*, solves that difficult *problem*, why *Urinators* or *Divers*, and others, who descend to the bottom of the Sea, are not oppressed with the weight of the incumbent water? where, among other solutions, *that* is examined, which occurs in a printed Letter of Monsieur *des Cartes*, but is found unsatisfactory.

II. *Nicolai Stenonis de Musculis & Glandulis Observationum Specimen; cum duabus Epistolis Anatomicis.* In the *Specimen* it self, the Author, having described in *general*, both the *Structure* and the *Function* of the *Muscles*, applies that description to the *Heart*, to demonstrate that *that* is also a *true Muscle*: Observing *first*, that in the substance of the *Heart* there appears nothing but *Arteries, Veins, Nerves, Fibres, Membrans*; and that that, & nothing else is found in a *Muscle*; affirming withall, that which is commonly taught of the *Muscles*, and particularly of the *Heart's Parenchyma*, as distinct from *Fibres*, is due, not to the *Senses*, but the *Wit* of *Anatomists*: so that he will not have the *Heart* made up of a substance peculiar to it self, nor considered as the principle of *Innate heat*, or of *Sanguification*, or of *vital spirits*. He observes *next*, that the *Heart* performs the like *operation* with the *Muscles*, to wit, to contract the Flesh; which action how it can have a different cause from that of the Contraction made in the *Muscles*, where there is so great a parity and agreement in the *Vessels*, he sees not. And as for the *Phænomena*, that occur, of the *Motion* of the Heart, he undertakes to explicate them all, from the *Ductus* or *Position* of the *Fibres*; but refers for the performance of this undertaking to another *Treatise*, he intends to publish.

Conglobate *Glanduls are called those, that do consist, as it were, of one continued substance, having an even superficies; whereof there are many in the* Mesentery, *and in other places: contra distinguisht to those, that bear the name of* Conglomerate *Glanduls, which are made up of several small Kernels, such as the* Pancreas, *the* Salivating Glanduls, *&c.*

As to his Observations about *Glanduls*, he affirms, that he has been the First, that has discover'd that Vessel, which by him is call'd {177} *Salivare Exterius*, passing from the *Parotides* (or the two chief Arteries that are on the right and left side neer the Throat) into the Mouth, and conveying the *Spittle*: Where he also gives an account of several other Vessels and Glanduls, some about the *Lips*; others under the *Tongue*; others in the *Pallate* &c. To which he adds the Vessels of the *Eye-lids*, which have their root in the *Glanduls* that are about the Eyes, and serve for the *shedding of Tears*. He mentions also several things about the *Lymphatick vessels*, and is of opinion, that the knowledge thereof may be much illustrated by that kind of *Glanduls* that are called *Conglobatæ*, and by their *true* insertion into the veins; the mistake of the latter whereof, he conceives to have very much misled the Noble *Ludovicus de Bills*, notwithstanding his excellent method of *dissection*. And here he observes *first*, that all the *Lymphatick vessels* have such a commerce with the *Glanduls*, that none of them is found in the body, which either has not its origine *from*, or is inserted *into* a *Glandule*: And *then*, that *Glanduls* are a kind of *Strainers*, so form'd, that whilst the Blood passes out of the Arteries into the Veins through the small *Capillary* vessels, the *Serous* parts thereof, being freed from the *Sanguineous*, are by vertue of the beat expell'd through fit pores into the *Capilaries* of the *Lymphaticks*, the direction of the *Nerves* concurring.

Of the two annex'd *Epistles*, the *First* gives an account of the dissection of two *Raja's* or *Skates*, and relates that the Author found in the bellies of these Fishes a *Haddock* of 1½ span long, and a *Sole*, a *Plaise*, and nine middle-sized *Sea crafishes*; whereof not only the three former had their flesh, in the fishes stomack, turn'd into a *fluid*, and the Gristles or Bones into a *soft* substance, but the *Crafishes* had their shels comminuted into very small particles, tinging here and there the *Chyle* near the *Pylorus*, which he judges to be done not so much by the heat of the Fishes stomack, as by the help of some digesting juyce. Coming to the *Uterus* of these Fishes, he takes occasion to examine, with what ground several famous *Naturalists* and *Anatomists* have affirm'd, that Eggs are the *uterus* exposed or ejected out of the body of the Animal. Taking a view of their *Heart*, he there finds but *one* ventricle, and discourses of the difficulty arising from thence. As for the *Lungs*, he saw no clearer footsteps of them in these, than he had done in other Fishes: but within the mouth he trac'd several *gaping fissures*, and found the recesses of the *Gills* so form'd, that the water taken in at the mouth, being let out by these dores, cannot by them re-enter, by reason of a skin outwardly passing over every hole, and covering it. Where he intimates, that though Fishes have not *true* Lungs, yet they want not a *Succedaneum* thereto, to wit, the *Gills*; and if *water* may be to Fishes, what *Air* is to terrestrial Animals, for Respiration: affecting, that whereas nothing is so necessary for the conservation of Animal life as a reciprocal Access and Recess of the *Ambient* to the sanguineous vessels, tis all one, whether that be done by receiving the Ambient *within* the body, or by its gentle passing *by* the *Prominent* vessels of the *Gills*.

The other *Epistle*, contains some Ingenious Observations, touching the way, by which the Chicken, yet in the shell, is nourish't, *videl*. not by the conveyance of the *Yolk* into the *Liver* by the *Umbilical* vessels, nor into the *Stomack* by the {178} *Mouth*, but by a Peculiar *ductus*, by him described, into the *Intestins*, where, according to his alledged experience, it is turn'd into *Chyle*: which he affirms, he hath discover'd, by taking an Egge from under a brooding Hen, when the Chicken was ready to break forth, and when he was looking for the passage of the *Yolk*, out of its integument into the *Liver*, by finding it pass thence into the *Intestins*, as he found the *White* to do by the *mouth* into the *belly*. Whence he inclines to infer, that, since every *fætus* takes in at the mouth the liquor it swims in, and since the Chicken receives the *white* of the Egge into the *mouth*, and the *yolk* by the new discover'd *ductus* into the *Intestins*, it cannot be certainly made out, that a *part* of the *Chyle* is conveyed into the *Liver*, before it passes into the *Heart*; Exhorting in the mean time the *Patrons* of the *Liver*, that they would produce Experiments to evince their Ratiocinations.

III. *Regneri de Graeff, de Succi Pancreatici Natura & usu, Exercitatio Anatomico-medica.* In this Tract, the Industrious Author, after he has enumerated the various opinions of *Anatomists* concerning the use of that kernelly substance; call'd *Pancreas* (in *English*, the *Sweetbred*) endeavours to prove experimentally that this *Glandule* was not form'd by Nature, to separate any *Excrementitious* humor, and to convey it into the *Intestins*, but to prepare an *useful* juyce out of the Blood and Animal Spirits, of a somewhat *Acid* taste, and to carry the same into the Gut, call'd *Duodenum*, to be there mixt with the Aliment, that has been in some degree already fermented in the Stomack, for a further fermentation, to be produced by the conflux of the said acid *Pancreatick* juyce and some *Bilious* matter, abounding with volatile Salt, causing an Effervescence; which done, that juyce is, together with the purer part of the nourishment, carried into the *Milkie* veins, thence into the *common receptacle* of the *Chyle* and *Lymphatick liquor*, and so through the *ductus Thoracicus* into the right Ventricle of the Heart.

This Assertion, first advanced (saith the *Author*) partly by *Gothofredus Mobius*, partly by *Franciscus de le Boe Sylvius*, he undertakes to prove by experiments; which, indeed, he has with much industry, tried upon several Animals, to the end that he might collect some of this juyce of the *Pancreas* for a taste: which having at last obtained, and found it somewhat *acid*, he thereupon proceeds to deliver his opinion both of the *constitution* and quantity of this *Succus* in *healthy* Animals, and the vices thereof, in the *unhealthy*: deriving most diseases *partly* from its too great Acidity, or from its saltness, or harshness; *partly* from its paucity or redundancy: but especially, endeavouring to reduce from thence, as all *intermittent Feavers* (of all the *Phænomena* whereof he ventures to assign the causes from this *Hypothesis*) so also the *Gout, Syncope's, Stranguries, Oppilations, Diarrhæas, Dysenteries, Hysterical* and *Colick passions,* &c. All which he concludes with mentioning the waies and remedies to cure the manifold peccancy of this juyce by Evacuations and Alterations.

This seeming to be a *new* as well as a *considerable* discovery, it is hop'd, that others will by this intimation be invited to prosecute the same by further experiments, either to confirm what this Author has started, if true, or to rectifie it, if he be mistaken.

NOTE.

In *Fig.* 1. of *Num.* 9 of these Tracts the Graver hath placed the bended *end* of the *Springing Wire* C F, above the *Wire-staple* B, between it and the *Ring* E, of the *Weight* D; whereas *that* end should have been so expressed, as to pass *under* the *Wire-staple*, betwixt its two Wires, into the said *Ring*.

London, Printed for *John Martyn*, and *James Allestry*, Printers to the Royal Society. 1666.
{179}

Num. 11.

PHILOSOPHICAL
TRANSACTIONS.

Munday, April. 2. 1666.

The Contents.

A Confirmation of the former Account, touching the late Earth-quake *near* Oxford, *and the Concomitants thereof, by Mr.* Boyle. *Some Observations and Directions about the* Barometer, *communicated by the same Hand. General Heads for a* Natural History *of a Country, small or great, proposed by the same. An Extract of a Letter, written from* Holland, *about* Preserving Ships from being Worm-eaten. *An Account of Mr.* Boyle's *lately publish't Tract, entituled,* The Origine of Forms and Qualities, *illustrated by Considerations and Experiments.*

A Confirmation of the former Account touching the late Earth-
quake *near* Oxford, *and the Concomitants thereof.*

This Confirmation came from the Noble Mr. *Boyle* in a Letter, to the *Publisher*, as followeth:

As to the *Earth-quake*, your curiosity about it makes me sorry, that, though I think, I was the first, that gave notice of it to several of the *Virtuosi* at *Oxford*; yet the Account, that I can send you about it, is not so much of the *Thing* it self, {180} as of the *Changes of the Air*, that accompanied it. To inform you of which, I must relate to you, that riding one Evening somewhat late betwixt *Oxford* & a Lodging, I have at a place, 4 miles distant from it, the weather having been for a pretty while Frosty, I found the Wind so very cold, that it reduced me to put on some defensives against it, which I never since, nor, if I forget not, all the foregoing part of the Winter was obliged to make use off. My unwillingness to stay long in so troublesome a Cold, which continued very piercing, till I had got half way home-ward, did put me upon galloping at no very lasy rate; and yet, before I could get to my Lodgings, I found the Wind turned, and felt the Rain falling; which, considering the shortness of the time, and that this Accident was preceded by a setled Frost, was surprising to me, and induced me to mention it at my return, as one of the greatest and suddainest Alterations of Air, I have ever observ'd: And what changes I * *See* Num. 10. Phil. Transactions p. 166-171; *at the time of the printing whereof, this Relation of Mr.* Boyle*was not yet come to hand.*found, have been taken notice of in the *Gravity* of the *Atmosphere* at the same time by that Accurate Observer * Dr. *Wallis*, who then suspected nothing of what follow'd; as I suppose, he has ere this told you himself. Soon after, by my guess about an hour, there was a manifest *Trembling* in the House where I was (which stands high in comparison of *Oxford*.) But it was not there so great, but that I, who chanced to have my thoughts busied enough on other matters, than the weather, should not have taken notice of it as an *Earth-quake*, but have imputed it to some other cause, if one, that you know, whose hand is employed in this Paper, and begins to be a diligent observer of Natural things, had not advertis'd me of it; as being taken notice of by him and the rest of the people of the House. And soon after there hapned a brisk Storm: whereupon I sent to make inquiry at a place call'd *Brill*, which standing upon a much higher ground, I supposed might be more obnoxious to the effects of the *Earth-quake* (of which, had I had any suspition of it, my having formerly been in one neer the *Lacus Lemanus*, would have made me the more observant:) But the person I sent to, being {181}disabled by sickness to come over to me (which he promis'd to do, as soon as he could) writ me only a *Ticket*, whose substance was, That the*Earth-quake* was there much more considerable, than where I lodged, and that at a Gentlemans house, whom he names (the most noted Person, it seems, of the neighbourhood) the House trembled very much, so as to make the Stones manifestly to move to and fro in the Parlour, to the great amazement and fright of all the Family. The Hill, whereon this *Brill*stands, I have observ'd to be very well stor'd with Mineral substances of several kinds; and from thence I have been inform'd by others, that this Earth-quake reach'd a good many miles; but I have neither leasure, nor inclination to entertain you with uncertain reports of the Extent and other Circumstances, especially since a little further time an inquiry may enable me to give you a better warranted account.

Some Observations and Directions about the Barometer, communicated by the same Hand, to the Author of this Tract.

These shall be set down, as they came to hand in another Letter; *videl.*

* *See* Num. 9. *of the*Phil. Transact. *p. 159the last* paragraph.

As to the *Barometrical* Observations (as for brevities sake I use to call them) though you * guessed aright, that, when I saw those of the Learned and Inquisitive Dr. *Beale*, I had not Mine by me, (for I left them, some years since, in the hands of a *Virtuoso*, nor have I now the leasure to look after those Papers;) yet since by the Communication, you have made publick, 'tis probable, that divers Ingenious men will be invited to attempt the like Observations, I shall (notwithstanding my present haste) mention to you some particulars, which perhaps will not appear unseasonable, that came into my mind upon the reading of what you have presented the Curious.

* *Some whereof have been since invited by the* Publisher, *to give their concurrence herein.*

When I did, as you may remember, some years agoe, publickly express and desire that some Inquisitive men would {182}make *Baroscopical*Observations in several parts of *England* (if not in forrain Countries * also;) and to assist them, to do so, presented some of my Friends with the necessary Instruments: The declared reason of my desiring this Correspondence was (among other things) that by comparing Notes, *the Extent of the Atmospherical Changes, in point of Weight, might be the better estimated.* But not having hitherto received some account, that I hoped for, I shall now, without staying for them, intimate thus much to you: That it will be very convenient, that the Observers take notice not only of the *day*, but as near as they can, of the *Houre* wherein the height of the*Mercurial Cylinder* is observ'd: For I have often found, that within less than the compass of one day, or perhaps half a day, the Altitude of it has so considerably vary'd, as to make it in many cases difficult, to conclude any thing certainly from Observations, that agree but in the day.

It will be requisite also, that the Observers give notice of the *Scituation of the place*, where their *Barometers* stand, not only, because it will assist men to Judge, whether the Instruments were duely perfected, but principally, because, that though the *Baroscope* be good (nay, because it is so) the Observations will much disagree, even when the *Atmosphere* is in the same state, as to Weight, if one of the Instruments stand in a considerably higher part of the Countrey, than the other.

To confirm *both* the foregoing admonitions, I must now inform you, that, having in these parts two Lodgings, the one at *Oxford*, which you know stands in a bottom by the *Thames*-side, and the other at a place four miles thence, seated upon a moderate *Hill*, I found, by comparing two *Baroscopes*, that I made, the one at *Oxford*, the other at *Stanton St. Johns*, that, though the former be very good, and have been noted for such, during some years, and the latter was very carefully fill'd; yet by reason, that in the *Higher* place, the incumbent part of the *Atmosphere* must be lighter, than in the *Lower*, there is almost {183} always between 2 and 3 Eights of an Inch difference betwixt them: And having sometimes order'd my servants to take notice of the Disparity, and divers times carefully observ'd it my self, when I pass'd to and fro between *Oxford* and *Stanton*, I generally found, that the *Oxford* Barometer and the *other*, did, as it were by common consent, rise and fall together so, as that in the former the *Mercury* was usually ⅜ higher, than in the latter.

Which Observations may teach us, that the Subterraneous steams, which ascend into the Air, or the other Causes of the varying Weight of the *Atmosphere*, do, many times, and at least in some places, uniformly enough affect the Air to a greater height, than, till I had made this tryall, I durst conclude.

But, as most of the *Barometricall* observations are subject to exception, so I found the formerly mentioned to be. For (to omit lesser variations) riding one evening from *Oxford* to *Stanton*, and having, before I took horse, look't on the *Baroscope* in the former of these 2. places, I was somewhat surprised, to find at my comming to the latter, that in places no farther distant, and notwithstanding the shortness of the time (which was but an hour and a half, if so much) the *Barometer* at *Stanton* was short of its usual distance from the *other*, near a quarter of an *Inch*, though, the weather being fair and calm, there appear'd nothing of manifest change in the Air, to which I could adscribe so great a Variation; and though also, since that time, the *Mercury* in the two Instruments hath, for the most part, proceeded to rise and fall as before.

And these being the only Observations, I have yet met with, wherein *Baroscopes*, at some *Distance of Place*, and *Difference of Height*, have been compar'd (though I cannot now send you the Reflexions, I have else where made upon them;) as the opportunity I had to make them my self, rendred them not unpleasant to me, so perhaps the Novelty will keep them from being unwelcome to you. And I confess, I have had some flying suspicions, that the odd *Phænomena* of the *Baroscope*, which have hitherto more pos'd, than instructed us, may in time, if a {184} competent number of Correspondents do diligently prosecute the Inquiries (especially with *Baroscopes*, accommodated with Mr. *Hooks* ingenious additions) make men some *Luciferous* discoveries, that possibly we do not yet dream off.

This hath been inquired into, and is found, that several Accurate and Curious persons (as the Most Noble President of the Royal Society, *the* Lord *Viscount* Brounker, Doctor Beale, Mr. Hook &c.) *have observed the same.*

I know not, whether it will be worth while to add, that since I was oblig'd to leave *London*, I have been put upon so many lesser removes, that I have not been able to make *Baroscopical* Observations with such a constancy, as I have wished, but, as far as I remember, the *Quick-silver* has been for the most part, so high, as to invite me to take notice of it; and to desire you to do me the favour to inquire among your correspondents whether they have observ'd the same thing. * For, if they have, this lasting (though not uninterrupted) Altitude of the *Quick-silver*, happening, when the Seasons of the year have been extraordinary dry (so much as to become a grievance, and to dry up, as one of the late *Gazettes* informs us, some springs near *Waymouth*, that used to run constantly) it may be worth inquiry, whether these obstinate Droughts, may not be cleaving of the ground too deep, and making it also in some places more porous and as it were, spungy, give a more copious Vent, than is usual, to subterraneal steams, which adscending into the Air, increase the gravity of it. The inducements I have to propose this inquiry, I must not now stay to mention. But perhaps, if the Observation holds, it may prove not useless in reference to some Diseases.

* *See Number 9.* Phil. Transact. *p. 157. 5. 8 & 9. where the Word,*Generally, *signifies no more, than* for the most part.

Perhaps it will be needless to put you in mind of directing those*Virtuosi*, that may desire your Instructions about *Baroscopes*, to set down in their Diarys not only the day of the month, and the hour of the day, when the *Mercuries* height is taken, but (in a distinct *Columne*) the weather, especially the Winds, both as to the Quarters, whence they blow (though that be not always so easy nor necessary,) and as to the Violence or Remisness, wherewith they blow. For, though it be more difficult, {185}than one would think, to settle any general rule about the rising and falling of the*Quick-silver*, yet in these parts one of those, that seem to hold oftnest, is, * that when high winds blow, the *Mercury* is the lower; and yet that it self does sometimes fail: For, this very day (*March* 3.) though on that hill, where I am, the somewhat Westerly Winds have been blustering enough, yet ever since morning the *Quick-silver* has been rising, and is now risen near ⅜ of an *Inch*.

I had thoughts to add something about another kind of *Baroscope* (but inferiour to that in use) whereof I have given some intimation in one of the *Præliminaries* to the *History of Cold.* But you have already too much of a letter, and my occasions, *&c.*

* *Dr.* Beale *concurs with this Observation, when he saith, in a late Letter of* March 19. *to his Correspondent in*London; By change of Weather and Wind, the *Mercury* is sunk more than an Inch, since I wrote to you on *Munday* last.*March* 12. This last night, by Rain and South wind, 'tis sunk*half an Inch.*

So far that Letter. Since which time, another from the same Noble Observer intimates, That, as for that cause of the height of the *Quick-silver* in Droughts, which by him is suspected to be the elevation of steams from the *Crust* or Superficial parts of the Earth, which by little and little may add to the Weight of the *Atmosphere*, being not, as in other seasons, carried down from time to time by the falling Rain, it agrees not ill with what he has had since occasion to observe. For, whereas about *March* 12th, at *Oxford*, The *Quick-silver* was higher, than, for ought he knew, had been yet observ'd in *England*, viz. above⁵/₁₆ above 30. *Inches*, upon the first considerable showers, that have interrupted our long Drought, as he affirms, he foretold divers hours before that the *Quick-silver* would be very low, (a blustering Wind concurring with the Rain) so he found it at *Stanton* to fall ⅜ beneath 29.*Inches.**

{186}

General Heads for a **Natural History of a Countrey**, *Great or Small, imparted likewise by Mr.* **Boyle.**

It having been already intimated (*Num. 8 of Phil. Transact.* p. 140. 141.) that divers*Philosophers* aime, among other things, at the Composing of a good Natural History, to superstruct, in time, a *Solid* and *Useful* Philosophy upon; and it being of no slight importance, to be furnisht with pertinent Heads, for the direction of Inquirers; that lately named *Benefactour to Experimental Philosophy*, has been pleased to communicate, for the ends abovesaid, the following *Articles*, which (as himself did signifie) belong to one of his*Essays* of the unpublisht part of the *Usefulness of Nat. and Experimen. Philosophy.*

But first he premises, that what follows, is design'd only to point at the more *General* heads of Inquiry, which the proposer ignores not to be Divers of them very comprehensive, in so much, that about some of the *Subordinate* subjects, perhaps too, not the most fertile, he has drawn up *Articles* of inquisition about particulars, that take up near as much room, as what is here to be deliver'd of this matter.

The *Heads* themselves follow;

The things, to be observ'd in such a History, may be variously (and almost at pleasure) divided: As, into *Supraterraneous, Terrestrial,* and *Subterraneous*; and otherwise: but we will at present distinguish them into those things, that respect the *Heavens*, or concern the*Air,* the *Water*, or the *Earth.*

1. To the *First* sort of Particulars, belong the Longitude and Latitude of the Place (that being of moment in reference to the observations about the Air *&c.*) and consequently the length of the longest and shortest days and nights, the Climate, parallels *&c.* what fixt starrs are and what not seen there: What Constellations 'tis said to be subject to? Whereunto may be added other Astrological matters, if they be thought worth mentioning.{187}

2. About the *Air* may be observ'd, its Temperature, as to the first four Qualities (commonly so call'd) and the Measures of them: its Weight, Clearness, Refractive power: its Sublety or Grossness: its abounding with, or wanting an *Esurine* Salt: its variations according to the seasons of the year, and the times of the day; What duration the several kinds of Weather usually have: What *Meteors* it is most or least wont to breed; and in what order they are generated; and how long they usually last: Especially, what Winds it is subject to; whether any of them be stated and ordinary, *&c.* What diseases are Epidemical, that are supposed to flow from the Air: What other diseases, wherein *that* hath a share, the Countrey is subject to; the Plague and Contagious sicknesses: What is the usual salubrity or insalubrity of the Air; and with what Constitutions it agrees better or worse, than others.

3. About the *Water*, may be observ'd, the Sea, its Depth, degree of Saltness, Tydes, Currents,*&c. Next*, Rivers, their Bigness, Length, Course, Inundations, Goodness, Levity (or their Contraries) of Waters, *&c. Then*, Lakes, Ponds, Springs, and especially Mineral waters, their Kinds, Qualities, Vertues, and how examined. To the *Waters* belong also *Fishes*, what kinds of them (whether Salt or Fresh-water fish) are to be found in the Country; their Store, Bigness, Goodness, Seasons, Haunts, Peculiarities of any kind, and the wayes of taking them, especially those that are not purely *Mechanical.*

4. In the *Earth*, may be observed,

1. *It self.*

2. Its *Inhabitants*, and its *Productions*, and these *External*, and *Internal.*

First, in the Earth *it self*, may be observ'd, its dimensions, scituation, East, West, North, and South: its Figure, its Plains, and Valleys, and their Extent; its Hills and Mountains, and the height of the tallest, both in reference to the neighbouring Valleys or Plains, and in reference to the Level of the Sea: As {188}also, whether the Mountains lye scattered, or in ridges, and whether those run North and South, or East and West, *&c.* What Promontories, fiery or smoaking Hills, *&c.* the Country has, or hath not: Whether the Country be coherent, or much broken into Ilands. What the Magnetical Declination is in several places, and the Variations of that Declination in the same place (and, if either of those be very considerable, then, what circumstances may assist one to guess at the Reason as Subterraneal fires, the Vicinity of Iron-mines, *&c.*) what the Nature of the Soyle is, whether Clays, Sandy, *&c.* or good Mould; and what Grains, Fruits, and other Vegetables, do the most naturally agree with it: As also, by what particular Arts and Industries the Inhabitants improve the Advantages, and remedy the Inconveniences of their Soyl: What hidden qualities the Soyl may have (as that of*Ireland*, against Venemous Beasts, *&c.*)

Secondly, above the ignobler *Productions* of the Earth, there must be a careful account given of the *Inhabitants* themselves, both *Natives* and *Strangers*, that have been long settled there: And in particular, their Stature, Shape, Colour, Features, Strength, Agility, Beauty (or the want of it) Complexions, Hair, Dyet, Inclinations, and Customs that seem not due to Education. As to their Women (besides the other things) may be observed their Fruitfulness or Barrenness; their hard or easy Labour, *&c.* And both in Women and Men must be taken notice of what diseases they are subject to, and in these whether there be any symptome, or any other Circumstance, that is unusual and remarkable.

As to the *External* Productions of the Earth, the Inquiries may be such as these: What Grasses, Grains, Herbs, (Garden and Wild) Flowers, Fruit-trees, Timber-trees (especially any Trees, whose wood is considerable) Coppices, Groves, Woods, Forrests, *&c.* the Country has or wants: What peculiarities are observable in any of them: What Soyles they most like or dislike; and with what Culture they thrive best. What *Animals* the Country has or wants, both as to wild Beasts, Hawks, and other Birds of Prey; and as to Poultrey, and {189}Cattle of all sorts, and particularly, whether it have any *Animals*, that are not common, or any thing, that is peculiar in those, that are so.

The *Internal* Productions or Concealments of the Earth are here understood to be, the riches that ly hid under the Ground, and are not already referr'd to other Inquiries.

Among these *Subterraneal* observations may be taken notice of, what sorts of Minerals of any kind they want, as well as what they have; *Then*, what Quarries the Country affords, and the particular conditions both of the Quarries and the Stones: As also, how the Beds of Stone lye, in reference to North and South, *&c*. What Clays and Earths it affords, as Tobacco-pipe-clay, Marles, Fullers-earths, Earths for Potters wares, Bolus's and other medicated Earths: What other Minerals it yields, as Coals, Salt-Mines, or Salt-springs, Allom, Vitrial, Sulphur,*&c*. What Mettals the Country yields; and a description of the Mines, their number, scituation, depth, signs, waters, damps, quantities of ore, goodness of ore, extraneous things and ways of reducing their ores into Mettals, *&c*.

To these General Articles of inquiries (saith their *Proposer*) should be added; 1 *Inquiries*.about *Traditions* concerning all particular things, relating to that Country, as either peculiar to it, or at least, uncommon elsewhere, 2 *Inquiries*, that require *Learning* or *Skill* in the Answerer: to which should be subjoyned *Proposals* of ways, to enable men to give Answers to these more difficult inquiries.

Thus far our Author, who, as he has been pleased to impart these *General* (but yet very*Comprehensive* and greatly *Directive*) Articles; so, 'tis hoped from his own late intimation, that he will shortly enlarge them with *Particular* and *Subordinate* ones. These, in the mean time, were thought fit to be publisht, that the Inquisitive and Curious, might, by such an Assistance, be invited not to delay their searches of matters, that are so highly conducive to the improvement of *True Philosophy*, and the wellfare of *Mankind*.{190}

An Extract of a Letter, Written from Holland*, about* Preserving of Ships from being Worm-eaten.

This *Extract* is borrowed from the *French journal des Scavans* of *Febr.* 15. 1666. and is here inserted, to excite Inventive heads *here*, to overtake the Proposer in *Holland*. The letter runs thus:

Although you have visited our Port (*Amsterdam*) I know not whether you have noted the ill condition, our ships are in, that return from the *Indies*. There is in those Seas a kind of small worms, that fasten themselves to the Timber of the ships, and so pierce them, that they take water every where; or if they do not altogether pierce them thorow, they so weaken the wood, that it is almost impossible to repair them. We have at present a Man here, that pretends to have found an admirable secret to remedy this evil. That, which would render this secret the more important, is, that hitherto very many ways have been used to effect it, but without success. Some have imployed Deal, Hair and Lime, *&c*. and therewith lined their ships; but, besides that this does not altogether affright the worms, it retards much the ship's Course. The *Portugals* scorch their ships, insomuch that in the quick works there is made a coaly crust of about an *Inch* thick. But as this is dangerous, it happening not seldom, that the whole vessel is burnt; so the reason why worms eat not thorow *Portugal* ships, is conceived to be the exceeding hardness of the Timber, employed by them.

We expect with impatience the nature and effect of this Proposition. Many have already ventur'd to give their thoughts concerning it. Some say, there needs no more, but to build Ships of a harder kind of Wood, than the usual. Others having observed, that these Worms fasten not to a kind of wild *Indian* Pear-tree, which is highly bitter, do thereupon {191}suggest, that the best Expedient would be, to find out a Wood having that quality. But certainly there being now no Timber, fit for Ships, that is not known, 'tis not likely that any will be found either more hard, or more bitter, than that, which has been hitherto employed. Some do imagine, that the Proposer will, by certain *Lixiviums*, give to the ordinary Wood such a quality and bitterness, as is found in the already mention'd *Indian* Pear-tree. But this also will hardly succeed, since it will be requisite not only to make *Lixiviums*, in great quantities at an easie rate, and strong enough to penetrate the thick sides of a Ship, but also to make them durable enough, not to be wash't out by the Sea. Yet notwithstanding, in these matters one ought to suspend on's judgement, untill experience do shew, what is to be believed of them.

So far the Extract. To which it may perhaps not be unseasonable to add, that a very worthy person in *London*, suggests the Pitch, drawn out of Sea coles, for a good Remedy to scare away these noysome insects.

An Account of a Book, very lately publish't, entituled, The Origine of Forms and Qualities, *illustrated by Considerations and Experiments, by the* Honourable Robert Boyle.

This Curious and Excellent Piece, is a kind of *Introduction* to the *Principles* of the *Mechanical Philosophy*, explicating, by very Considerable Observations and Experiments, what may be, according to such Principles, conceived of the *Nature and Origine of Qualities and Forms*; the knowledge whereof, either makes or supposes the Fundamental and Useful part of *Natural Philosophy.* In doing of which, the Author, to have his way the clearer, writes rather for the *Corpuscularian* Philosophers (as he is pleased to call them) in *General,* than any {192}*Party* of them, keeping himself thereby disengaged from adopting an *Hypothesis,* in which perhaps he is not so throughly satisfied, and of which he does not conceive himself to be necessitated to make use here; and accordingly forbearing to employ Arguments, that are either grounded on, *or* suppose *Atoms,* or any *Innate Motion* belonging to them; *or* that the Essence of Bodies consists in Extension; *or* that a *Vacuum* is impossible; *or* that there are such *Globuli Cœlestes, or* such a *Materia Subtilis,* as the *Cartesians* imploy to explicate most of the *Phænomena* of Nature.

The *Treatise* consisting of a *Speculative,* and an *Historical* part, the Author, with great modesty leaves the *Reader* to judge; *Whether* in the *First* part he hath treated of the *Nature* and *Origine of Forms and Qualities* in a more Comprehensive way, than others; *Whether* he has by fit Examples, and other means, rendred it more intelligible, than they have done: *Whether* he has added any considerable number of Notions and Arguments towards the compleating and confirming of the proposed *Hypothesis. Whether* he has with reason dismissed Arguments unfit to be relied on; and *Whether* he has proposed some Notions and Arguments so warily, as to keep them from being liable to Exceptions and Evasions, whereto they were obnoxious, as others have proposed them. And, as to the *Second* and *Historical* part, he is enclin'd to believe that the *Reader* will grant, he hath done that part of *Physicks,* he is treating of, some service, by strengthning the doctrines of the *New Philosophy* (as 'tis call'd) by such particular Experiments, whose Nature and Novelty will render them as well Acceptable as Instructive.

The *summe* of the *Hypothesis,* fully and clearly explicated in the *First* Part, is this;

That all Bodies are made of *one Catholick matter,* common to them all, and differ but in *Shape, Size, Motion* or *Rest,* and *Texture* of the small parts, they consist off; from which{193}Affections of Matter, the *Qualites,* that difference particular Bodies, result: whence it may be rationally concluded, that one kind of Bodies may be transmuted into another; *that* being in effect no more, than that one Parcel of the Universal Matter, wherein all Bodies agree, may have a *Texture* produced in it, like the *Texture* of some other Parcel of Matter, common to them both.

To this *Hypothesis,* is subjoin'd an Examination of the *Scholastick* opinion of *Substantial Forms;* where the Author, *first,* States the Controversie; *next,* gives the Principal reasons, that move him to oppose that Opinion; *then,* answers the Main arguments employed to evince it; *further,* assigns both the *First* Cause of Forms (*God;*) and the Grand *Second* Cause thereof (*Local Motion:*) and *lastly,* proves the *Mechanical* Production of *Forms;* grounding his proof, *partly* upon the Manner, by which such a *Convention of Accidents,* as deserve to pass for a *Form,* may be *produced;* as that the Curious Shapes of *Salts* (believed to be the admirablest Effects and strongest Proofs of *Substantial Forms*) may be the Results of *Texture, Art* being able to produce Vitriol, as well as *Nature: partly,* upon the possibility of *Reproducing* Bodies by skill, that have been deprived of their reputed *Substantial Forms.* Where he alledges the *Redintegration of Saltpetre,* successfully performed by himself; though his Attempts, made upon the dissipation and re-union of *Amber, Allum, Sea-Salt,* and *Vitriol,* proved (by reason of *accidental* hindrances rather, than of any impossibility in the Nature of the Thing) less successful.

In the *Second* and *Historical* Part, the Author, appealing to the Testimony of Nature, to verifie his Doctrine, sets down, *both* some *Observations,* of what Nature does without being over-ruled by the power and skill of man; and some *Experiments,* wherein Nature is guided, and as it were, mastered by Art.

The *Observations* are four.

1. The *First* is taken from what happens in the *Hatching of* {194} *an Egge*; out of the *White* whereof, which is a substance Similar, insipid, soft, diaphanous, colourless, and readily dissoluble in cold water, there is by the *New* and *Various* contrivence of its small parts, caused by the Incubation of the Hen, an Animal produced, some of whose parts are opacous, some red, some yellow, some white, some fluid, some consistent, some solid and frangible, others tough and flexible, some well, some ill-tasted, some with springs, some without springs, *&c.*

2. The *Second* is fetcht from *Water,* which being fluid, tastless, inodorous, diaphanous, colourless, volatile, *&c.* may by a *Differing Texture* of its parts, be brought to constitute Bodies, having qualities very distant from these, as *Vegetables,* that have firmness, opacity, odors, tasts, colours, Medicinal vertues; yielding also a true *Oyle,* that refuses to mingle with *Water, &c.*

3. The *Third,* from *Inoculation*; wherein, a small *Bud* is able to transmute all the sap, that arrives at it, as to make it constitute a Fruit quite otherwise qualified, then that, which is the *genuine* production of the Tree, so that the same sap, that in one part of the Branch constitutes (for Instance) a *Cluster of Haws,* in another part of the same Branch, may make a *Pear.* Where the Author mentions divers other very considerable Effects of Inoculations, and inserts several Histories, all countenancing his doctrine.

4. The *Fourth,* from *Putrified Cheese*; wherein, the *rotten* part, by the alteration of its Texture, will differ from the *Sound,* in colour, odor, taste, consistence, vermination, *&c.*

The Experiments are ten.

1. *A Solution of Vitriol and Camphire*; in which by a change of Texture, appear'd the Production of a deep colour from a {195} white Body, and a clear Liquor without any external heat: The destruction of this Colour, by adding only some fair water: The change of an Odorous Body, *as Camphire,* into an Inodorous, by mixing it with a Body, that has scarce any sensible odour of its own: The sudden restauration of the *Camphire* to its native scent and other qualities, by common water, *&c.*

2. *Sublimate, distill'd from Copper and Silver,* which both did wholly loose their Metalline forms, and were melted into brittle lumps, with colours quite differing from their own; both apt to imbibe the moisture of the Air, *&c.*

3. *A solution of silver into Luna Cornea:* Whereby the opacous, malleable and hardly fusible Body of *Silver,* was, by the addition of a little spirit of salt, reduced into Chrystals, differing from those of other Mettals; diaphanous also, and brittle, and far more easily fusible, than Silver; wholly unlike either a Salt or a Mettal, but very like to a piece of *Horn,* and withall insipid, though the Solution of Silver, be very bitter, and the spirit of salt, highly sowre, *&c.*

4. *An Anomalous Salt*; (which the Author had not, it seems the liberty to teach the Preparation off) whose Ingredients were purely Saline, and yet the Compound, made up only of salt, sowre, and strongly tasted Bodies, was rather *really* sweet, than of any other taste , and when a little urged with heat, its odour became stronger, and more insupportable than that of *Aqua fortis, distilled Urine* and even *spirit of salt Ammoniack*; but yet when these Fumes settled again into salt, their odour would again prove inoffensive, if not pleasant *&c.*

5. *A Sea-salt, whence Aqua fortis had been distilled*: Where the Liquor, that came over, proved an *Aqua Regis*: the substance in the bottom, had not onely a mild taste, and {196} affected the Pallat much more like salt-peter, than Common salt; but was also very fusible, and inflammable, though produced of two un-inflammable bodies: and the same substance, consisting of *Acid* salts, by a certain way of the Author, produced a *Fixt* salt.

6. *Oyle of Vitriol poured upon a Solution of Bay-salt:* whence was abstracted a liquor, that by the smell and Taste appeared to be a spirit of salt. In which operation, the mixture, by working a great change of Texture, did so alter the nature of the compounding Bodies, that the sea-salt, though a considerably fixt Body, was distill'd over in a moderate Fire of sand,

whilst the Oyl of Vitriol, though no such gross salt, was by the same operation so fixt, as to stay behind: Besides that the same, by a competent heat yeilded a substance, though not insipid, yet not at all of the taste of Sea-salt, or of any other pungent one, much less having the highly corrosive acidity of oyl of Vitriol, &c.

7. *A dissolvent, made by pouring a strong spirit of Nitre on the rectified Oyl of the Butter of Antimony, and then distilling off all the liquor, that would come over, &c.* This *Menstruum*(called by the Author *Peracutum*) being put to highly refined Gold, destroyed its Texture, and produced, after the method prescribed in the book, a *true Silver*, as its whiteness in colour, dissolublenes in *Aqua fortis*, and odious Bitterness, did manifest: which change of a Mettal, commonly esteemed to be absolutely indestructible by Art, though it be far from being *Lucriferous*, is yet exceedingly *Instructive*; as is also the way, the Author here adds, of *Volatilizing* Gold, by the power of the same *Dissolvent*.

8. *Aqua fortis, concoagulated with differing Bodies*, produced very differing Concretes: And the same Numeral Saline Corpuscles, that being associated with those of one Mettal, had already produced a Body eminent in one Taste, did {197}afterwards, being freed from that Body, compose a Liquor of a very differing taste; and after *that* too, being combin'd with the parties of another Mettal, did with them constitute a Body of a very eminent Taste, as opposite as any one can be to both the other Tasts; and yet these Saline Corpuscles, being instead of this second Mettal, associated with such a one as that, they are driven from, did therewith exhibit again the first of the three mention'd Tasts.

9. *Water transmuted into Earth*, though the Author saith of this Transmutation, that it was not so perfect, as he wish'd, and as he hopes to make it.

10. *A mixture of Oyle of Vitriol and Spirit of Wine.* These two Liquors, being of odd Textures in reference to each other, their conjunction and distillation made them exhibit these *Phænomena*: *vid.* That, whereas Spirit of Wine has no great, nor good scent, and moderately dephlegm'd Oyl of Vitriol is wont to be inodorous; the Spirit, that first came over from their mixture, had a scent not only very differing from Spirit of Wine, but from all things else, that the Author ever smelt; the Odor being very fragrant & pleasant, and so subtle, that in spight of the care taken in luting the Glasses exactly together, it would perfume the neighbouring parts of the *Laboratory*, and afterwards smell strongly at some distance from the Viol, wherein it was put, though stopt with a close Cork covered with two or three several Bladders. But, after this volatile and odoriferous Spirit was come over, and had been follow'd by an Acid Spirit, it was at last succeeded by a strongly stinking Liquor,*&c.*

But *Manum de Tabula*: the Book it self will certainly give a satisfaction far beyond what here can be said of it.{198}

Some New observations about the Planet Mars, *communicated since the Printing of the former sheets.*

There was very lately produced a Paper, containing some observations, made by Mr. *Hook*, about the Planet *Mars*; in the *Face* whereof he affirmed to have discovered, in the late months of *February* and *March*, that there are several *Maculæ* or *Spotted parts*, changing their place, and not returning to the same Position, till the next ensuing night near about the same time. Whence it may be collected, that *Mars* (as well as *Jupiter*, and the *Earth*, *&c.*) does move about his own *Axis*, of which a fuller account will be given hereafter, God permitting. This short and hasty intimation of it, is intended onely to invite others, that have opportunity, timely to make Observations, (either to confirm, or rectify) before *Mars* gets out of sight.

Printed with Licence for *John Martyn*, and *James Allestry*, Printers to the Royal Society.
1666.

{199}

PHILOSOPHICAL
TRANSACTIONS.

Munday, May 7. 1666.

The Contents.

A way of Preserving Birds taken out of the Egge, and other small Fetus's; *communicated by* Mr. Boyle. *An Extract of a Letter, lately sent to* Sr. Robert Moray *out of* Virginia, *concerning an unusuall way of Propagating Mulberry-trees there, for the better improvement of the* Silk-Work; *together with some other particulars, tending to the good of that* Royall *Plantation. A Method, by which a Glass of a small Plano-Convex Sphere may be made to refract the Rayes of Light to a* Focus *of a far greater distance, than is usuall. Observations about* Shining Worms *in* Oysters. *Observations of the Effects of* Touch *and* Friction. *Some particulars, communicated from forrain Parts, concerning the Permanent* Spott *in* Jupiter; *and a contest between two Artists about* Optick-Glasses, *&c. An Account of a Book written by* Dr. Thomas Sydenham, *entituled,* Methodus Curandi Febres, propriis Observationibus superstructa.

A way of preserving Birds taken out of the Egge, and other small Fætus's; *communicated by* Mr. Boyle.

This was imparted in a Letter, as follows;

The time of the year invites me to intimate to you, that among the other Uses of the Experiment, I long since presented the *Society*, of preserving Whelps taken out of the Dams womb, and other *Fœtus's*, or parts of them, in *Spirit of Wine*; I {200} remember, I did, when I was sollicitous to observe the Processe of Nature in the Formation of a Chick, open Hens Eggs, some at such a day, and some at other daies after the beginning of the Incubation, and carefully taking out the *Embryo's*, embalmed each of them in a distinct Glass (which is to be carefully stopt) in *Spirit of Wine*: Which I did, that so I might have them in readinesse, to make on them, at any time, the Observations, I thought them capable of affording; and to let my Friends at other seasons of the year, see, *both* the differing appearances of the Chick at the third, fourth, seventh, fourteenth, or other daies, after the Eggs had been sate on, *and*(especially) some particulars not obvious in Chickens, that go about; as the hanging of the Gutts out of the *Abdomen, &c.* How long the tender *Embryo* of the Chick soon after the *Punctum saliens* is discoverable, *and* whilst the Body seems but a little Organized Gelly, *and* some while after *That*, will be this way preserv'd, without being too much shrivel'd up, I was hindred by some mischances to satisfie my self: but when the *Fœtus's*, I took out, were so perfectly formed as they were wont to be about the seventh day, and after, they so well retain'd their shape and bulk, as to make me not repent of my curiosity: And some of those, which I did very early this Spring, I can yet shew you. I know I have mention'd to you an easie application of what I, some year since, made publick enough; but not finding it to have been yet made by any other, and being perswaded by Experience, that it may be extended to other *Fœtus's*, which this season (the *Spring*) is time to make provision off, I think the *Advertisement* will not seem unseasonable to some of our Friends; though being now in haste, and having in my thoughts divers particulars, relating to this way of Preserving Birds taken out of the Egge, and other small *Fœtus's*, I must content my self to have mention'd that, which is *Essential,* leaving divers other things, which a little practise may teach the Curious, unmention'd. Notwithstanding which, I must not omit these two Circumstances; the *one*, that when the Chick was grown big, before I took it out of the Egge, I have (but not constantly) {201}* *In the Usefulness of Experimental Philosophy.* mingled with the *Spirit of Wine*, a little Spirit of *Sal Armoniack*, made (as I have elsewhere delivered) * by the help of *Quick-lime*: which Spirit I choose, because, though it abounds in a Salt not Sowre, but Urinous, yet I never observed it (how strong soever I made it) to coagulate Spirit of Wine. The *other* circumstance is, that I usually found it convenient, to let the little *Animals,* I meant to imbalme, lie for a little while in ordinary Spirit of Wine, to wash off the looser filth, that is wont to adhere to the Chick, when taken out of the Egge; and then, having put either the same kind of Spirit, or better upon the same Bird, I suffer'd it to soak some hours (perhaps some daies, *pro re nata*) therein, that the Liquor, having drawn as it were what Tincture it could, the *Fœtus* being remov'd into more pure and well dephlegm'd Spirit of Wine, might not discolour it, but leave it almost as limpid, as before it was put in.

An Extract of a Letter, sent lately to Sir Robert Moray out of Virginia, concerning an unusual way of propagating Mulberry trees there, for the better improvement of the Silk-Work; together with some other particulars, tending to the good of that Plantation.

I am disappointed at this time of some Rarities of Minerals, Mettals, and Stones; but you may have them any other time, as conveniently, *&c.* I have planted here already ten thousand *Mulberry trees;* and hope, within two or three years, to reap good silk of them. I have planted them in a way unusual here, which advances them two or three years growth, in respect of their being sown in seed: And they are now, at writing hereof all holding good, although this has been a very long and bitter winter with us, much longer and colder, than ever I did find it in *Scotland* or *England.* I intend likewise to plant {202} them all, as if they were *Currants* or *Goos-berries,* so thick as hedges; whereby one man may gather as many of them, as otherwise, when they are planted in trees at distance, four persons my do. Expedient is the benefit of this Trade. Having discoursed of this new way to all here; they are generally inclinable to it; considering that the Planting their Trees, as before, at distance, and letting them grow high, has been the main obstruction of that work hitherto, and the loss of their time and gain: but being in hedges, they will be always young tender plants; and consequently will be easily cut in great quantities with a pair of Garden Sizzers. But there may be suggested yet another, and perhaps a better way; which is, to sowe some Acres with *Mulberry seed,* and to cut it with a sith, and ever to keep it under. I have also bethought my self of a new way, for a few hands to serve many Worms, and that more cleanly than before: which also will be a means, without more trouble or pains, to separate unhealthy worms from healthful; and by which a great many more may be kept in a room, than otherwise upon shelves, as is usual here. Besides this, I have sown a little *French Barley* and *Rice seed,* and am thinking on a way of un-husking them with expedition, and so preparing them for the Merchant, as they use to be: But if you can inform me, how they are prepared, you may save me some labour. If I had any *Coffee* in husks, or any other vegetable commodity, from the Streights to try, I would here make tryal with them. Its like, that some of those Merchants that are of your *Society,* and keep a Correspondency there, may assist in procuring them. By the latter ships I intend to send you a New sort of sweet sented *Tobacco,* which I have not yet had time to improve.

A Method, by which a Glass of a small Plano-convex Sphere may be made to refract the Rayes of light to a Focus of a far greater distance, than is usual.

This is proposed by Mr. *Hook,* in consequence of what was {203} mention'd from him in *Numb.* 4 *pag.* <u>67</u>, of these *Transactions.*

Prepare (*saith he*) two Glasses, the one exactly flat on both sides, the other flat on the one side, and convex on the other, of what Sphere you please. Let the flat Glass be a little broader than the other. Then let there be made a Cell or Ring of Brass, very exactly turn'd, into which these two Glasses may be so fastened with Cement, that the plain surfaces of them may lye exactly paralell, and that the Convex-side of the Plano-convex-Glass may lye inward; but so, as not to touch the flat of the other Glass. These being cemented into the Ring very closely about the edges, by a small hole in the side of the Brass-ring or Cell, fill the interposed space between these two with *Water, Oyl of Turpentine, Spirit of Wine, Saline Liquors, &c;* then stop the hole with a screw: and according to the differing refraction of the interposed Liquors, so shall the *Focus* of the compound Glass be longer or shorter.

But this (adds the *Proposer*) I would only have look't upon, as one instance of many (for there may be others) of the *Possibility* of making a Glass, ground in a smaller Sphere, to constitute a Telescope of a much greater length: Though (not to raise too great exspectation) I must add, That of *Spherical* object glasses, those are the best, which are made of the greatest Sphere, and whose substance hath the greatest refraction.

Observations about Shining Worms in Oysters.

93

These Observations occur in the *French Journal* of *April* 12. 1666. in two letters, written by M. *Auzout* to M. *Dela Voye*; whereof the substance may be reduced to the following particulars.

1. That M. *Dela Voye* having observed, as he thought, {204} some shining Worms in Oysters; M.*Auzout*, being made acquainted with it, did first conceive, they were not Worms (unless they were crushed ones) that shin'd, as having not been able then to discern any parts of a Worm; but only some shining clammy moysture; which appeared indeed like a little Star of a blewish colour, and stuck to the Oyster-shell; being drawn out, shone in the Air its whole length (which was about four or five lines,) and when put upon the *Observers* hand, continued to shine there for some time.

2. That M. *Auzout* afterwards, causing more than 20. douzen of Oysters to be open'd at Candle-light, really saw, in the dark, such shining worms in them; and those of three sorts. *One* sort was whitish, having 24. or 25. feet on each side, forked; a black speck on one side of the head (taken by him for a *Chrystallin*) & the back like an Eele, stript off her skin. The *second*, red, and resembling the common *Glow-worms*, found at Land, with folds upon their backs, and feet like the former; and with a nose like that of a dog, and one eye in the head. The *third* sort was speckled, having a head like that of a Sole, with many tufts of whitish hair on the sides of it,

3. That, besides these, the *Observer* saw some much bigger, that were grayish, with a big head, and two horns on it, like those of a Snayl, and with 7. or 8. whitish feet, but these, though kept by him in the night, shin'd not.

4. That the two first sorts are made of a matter easily resoluble, the least shaking or touch turning them in into a viscous and aqueous matter; which falling from the shell, stuck to the *Observers* fingers, and shone there for the space of 20. seconds: and if any little part of this matter, by strongly shaking the shell, did fall to the ground, it appear'd like a little piece of a flaming Brimstone; and when shaken off nimbly, it became like a small shining Line, which was dissipated before it came to the ground.

{205}

5. That this shining matter was of different colour; some, whitish, some, reddish; but yet that they afforded both, a light which appear'd a violet to his eye.

6. That it is very hard to examine these worms entire (especially the white ones) because that at the least touch they doe burst, and resolve into a glutinous moysture; whence also if it were not for their feet, that are discover'd in their matter, none would judge them to be Worms.

7. That among those, which he observed, he saw two more firm, than the rest, which shone all over; and when they fell from the Oyster, twinkled like a great star, shining strongly, and emitting rays of a violet-light by turns, for the space, (as touch't above) of 20. seconds. Which Scintillation the *Observer* imputes to this, that those worms being alive, and sometimes raising their head, sometimes their tayle, like a Carpe, the light increased and lessened accordingly; seeing that, when they shone not, he did, viewing them by a Candle, find them dead.

8. That forcibly shaking the Oyster-shells in the dark, he sometimes saw the whole shell full of lights, now and then as big as a fingers end; and abundance of this clammy matter, both red and white, (which he judges to have been Worms) burst in their holes.

9. That in the shaking he saw all the Communications of these little Verminulous holes, like to the hole of Worms in Wood.

10. That in more than 20 douzen of Oysters he shook no shell (10. or 12. excepted) but it emitted light: And found some of this light in sixteen of the Oysters themselves.

11. That this light occurs more frequently in big, than small Oysters; in those that are pierced by the Worm, oftner, than {206} in those that are not, and rather upon the Convex-side, than the other; and more in fresh ones; than in the stale.

12. That having somewhat scaled the Convex-side of the shell, and discover'd the Communication of the holes, wherein the often-mention'd viscous moysture, that has any form of insects, is found; he smelt a scent, that was like the water of a squeesed Oyster.

13. That the Worms give no light, when irritated, but if they do, the light lasts but a very little time, whereas that which appears in those, that were not angred before, continues a great while; the *Observer* affirming to have kept of it above 2 hours.

So far the *Journal des Scavans*; which intimates withal, that if the *Observers* had had better*Microscopes*, they could have better examin'd this matter.

But since the curious here in *England* are so well furnish with good ones, 'tis hoped, that they will employ some of them for further and more minute Observations of these Worms; it being a matter, which, joyned with other Observations, already made by some excellent persons here, (especially Mr. *Boyle*) upon this subject of Light, may prove very luciferous to the doctrine of it, so much yet in the dark.

Some Observations of the Effects of Touch *and* Friction.

The Operations and Effects of *Touch* and *Friction* having been lately much taken notice off, and being lookt upon by some, as a great *Medical* Branch, for the curing of many diseases and infirmities; it will perhaps not be unseasonable to mention (here also) some Observations relating thereunto; which may give an occasion to others, to consider this subject more, than has been done heretofore, and to make {207}further Observations and Tryals concerning the power of the same.

And *First*, the Illustrious Lord of *Verulam*, in his *History of Life and Death*, Histor. 6. §. 3. observes, That *Motion* and *Warmth* (of which two, *Friction* consists) draws forth, into the parts, New Juyce and Vigour. And *Canon*. XIII. he affirms, That *Frictions* conduce much to*Longevity*. See the same, *Connex*. ix. §. 26. &c.

Secondly, The Honourable *Robert Boyle*, in his *Usefulness of Experimental Philosophy*, *sect*2. *ch*. 15. considering the Body of a Living man or any Animal, as an Engine, so composed, that there is a conspiring communication betwixt its parts, by vertue whereof a very slight impression of adventitious matter upon some one part, may be able to work, on some other distant part, or perhaps on the whole Engine, a change far exceeding, what the same adventitious matter could do upon a Body not so contrived: Representing, I say, an Animal in this manner, and thence inferring, how it may be alter'd for the better or worse by motions or impulses, confessedly *Mechanicall*, observes, How some are recover'd from swouning fits by pricking; others grow faint and do vomit by the bare motion of a Coach; others fall into a troublesome sickness by the agitation of a Ship, and by the Sea-air (whence they recover by rest, and by going a shore.) Again, how in our Stables a Horse well-curried is half-fed: How some can tell by the Milk of their Asses, whether that day they have been well curried or not: Arguing hence, that if in *Milk* the alteration is so considerable, it should be so likewise in the*Blood*, or other Juyces, of which the Blood is elaborated, and consequently in divers of the principal parts of the Body. Where also (upon the authority of *Piso*) he refers the Reader to the *Brasilian* Empiricks, whose {208}wild *Frictions*, as unskilfully as they order them, do strange things, both in *preserving health*, and *curing diseases*; curing Cold and *Chronical* ones by*Friction*, as they do *Acute* ones, by *Unction*.

Thirdly, The learned Dr. *John Beale*, did not long since communicate by some Letters; *First*, that he could make good proof of the curing or killing a very great and dangerous *Wen* (that had been very troublesome for two or three years,) by the application of a dead mans hand, whence the Patient felt such a cold stream pass to the Heart, that it did almost cause in him a fit of swouning. *Secondly*, that, upon his brothers knowledge, a certain Cook in a Noble Family of *England* (wherein that brother of his then lived) having been reproached for the ugliness of his *Warty* hands, and return'd for answer, that he had tried many remedies, but found none, was bid by his Lord, to rub his hand with that of a dead man; and that this Lord dying soon after, the Cook made use both of his Lords advise and hand, and speedily found good effect. (Which is also confirm'd by what Mr. *Boyle* relates in his lately mentioned*Book*, of Dr. *Harvey's* frequently succesfull triall, of curing some Tumors or Excrescencies, by holding on them such a Hand.) Here is *Friction* or *Touch*, to mortifie Wens, to drive away swellings and Excrescencies: And why not to repell or dissipate Spirits, that may have a dangerous influence upon the Brain, or other parts; as well as to call forth the retired ones into the habit of the Body, for Invigoration? *Thirdly*, that a Gentleman, who came lately out of *Ireland*, lay at his House, and inform'd him of an aged Knight there, who having great pain in his feet, insomuch that he was unable to use them, suffered, as he was going to bed, a loving *Spaniell* to lick his feet; which was for the present very pleasing to him, so that he used it mornings and evenings, till he found the pain appeased, and the use of his feet restored. This, saith {209} the *Relater*, was a gentle touch, and transpiration; for he found the Spirits transpire with a pleasing Kind of Titillation. *Fourthly*, that he can assure of an honest Blacksmith, who by his healing hand converted his Barrs of Iron into Plates of Silver; and had this particular faculty, that he caused Vomitings by stroaking the Stomack; gave the Stool by stroaking the Belly; appeased the Gout, and other paines, by stroaking the parts affected.

Some particulars, communicated from forraign parts, concerning the Permanent Spott *in* Jupiter; *and a Contest between two Artists about* Optick Glasses, &c.

See Numb. 1. *of these*Transactions; *by the date whereof it will appeare, that that*Spot *was observed in*England, *a good while before any such thing was so much as heard of.*

Eustachio de Divinis (saith the *Informer*,) has written a large Letter, wherein he pretends, that the Permanent Spot in *Jupiter* hath been first of all discovered with *his* Glasses; and that the P. *Gotignies* is the first that hath thence deduced the Motion of *Jupiter* about his *Axis*; and that Signior *Cassini* opposed it at first; to whom the said *Gotignies* wrote a letter of complaint thereupon.

The same *Eustachio* pretends likewise, that his great Glasses excell those of *Campani*; and that in all the tryals, made with them, they have performed better; and that *Campani* was not willing to do, what was necessary for well comparing the one with the other. *viz.* To put equall *Eye-glasses* in them, or to exchange the same Glasses.

The said *Divini* affirms also, that he hath found a way to {210}know, whether an Object glass be good or not, onely by looking upon it, without trying. This would be of good use, especially if it should extend so far as to discerne the goodness of such a glass, whilst it is yet on the Cement.

An Account of Dr. Sydenham's *Book, entituled,* Methodus Curandi Febres, Propriis observationibus superstructa.

This *Book* undertakes to deliver a more certain and more genuine Method of curing Feavers and Agues, than has obtained hitherto: And it being premised, *First*, that a Fever is Natures Engine, she brings into the field, to remove her enemy; or her handmaid, either for evacuating the impurities of the blood, or for reducing it into a New State: *Secondly*, that the true and genuine cure of this sickness consists in such a tempering of the Commotion of the Blood, that it may neither exceed, nor be too languide: This, I say, being premised by the Author, he informs the Reader;

In the *First Section*, of the different Method, to be employed in the cure of Feavers, not only in respect of the differing constitutions and ages of the patients, but also in regard of the differing seasons of one and the same year, and of the difference of one year from another. As to the *Former*, he shews, in what sorts of *Patients*, and at what time of the Feaver, Phlebotomy, or Vomiting, or both, are to be used; and when and where not: In what space of time the *Depuration* if nature be not disturbed or hindred in her work, will be perform'd: When *Purgatives* are to be administred: How that *Diarrhea's* happen, if the *Patient* had in the {211}beginning of the Feaver an inclination to vomit, but no vomit was given; and that those symptoms, which commonly are imputed to a malignity, do, for the most part, proceed from the Relaxation of the tone of the Bloud, caused by Medicines too refrigerating, or by the unseasonable use of Glisters in the declination of the disease. As to the *Latter*, he observes, that one of the chief causes, rendring the Cure of Feavers so uncertain and unsuccessfull, is, that *Practitioners* do accommodate their observations, they take from the successful cure of some Feavers in one season or the year, or in some one year, to that of all Feavers in any season, or in any year whatsoever. And here he observes, *first*, how vigorous the blood is in the *Spring*, and how dispirited in *Autumn*; and thence regulates the letting of bloud, and Vomiting, and the giving of Glisters. *Next*, how difficult it is, to assign the cause of the difference between the Feavers of *Several years*; and to prognosticate of the salubrity or insalubrity of the following part of the year: where yet he insinuates, that, when *Insects* do swarm extraordinarily, and when Feavers and Agues (especially *Quartans*) appear very early, as about *Midsummer*, then *Autumn* commonly proves very sickly. *Lastly*, what method and Cautions are to be used in the Cure of *Epidemical* Feavers.

In the *Second Section*, he treats of the *Symptoms*, accompanying *Continued* Feavers; as *Phrensies, Pleurisies, Coughs, Hicoughs, Fluxes, &c.* Shewing, both whence they are caused, and how they are to be cured: Where having inserted a considerable *Paragraph*, touching a certain *Symptomatical* Feaver in the *Spring*, to be cured like Plurisies; he mentions among many Observables, this, as a chief one, that *Laudanum*, or any other *Narcotick* given against the *Phrensy*, in the beginning, progress, or height of a Feaver, does rather hurt, than good, but in the declination thereof, is used with good success. To all which he subjoins a particular {212} accompt of the *Iliac Passion* (esteem'd by him to be sometimes a *Symptome* also of Feavers;) not only discoursing of its cause (a preposterous inversion of the Intestins, proceeding either from Obstruction, or Irritation,) but adding also a very plain way of Curing the same; and that not by the use of *Quick-silver* or *Bullets* (by him judged to be frequently noxious) but only by *Mint-water*, and the application of a Whelp to the Patients stomach; to strengthen the same, and to reduce it again to its natural motion.

In the *Third Section*, he treats of *Intermittent* Feavers, or of *Agues*. Where he discourses of the times of the *Cold* and *Hot* fits, and of *that* of the *Separation* of the subdued aguish matter: Finds difficulty in giving a satisfactory accompt of the *return of Fits*. distinguishes Agues into *Vernal* and *Autumnal*. Takes notice, that as there are few *Continued* Feavers, so generally there are only *Quotidians* and *Tertians*, in the *Spring*; and only *Tertians* and *Quartans* in *Autumn*; Of which having offered Reasons, that seem considerable, he proceeds to his Method of curing them; and, laying much weight upon the said difference, he prescribes and urges different ways to be used in that cure: Interserting among other things these notes; *First*, that the Period of Fermentation in Feavers, both *Continued* and *Intermittent*, is (if left to Natures own conduct, and well regulated, if need be, by Art) perform'd in about 336. hours or 14 dayes, subducting in *Intermittent* ones, the hours of intermission, and counting 5½ hours for every Paroxism; and imputing the excursion beyond that time to the disturbance given to nature by the error of Practitioners. *Secondly*, that whoever hath had a *Quartan* formerly, though many years be pass'd, shall, if he chance to have another, be *soon* freed from it; and that a Physician knowing *that*, may confidently predict *this*. {213}

In the *Fourth Section*, the Author, in conformity to the Custom of those that write of Feavers, discourses of the *Small-pox*; and *First*, examining the cause of this sickness and its universality, delivers his peculiar opinion of the bloud's endeavouring a Renovation or a New Texture (once at least in a Mans life) and is inclin'd to preferr the same to the received doctrine of its malignity. *Then*, having laid down, for a foundation of the Cure, the two times, of *Separation* and *Expulsion*, he argues as well against too high an Ebullition or too hasty a separation (by a hot diet or high Cordials) as against too languid a one (by Blooding, Purges, and Cooling medicines.) The like he does to the Time of *Expulsion*, forbidding *both* immoderate Heat (whereby Nature's expelling operation is disturbed by a precipitated and too thick a crowd of the protruded pustuls,) *and* too much Cooling, whereby due Expulsion is hindred. In short, he advises, to permit Nature to do her own work, requiring nothing of the Physician, but to regulate her, when she is exorbitant, and to fortifie her, when she is too weak. He concludes all, with delivering a Model of the Method, he would use for his own only Son, if he should fall into this Sickness.

Advertisement.

Whereas 'tis taken notice of, that several persons perswade themselves, that these Philosophical *Transactions are publish't by the* Royal Society, *notwithstanding many circumstances, to be met with in the already publish't ones,* {214} *that import the contrary; The Writer thereof hath thought fit, expresly here to declare, that that perswasion, if there be any such indeed, is a meer mistake; and that he, upon his* Private *account (as a Well-wisher to the advancement of usefull knowledge, and a Furtherer thereof by such Communications, as he is capable to furnish by that Philosophical Correspondency, which he entertains, and hopes to enlarge) hath begun and continues both the composure and publication thereof: Though he denies not, but that, having the honour and advantage of being a* Fellow *of the said* Society, *he inserts at times some of the Particulars that are presented to them; to wit, such as he knows he may mention without offending them, or transgressing their Orders; tending only to administer occasion to others also, to consider and carry them further, or to Observe or Experiment the like, according as the nature of such things may require.*

Printed with Licence for *John Martyn,* and *James Allestry,* Printers to the Royal Society.
1666.

{215}

Numb. 13.

PHILOSOPHICAL
TRANSACTIONS.

Munday, June 4. 1666.

The Contents.

Certain Problems *touching some Points of Navigation: Of a new Contrivance of* Wheel-Barometer, *much easier to be prepar'd, than others. An account of* Four Suns *which lately appear'd in* France; *and of two, unusually posited,* Rainbows, *seen in the same Kingdom. A Relation of an Accident, by Thunder and Lightning, in* Oxford. *An Experiment, to examine, what* Figure *or Celerity of Motion begetteth or increaseth* Light *and* Flame. *Some Considerations touching a Letter in the* Journal des Scavans *of* May 24. 1666.

Certain Problems *touching some Points of* Navigation.

These *Problems* are presented by the Learned and Industrious *Nicolaus Mercator,* for the advancing of that Excellent and Beneficial Science, *Navigation,* as follows:

The line of *Artificial Tangents,* or the *Logarithmical Tangent-line,* beginning at 45 deg. and taking every half *degree* for a whole one, is found to agree pretty near with the *Meridian-line* of the *Sea-Charte;* they both growing, as it were, after the same Proportion. But the Table of *Meridional* degrees being calculated only to every *Sexagesimal* minute of a degree, shews some small difference from the said *Logarithmical Tangent-line.* Hence it may be doubted, whether that difference do not arise from that little errour, which is committed by calculating the Table of *Meridional* degrees *only* to every minute. {216}

Mr. *Oughtred* in the VI. *Chap.* of his *Navigation,* annexed to the Book, entituled, *The Circles of Proportion, and the Horizontal Instrument* &c. mentions an Artifice, by himself discover'd, by which it may be effected, that the small Parts of the *Meridian* be not one minute (which on the face of the *Earth* answers to above an *English* Mile) but the hundred-thousanth, or, if need be, the millioneth part of a minute, scarce exceeding one fifteenth part of an Inch: Which thing, *he saith,* he is able to perform in *Tables* unto the *Radius* 10000000; yet nothing at all differing either in their form or manner of working from those that are now commonly in use.

But which way this is to be done, this *Author* hath not made known to the Publick. And, though such *Tables* unto the *Radius* 10000000, had been brought to light, yet would they not be sufficient to prove the identity or sameness of the said two Lines, as to continue the comparison between them as far, as the one of them, *videl.* the *Logarithmicall Tangent-line,* is already calculated, that is; to Ten places, besides the *Charactoristick.*

Now therefore, if a certain Rule could be produced, by which the Agreement or Disagreement of the said two Lines might be shew'd, not only to that Extent of places, to which that *Tangent Line* is already calculated, but also to as many more, as the same may be yet further extended unto, in *infinitum usque;* surely that rule would not only save us the labour of making *Tables* unto the *Radius* 10000000; but also the *Helix* or Spiral Line of the Ships Course would be reduced to a more precise exactness, than ever was pretended by Him: and this most Noble and Useful Science (as He justly calls it) which is the Bond of most disjunct Countries, and the Consociation of Nations farthest remote, would attain its full lustre and perfection.

Besides, that the same Rule would also discover a far easier way of making *Logarithmes*, than ever was practised or known; and therefore might serve, when ever there should be occasion, to extend the *Logarithmes* beyond that number of places, that is already extant.

Moreover such a rule would enable men to draw the *Meridian* line *geometrically*, that is, without *Tables* or *Scales*: which indeed {217} might also be done, by setting of the *Secants* of every whole or half degree, if there were not this Inconveniency in it (which is not in my Rule:) That a Line composed of so many small parts, would be subject to many errours, especially in a small compass.

The same Rule also will serve, to find the Course and Distance between two Places assigned, as far, as practice shall require it; and that, without any Table of *Meridional* parts, and yet with as much ease and exactness.

And seeing all these things do depend on the solution of this Question, *Whether the Artificial Tangent-line be the true Meridian-line?* It is therefore, that I undertake, by God's assistance, to resolve the said Question. And to let the world know the readiness and confidence, I have to make good this undertaking, I am willing to lay a *Wager* against any one or more persons that have a mind to engage, for so much as *another Invention* of mine (which is of less subtlety, but of far greater benefit to the publick) may be worth to the Inventor.

For, the great advantage, that all Merchants, Mariners, and consequently the Common-wealth, may receive from this *other Invention*, is, in my judgment, highly valuable; seeing it will oftentimes make a ship sail, though, according to the common way of sailing, the wind be quite contrary, and yet as near to the place intended, as if the wind had been favourable: Or, if you will, it will enable one to gain something in the intended way, whether the wind be good or no (except only when you go directly South or North) but the advantage will be most, where there is most need of it, that is, when the Wind is contrary: So that one may very often gain a fifth, fourth, third part, or more of the intended voyage; according as it is longer or shorter, *viz.* always more in a longer Voyage, where the gain is more considerable, and more welcome; not only by saving Time, but also Victuals, Water, Fuel, Mens health, and so much Room in the ship.

All this, which is here pretended, the Proposer is to make good by the Verdict of some able Men, who also may give a guess, what this latter Invention may be worth to the owner: And for so much, and no more, he will stand engaged against {218} any one or more Persons, that he will and shall resolve the *Question* above-mention'd, *viz. Whether the Artificial Tangent-line be the true Meridian-line, yea or no?* And if he do not, that then he will loose, and transport to the other Party the whole benefit of the last mentioned invention. But if, on the contrary, he do prove or disprove the Identity of the said two lines, to the Judgment of some able *Mathematicians*, That then so much money be paid him by the other Party, as the said Invention was valued.

And, whereas there are often Wagers laid about things that concern the Engagers little or nothing; 'tis thought, that it would concern all Merchants, Mariners, and all Lovers of the common good, rather to lay wagers against one another about Things of this nature, where the Gainer doth gain as well, as if he had laid his wager about something else, and the Looser hath so far the benefit as well as the Gaine, That he seeth thereby promoted the thing, that concerns them both alike.

Now therefore, to the end, that the Looser may have his benefit by it, as well as the Gainer, it would not be amiss, that the condition were made thus, that the latter should grant the moity of his gain to the Proposer; that thereby he might be enabled to bring to light both those, and some other useful inventions, for the Service of Mankind. And to manifest, that it is not for his own interest only, that the *Proposer* mentions this; he is willing to impart from that moity, so received, the full moity again to any other person within his Majesty's Dominions, who shall first of all give notice of his Undertaking to prove or disprove the said Identity, and perform it accordingly within the space of two Months, to be computed from the present Date. Those that have a mind to engage, may repair to the Printers of these *Tracts*, where they may know further.

A new Contrivance of **Wheel-Barometer,** *much more easy to be prepared, than that, which is described in the* **Micrography;** *imparted by the Author of that Book.*

This is only an easy way of applying an *Index* to any *Common Barascope*, whether the Glass be only a Single Cane, or have a round Bolthead at the top. And by the means thereof, the {219}Variation of the Altitude of the *Mercurial* Cylinder, which at most is hardly three Inches, may be made as distinguishable, as if it were three Foot, or three Yards, or as much more, as is desired.

The manner hereof is visible enough by *Figure* I: where A B C represents the Tube, which may be either Blunt, or with a Head, as A B C (by which latter shape, more room is allow'd for any remainder of Air, to expand the better.) This is to be filled with Quick-silver, and inverted as commonly; but into a Vessel of Stagnant Mercury, made after the fashion of I K, that is, having its sides about 3 or 4 inches high, and the Cavity of it equally big both above and below; and if it can be (besides that part, which is fill'd by the end of the *Mercurial* Tube, that stands in it) of equal capacity with the hollow of the Cane about B: For then the Quicksilver rising as much in the hollow of I, as it descends at B, the difference of the height in the Receiver I, will be just half the usual difference, And if the receiving Vessel I K have a bigger Cavity, the difference will be less, but if less, the difference will be greater: But, whether the difference be hereby made bigger or less, 'tis no great matter, since by the contrivance of the *Wheel* and *Index* (which is more fully described in the *Preface* to the *Micrography*) the least variation may be made as sensible as is desired, by diminishing the bigness of the Cylinder E, and lengthening the *Index* F G, according to the Proportion requisite.

An Account of **Four Suns,** *which very lately appear'd in* **France,** *and of* **two** **Raine-bows,** *unusually posited, seen in the same Kingdom, somewhat longer agoe.*

These *Phænomena* are thought worthy to be inserted here, for the Speculation of the Curious in those Kingdoms; as they were publisht in the French *Journal des Scavans*, of May 10, 1666. *viz.*

The 9th of *April* of this present year, about half an hour past nine, there appear'd three Circles in the Sky. *One* of them was very great, a little interrupted, and white every where, without {220} the mixture of any other colour. It passed through the midst of the Sun's *Disk*, and was parallel to the *Horizon*. Its *Diameter* was above a hundred degrees, and its *Center* not far from the *Zenith*.

The *Second* was much less and defective in some places, having the Colours of a Rainbow, especially in that part, which was within the great Circle. It had the true Sun for its Center.

The *Third* was less, than the first, but greater than the second; it was not entire, but only an Arch or Portion of a Circle, whose Center was far distant from that of the Sun, and whose circumference did, by its middle, join to that of the least Circle, intersecting the greatest Circle by its two extreams. In this Circle were discerned also the Colours of a Rainbow, but they were not so strong, as those of the *Second*.

At the place, where the circumference of this *Third* Circle did close with that of the *Second*, there was a great brightness of Rainbow-Colours, mixt together: And at the two extremities, where this *Second* Circle intersected the *First*, appear'd two *Parhelia's* or Mock-suns; which shone very bright, but not so bright, nor were so well defined, as the true Sun. The False Sun, that was towards the *South*, was bigger, and far more luminous, than that towards the *East*. Besides those two *Parhelia's*, which were on the two sides of the true Sun, in the intersection of the *First* and *Third* Circle, there was also upon the *First* great Circle, a *third* Mock-sun, situated to the *North*, which was less and less bright, than the two others. So that at the same time there were seen *Four* Suns in the Heavens.

Figure II. will illustrate the Position of this *Phænomenon*.
A. *The Zenith or the Point Vertical to the place of Observation.*
B. *The true Sun.*

100

S C H N. *The great Circle, altogether White, almost parallel to the Horizon, which pass'd through the true Sun's Diske, and upon which were the false Suns.*

D E B O. *A Rain-bow about the Sun, forming an entire Circle, but interrupted in some places.*

H D N. *A portion of a Circle, that was Excentrick to the Sun, and greater than the Circle* D E B O, *which touch'd* D E B O, *and was confounded with it in the point* D. {221}H N. *The two Mock-Suns, in the intersection of the Semicircle* H D N, *and the Circle* S C H N: *The midst of which two False-Suns was white and very luminous; and their Extremities towards* D I*were tinged with the Colours of a Rainbow. The False Sun, mark'd* N, *was fainter than that, which is mark'd* H.

C. *The Mock-Sun, all white, and far less shining, than the two others.*

I. *A space very dark betwixt* R. *and* D.

* *Those Five Suns, that appear'd the 29*March, *A. 1629. at*Rome, *between 2 or 3 of the Clock, in the afternoon, were thus posited; that the two of them, which were in the intersection of two Circles, appear'd in that of a Circle, which passed through the Sun's Diske, with another, that was*Concentrick *to the Sun: as may be seen in* Figure III. *borrow'd (for the easier comparing them together) out of*Des-Cartes *his*Meteors, *cap. X.*

This Appearance is look't upon as one of the notablest, that can be seen, by reason of the *Excentricity* of the Circle H D N, and because that the*Parhelia* * were not in the Intersection of the Circle D E B O with the great Circle S C H N, but in that of the Semi-circle H D N.

As for the two odd *Rainbows*; they appear'd at *Chartres* the 10. of*August*, 1665. about half an hour past six in the Evening; and did cross one another almost at right Angles, as may be seen by *Fig.* IV.

The Rainbow, which was opposite to the Sun, in the usual manner, was more deeply colour'd, than that, which cross'd it; though even the Colours of the first*Iris* were not so strong, as they are now and then seen at other times.

The greatest height of the stronger Rainbow, was about 45. degrees; the feebler Rainbow lost one of its Legs, by growing fainter, about 20 degrees above the stronger; and the Leg below appear'd continued to the *Horizon.*

These Rainbows did not *Just* decussate one another at right Angles; there was some 6 or 7 degrees difference. The fainter, seem'd to be a Portion of a great Circle; and the stronger was but a Portion of a small Circle, as usually.

The Sun, at their appearance, was about 6 degrees high above the *Horizon*, and towards the 17 *Azimuth* of the West, Northward.

{222}

The Observer, M. *Estienne*, notes, that, when he made this Observation, the River of*Chartres*, which runs very near from *South* to *North*, was betwixt him and the Rainbow; and that he stood Level with this River, whence he was distant not above 150 paces: which he adds, that the Curious may the better judge of this Observation.

A Relation of an Accident by Thunder and Lightning, at Oxford.

This was imparted by Dr. *Wallis* in a Letter, written at *Oxford*, May 12, 1666. to the*Publisher*, as follows:

I should scarce have given you so soon the trouble of another Letter, were it not for an Accident which hapn'd here *May* 10. I had that afternoon, about 4 of the clock heard it thunder at some distance. About 5 of the clock the Thunder coming nearer to us; it began to rain, and soon after (the rain withal increasing) the Thunder grew very loud, and frequent, and with long ratling Claps (though not altogether so great, as I have some other times heard:) and the Lightning with flashes very bright (notwithstanding the clear day-light) and very frequent, (when at the fastest, scarce a full minute between one flash and another; many times not so much, but a second flash before the Thunder of the former was heard:) The Thunder for the most part began to be heard about 8 or 10 second minutes after the flash; as I observ'd for a great part of the time by my Minute-Watch: but once or twice I observ'd it to follow (in a manner) immediately upon it, as it were in the same moment; and the lightning extream red and fiery. I do not use to be much apprehensive of Thunder and Lightning, but I was at this time (I know not well, why?) very apprehensive, more than ordinary, of mischief to be done by it, for it seem'd to me to be very low and near us (which made me so particular, as to observe the distance of the flash by the noise) and very frequent, and bright, so that, had it been by night as it was by day, it would have been very terrible. And, though I kept within doors, yet I sensibly discover'd a stinking sulphureous smell in the Air. About 7 of the clock it ended, before which time I had news brought me of a Sad Accident upon the{223}water at *Medley* about a Mile or somewhat more distant from hence. Two Schollars of*Wadham*-Colledge, being alone in a Boat (without a Water-man) having newly thrust off from shore, at *Medley*, to come homewards, standing near the Head of the Boat, were presently with a stroke of Thunder or Lightning, both struck off out of the Boat into the Water, the one of them stark dead, in whom, though presently taken out of the Water (having been by relation, scarce a minute in it) there was not discerned any appearance of life, sense, or motion: the other was stuck fast in the Mud (with his Feet downwards, and his upper parts above water) like a post not able to help himself out; but, besides a present stonying or numness, had no other hurt; but was for the present so disturb'd in his senses, as that he knew not, how he came there out of the Boat, nor could remember either Thunder or Lightning, that did effect it: and was very feeble and faint upon it; which (though presently put into a warm Bed) he had not thoroughly recover'd by the next Night; and whether since he have or no, I know not.

Others in another Boat, about 10 or 20 yards from these (as by their description I estimate) felt a disturbance and shaking in their Boat, and one of them had his Chair struck from under him, and thrown upon him; but had no hurt. Those immediately made up to the others, and (some leaping into the Water to them) presently drew them either into the Boat or on Shore; yet none of them saw these two fall into the Water (not looking that way) but heard one of them cry out for help presently upon the stroke, and smelt a strange stinking smell in the Air; which, when I asked him, that told it me, what kind of stink? he said, like such a smell, as is perceived upon the stricking of Flints together.

He that was dead (when by putting into a warm Bed, and rubbing, and putting strong waters into his Mouth, &c. no life could be brought into him) was the next morning brought to town; where, among the multitudes of others, who came to see, Dr. *Willis*, Dr. *Mellington*, Dr. *Lower*, and my self, with some others, went to view the Corps: where we found no wound at all in the skin, the face and neck swart and black, but not more, than might be ordinary, by the settling of the blood: On the right side of the neck was a little blackish spot about an inch long, and {224}about a quarter of an inch broad at the broadest, and was, as if it had been sear'd with a hot iron; and, as I remember, one somewhat bigger on the left side of the neck, below the Ear. Streight down the breast, but towards the left side of it, was a large place about three quarters of a Foot in length, and about two inches in breadth, in some places more, in some less, which was burnt and hard, like Leather burnt with the fire, of a deep blackish red Colour, not much unlike the scorch'd skin of a rosted Pig. And on the fore-part of the left Shoulder such another spot about as big as a Shilling; but that in the neck was blacker and seem'd more sear'd. From the top of the right shoulder, sloping downwards towards that place in his Breast, was a narrow Line of the like scorched skin; as if somewhat had come in there at the neck, and had run down to the breast, and there spread broader.

The buttons of his *Doublet* were most of them off; which, some thought might have been torn off with the blast, getting in at the neck, and then bursting its way out: for which the greatest presumption was (to me) that, besides 4 or 5 buttons wanting towards the bottom of the Breast, there were about half a dozen together clear off from the bottom of the collar downwards, and I do not remember, that the rest of the buttons seem to be near worn out, but almost new. The collar of his doublet just over the fore-part of the left shoulder was quit broken asunder, cloth and stiffening, streight downwards, as if cut or chop'd asunder, but with a *Blunt* tool; only the inward linnen or fustian lineing of it was whole, by which, and by the view of the ragged Edges, it seem'd manifest to me, that it was by the stroak inward (from without) not outwards from within.

His *Hat* was strangely torn, not just on the Crown, but on the side of the hat, and on the brim. On the side of it was a great hole, more than to put in ones fist through it: some part of it being quite struck away, and from thence divers gashes every way, as if torn, or cut with a *Dull* tool, and some of them of a good length, almost quite to the edges of the brim. And, beside these, one or two gashes more, which did not communicate with the hole in the side. This also I judged by a stroke inwards; not so much from the view of the edges of those gashes (from which there was scarce any judgement to be made either way) but {225} because the lining was not torn, only ript off from the edge of the hat (where it was sow'd on) on that side, where the hole was made. But his hat not being found upon his head, but at some distance from him, it did not appear, against what part of the head that hole was made.

Upon the rest of his Cloaths, I do not know of any further effect, nor did we smell any sulphurous scent about them: which might be, *Partly* because it was now a good while after the time, and *Partly* by reason of their being presently drenched in the water into which he fell.

The night following, the three *Doctors* above mentioned, and my self, with some Chirurgions (besides a multitude of others) were present at the opening of the head, to see if any thing could be there discover'd; but there appear'd no sign of contusion; the brain full and in good order; the nerves whole and sound, the vessels of the brain pretty full of Blood. But nothing was by any of them discern'd to be at all amiss. But it was by candle-light, and they had not time to make very nice Observations of it (the Body being to be buried by and by) and the croud of People was a further hindrance. But if any thing had been considerably out of order to the view, it would surely have been by some of them discover'd. Some of them thought, they discern'd a small fissure or crack in the skull; and some who held it, while it was sawing off, said, they felt it Jarring in their hands, and there seem'd to the eye something like it, but it was so small, as that by candle-light we could not agree it certainly so to be.

Some of the *Hair* on the right Temple was manifestly singed, or burnt; and the lower part of that Ear blacker, than the parts about it, but soft; and it might be only the settling of the Blood. The upper part of the left shoulder, and that side of the neck, were also somewhat blacker than the rest of the Body, but whether it were by the blow, which broke the collar, and scorch'd the round red spot thereupon, or only by settling of the Blood, I cannot say; yet I think, it might very well be, that both on the head, and on this side of the neck, there might be a very great blow, and a contusion upon it (and seems to have been so, by the tearing of the hat, and breaking the collar, if not also cracking of the skull) and yet no sign of such contusion, because dying so immediately, there was not time for the Blood to gather {226} to the part and stagnate there (which in bruises is the cause of blackness) and it was but as if such a blow had been given on a Body newly dead; which does not use to cause such a symptom of a bruise, after the Blood ceases to circulate.

Having done with, the Head, they open'd the *Breast*, and found that burning to reach quite through the skin, which was in those scorch'd places hard and horney, and shrunk up, so as it was not so thick as the soft skin about it: but no appearance of any thing deeper than the skin; the Muscles not at all disorder'd or discolour'd (perhaps, upon the reason, that was but now said of the Head, Neck and Shoulder). Having then taken off the *Sternum*, the Lungs and Heart appear'd all well, and well-colour'd without any disorder.

This is the sum of what was observ'd; only that the whole Body was, by night, very much swell'd, more than in the morning; and smelt very strong and offensively: Which might be by the hotness of the weather, and by the heat of the place occasion'd by the multitude of People.

An Experiment to examine, what Figure, *and* Celerity *of* Motion *begetteth, or encreaseth* Light *and* Flame.

This was communicated by Dr. *Beale*, as follows;

May 5. 1665. fresh Mackrels were boyl'd in Water, with salt and sweet herbs; and, when the Water was perfectly cold, the next morning, the Mackrels were left in the Water for pickle.

May 6. more fresh Mackrels were boyl'd in like Water; and *May* 7. both Water and Mackrels were put into the former Water, together with the former Mackrels. (Which circumstances I do particularize, because, whether, the mixture of the pickle of several ages, and a certain space of time, or whatever else was necessary, and wanting, the trial did not succeed with like effect at other times).

But now on the next *Munday* (*May* 8). evening, the Cook stirring the Water, to take out some of the Mackrels, found the Water at the first motion become very luminous, and the Fish shining through the Water, as adding much to the Light, which the water yielded. The water by the mixture of Salt and Herbs, {227} in the boyling, was of it self thick and rather blackish, than of any other clear colour: yet being stirr'd, it shin'd, and all the fish appear'd, more brightly luminous in their own shapes.

Wherever the drops of this water (after it was stirr'd) fell on the Ground, or Benches, they shin'd: And the Children took drops in their hands, as broad as a penny, running with them about the house, and each drop, both near and at distance, seem'd by their shining as broad as a six pence, or a shilling, or broader.

The Cook turn'd up the side of the Fish, which was lowest, and thence came no shining: and after the water was for some good time settled, and fully at rest, it did not shine at all.

On *Tuesday* night (*May* 9). we repeated the same Trial, and found the same effects. The water, till it was stirr'd, gave no light, but was thick and dark, as we saw by day-light, and by candle-light. As soon as the Cook's hand was thrust into the water, it began to have a glimmering; but being gently stirr'd by the hand moving round (as the Dairy-maid do to gather the Curds for Cheese) it did so shine, that they, who look'd on it at some distance, from the farther end of another room, thought verily, it was the shining of the Moon through a Window upon a Vessel of Milk; and by brisker Circulation it seem'd to flame.

The Fish did then shine as well from the Inside, as the Outside, and chiefly from the Throat, and such places, as seem'd a little broken in the boyling.

I took a piece that shin'd most, and fitted it as well as I could devise in the night, both to my great *Microscope*, and afterwards to my little one; but I could discern no light by any of these Glasses; nor from any drops of the shining water, when put into the Glasses. And *May*10. in the brightest rayes of the Sun, I examin'd, in my great *Microscope*, a small broken piece of the Fish, which shin'd most the night before. We could find nothing on the surface of the Fish very remarkable. It seem'd whitish, and in a manner dried, with deep inequalities. And others, as well as my self, thought, we saw a stream, rather darkish, than luminous, arising like a very small dust from the Fish: And rarely here and there, a very small; and almost imperceptible sparkle in the Fish. Yet of these *sparkles* we are *certain*; we numbered them, and agreed in the number, order and place. Of the *steam* I am not confident, but do suspect our Eyes in the {228} bright Sun, or that it might be some dust in the Aire.

The great *Microscope* being fitted in the day-light for this piece of Fish, we examin'd it that night, and it yielded no light at all, either by the view of the Glass, or otherwise.

Finding it dry, I thought that the moisture of Spittle, and touching of it, might cause it to shine: and so it did, though but a very little, in a few small sparks, which soon extinguish'd. This we saw with the bare eye; not in the Glass.

The Fish were not yet fetide, nor insipid to the best discerning palats: And I caused two Fish to be kept for further Tryal, two or three days longer, till they were fetide in very hot weather; and then I expected more brightness, but could find none, either in the water, by stirring it, or in the Fish, taken out of the water.

And some Trials I made afterwards with other boyl'd Mackrels (as is above said) with like pickle, but failed of the like success.

This season serves for many Trials in this kind, and by better *Microscopes*, or better ordered. And in these Vulgarities we may perhaps as well trace out the cause and nature of Light, as in Jewels of greatest value, &c.

Some Considerations touching a Letter in the Journal des Scavans *of* May 24. 1666.

In *Num.* 9. of these *Transactions* were publish'd the *Schemes* and *Descriptions* of certain Ways of *Sounding the Depth of the Sea without a Line*; and of *Fetching up Water from the bottom of it*; together with some Experiments already made with the former of these two Contrivances. The Author of the French *Journal des Scavans* found good, to insert them both in his *Journal* of *May* 3. but in another of *May* 24. intimates, that the said *Schemes* and their *Descriptions* are not very clear and intelligible (he means, that they were not well understood by *French* Readers) proposing also some Difficulties, relating to that Subject, and esteemed by him necessary to be satisfied, before any use could be made of the said Instruments.

Upon this occasion, the Author of these *Tracts* thinks fit, here to represent,{229}

First, That *Englishmen* and such others, as are well versed in the *English* tongue, find no difficulty in understanding the descriptions of these *Engines*, nor in apprehending their structure, exhibited by the *Figures*, especially if notice be taken of the Emendation, expressed at the end of *Num.* 10. about the misgraving the *Bended end* of the *Springing Wire* (which it seems has not been noted in *France*, tho' the said *Num.* 10 is known to have been seen there a pretty while before their *Journal* of *May* 24. was publish'd). And as for the particular of the *Bucket*, fetching water from the bottom of the Sea, both the *Figure* and the annexed *Description* thereof are so plain and clear, that 'tis some wonder here, that any difficulty of understanding them is pretended by any, that hath but ordinary skill in *Cutts* and the *English* language. Mean while, that way, which the *French* Author recommends for this purpose as more simple, *Videl. a Brass-Pump with double Valves*, is not at all unknown in*England*, nor has bin left untried there; but was found inconvenient, in respect that the Valves in descending did not fully open, and give the water a free passage through the Cavity of the Vessel, nor in ascending shut so close, as to hinder the water from coming in at the top: Whereas by the way proposed in *Num.* 9. both is perform'd with great ease and security.

Secondly, Whereas the *French* Author is of opinion, that 'tis unknown, how much time a Heavy Body requires to sink in water, according to a certain depth; he may please to take notice, that that hath been made out in *England* by frequent Experiments; by which, several Depths, found by this Method of sounding *without* a Line, were examin'd by trying them over again in *the same* place *with* a Line, after the common way. And as to that *Quære* of his, Whether a heavy Body descends in the same *Proportion* of swiftness in *Water*, that it would do in *Air*? The Answer is, that it does not; but that, after it is sunk one or two fathoms into the Water, it has there arrived to its greatest swiftness, and keeps, after that, an equal degree of velocity; the *Resistance* of the water being then found equal to the *Endeavour* of the heavy Body downwards.

Thirdly, When the same *Author* alledges that it must be known, when a Light Body reascends from the bottom of the water to {230} the top, in what proportion of time and swiftness it rises. He seems not to have considered, that in this Experiment, the times of the descent and assent are both taken and computed together; so that for this purpose, there needs not that nicety, he discourses of.

Fourthly, Whereas it is further excepted, That this way of Sounding Depths is no new Invention; The answer is ready, that neither is it pretended to be so, in the often quoted*Tract*; it being only intimated there, that the manner of performing it, as it is in that place represented and described, is new.

Lastly, To rectifie the said Author's mistake, as if the instrument of fetching up Water from the bottom of the Sea, were chiefly contriv'd, to find out, Whether in some places of the Sea any *Sweet* Water is to be met with at the bottom: There will need no more, than to direct him to the Book it self *Num.* 9. where p. 149. towards the end, the *First* use of this *Bucket* is express'd to be, to know the *degrees of Saltness* of the Water according to its nearness to the top or bottom; or rather to know the constitution of the Sea-water in several depths of several*Climates*, which is a matter, much better to be found out by *Trial*, than *Discourse*. Neither is it any where argued in that Book (as the *French Journal* insinuates) that, because sweet water is found at the Bottom of the Sea of *Baharem*, therefore it *must*, but only that it *may*, be found so elsewhere. And since the same *Journal* admits, that those Sweet water-springs, which yield the sweet water, that is found at the said place, have been formerly on the*Continent*, far enough from the Sea, which hath afterwards covered them. It will be, it is presumed, lawful to ask, Why in many other places there may not be found the like? And besides, how we do know, but that there may be in other parts, Eruptious of large Springs at the bottom of the Sea, as well as there?

Printed with Licence for *John Martyn*, and *James Allestry*, Printers to the Royal-Society.
1666.

{231}

PHILOSOPHICAL
TRANSACTIONS.

Munday, July 2. 1666.

The Contents.

An Account of a New *kind of* Baroscope, *which may be call'd* Statical*; and of some Advantages and Conveniencies it hath above the* Mercurial*; communicated by Mr.*Boyle. *The Particular Observations of the Planet* Mars, *formerly intimated to have been made by Mr.* Hook *in* February *and* March *last. Some Observations, made in*Italy, *confirming the former; and withall fixing the* Period *of the said Planet's Revolution. Observations, lately made at* London, *of the Planet* Jupiter: *as also of*Saturn. *A Relation of a sad Effect of Thunder and Lightning. An Account of some Books, lately publish'd;* videl. *The Relations of divers Curious Voyages, by Mons.*Thevenot: *A Discourse about the Cause of the Inundation of the* Nile, *by Mons.* de la Chambre, *both* French: De Principiis & Ratiocinatione Geometrarum, Contra Fastum Professerum Geometriæ, *by Mr.* Hobbes: King Salomons Pourtraiture of Old Age, *by*J. Smith, M. D.

An Account of a **New** *kind of* **Baroscope,** *which may be called* **Statical;** *and of some Advantages and Conveniencies it hath above the* **Mercurial:** *Communicated, some while since, by the* **Honourable** **Robert Boyle.**

* See *Num. 11. p.185. Phil. Transactions.*

As for the *New* kind of *Baroscopes,* which, not long agoe, * I intimated to you, that my haste would not permit me to give you an account off; since your Letters acquaint me, that you still design a Communicating to the {232}Curious as much Information, as may be, in reference to*Baroscopes,* I shall venture to send you some Account of what I did but name (in my former Letter) to you.

* *The Scales here meant were before competent Eyewitnesses made to turn manifestly with the thousandth part of a grain.*

Though by a Passage, you may meet with in the 19th and 20th Pages of my *Thermometrical Experiments and Thoughts,* you may find, that I did some years agoe think upon this New kind of Baroscope; yet the Changes of the Atmosphere's Weight not happening to be then such, as I wish'd, and being unwilling to deprive my self of all other use of the exactest Ballance *, that I (or perhaps any man) ever had, I confess to you, that successive avocations put this attempt for two or three years out of my thoughts; till afterwards returning to a place, where I chanc'd to find two or three pairs of Scales, I had left there, the sight of them brought it into my mind; and though I were then unable to procure exacter, yet my desire to make the Experiment some amends for so long a neglect, put me upon considering, that if I provided a*Glass-buble,* more than ordinary large and light, even such Ballances, as those, might in some measure perform, what I had tried with the strangely nice ones above-mention'd.

I caused then to be blown at the Flame of a Lamp some *Glass-bubles* as large, thin and light, as I could then procure, and choosing among them, one, that seem'd the least unfit for my turn, I counterpoised it in a pair of Scales, that would loose their *Æquilibrium* with about the 30th part of a Grain, and were suspended at a Frame. I placed both the Ballance and the Frame by a good Baroscope, from whence I might learn the present weight of the Atmosphere. Then leaving these Instruments together; though the Scales, being no nicer than I have express'd, were not able to shew me all the Variations of the Air's weight that appear'd in the *Mercurial* Baroscope, yet they did what I expected, by shewing me variations no greater, than alter'd the height of Quicksilver half a quarter of an Inch, and perhaps much smaller than those: Nor did I doubt, that, if I had had either tender Scales, or the means of supplying the experiment with convenient accommodations, I should have {233}discerned far smaller Alterations of the Weight of the Air, since I had the pleasure to see the Buble sometimes in an *æquilibrium* with the counterpoise; sometimes, when the Atmosphere was high, preponderate so manifestly, that the Scales being gently stirr'd, the Cock would play altogether on that side, at which the Buble was hung; and at other times (when the Air was heavier) that, which was at the first but the Counterpoise, would preponderate, and, upon the motion or the Ballance, make the Cock vibrate altogether on its side. And this would continue sometimes many daies together, if the Air so long retain'd the same measure of gravity; and then (upon other changes) the Buble would regain an *æquilibrium*, or a preponderance; so that I had oftentimes the satisfaction, by looking first upon the *Statical*Baroscope (as for distinctions sake it may be call'd) to foretell, whether in the *Mercurial*Baroscope the Liquor were high or low. Which Observations though they hold as well in Winter, and several times in Summer (for I was often absent during that season) as the Spring, yet the frequency of their Vicissitudes (which perhaps was but accidental) made them more pleasant in the latter of these seasons.

So that, the matter of Fact having been made out by variety of repeated Observations, and by sometimes comparing severall of those new *Baroscopes* together, I shall add some of those Notes about this Instrument, which readily occur to my memory, reserving the rest till another opportunity.

And *First*, if the ground, on which I went in framing this *Baroscope*, be demanded, the answer in short may be; 1. That, though the Glass-buble, and the Glass-counterpoise, at the time of their first being weigh'd, be in the Air, wherein they both are weigh'd, exactly of the same weight; yet they are nothing near of the same bulk; the Buble, by reason of its capacious cavity (which contains nothing but Air, or something that weighs less than Air) being perhaps a hundred or two hundred times (for I have not conveniency to measure them) bigger than the Metalline counterpoise. 2. That according to a *Hydrostatical* Law (which you know I have lately had occasion to make out) If two Bodies of equal gravity, but unequal bulk come to be weigh'd in another *Medium*, they will be no longer {234} equiponderant; but if the new *Medium* be heavier, the greater Body, as being lighter in *Specie*, will loose more of its weight, than the lesser and more compact; but if the new *Medium* be lighter than the first, then the bigger Body will outweigh the lesser; And this disparity, arising from the change of*Medium's*, will be so much the greater, by how much the greater inequality of bulk there is between the Bodies formerly equiponderant. 3. That, laying these two together, I consider'd, that 'twould be all one, as to the effect to be produced, whether the Bodies were weighed in*Mediums* of differing gravity, or in the same *Medium*, in case its (*specifick*) gravity were considerably alter'd: And consequently, that since it appear'd by the *Baroscope*, that the weight of the Air was sometimes heavier, and sometimes lighter, the alterations of it, in point of gravity, from the weight, it was off at first counterpoising of the Buble of it, would*unequally* affect so large and hollow a Body, as the Buble, and so small and dense a one, as a Metallin weight: And when the Air by an increase of gravity should become a heavier*Medium*, than before, it would buoy up the Glass more than the Counterpoise; and if it grew lighter, than it was at first, would suffer the former to preponderate: (The Illustrations and Proof can scarce be added in few words; but, if it be desired, I may, God permitting, send you them at my next leasure:) And though our English Air be about a thousand times lighter, than water, the difference in weight of so little Air, as is but equal in bulk to a Buble, seem'd to give small hopes, that it would be sensible upon a Ballance; yet, by making the Buble very large and light, I supposed and found the Event, I have already related.

Secondly, The hermetically seal'd Glass-buble, I employed, was of the bigness of a somewhat large *Orange*, and weigh'd about 1. drachme and 10. grains. But I thought it very possible, if I had been better furnish'd with conveniencies (wherein I afterwards found, I was not mistaken) to make (among many, that might be expected to miscarry) some, that might be preferable to this, either for capacity or lightness, or both; especially if care be taken, that they be not seal'd up, whilst they are too hot. For, though one would think, that it were{235}advantagious to rarify and drive out the Air as much as is possible, because in such seal'd Bubles the Air it self (as I have elsewhere shewn) has a weight; yet this advantage countervails not the inconvenience of being obliged to increase the weight of the Glass, which when it includes highly rarified Air, if it be not somewhat strong, will be broken by the pressure of the External Air, as I have sufficiently tryed.

Thirdly, I would have tryed, whether the *Dryness* and *Moisture* of the Air would in any measure have alter'd the weight of the Buble, as well as the Variation of Gravity produced in the *Atmosphere* by other causes; but the extraordinarily constant absence of Fogs, kept me from making Observations of this kind; save that one morning early, being told of a mist, I sent to see (being my self in bed) whether it made the Air so heavy as to buoy up the Buble; but did not learn, that that mist had any sensible operation on it.

Fourthly, By reason of the difficulties and casualties, that may happen about the procuring and preserving such large and light Bubles, as I have been lately mentioning; it may in some cases prove a convenience to be inform'd, That I have sometimes, instead of one sufficiently large Buble, made use of two, that were smaller. And, though a single Buble of competent bignes be much preferable, by reason that a far less quantity and weight of Glass is requisite to comprise an equal capacity, when the Glass is blown into a single Buble, than when it is divided into two; yet I found, that the employing of two instead of one, did not so ill answer my exspectations, but that they may for a need serve the turn instead of the other; than which they are more easier to be procured; And if the Ballance be strong enough to bear so much Glass, without being injur'd: by employing two or a greater number of large Bubles, the effect may be more conspicuous, than if only a single Buble (though a very good one) were employed.

This instrument may be much improved by divers Accommodations, As

First, There may be fitted to the *Ansa* (or Checks of the Ballance) an Arch (of a Circle) divided into 15. or 20. deg. (more or less, according to the goodness of the Ballance) that the Cock resting over against these Divisions, may readily {236} and without Calculation shew the quantity of the Angle, by which, when the scales propend either way, the Cock declines from the Perpendicular, and the beam from its Horizontall parallelism.

Secondly, Those, that will be so curious, may, instead of the Ordinary Counterpoise (of Brass) employ one of Gold, or at least of Lead, whereof the *latter* being of equal weight with Brass, is much less in Bulk, and the *former* amounts not to half its bigness.

Thirdly, These parts of the Ballance, that may be made of Copper or Brass, without any prejudice to the exactness, will, by being made of one of those Mettals, be less subject, than Steel, (which yet, if well hardned and polish'd, may last good a great while) to rust with long standing.

Fourthly, Instead of the scales, the Buble may be hung at one end of the Beam, and only a Counterpoise to it at the other, that the Beam may not be burthen'd with unnecessary weight.

Fifthly, The whole instrument, if placed in a small Frame, like a square Lanthorn with Glass-windows, and a hole at the top for the Commerce of the internal and external Air, will be more free from dust, and irregular agitations; to the latter of which, it will otherwise be sometimes incident.

Sixthly, This instrument being accommodated with a light Wheele and an Index (such as have been applyed by the excellent Dr. *Chr. Wren* to open Weather glasses, and by the ingenious Mr. *Hook* to *Baroscopes*) may be made to shew much more minute variations, than otherwise.

Seventhly, And the length of the Beam, and exquisitness of the Ballance, may easily, *without* any of the foregoing helps (and much more *with* them) make the instrument far exacter, than any of those, I was reduced to employ. And to these Accommodations divers others may be suggested by a farther consideration of the nature of the thing, and a longer practice.

Though in some respects this *Statical* Baroscope be inferior to the *Mercurial*, yet in others it has its own advantages and conveniencies above it.

And 1: It confirms *ad oculum* our former Doctrine, that the falling and rising of the *Mercury* depends upon the varying weight of the Atmosphere; since in this Baroscope it cannot {237} be pretended, that a *Fuga vacui*, or a *Funiculus*, is the cause of the changes, we observe. 2. It shews, that not only the Air has weight, but a more considerable one, than some Learned men, who will allow me to have prov'd, it has some weight, will admit; since

108

even the variation of weight in so small a quantity of Air, as is but equal in bulk to an *Orange*, is manifestly discoverable upon such Balances, as are none of the nicest. 3. This *Statical*Baroscope will oftentimes be more parable, than the other: For many will finde it more easie, to procure a good pair of Gold-scales, and a Buble or two, than a long Cane seal'd, a quantity of *Quick-silver*, and all the other requisits of the *Mercurial* Baroscope; especially if we comprise the trouble and skill, that is requisite to free the deserted part of the Tube from Air. 4. And whereas the difficulty of removing the *Mercurial* Instrument has kept men from so much as attempting to do it, even to neighbouring places; the Essential parts of the *Scale*-Baroscope (for the Frame is none of them) may very easily in a little room be carried, whither one will, without the hazard of being spoil'd or injur'd. 5. There is not in *Statical*Baroscopes, as in the other, a danger of uncertainty, as to the goodness of the Instruments, by reason, that in *these* the Air is, in some more, and in some less perfectly excluded; whereas in *those*, that consideration has no place. (And by the way, I have sometimes, upon this account, been able to discover by our new Baroscope, that an esteem'd *Mercurial* one, to which I compared it, was not well freed from Air.) 6. It being, as I formerly intimated, very possible to discover *Hydrostatically*, both the bigness of the Buble, and the Contents of the cavity, and the weight and dimensions of the Glassie substance (which together with the included Air make up the Buble,) much may be discover'd by this Instrument, as to the Weight of the Air, *absolute* or *respective*. For, when the *Quick-silver* in the *Mercurial*Baroscope is either very high, or very low, or at a middle station between its greatest and least height, bringing the *Scale*-Barometer to an exact *Æquilibrium* (1 with very minute divisions of a Graine,) you may, by watchfully observing, when the *Mercury* is risen or faln just an inch, or a fourth, of half an inch &c. and putting in the like minute divisions of a Grain to the lighter Scale, till you have again brought the Ballance to an {238}exquisit*Æquilibrium*; you may, I say, determine, What known weight in the *Statical* Baroscope answers such determinate Altitudes of the ascending and descending Quick-silver in the*Mercurial*. And if the Ballance be accommodated with a divided Arch, or a Wheel and Index, these Observations will assist you for the future to determine readily, by seeing the inclination of the Cock or the degree mark'd by the Index, what pollency the Buble hath, by the change of the *Atmospheres* weight, acquired or lost. Some Observations of this nature I watchfully made, sometimes putting in a 64[th.] sometimes a 32[th.] sometimes a 16[th.] and sometimes heavier parts of a Grain, to the lighter Scale. But one, that knew not, for what uses those little papers were, coming to a window, where my Baroscopes stood, so unluckily shook them out of the Scales, and confounded them, that he robb'd me of the opportunity of making the nice Observations I intended, though I had the satisfaction of seeing, that they were to be made. 7. By this *Statical* Instrument we may be assisted to compare the *Mercurial*Baroscopes of *several* places (though never so distant) and to make some Estimates of the Gravities of the Air therein. As if, for instance, I have found by Observation, that the Buble, I employ, (and one may have divers Bubles of several sizes, that the one may repaire any mischance, that may happen to another) weigh'd just a Drachme, when the *Mercurial*Cylinder was at the height of 29½ inches (which in some places I have found a *moderate*altitude;) and that the Addition of the 16th part of a gr. is requisite to keep the Buble in an*Æquilibrium*, when the *Mercury* is risen an 8th, or any determinate part of an inch above the former station: When I come to another place, where there is a *Mercurial* Barometer, as well freed from Air as mine (for that must be supposed) if taking out my *Scale* instrument, it appeare to weigh precisely a Drachme, and the *Mercury* in the Baroscope there stand at just 29½ inches, we may conclude the Gravity of the Atmosphere not to be sensibly unequal in both those two places, though very distant. And though there be no Baroscope there, yet if there be an additional weight, as for instance, the 16th part of a Grain requisite to be added to the Buble, to bring the scales to an *Æquilibrium*, it will appear that the Air at this second place is, at that time {239}so much heavier, than the Air of the former place was, when the*Mercury* stood at 29½ inches.

But in making such comparisons, we must not forget to consider the Situation of the several places, if we mean to make Estimates not only of the weight of the Atmosphere, but of the weight and density of the Air. For, though the Scales wil shew (as has been said) whether there be a difference of weight in the Atmosphere at the two places; yet, if one of them be in a Vale or bottom, and the other on the top or some elevated part of a Hill, it is not to be excpected, that the Atmosphere, in this latter place, should gravitate as much, as the Atmosphere in the former, on which a longer Pillar of Air does lean or weigh.

And the mention, I have made of the differing Situation of Places, puts me in mind of something, that may prove another use of our *Statical* Baroscope, and which I had thoughts of making tryal off, but was Accidentally hindred from the opportunity of doing it. Namely, that by exactly poysing the Buble at the foot of a high Steeple or Hill, and carrying it in its close Frame to the top, one may, by the weight requisite to be added to Counterpoise there to bring the Beam to its Horizontal position, observe the difference of the weight of the Air at the bottom, and at the top; and, in case the Hill be high enough, at some intermediate Stations. But how far this may assist men, to estimate the *Absolute* or *Comparative* height of Mountains, and other elevated Places; and what other Uses the Instrument may be put to, when it is duly improved; and the Cautions, that may be requisite in the several cases, that shall be proposed, I must leave to more leasure, and farther Consideration.

The Particulars of those Observations of the Planet Mars, formerly intimated to have been made at London in the Months of February and March A.166⁵/₆.

To perform, what was promised *Num.* 11. of these Papers, *pag.* 198; 'tis thought fit now to publish the Particular Observations, concerning the spots in *Mars*, and their motion, as they were made with a 36 foot Telescope, and produced in {240}writing before the *Royal Society*, the 28 *March* 1666. by Mr. *Hook*, as follows;

Having a great desire (saith he) to observe the Body of *Mars*, whilst *Acronycal* and *Retrograde* (having formerly with a Glass of about 12. foot long, observ'd some kind of Spots in the Face of it,) though it be not at present in the *Perihelium* of its Orbe, but nearer its *Aphelium*, yet I found, that the Face of it, when neer its Opposition to the Sun (with a Charge, the 36. foot-glass, I made use off, would well bear) appear'd very near as big, as that of the Moon to the *naked* eye; which I found, by comparing it with the Full Moon, near adjoyning to it, *March* 10.

But such had been the ill disposition of the Air for several nights, that from more than 20. Observations of it, which I had made since its being *Retrograde*, I could find nothing of satisfaction, though I often imagin'd, I saw Spots, yet the *Inflective veins* of the Air (if I may so call those parts, which, being interspers'd up and down in it, have a greater or less Refractive power, than the Air next adjoyning, with which they are mixt) did make it so confus'd and glaring, that I could not conclude upon any thing.

On the third of *March*, though the Air were still bad enough yet I could see now and then the Body of *Mars* appearing of the form A: which I presently described by a *Scheme*; and about 10. minutes after, as exactly representing what I saw through the Glass, as I could, I drew the *Scheme* B. This I was sufficiently satisfied (by very often observing it through the Tube, and changing my Eye into various positions, that so there might be no kind of Fallacy in it) could be nothing else, but some more *Dusky* and *Spotted* parts of the Face of this Planet.

March 10. finding the Air very bad, I made use of a very shallow Eye-glass, as finding nothing *Distinct* with the greater *Charge*; and saw the appearance of it as in C, which I imagin'd, might be the Representation of the former Spots by a lesser charge. About 3 of the Clock the same morning, the Air being *very bad* (though to appearance *exceeding clear*, and causing all the Stars to twinkle, and the minute Stars to appear very thick) the body seem'd like *D*; which I still suppos'd to be {241}the Representation of the same Spots through a more confused and glaring Air.

But observing *March* 21. I was surprised to find the Air (though not so clear, as to the appearance of small Stars) so *exceeding transparent*, and the Face of *Mars* so very well *defined*, and round, and distinct, that I could manifestly see it of the shape in E. about half an hour after Nine at night. The *Triangular* spot on the right side (as it was inverted by the Telescope, according to the appearances, through with all the preceeding *Figures* are drawn) appear'd very black and distinct, the other towards the left more dim; but both of them sufficiently plain and defin'd. About a quarter before 12. of the Clock the same night, I observ'd it again with the same Glass, and found the appearance exactly, as in F; which I imagin'd to shew me a *Motion* of the former triangular spot: But designing to observe it again about 3. of the Clock the same Morning, I was hindred by cloudy weather.

But *March* 22. about half an hour after 8. at night, finding the same Spots in the same posture, I concluded, that the preceeding Observation was only the appearance of the same Spots at another height and thickness of the Air: And thought my self confirm'd in this Opinion, by finding them in much the same posture, *March* 23. about half an hour after 9. though the Air was nothing so good as before.

And though I desired to make Observations, about 3. of the Clock those mornings; yet something or other interven'd, that hindred me, till *March* 28. about 3 of the Clock, the Air being light (in weight) though moist and a little hazy; when I plainly saw it, to have the form, represented in I; which is not reconcileable with the other Appearances, unless we allow a *Turbinated* motion of *Mars* upon its Center: Which, if such there be, from the Observations made *March* 21. 22. and 23. we may guess it to be once or twice in about 24. hours unless it may have some kind of *Librating* motion; which seems not so likely. Now, whether certainly so or not, I shall endeavour, as oft as I have opportunity, further to observe.

A particular direction to the *Figures* mentioned in the precedent discourse.

A. *March* 3ᵈ· 00ʰ· 20ᵐ· *in the morning: the Air having many* {242}*inflecting parts dispersed up and down in it; by the* Wheel Barometer, *heavy,*

B. *Another Scheme, which I drew from my Observation, about* 10. *minutes after, the same morning. Both these were observed with a very deep Eye-glass.*

C. *March* 10ᵈ· 00ʰ· 20ᵐ· *in the morning: the Air heavy and inflective. Use was made of a shallow or ordinary Charge.*

D. *March* 10ᵈ· 3ʰ· 00ᵐ· *in the Morning; the Air very heavy and Inflective, which made it glare and radiate, and be more confused, than about* 3. *hours before. A shallow Charge.*

E. *March* 21ᵈ· 9½ʰ· *post merid; the Air light (in weight) and clear, without inflecting parts; the Face appear'd most distinctly of this Forme. A shallow Charge.*

F. *March* 21ᵈ· 11¾ʰ· *post merid; the Air continuing very light and clear, without inflecting vapours. A shallow Charge.*

G. *March* 22ᵈ· 8½ʰ· *post mer. the Air clear, with few inflecting veins in it, and indifferent light. A shallow Charge.*

H. *March* 23ᵈ· 9½ʰ· *post mer. the Air pretty light, but moist, and somewhat thick and hazy, but seem'd to have but few veins, or inflecting parts.*

I. *March* 28ᵈ· 3ʰ· *p. m. much the same kind of Air with that of March* 23; *light, moist, and a little hazy, with some very few veins.*

Observations made in **Italy***, confirming the former, and withall fixing the* **Period** *of the Revolution of* **Mars.**

These Observations we shall summarily present the Curious in these parts with, as they were lately presented (by Letter from his Excellency the Ambassadour of *Venice*, now residing at the Court of *France*) to the *Royal Society*, in some printed sheets of Paper, entituled,*MARTIS, circa Axem proprium Revolubilis, Observationes, BONONIÆ à JO. DOMINICO CASSINO habitæ;* come to hand *June* 3. 1666.

In these Papers the Excellent *Cassini* affirms;

1. That with a *Telescope* of 24. *Palmes,* or of about 16 *Foot,* wrought after S. *Campani's*way, he began to observe *February* 6. 1666 (st.n.) in the morning, and saw two dark Spots in the *first* Face of *Mars.*{243}

2. That with the same Glass he observ'd *Febr.* ¹⁴/₂₄. in the Evening, in the *other* Face of this Planet, two other Spots, like those of the first, but bigger.

3. That afterwards continuing the Observations, he found the Spots of these two Faces to turn by little and little from *East* to *West*, and to return at last to the same situation, wherein he had seen them first.

4. That S. *Campani,* having also observ'd at *Rome* with Glasses of 50. *Palmes* or about 35*Foot*, likewise of his own contrivance, had seen in the same Planet the same *Phenomena.*

5. That sometimes he hath seen, during the same night, the two Faces of *Mars*, one, in the Evening, the other in the Morning.

6. That the Motion of these Spots in the inferior part of the apparent Hemisphere of *Mars*, is made from *East* to *West*, as that of all the other Celestial Bodies, and is peform'd by Parallels, that decline *much* from the *Equator*, and *little* from the *Ecliptick*.

7. That the Spots return the next day to the same situation, 40. minuts later, than the day before; so that in every 36. or 37. daies, about the same hour, they come again to the same place.

8. He promises shortly to give us the particular *Tables* of this Motion and of its Inequalities, together with the *Ephemerides* themselves.

9. He represents, that some other *Astronomers* have also made at *Rome* several Observations of these Spots of *Mars*, from *March* ¹⁴/₂₄. to *March* ²⁰/₃₀. with Glasses, wrought by *Eustachio Divini*, of 25. and 45. Palmes; Which Spots he makes little differing from his own, of the first Face; as will by and by appear, by the direction to the *Schemes*.

10. But he adds, that those other *Roman* Astronomers, that have observ'd with *Divini's* Glasses, will have the Conversion of *Mars* to be performed, not in 24 h, 40 m. (as he maintains it is) but in about 13 h.

11. And to evince, that they are mistaken in these Observations of theirs; he alledges, That they assure that the Spots, which they have seen in this Planet, (by an *Eustachian* Telescope) the ²⁰/₃₀ of *March*, were small, very distant from one another, remote from the middle of the Disk, and the *Oriental* Spot was less, than the *Occidental* (as is represented by the Fig. O; like that of the first Face of *Mars*.) whereas, on the contrary, {244} He (*Cassini*) pretends to evidence by his Observations, made at the same time at *Bononia*, that, the same day and hour, those Spots were very large, neer one another, in the midst of the Disk, the Oriental bigger than the Occidental (as appears by *Fig.* P, which is that of the second Face of *Mars*.)

12. Besides, he declares, that those *Astronomers* were too hasty, in determining, after 5 or 6 Observations only, in how much time *Mars* finish's his Revolution; and denies it to be perform'd in 13 hours: adding, that, though Himself had observ'd for a much longer time, than they; yet he durst not for a great while define, Whether *Mars* made but *one* Turn in 24 hours 40 minuts or *two*; and that all, that he could, for a long time affirm, was onely this, that after 24 h. 40 m. this Planet appear'd in the same manner he did before.

13. But since those first Observations, He affirms to have found cause to determine, that the Period of this Conversion is made in the said space of 24 h. 40 m; and not oftner than once within that time; Alledging for proof;

1. That, whereas *Febr.* 6. (st.n.) he saw the Spots of the first Face of *Mars*, moving from eleven of the Clock in the night, until break of day, they appear'd not afterwards in the Evening after the rising of that Planet (witness several intelligent persons, which he names, that were present at the Observations) Whence he infers, that after 12 hours and 20 minuts, the same Spots did not come about; since that the same, which in the morning were seen in the middle, upon the rising of *Mars*; after 13 or 14 hours, might have appear'd neer the Occidental Limb. But, because he might be imposed upon by Vapors, whilst *Mars* was yet so neer the *Horizon*, he gives this other determination, *vid.*

2. Whereas he saw the first Face of *Mars* the 6 of *February* at 11 of the clock of the night following; he did not see the same after 18 daies at the same hour; as he ought to have done, if the Period were absolved in the space of 12 h. 20 m.

3. Again, whereas he saw *Febr.* 24. in the Evening, the other Face of *Mars*, he could not see the same, the 13. and 15. day of *March*, to wit after 17 and 19 days; as he should have done, if the Revolution were made in the newly mention'd time.

4. Again, whereas the 27. of *March* in the Evening he saw {245} the second Face of *Mars*, he could not see it the 14. and 16. of *April.*

From all which Observations he Judges it to be evident, that the Period of this Planets Revolution is not perform'd in the space of 12. hours 20, minutes, but in about 24 hours 40 minutes; more exactly to be determin'd by comparing distant Observations: And that those who affirm the former, must have been deceived by not well distinguishing the two Faces, but that having seen the second, taken it for the first.

All which he concludes with this Advertisement, that, when he defines the time of the Revolution of *Mars*, he does not speak of its *Mean* Revolution, but onely of that, which he observ'd, whilst *Mars* was opposite to the Sun; which is the shortest of all.

The Figures of the Principal *Observations, represented in the Book here discoursed of, may be seen in the annexed* Scheme; videl.

K. *One of the Faces of Mars, as S.* Cassini *observed it* March 3. (*st.n.*) 1666 *in the Evening, with a Glass of 24 Palmes.*

L. *The other Face, as he saw it* Febr. $^{14}/_{24}$ *in the Evening.*

M. *The first Face, as S.* Campani *saw at Rome,* March 3. 1666. *in the Evening, with a Glass of 50 Palmes.*

N. *The second Face, as the same* Campani *observed it* March $^{18}/_{28}$. *in the Evening.*

O. *The figure of* Mars *as it was seen at* Rome *by a Telescope of* Divini *of 45 Palmes,* March$^{20}/_{30}$.

P. *The Figure of the said Planet, as it was seen the same day and hour at Bononia by* Cassini; *being that of the second Face.*

Some Observations lately made at London concerning the Planet Jupiter.

These, as they were made, so they were imparted, by Mr. *Hook*, as follows:

A. 1666, *June* 26. between 3. and 4. of the Clock in the morning, I observed the Body of *Jupiter* through a 60 foot-glass, and found the apparent Diameter of it through the Tube, to be somewhat more than 2. degrees, that is, about four {246} times as big, as the Diameter of the *Moon* appears to the *naked* Eye. I saw the Limb pretty round, and very well defin'd without radiation. The parts of the *Phasis* of it had various degrees of Light. About *a* and *f*, the *North* and *South* poles of it (in the *Fig Q.*) 'twas somewhat darker, and by degrees it grew brighter towards *b*. and *e*, two Belts or Zones; the one of which (*b*) was a small dark *Belt* crossing the Body Southward; Adjoyning to which was a smal Line of a somewhat lighter part; and below that again, Southwards, was the great black Belt *c*. Between that, and *e*, the other smaller black Belt, was a pretty large and bright *Zone*; but the middle *d*, was somewhat darker than the edges. I perceiv'd about 3$^{h.}$15$^{m.}$ near the middle of this, a very *dark round Spot*, like that represented at *g*, which was not to be perceiv'd about half an hour before: And I observed it, in about 10. minutes time to be gotten almost to *d*, keeping equal distance from the *Satelles h*, which moved also Westwardly, and was joyn'd to the Disk at *i*, at 3$^{h.}$ 25$^{m.}$ After which, the Air growing very hazy, and (as appeared by the *Baroscope*) very light also (in weight) I could not observe it: So that it was sufficiently evident, that this black Spot was nothing else, save the shadow of the *Satelles h*, Eclipsing a part of the Face of Jupiter. About two hours before, I had observed a large darker spot in the bigger *Belt* about *k*, which in about an hour or little more (for I did not exactly observe the time, nor draw the *Figure* of it) moving Westwards, disappear'd. About a week before, I discover'd also, together with a Spot in the *Belt c*, another Spot in the *Belt e*, which kept the same way and velocity with that of the *Belt c*. The other three *Satellites* in the time of this Eclipse, made by the *Satelles*, were Westwards of the Body of *Jupiter*; appearing as bright through the Tube, as the Body of *Jupiter* did to the naked Eye, and I was able to see them longer through the Tube, after the day-light came on, than I was able to see the Body of *Jupiter* with my naked eye.

A late Observation about Saturn made by the same.

June 29 1666. between 11. and 12. at night I observed the Body of *Saturn* through a 60. foot Telescope, and found it {247} exactly of the shape represented in the *Figure* R. The *Ring* appear'd of a somewhat brighter Light than the *Body*; and the black lines *a a*, crossing the Ring, and *b b* crossing the Body (whether Shadows or not, I dispute not) were plainly visible: whence I could manifestly see, that the *Souther*-most part of the Ring was on *this* side of the Body, and the *Northern* part, behind, or covered by the Body.

A Relation of a sad effect of Thunder and Lightning:

This Relation was written by that worthy Gentleman, *Thomas Neale* Esquire, (the then *High Sheriff* of the County of *Hampshire*, when this disaster hapned) to a Friend of his in *London*, as follows;

On the 24 of *January* 166⁵/₆, one Mr. *Brooks* of *Hampshire*, going from *Winchester* towards his house near *Andover* in very bad Weather, was himself slain by Lightning, and the Horse, he rode on, under him. For about a mile from *Winchester* he was found with his Face beaten into the ground, one leg in the stirrup, the other in the Horses mane; his Cloaths all burnt off his back, not a piece as big as a handkerchief left intire, and his hair and all his body singed. With the force, that struck him down, his nose was beaten into his face, and his Chin into his Breast; where was a wound cut almost as low, as to his Navil; and his cloaths being, as aforesaid, torn, the pieces were so scatter'd and consum'd, that not enough to fill the crown of a hat could be found. His gloves were whole, but his hands in them sing'd to the bone. The hip-bone and shoulder of his Horse burn't and bruised; and his saddle torn in little pieces. This was what appear'd to the Coroners inquest, and so is likely to be as near truth, as any is to be had.

So far this Letter. Which, if it had come soon enough to the hands of the *Publisher*, would have been joyned to a like *Relation*, inserted in the next foregoing Papers (*Num.* 13.) of an accident hapn'd at a later time. With both which may be compared the Account, formerly published in Latin by the Learned Dr. *Charleton*, concerning the Boy, that was {248}Thunder-struck near *Nantwich in Cheshire;* the Title of the Book being *Anatome Pueride Cælo tacti*: such Relations, when truly made, well deserving to be carefully recorded for farther consideration.

Of some Books lately publish't.

RELATIONS OF DIVERS CURIOUS VOYAGES, by *Mons. Thevenot*, the third *Tome*, in *French*. This Book contains chiefly, the Ambassie of the *Dutch* into *China*, translated out of the Dutch manuscript: A Geographical description of *China*, translated out of a Chinese Author by *Martinius*: And the Account, which the Directors of the Dutch East-India Company made to the States General, touching the state of affairs in the East-Indies, when their late Fleet parted from thence. To touch some things of a *Geographical* and *Philosophical* nature, contained therein, we shall take notice;

1. How the Kingdom of *China* is peopled; there being according to the best computation (which is there made with singular care) above 58 millions of Men, not counting Magistrates, Soldiers, Priests, Eunuchs, Women and Children; so that it may not be altogether strange, if one should affirm, there were 200 millions of people, of all sorts, in that Kingdom.

2. That *Catay* is nothing else, but the *Six* Northern Provinces of *China*, separated from the other *Nine*, by the great River *KIANG*; and that the City *Cambalu* is the same with that of *Peking*; the *Tartars*, who carry every three years their Tribute to the Emperor of *China*, constantly calling the said Provinces and City by those names of *Catay*, and *Cambalu*.

3. That *China* is so well furnisht with Rivers, and cut Channels, that men may go from the most Southern to the most Northern part thereof by water, except one daies journey; as the Dutch Ambassadours did, embarking at *Canton*, which is 23d. 48m. Northern Latitude, and landing at *Peking*, which is about 40d; having only travell'd one daies journey over some Mountains of the Province *Kiamsi*.

4. That the people of *China* are exceeding industrious {249}Husbandmen making, among other waies of improving their soile, great use of Flouding.

5. That the *Physicians* of *China* do cure Sicknesses with much ease, and in a short time: That they have very ancient Books of the nature and vertues of Herbs, Trees and Stones: That their Modern Physicians (as well as their Ancient ones did) write of the Prognosticks, Causes, Effects, &c. of Diseases. That their Remedies consist for the most part of *Simples* and *Decoctions, Cauteries, Frictions*; without the use of *Bloud letting:* That they have such an excellent skill and method in feeling the *Pulse*, that by the means thereof they discover even the most latent causes of Diseases; taking a good half hour, when they visit a Patient, in feeling and examining his Pulse: That they prescribe much the use of *The*; and the

drinking alwayes warme, whatever they drink: To the custome of both which it's imputed, that the inhabitants of *China* do spit very little, nor are subject to the Stone or Gout: That they prise highly the Root *Ginseng*, as an extraordinary Restorative and Cordiall, recovering frequently with it agonizing persons; one pound of it being paid with 3 pounds of silver. As for their*Chymists*, (of which they have also good store) they go beyond ours, promising not only to make Gold, but to give Immortality.

6. That their *Nobility* is raised from Learning and Knowledge, without regard to Bloud or Parentage, excepting the Royall Family.

7. That in *CHEKIAN*, a maritime Province, whence is the shortest cut of *China* to *Japan*, is the best and plentifullest *Silk-trade* in the world: And that there every year the Mulberries are cutt, and kept down, that they grow not into Trees for the easier gathering of the Leaves, there being a *double* Silk-harvest in that Country, as there is in severall other parts of the East-indies; (both which there is hope, will shortly be imitated in *Virginia*.)

8. That the way of making *Porcelane* is this: (*Which is the rather inserted here, because it agrees so well with an Account, we received a while since from a very Curious and intelligent Person of Amsterdam.*) There is in the Province of *Nankin* a Town, call'd {250} *Goesifols* whence they draw the Earth for *Porcelaine*, which is found between the Rocks of Mountains. This Earth they beat very small, and stamp it to a very fine Powder, and then put it into Tubs fill'd with water; where the finest part sinks to the bottom. Afterwards 'tis kneaded in the form of small Cubes, of the weight of about 3. *Catti* (a *Catti* being 20 Ounces.) These pieces thus wrought are sold to the people, that commonly in great numbers fetch them, coming from the Town *Sintesimo* (otherwise *Jontiou*) in the Province of *Kiansy*, being about 50 miles distant from *Wotsing*, neer the City *KIANSY*; which people transport them to their homes, and there bake them in this manner: They heat their Ovens well, for the space of 15 daies successively, and then keep them so close, that no Air may get in; and after 15 *other* daies are pass'd, they open the Oven in the presence of an Officer, who takes every fifth vessel of each fashion for the service of the Emperor: Which done, the rest is sold to those of *Ucienien*, whence it is transported all over the Country. So that the Earth is not prepared, in *Nankin*, where 'tis found, because the people of that Province have not the skill of working it, as the other above-mention'd; who also alone have the Art of coloring it, which they keep as a great Secret, not teaching it to any, but their Children and next Kindred.

9. That *Musk* is nothing else, but the Testicles of a Beast like a Dear, found in the Province of *Honan*; and that, when tis good and unmixt, as it comes from the Animal, they sell it even in *Nankin* and *Pekin*, for 30. or 35. *Teyls* (that is, about so many Crowns) the *Catti*.

Many other curious informations might be borrow'd from this Author, concerning the Customs, Studies, Exercises of the *Chinese*; of the number of the people of each Province; of the Natural productions of the Earth and Rivers there; of the Structure and Antiquity of their Wall; of the Magnificence of their Porcelain Tower &c.; but, remitting for these things to the Book it self, we shal only add a piece of Oeconomy, used by the *Holland*-Merchants in their Commerce with *China*, which is, that they dry abundance of Sage-leaves, role them up, and{251}prepare them like *The*, and carrying it to *China*, as a rare drogue, get for one pound of it, fourtimes as much *The*.

A DISCOURSE ABOUT THE CAUSES OF THE INUNDATION OF THE NILE, in *French*. The Author of this Book is Monseiur *dela Chambre*, who being perswaded from several Circumstances, that accompany the Overflowing of this River, that it cannot proceed from Rain, ventures to assign for a Cause of *it*, and of all the other effects that happen at the time of its swelling, the *Niter*, wherewith that water abounds.

The discourse having six parts, the Author endeavours to shew in the

First, that the Waters of the *Nile* are Nitrous, explicating the Nature of Salt, and Saltpeter, and imputing the fertility of the Earth, as well us the fecundity of Animals, to Salt. Where he shews, that all things, that serve to improve Land, are full of Salt; and that 'tis observ'd, that grain steep'd in Vrine, before sowing, rises sooner, and becomes fuller and stronger, than else. Adding, that that, which renders the Seed of Animals prolifick, is, that one of the *Spermatick* veins hath its Origine from the *Emulgent*, through which the Nitrous and Saline Serosities, that discharge themselves into the Kidneys and Bladder, do pass.

In the *Second*, he examins, what is Fermentation, and how 'tis perform'd; affirming, that, what thrusts forth Plants in the Spring, is, that the Earth being fermented by the *Niter*, it harbours, the Nitrous spirits insinuate themselves into their Pores.

In the *Third* he treats of all the Circumstances, observable in the Inundation of the Nile. 'Tis affirm'd, that 3 or 4 days before that River begins to overflow, all its water is troubled: that then there falls a certain Dew, which hath a fermenting vertue, and leavens a Paste exposed to the Air: that the Mud, which has been drawn out of the water, grows heavier, when the overflowing begins, then it was before, and that by the increase of the weight of that Mud, they judge of the greatness of the approaching inundation. The Author pretends, that {252} the Niter, which the *Nile* is stored with, is the cause of all these strange effects, and of many others, by him alledged. For, *saith he*, when the Nitre is heated by the heat of the Sun, it ferments, and mingling with the water, troubles it, and swells it, and makes it pass beyond its banks; after the same manner, as the Spirits in new Wine render it troubled, and make it boyle in the vessel. And it seems not likely to him, that the Mud, found in the *Nile*, should come a far off; for then it would at last so raise the banks of this River, that it would not be able to overflow them any longer. Whereas 'tis more than 2000 years, that the banks thereof are not grown higher, there being now requisite but 16. cubits for overflowing the Land, no more than there was in the time of *Herodotus*. Which shews, *saith he*, that this Mud is nothing but a volatil *Niter*, which exhaling, doth not increase the Earth. As for the *Ægyptian* Dew, and the increase of the weight of the Mud, he adscribes them to the same Cause. For the spirits of Nitre abounding in the *Nile*, when raised into the Air with the vapors, that exhale continually from this River, there is made out of their mixture, a Dew, that refreshes the Air, makes sickness to cease, and produces all those admirable effects, that make the *Ægyptians* wish for it so passionately. And the same spirits of Niter, being joyned to the Paste, and to the Mud, raise the one, and augment the weight of the other. That, which Mr. *Buratini* observes, that at the time of this inundation, the Niter-pits of the neighboring places vomit out liquid Niter, and that one may see issue out of the Earth abundance of Chrystals of Nitre, is alledged to fortify this conjecture; Which is yet more confirm'd by the Fertility, communicated to the Earth by the Mud of this River. For, plants do grow there in such abundance, that they would choak one another, if it were not remedied by throwing Sand upon the Fields; insomuch that the *Ægyptians* must take as much pains to spread Sand to lessen the fatness of their Land, as other Nations do, to spread dung or other manure upon theirs to increase the fatness.

In the *Fourth* and *Fifth*, the Author undertakes to prove, that all those strange effects cannot be attributed to Rain or Snow, {253} and that the overflowing of the *Nile* always happens at a certain day.

In the *Last*, he alledges some Relations, serving to confirm his Opinion; Which are too long here to insist upon.

DE PRINCIPIIS ET RATIOCINATIONE GEOMETRARUM, Contra Fastum Professorum Geometriæ; Authore *Thoma Hobbes*. It seems, that this Author is angry with all Geometricians, but himself; yea he plainly saith in the dedication of his Book, that *he invades the whole Nation of them*; and unwilling, it seems, to be call'd to an account for doing so; He will acknowledge no judge of *this* Age; but is full of hopes, that posterity will pronounce for him. Mean while he ventures to advance this *Dilemma; Eorum qui de iisdem rebus mecum aliquid ediderunt, aut solus insanio Ego, aut solus non insanio; tertium enim non est, nisi (quod dicet forte aliquis) insaniamus omnes.* Doubtless, one of these will be granted him.

As to the Book it self, he professes, that he doth not write it against *Geometry*, but *Geometers*; and that his design in it is, to shew, That there is no less uncertainty and falsity in the writings of *Mathematicians*, than there is in those of *Naturalists, Moralists,* &c., though he judges, that *Physicks, Ethicks, Politicks,* if they were well demonstrated, would be as certain as the *Mathematicks*.

Attacking the Mathematical Principles as they are found in Books, and withall some Demonstrations, he takes to task *Euclid* himself, instead of all, as the Master of all

Geometricians, and with him his best interpreter, *Clavius*, examining in the *First* place, the*Principles* of *Euclid*: *Secondly*, Declaring false, what is superstructed upon them, whether by*Euclid*, or *Clavius*, or any *Geometer* whatsoever that hath made use of those or other (as he is pleased to entitle them) *false* Principles. *Thirdly*, Pretending, that he means so to combat all, both Principles and Demonstrations, undertaken by him, as that he will substitute better in their room, least he should seem to undermine the Science it selfe.{254}

The particulars, which he undertakes to reform, are,
Punctum.
Linea.
Terminus.
Linea Recta.
Superficies.
Superficiei Termini.
Superficies Plana,
Angulus (Where he is large upon the *Angulus Contactus.*)
Petitio prima Elem. 1. Euclidis.
Ratio.
Radix & Latus.
Prop. 16. El. 3.
Dimensio Circuli.
Magnitudo Circuli Hugeniana.
Sectio Anguli.
Ratio, quam habet recta composita ex Radio & Tangente 30. grad, ad Radium ipsum.
Propos. 47æ. Elem. 1. Demonstratio.
Addita est Appendix de Mediis proportionalibus in genere.

KING SALOMONS POUTRAITURE OF OLD AGE; by *John Smith*, M.D. This Treatise being a *Philosophical* Discourse, though upon a *Sacred* Theme, may certainly claim a place among *Philosophical* Transactions. Not here to mention the many other learned Notes, this Worthy Author gives upon that Hieroglyphical Description of Old Age, made by that Royal Pen-man of *Ecclesiastes*, cap. 12. We shall onely take notice of that surprizingly Ingenious one, there to be met with, concerning the Antiquity of the Doctrine of the *Blood's Circulation*: King *Salomon*, who lived neer 2700 years agoe, using such expressions, as may, to a considering Reader, very probably denote the same Doctrine, which the Sagacious Dr.*Harvey* has of late years so happily brought to light, and introduced into all the most Ingenuous Societies of Learned men: The *Pitcher*, mention'd in the quoted place, being Interpreted for the *Veines*, and the *Fountain* for the *Right Ventricle of the Heart*, as the*Cistern* for the *Left*; the *Wheele*, there spoken off, manifestly importing a *Circulation*, made by the *Great Artery* with its Branches, the principal Instrument thereof.

Printed with Licence for *John Martyn*, and *James Allestry*, Printers to the Royal Society.
1666.

{255}

PHILOSOPHICAL
TRANSACTIONS.

Wednesday, July 18. 1666.

The Contents.

A new Experiment, shewing, How a considerable degree of Cold may be suddenly produced without the help of Snow, Ice, Haile, Wind, *or* Niter, *and that at any time of the year. An Account of two Books, lately printed in* London; *whereof the one is entituled,* EUCLIDIS ELEMENTA

GEOMETRICA, novo ordine ac Methodo demonstrata; *the* *Author* Anonymus. *The other,* THE ENGLISH VINE-YARD VINDICATED, *by* JOHN ROSE.

A new Frigorifick Experiment shewing, how a considerable degree of **Cold** *may be suddenly produced without the help of* **Snow, Ice, Haile, Wind,** *or* **Niter,** *and that at any time of the year.*

This subject will it self, 'tis presumed, without any other *Preamble*, speak the Cause, why this present Paper is publish't at this (unusual) time of the Month: though, by the by, it may not be amiss to add on this occasion, that the Publisher of these *Tracts* never meant so to confine himself to a *Set* time, as not to retain the Liberty of taking any other, when there is occasion. And there being one given him, before another Month is come in, he does without any scruple or delay comply therewith, presenting the Curious with an Experiment which he thinks is both seasonable, and will not be unwellcome to them; furnish't out of the Ample Magazin of that Philosophical Benefactor, the Noble Mr. *Boyle*; Concerning which, thus much is further thought requisite to intimate on this occasion, that it, and some others of the same Gentlemans, that have been, and may be, mentioned in the *Transactions*, belong to certain Treatises, the Author hath lying by him; but that yet he denys not {256} to communicate them to his Friends, and to allow them to dispose thereof, upon a hope, that equitable Readers will be ready to excuse, if hereafter they should appear also in the Treatises they belong to, since he consents to this Anticipation, but to comply with those, that think the imparting of real and practical Experiments, may do the Publick some Service, by exciteing and assisting mens Curiosity in the interim.

As for the Experiment, you saw the other day at my Lodgings, though it belongs to some Papers about *Cold*, that (you know) could not be Publish't, when the rest of the *History* came forth, and therefore was reserved for the next *Edition* of that Book; yet the Weather having been of late very hot, and threatning to continue so, I presume, that to give you here in compliance with your Curiosity an Account of the Main and Practical part of the Experiment, may enable you to gratify not onely the Curious among your Friends, but those of the Delicate, that are content to purchase a Coolness of Drinks at a somewhat chargeable rate.

You may remember, that the Spring before the last, I shew'd you a particular Account of a way, wherein by a certain substance obtain'd from *Sal Armoniack*, I could presently produce a considerable degree of *Cold*, and that with odd Circumstances, without the help of *Snow, Ice, Niter* &c. But that Experiment being difficult and costly enough, and design'd to afford men *Information*, not *Accomodations*, I afterwards tryed, what some more cheap and facile mixtures of likely Bodies with *Sal Armoniack* would do towards the Production of Cold, and afterwards I began to consider, whether to that purpose alone (for my first experiment was design'd to exhibite other *Phænomena* too) those mixtures might not without inconvenience be omitted: and I was much confirm'd in my conjecture, by an accident, which was casually related to me by a very Ingenious Physician of my acquaintance, but not to be repeated to you in few words, though he complain'd, he knew not what to make of it.

Among the several ways, by which I have made infrigidating Mixtures with *Sal Armoniack*, the most simple and facile is this; Take one pound of powder'd *Sal Armoniack* and about three Pints (or pounds) of Water, put the Salt into the Liquor, *either* altogether, if your design be to produce an intense, though {257} but a short coldness; *or* at two, three, or four several times, if you desire, that the produced coldness should rather last somewhat longer than be so great. Stirre the powder in the Liquor with a stick or whalebone (or some other thing that will not be injur'd by the fretting Brine, that will be made) to hasten the dissolution of the Salt; upon the quickness of which depends very much the intensity of the Cold, that will ensue upon this Experiment. For the clearing up whereof, I shall annex the following particulars.

1. That a considerable degree of Cold is really produced by this operation, is very evident: *First* to the touch; *Secondly*, by this, that if you make the Experiment (as for this reason I sometimes chuse to do) in a Glass-Body or a Tankard, you * *In the History of Cold.* may observe, that, whilst the Solution of the Salt is making, the outside of the Metalline Vessel will, as high as the mixture reaches within, be bedew'd (if I may so speak) with a

multitude of little Drops of Water as I have * elsewhere shown that it happens, when mixtures of Snow and Salt, being put into Glasses or other Vessels, the aqueous vapors that swim to and fro in the Air, and chance to glide along the sides of the Vessels, are by the coldness thereof condens'd into Water. And in our Armoniack Solution you may observe, that if you wipe off the Dew from any particular part of the outside of the Vessel, whilst the solution does yet vigorously goe on, it will quickly collect fresh Dew, which may be sometimes copious enough to run down the sides of the Vessel. But *Thirdly*, the best and surest way of finding out the Coldness of our Mixture is that, which I shew'd you by plunging into it a good seal'd Weatherglass furnish't with tincted Spirit of Wine. For the Ball of this being put into our frigorifick mixture, the Crimson Liquor will nimbly enough descend much lower, than when it was kept either in the open Air, in common Water, of the same temper with that, wherein the *Sal Armoniack* was put to dissolve. And if you remove the Glass out of our Mixture into common water, the tincted Spirit will, (as you may remember, it did) hastily enough reascend for a pretty while, according to the greater or lesser time, that it continued in the *Armoniack* Solution. And this has succeeded with me, when instead of removing the Mixture into *Common* Water, I removed it into water newly impregnated with *Salt-peter*.

{258}

2. The *Duration* of the Cold, produc'd by this Experiment, depends upon several Circumstances; as *First*, upon the Season of the year, and present temperature of the Air; For, in Summer and Hot weather the Cold will sooner decay and expire. *Secondly*, upon the Quantity of Salt and Water: For, if both these be great, the effect will be as well more lasting, as more considerable. *Thirdly*, for ought I yet know, we may here add the Goodness & Fitness of the particular parcel of Salt, that is imploy'd; for, though it be hard to discern beforehand, which will be the more, and which the less proper; yet some trials have tempted me to suspect, that there may be a considerable disparity, as to their fitness to produce Cold, betwixt parcels of Salt, that are without scruple look't upon as Sal Armoniack: Of which difference it were not perhaps very difficult to assign probable reasons from the Nature of the Ingredients of this compound Concrete, and the wayes of preparing it. But the Duration of the Cold may be conceived to depend also. *Fourthly*, upon the Way of putting in the Salt into the Water. For, if you cast it in all at once, the Water will sooner acquire an intense degree of Coldness, but it will also the sooner return to its former temper; Whereas, if you desire but an inferiour degree of that Quality, but that may last longer (which wil usually be the most convenient for the Cooling of Drinks), then you may put in the Salt by little and little. For, keeping a long Weather-glass for a good while in our impregnated Mixture, I often purposely try'd, that, when the tincted liquor subsided but slowly, or was at a stand, by putting in, from time to time, 2 or 3. spoonfuls of fresh Salt, and stirring the Water to quicken the Dissolution, the Spirit of Wine would begin again to descend, if it were at a stand or rising, or subside much more swiftly than it did before. And if you would lengthen the Experiment, it may not be amiss, that part of the Sal Armoniack be but grosly beaten, that it may be the longer in dissolving, and consequently in Cooling the Water. Whilst there are dewy drops produced on the outside of the Vessel, 'tis a sign, that the Cold within continues pretty strong; for when it ceases, these drops especially in warm weather, will by degrees vanish. But a *surer* way of measuring the duration of the Cold, is, by removing from time to time the Seal'd Weather-glass out of the Saline Mixture into the same common Water, with part of which it was made. And though it be not easie to determin any thing particularly about this matter; yet it may somewhat assist you in your Estimates, to be inform'd, That I have in the Spring by a good Weather-glass found a sensible adventitious Cold made by a pound of Sal Armoniack at the utmost, to last about 2 or 3 hours.

3. To cool Drinks with this Mixture, you may put them in *thin* Glasses, the thinner the better; which (their orifices being stopp'd, and still kept above the Mixture) may be moved to and fro in it, and then be immediately pour'd out to be drunk: Though when in the Glass, I imployed, was conveniently shap'd as, like a Sugar-loaf, or with a long Neck, I found it not amiss to drink it out of that, without pouring it into any other; which can scarce be done without lessning the Coolness. The refrigeration, if the Glass viall be convenient, is quickly perform'd: And if one have a mind to cool his hands, he may readily do it by applying them

119

to the outside of the Vessel, that contains the refrigerating Mixture; by whose help, pieces of Chrystal, or Bullet for the cooling of {259} the Mouths or Hands of those patients, to whom it may be allow'd, may be potently cool'd, and other such refreshments may be easily procur'd.

4. How far Sal Armoniack, mingl'd with Sand or Earth, and not dissolv'd, but only moistn'd with a little Water sprinkl'd on it, will keep Bottles of Wine or other liquors more coole, than the Earth or that Sand alone will do, I have not yet had opportunity by sufficient trials fully to satisfie my self, and therefore resign that Enquiry to the Curious.

5. For the cooling of Air, and Liquors, to adjust Weather-glasses (to be able to do which at all times of the year, was one of the chief aimes, that made me bethink my self of this Experiment;) or to give a small quantity of Beer &c. a moderate degree of coolness, it will not be requisite, to employ neer so much as a whole pound of Sal Armoniack at a time. For, you may easily observe by a seal'd Weather-glass, that a very few ounces, well pouder'd and nimbly dissolv'd in about 4. times the weight of Water, will serve well enough for many purposes.

6. And that you may the less, scruple at this, I shall tell you, that even before and after Midsummer, I have found the Cold producible by our Experiment to be considerable and useful for refrigerating of Drinks, &c. but if the Sal Armoniack be of the fittest sort (for I intimated above, that I suspected, 'tis not equally good) and if the season of the year do make no disadvantagious difference, the degree of Cold, that may be produced by no more than one pound (if not by less) of Sal Armoniack, may, within its own Sphere of Activity, be much more vehement, than, I presume, you yet imagine, and may afford us excellent Standards to adjust seal'd Weather glasses by; and for several other purposes, For I remember that in the Spring, about the end of *March*, or beginning of *April*, I was able with one pound of Sal Armoniack, and a requisite proportion of Water, to produce a degree of Cold much greater, than was necessary the preceding Winter, to make it frosty Weather abroad; nay I was able to produce real Ice in a space of time, almost incredibly short. To confirm which particulars, because they will probably seem strange to you, I will here annex the Transcript of an entry, that I find in a Note book of the *Phænomena* and success of one of those Experiments, as I then tryed it; though I should be asham'd to expose to your perusal a thing so rudely pen'd; if I did not hope, you would consider, that 'twas hastily written onely for my own Remembrance. And that you may not stop at any thing in the immediately annext Note, or the two, that follow, it will be requisite to premise this Account of the seal'd Thermoscope; (which was a good one) wherewith these Observations were made; That the length of the Cylindrical pipe was 16. Inches; the Ball, about the bigness of a somewhat large Walnut, and the Cavity of the Pipe by guess about an eight or ninth part of an inch Diameter.

The First Experiment is thus registered. *March* the 27th, in the Seal'd Weather glass, when first put into the Water, the tincted Spirit rested at $8\frac{5}{8}$ inches; being suffered to stay there a good while, and now and then stirr'd to and fro in the Water; it descended at length a little beneath $7\frac{5}{8}$ inches; then the *Sal Armoniack* being put in, within about a quarter of an hour or a little more it descended to $2^{11}/_{16}$ inches, but before that time, in half a {260} quarter of an hour it began manifestly to freeze the vapours and drops of water on the outside of the Glass. And when the frigorifick power was arriv'd at the height, I several times found, that water, thinly plac'd on the outside, whilst the mixture within was nimbly stirr'd up and down, would freeze in a quarter of a minute (by a Minute-watch.) At about $\frac{3}{4}$ of an hour after the infrigidating Body was put in, the Thermoscope, that had been taken out a while before, and yet was risen but to the lowest freezing mark, being again put in the liquor, fell an inch beneath the mark. At about $2\frac{1}{2}$ houres from the first Solution of the Salt I found the tincted liquor to be in the midst between the freezing marks, whereof the one was at $5\frac{1}{2}$ inches (at which height when the Tincture rested, it would usually be, some, though but a small, frost abroad;) and the other at $4\frac{3}{4}$ inches; which was the height, to which strong and durable Frosts had reduced the liquor in the Winter. At 3 hours after the beginning of the Operation, I found not the Crimson liquor higher than the upper Freezing mark newly mention'd; after which, it continued to rise very slowly for about an hour longer; beyond which time I had not occasion to observe it.

Thus far the *Note-book*; wherein there is mention made of a Circumstance of some former Experiments of the like kind, which I remember was very conspicuous in this newly recited. For, the frigorifick mixture having been made in a Glass body (as they call it) with a large and flattish bottom, a quantity of water, which I (purposely) spilt upon the Table, was by the operation of the mixture within the Glass, made to freeze, and that strongly enough, the bottom of the Cucurbite to the Table; that stagnant liquor being turn'd into solid ice, that continued a considerable while unthaw'd away, and was in some places about the thickness of a half Crown piece.

Another Observation, made the same Spring, but less solemn, as meant chiefly to shew the Duration of Cold in a high degree, is recorded in these terms: The first time, the Seal'd Weather-glass was put in, before it touch'd the common water, it stood at 8⅛, having been left there a considerable while, and once or twice agitated the water, the tincted liquor sunk but to 7⅞, or at furthest, 7⁶/₈; then the frigorifick liquor being put into the water with circumstances disadvantagious enough in (about) half a quarter of an hour the tincted liquor fell beneath 3¼, and the Thermoscope, being taken out, and then put in again, an hour after the water had been first infrigidated subsided beneath 5 inches, and consequently within ¼ of an inch of the mark of the strongly freezing weather.

7. Whereas the grand thing, that is like to keep this Experiment from being as generally *Useful*, as perhaps it will prove *Luciferous*, is the Dearness of Sal Armoniack, two things may be offered to lessen this Inconvenience. For *first*, Sal Armoniack might be made much cheaper, if instead of fetching it beyond-sea, our Country-men made it here at home; (which it may easily be and I am ready to give you the Receipt, which is no great Secret.) But *next*, I considered, that probably the infrigidating vertue of our mixture might depend upon the peculiar Texture of the Sal Armoniack whereby, whilst the Water is dissolving it, either some Frigorifick particles are extricated and excited or (rather) some particles which did before more agitate the minute parts of the water, are expell'd (or invited out by the ambient Bodies) or {261} come to be clogg'd in their motion: Whence it seem'd reasonable to expect that upon the Reunion of the Saline particles into such a Body, as they had constituted before, the redintegrated Sal Armoniack having, neer upon, the same Texture, would, upon its being redissolv'd, produce the same, or a not much inferior degree of Coldness: And hereupon, though I well enough foresaw that an Armoniack solution, being boyl'd up in Earthen vessels (for Glass ones are too chargeable) would, by piercing them, both lose some of the more subtle parts, and thereby somewhat impaire the texture of the rest; yet I was not deceiv'd in Expecting, that the dry Salt, remaining in the pipkins, being redissolv'd in a due proportion of water, would very considerably infrigidate it; as may further appear by the Notes, which for your greater satisfaction you will find here subjoyn'd, as soon as I have told you, that, though for want of other vessels I was first reduc'd to make use of Earthen ones, and the rather, because some Metallin Vessels will be injur'd by the dissolv'd Sal Armoniack, if it be boyl'd in them; yet I afterwards found some conveniencies in Vessels of other Mettall, as of Iron; whereof you may command a further Account.

March the 29th, the Thermoscope in the Air was at 8⅞ inches; being put into a somewhat large evaporating glass, fill'd with water, it fell (after it staid a pretty while, and had been agitated in the liquor) to 8. inches: then about half the Salt, or less, that had been used *twice* before, and felt much less cold than the water, being put in and stirr'd about, the tincted Spirit subsided with a visible progress, till it was faln manifestly beneath 4. inches; and then, having caused some water to be freshly pump'd and brought in; though the newly mention'd Solution were mixt with it, yet it presently made the Spirit of Wine manifestly to ascend in the Instrument, much faster, than one would have expected, *&c.*

And this much may suffice for this time concerning our *Frigorifick* Experiment; which I scarce doubt but the *Cartesians* will lay hold on as very favourable to some of their Tenents; which you will easily believe, it is *not* to the Opinion, I have elsewhere oppos'd, of those Modern Philosophers, that would have *Salt-petre* to be the *Primum Frigidum*. (though I found by trial, that, whilst 'tis actually dissolving, it gives a much considerabler degree of Cold, than otherwise.) But about the Reflexions, that may be made on this Experiment, and the Variations, and Improvements & Uses of it, though I have divers things lying by me; yet, since you have seen several of them already, and may command a sight of the rest, I shall forbear the mention of them here, not thinking it proper, to swell the bulk of this Letter with them.

An Account of two Books lately printed in London.

I. *EUCLIDIS ELEMENTA GEOMETRICA, novo ordine ac methodo demonstrata.* In this compendious and pretty Edition, the Anonymous Author pretends to have rendred these Elements more expeditious; by bringing all together into one place, what belongs to one and the same subject: Comprising 1. what *Euclid* hath said of *Lines*, Streight, Intersecting one another, and Parallel. 2. What he hath demonstrated of a *Single Triangle*, and of *Triangles Compared* one with another. 3. What of the *Circle*, and its Properties. 4. What of *Proportions* in Triangles and other Figures. 5. What of *Quadrats* and *Rectangles*, made of Lines diversly {262} cut. 6. What of *Plane Superficies's*. 7. What of *Solids*. After which follow the *Problems*. The *Definitions* are put to each *Chapter* as need requireth. The *Axioms*, because they are few, and almost every where necessary, are not thus distributed in *Chapters*. The *Postulata*, are not subjoyn'd to the *Axioms*, but reserv'd for the *Problems*, the Author esteeming, that they being *practical* Principles, had only place in *Problems*.

This for the *Order:* As to the *Manner* of Demonstrating, One and the same is observ'd in most Propositions; all with much brevity; to the end, that what is not of it self difficult, may not be made so, by multitude of Words and Letters.

II. *THE ENGLISH VINE-YARD VINDICATED.* The Author (Mr. *John Rose*, his Majesties Gardener at his Royal Garden in St. *James's*) makes it his business in this small Tract (a very thin Pocket-book) by a few short Observations made by himself, to direct *Englishmen* in the *Choice* of the *Fruit*, and the *Planting* of Vine-yards; heretofore very frequently cultivated, though of late almost quite neglected by them.

He discourses skilfully, 1. Of the *severall sorts* of *Vines*, and what *Grapes* are most sutable to the *Climate* of *England*; where he chiefly commends the small *Black-grape*, or *Cluster-grape*; the *Parsley-grape*; the White *Muscadine*; the *Frontiniack*; and a new *White-grape*, with a red Wood and a dark green Leaf: All these being early ripe fruit. 2. Of the *Soyle*, and *Scituation* of a Vine-yard in *England*: Where, as to the *First*, he pitches upon a *Light Soile*, having a bottom of *Chalk* or *Gravel*, and given to *Brambles* observing, that no Plant whatsoever is so connatural to the Vine for Soyl, as the *Bramble*. As for the *Scituation* he chooses that side or declivity of a Hill, that lies to the *South* or *Southwest*; and is favoured with *other Hills* somewhat higher, or *Woods* on the *North* and *East*, to break the rigour of those quarters. This direction he thinks of that importance, that he affirms, that the discouragement of the Culture of Vines in *England* has only proceeded from men's misinformation on this material article of *Choice* of *Soyle* and *Scituation*. 3. How to *prepare* the Ground for the Plantation, *vid.* by plowing up the *Swarth* in *July*, and by disposing the *Turf* in *small* heaps, and so burning them, and spreading the ashes over the Land; care being taken, that by heaping too much materials together, the Earth be not over-burnt by the excessive heat and fire, which they require to reduce them to ashes.

What is added, of the Manner of planting the *Sets*; of Dressing, Pruning, and Governing the Plantation; of the Ordering and Cultivating the Vine-yard after the first four years, till it needs renewing; as also of the *manner* and *time*, how and when to manure the Vine-yard, with Compost, will be better understood from the Book it self, than can be here described; the Author pretending, that, those few observations of his, as the native production of his own Experience, being practised with care, the Vine-yards in *England* may be planted, govern'd and perpetuated with undoubted success; and offering withall to furnish those, that have a desire to renew this Culture, and to store their grounds with *Sets* and *Plants* of all those sorts, which he recommends; he having a plentiful *stock* of them all.

Printed with Licence for *John Martyn*, and *James Allestry*, Printers to the Royal Society. 1666.

PHILOSOPHICAL
TRANSACTIONS.

Munday, August 6. 1666.

The Contents.

An essay of Dr. John Wallis, *exhibiting his* Hypothesis *about the* Flux and Reflux of the Sea, *taken from the consideration of the* Common Center of Gravity of the Earth and Moon*; together with an* Appendix *of the same, containing an* Answer *to some*Objections, *made by severall Persons against that* Hypothesis. *Some Animadversions of the same* Author *upon Master* Hobs'*s late Book,* De Principiis & Ratiocinatione Geometrarum.

An Essay of Dr. John Wallis, *exhibiting his* Hypothesis *about the* Flux and Reflux of the Sea.

How abstruse a subject in Philosophy, the *Flux and Reflux of the Sea* hath proved hitherto, and how much the same hath in all Ages perplexed the Minds even of the best of *Naturalists*, when they have attempted to render an Account of the Cause thereof, is needless here to represent. It may perhaps be to more purpose, to take notice, that all the deficiencies, found in the *Theories* or *Hypotheses*, formerly invented for that End, have not been able to deterre the Ingenious of *this* Age from making farther search into that Matter: Among whom that Eminent Mathematician Dr. *John Wallis*, following his happy *Genius* for advancing reall Philosophy, hath made it a part of his later Inquiries and Studies, to contrive and deduce a certain Hypothesis concerning that *Phænomenon*, taken {264} from the Consideration of the*Common Center of Gravity of the Earth and Moon*, This being by several Learned Men lookt upon, as a very rational Notion, it was thought fit to offer it by the Press to the Publick, that other Intelligent Persons also might the more conveniently and at their leisure examine the*Conjecture* (the Author, such is his Modesty, presenting it no otherwise) and thereupon give in their sense, and what Difficulties may occur to them about it, that so it may be either confirm'd or laid aside accordingly; As the *Proposer* himself expressly desires in the Discourse, we now, without any more *Preamble*, are going to subjoyn, as it was by him addressed, by way of Letter, from *Oxford* to Mr. *Boyle, April* 25. 1666. and afterwards communicated to the R. *Society*, as follows:

You were earnest with me, when you last went from hence, that I would put in writing somewhat of that, which at divers times, these three or four years last past, I have been discoursing with your self and others concerning the *Common Center of Gravity of the Earth and Moon*, in order to salving the *Phænomena* as well of the *Seas Ebbing and Flowing*, as of some perplexities in *Astronomical Observations* of the *Places* of the Celestial Bodies.

How much the World, and the great Bodies therein, are manag'd according to the *Laws of Motion*, and *Statick Principles*, and with how much more of clearness and satisfaction, many of the more abstruse *Phænomena* have been salved on such Principles, within this last Century of years, than formerly they had been; I need not discourse to you, who are well versed in it. For, since that *Galilæo* and (after him) *Torricellio*, and others, have applied*Mechanick* Principles to the salving of *Philosophical* Difficulties; *Natural Philosophy* is well known to have been rendered more intelligible, and to have made a much greater progress in less than an hundred years, than before for many ages.

The *Seas Ebbing and Flowing*, hath so great a connexion with the *Moons* motion, that in a manner all Philosophers (whatever other Causes they have joyned with it), have attributed much of its cause to the *Moon*, which either by some *occult quality*, {265} or *particular influence*, which it hath on moyst Bodies, or by some *Magnetick vertue*, drawing the water towards it, (which should therefore make the Water there *highest*, where the Moon is *vertical*) or by its gravity and pressure downwards upon the Terraqueous Globe (which would make it *lowest* where the Moon is *vertical*) or by whatever other means (according to the several Conjectures of inquisitive persons,) hath so great an influence on, or at least a connexion with, the Sea's Flux and Reflux, that it would seem very unreasonable, to seclude the consideration of the Moons motion from that of the Sea: The *Periods of Tides* (to say nothing of the greatness of them near the New moon and Full moon) so constantly waiting on the Moon's motion, that it may be well presumed, that either the one is governed by the other, or at least both from some common cause.

But the first that I know of, who took in the consideration of the *Earth's* motion, (*Diurnal* and *Annual*) was *Galilæo*; who in his *Systeme of the World*, hath a particular discourse on this subject: Which, from the first time I ever read it, seemed to me so very rational, that I could never be of other opinion, but that the true Account of this great *Phænomenon* was to be referred to the Earths motion, as the *Principal* cause of it: Yet that of the Moon (for the reasons above mentioned) not to be excluded, as to the determining the *Periods of Tides*, and other circumstances concerning them. And though it be manifest enough, that *Galilæo*, as to some particulars, was mistaken in the account which there he gives of it; yet that may be very well allowed, without any blemish to so deserving a person, or prejudice to the *main Hypothesis*. For that Discourse is to be looked upon onely as an *Essay* of the *general Hypothesis*; which as to *particulars* was to afterwards adjusted, from a good *General History of Tides*, which it's manifest enough that he had not; and which is in a great measure yet wanting. For were the matter of Fact well agreed on, it is not likely, that several Hypotheses should so far differ, as that one should make the Water *then* and *there* at the Highest, *where* and *when* the other makes it at the Lowest; as when the Moon is Vertical to the place. {266}

And what I say of *Galilæo*, I must in like manner desire to be understood of what I am now ready to say to you. For I do not profess to be so well skilled in the History of Tides, as that I will undertake presently to accommodate my *general Hypothesis* to the *particular cases*, or that I will indeed undertake for the certainty of it, but onely as an *Essay* propose it to further consideration; to stand or fall, as it shall be found to answer matter of Fact. And truly had not your importunity (which is to me a great Command) required me to do it, I should not so easily have drawn up any thing about it, till I had first satisfied my selfe, how well the Hypothesis would answer Observation: Having for divers years neglected to do it, waiting a time when I might be at leisure throughly to prosecute this design.

But there be two reasons, by which you have prevailed with me, at least to do something. *First*, because it is the common Fate of the *English*, that out of a modesty, they forbear to publish their Discoveries, till prosecuted to some good degree of certainty and perfection; yet are not so wary, but that they discourse of them freely enough to one another, and even to Strangers upon occasion; whereby others, who are more hasty and venturous, comming to hear of the notion, presently publish something of it, and would be reputed thereupon, to be the first Inventers thereof: though even that little, which they can then say of it, be perhaps much less, and more imperfect, than what the true Authors could have published long before, and what they had really made known (publikely enough, though not in print) to many others. As is well known amongst us as to the business of the *Lymphatick Vessels* in *Anatomy*; the *Injection of Liquors into the veins of Living animals*; the *Exhibiting of a straight line equal to a crooked*; the *spot in Jupiter*, whence his motion about his own Axis may be demonstrated; and many other the like considerable Inventions.

The *other* Reason (which, with me, is more really of weight, though even the former be not cotemptible) is, because, as I have been already for at least three or four years last past diverted from prosecuting the inquiry or perfecting the Hypothesis, as I had thoughts to do; so I do not know, but like Emergencies may divert me longer; and whether I shall ever so {267} do it, as to bring it to perfection, I cannot determine. And therefore, if as to my self any thing should *humanitus accidere*; yet possibly the notion may prove worth the preserving to be prosecuted by others, if I do it not. And therefore I shall, at least to your self, give some general account of my present imperfect and undigested thoughts.

I consider therefore, that in the Tides, or the Flux and Reflux of the Sea, besides extraordinary Extravagancies or Irregularities, whence great Inundations or strangly high Tides do follow, (which yet perhaps may prove not to be so meerly accidental as they have been thought to be, but might from the regular Laws of Motion, if well considered, be both well accounted for and even foretold;) There are these *three* notorious Observations made of the Reciprocation of Tides. *First*, the *Diurnal* Reciprocation; whereby twice in somewhat more than 24. hours, we have a Floud and an Ebbe; or a High-water and Low-water. *Secondly*, the *Menstrual*; whereby in one *Synodical* period of the Moon, suppose from Full-moon to Full-moon, the Time of those Diurnal Vicissitudes doth move round through the whole compass of the Νυχθήμερον, or Natural day of twenty four hours: As for instance, if at the Full-moon the full Sea be at such or such a place just at Noon, it shall be the next day (at the same place) somewhat before One of the clock; the day following, between One and Two; and so onward, till at the New moon it shall be at midnight; (the other Tide, which in the Full moon was at midnight, now at the New-moon coming to be at noon;) And so forward till at the next Full-moon, the Full sea shall (at the same place) come to be at Noon again: Again, That of the Spring-tides and Neap-tides (as they are called;) about the Full-moon and New-moon the Tides are at the Highest, at the Quadratures the Tides are at the Lowest: And at the times intermediate, proportionably. *Thirdly*, the *Annual*; whereby it is observed, that at sometimes of the year, the Spring-tides are yet much higher than the Spring-tides at other times of the year: Which Times are usually taken to be at the Spring and Autumne; or the two Æquinoxes; but I have reason to believe (as well from my own Observations, for many years, as of others who have been {268} much concerned to heed it, whereof more will be said by and by;) that we should rather assign the beginnings of *February* and *November*, than the two *Æquinoxes*.

Now in order to the giving account of these three Periods, according to the *Laws of Motion* and *Mechanick Principles*, We shall *first* take for granted, what is now adayes pretty commonly entertained by those, who treat of such matters; *That a Body in motion is apt to continue its motion, and that in the same degree of celerity, unless hindred by some contrary Impediment*, (like as a Body at rest, to continue so, unless by some sufficient mover, put into motion:) And accordingly (which daily experience testifies) if on a Board or Table, some loose incumbent weight, be for some time moved, & have thereby contracted an *Impetus* to motion at such a rate; if that Board or Table chance by some external obstacle, or otherwise, to be stopped or considerably retarded in its motion, the incumbent loose Body will shoot forward upon it: And contrarywise, in case that Board or Table chance to be accelerated or put forward with a considerably greater speed than before, the loose incumbent Body, (not having yet obtained an equal *Impetus* with it) will be left behind, or seem to fly backward upon it. Or, (which is *Galilæo*'s instance,) if a broad Vessel of Water, for some time evenly carried forward with the water in it, chance to meet with a stop, or to slack its motion, the Water will dash forward and rise higher at the fore part of the Vessel: And, contrarywise, if the Vessel be suddenly put forward faster than before; the Water will dash backwards, and rise at the hinder part of the Vessel. So that an Acceleration or Retardation of the Vessel, which carries it, will cause a rising of the Water in one part, and a falling in another: (which yet, by its own weight, will again be reduced to a Level as it was before.) And consequently, supposing the Sea to be but as a loose Body, carried about with the Earth, but not so united with it, as necessarily to receive the same degree of *Impetus* with it, as its fixed parts do: The acceleration or retardation in the motion of this or that part of the Earth, will cause (more or less, according to the proportion of it) such a dashing of the Water, or rising at one part, with a Falling at another, as is that, which we call the Flux and Reflux of the Sea. {269}

Now this premised, We are next, with him, to suppose the Earth carried about with a double motion; The one *Annual*, as (*Fig.* 1.) in B E C the great Orb, in which the Center of the Earth B, is supposed to move about the Sun A.

The other *Diurnal*, whereby the whole moves upon its own *Axis*, and each point in its surface describes a Circle, as D E F G.

It is then manifest, that if we suppose, that the Earth moved but by any one of these motions, and that regularly, (with an equal swiftness;) the Water, having once attained an equal *Impetus* thereunto, would still hold equal pace with it; there being no occasion, from the Quickening or Slackening of the Earths motion, (in that part where the Water lyeth) for the

Water thereon either to be cast Forward or fall Backward; and thereby to accumulate on the other parts of the Water: But the true motion of each part of the Earths surface being compounded of those two motions, the *Annual* and *Diurnal*, (the *Annual* in B E C being, as *Galilæo* there supposeth, about three times as fast as a *diurnal* motion in a great Circle, as D E F;) while a Point in the Earths surface moves about its Center B. from G. to D. and E. and at the same time, its Center B. be carried forwards to C; the true motion of that Point forwards, is made up of both those motions; to wit, of B to C, and of G to E; but while G moves by D to E, E moves backward by F to G, contrary to the motion of B to C; so that the true motion of E, is but the difference of B C, and E G: (for, beside the motion of B above the Center; G. is also put forward as much as from G to E; and E put backward as much as is G E, the Earths *Diameter*. Which would afford us a Cause of two Tides in twenty four hours; the One upon the greatest Acceleration of motion, the Other upon its greatest Retardation.

And thus far *Galilæo*'s Discourse holds well enough; But then {270}in this it comes short; that as it gives an Account of two Tides; so those two Tides are alwayes to be at F and D; that is, at *Noon* and *Midnight*; whereas Experience tells us, that the Time of Tides, moves in a *moneths space* through all the 24. hours. Of which he gives us no account. For though he do take notice of a Menstrual Period; yet he doth it onely as to the *Quantity* of the Tides; greater or less; not as to the *Time* of the *Tides*, sooner or later.

* *Vid. Riccioli Almagest. novum*, Tom. 1, lib. 4. cap. 10. n. 111. pag. 216. 2.

To help this, there is one (*Vid.* * *Jo. Baptista Balianus*) who makes the *Earth* to be but a *secondary* Planet; and to move, not directly about the Sun, but about the Moon, the Moon meanwhile moving about the Sun; in like manner as we suppose the Earth to move about the Sun, and the Moon about it.

But this, though it might furnish us with the foundation of a *Menstrual* Period of Accelerations and Retardations in the compound motion of several parts of the Earths surface; yet I am not at all inclined to admit this as a *true Hypothesis*, for divers Reasons, which if not demonstrative, are yet so consonant to the general Systeme of the World, as that we have no good ground to disbelieve them. For 1. The Earth being undeniably the greater Body of the two (whereof there is no doubt to be made) it cannot be thought probable, that this should be carried about by the Moon, lesser than it self: The contrary being seen, not onely in the *Sun*, which is bigger than any of the Planets, which it carryes about; but in *Jupiter*, bigger than any of his *Satellites*; and *Saturne*, bigger than his. 2. As the *Sun* by it's motion about it's own Axis, is with good reason judged to be the *Physical* cause of the *Primary* Planets moving about it; So there is the like reason to believe, that *Jupiter* and *Saturne* moving about their Axes, are the Physical cause of their *Satellites* moving about them, which motion of *Jupiter* hath been of late discover'd, by the help of a *fixed* Spot discern'd in him; and we have reason to believe the like of *Saturne:* Whether *Venus* and *Mercury* (about whom no *Satellites* have been yet observed) be likewise so moved; we have not yet the like ground to determine: But we have of *Mars*; from {271}the Observations of Mr. *Hook* made in *February* and *March* last, and by him communicated to the *Royal Society*, and since Printed in the *Transactions*, published *Apr.* 2. 1666. consonant to the like observations of *Jupiter*, made by him in *May.* 1664, and since communicated to the same *Society*; and then published in the *Transactions*, of *March.* 6. then next following. Now that the Earth hath such a motion about its own *Axis* (whereby it might be fitted to carry about the Moon) is evident by its *Diurnal* motion. And it seems as evident that the Moon hath not; because of the same side of the Moon alwaies turned towards us; which could not be, if the Moon carried the Earth about: Unlesse we should say, that it carries about the Earth in just the same Period, in which it turnes upon its own Axis: Which is contrary to that of the Sun carrying about the Planets: the shortest of whose Periods, is yet longer than that of the Suns moving about its own Axis. And the like of *Jupiter*, shorter than the Period of any of his *Satellites*; if at least the Period of his conversion about his Axis, lately said to be observed, prove true. (Of *Saturn* we have not yet any Period assigned; but it's likely to be shorter, than that of his *Satelles*.) And therefore we have reason to believe, not that by the Moons motion about its Axis the Earth should be carried by a contemporary Period (whereby the same face of the Moon should be ever towards us;) but that by the Earths revolution about its Axis in 24. hours, the Moon should be carried about it in about 29. dayes, without any motion on its own Axis: And accordingly, that the *Secondary* Planets about *Jupiter* and *Saturn*, are not (like their *Principals*) turned about their own Axis. And therefore I am not at all inclined to believe, that the *Menstrual* Period of the Tides with us, is to be salved by such an Hypothesis.

In stead of this, that *Surmise* of mine, (for I dare not yet, with confidence give it any better name,) of what I have spoken to you heretofore, (and which hath occasioned this present account which I am now giving you,) is to this purpose.

The Earth and Moon being known to be Bodies of so great connexion (whether by any Magnetick, or what other Tye, I will not determine; nor need I, as to this purpose;) as that {272}the motion of the one follows that of the other; (The Moon observing the Earth as the Center of its *periodick* motion:) may well enough be looked upon as *one Body*, or rather *one Aggregate of Bodies*, which have *one common center of Gravity*; which Center (according to the known Laws of *Staticks*) is in a streight Line connecting their respective Centers, so divided as that its parts be in reciprocal proportion to the Gravities of the two Bodies. As for Example; Suppose the Magnitude (and therefore probably, the Gravity) of the Moon to be about an *One and fourtieth part* of that of the Earth; (and thereabouts *Hevelius* in his*Selenography* page 203. doth out of *Tycho*, estimate the proportion; and an exact certainty is not necessary to our present businesse.) And the distance of the Moons Center from the Center of the Earth, to be about *fifty six Semidiameters* of the Earth, (as thereabouts he doth there estimate it, in its middle distance; and we need not be now very accurate in determining the numbers; wherein Astronomers are not yet very well agreed.) The distance of the Common Center of Gravity of the two Bodies, will be from that of the Earth, about a two and fourtieth part of fifty six Semidiameters; that is, about $^{56}/_{42}$ or $^4/_3$ of a Semidiameter; that is about $\frac{1}{3}$ of a Semidiameter of the Earth, above its surface, in the Air, directly between the Earth and Moon.

Now supposing the Earth and Moon, joyntly as one Body, carried about by the Sun in the great Orb of the *Annual* motion; this motion is to be estimated, (according to the Laws of*Staticks*, in other cases,) by the motion of the common Center of Gravity of both Bodies. For we use in *Staticks*, to estimate a Body, or Aggregate of Bodies, to be moved upwards, downwards, or otherwise, so much as its Common Center of Gravity is so moved, howsoever the parts may change places amongst themselves.

And accordingly, the Line of the *Annual* motion, (whether *Circular* or *Elliptical*; of which I am not here to dispute,) will be described, not by the Center of the Earth (as we commonly estimate it, making the Earth a Primary and the Moon a Secondary Planet,) nor by the Center of the Moon, (as they would do, who make the Moon the Primary and the Earth a {273}Secondary Planet, against which we were before disputing:) But by the *Common Center of Gravity of the Bodies, Earth and Moon*, as one Aggregate.

See Fig. 2. and 3.

Now supposing A B C D E to be a part of the great Orb of the *Annual*motion, described by the Common Center of Gravity, in so long time as from a *Full-Moon* at A to the next *New-Moon* at E; (which, though an Arch of a *Circle* or *Ellipse*, whose Center we suppose at a due distance below it; yet being put about $^1/_{25}$ of the whole, may well enough be here represented by a streight Line:) the Center of the Earth at T, and that of the Moon at L, must each of them (supposing their common Center of Gravity to keep the Line A E) be supposed to describe a *Periphery* about that Common Center, as the Moon describes her Line of *Menstrual* motion (Of which I have (in the *Scheme*) onely drawn that of the *Earth*; as being sufficient to our present purpose; parallel to which, if need be, we may suppose one described by the Moon; whose distance is also to be supposed much greater from T than in the *figure* is expressed, or was necessary to expresse.) And in like manner E F G H I, from that *New moon* at E, to the next *Full-moon* at I.

From A to E (from Full moon to New moon,) T moves (in its own *Epicycle*) upwards from the Sun: And from E to I, (from New moon to Full moon) it moves downwards, toward the Sun. Again, from C to G, (from last quarter to the following first quarter,) it moves *forwards according* to the *Annual* motion; But from G forward to C, (from the first Quarter to the ensuing last Quarter,) it moves *contrary* to the *Annual* motion.

It is manifest therefore, according to this Hypothesis, that from Last quarter to First quarter (from C to G, while T is above the Line of the *Annual* motion) its *Menstrual* motion in its Epicycle *adds* somewhat of Acceleration to the *Annual* motion, and most of all at E, the New-moon: And from the first to the last quarter (from G forward to C, while T is below the Line of the *Annual* motion,) it *abates* of the *Annual* motion; and most of all at I, or A the Full-moon.

So that in pursuance of *Galilæo's* Notion, the *Menstrual* {274} adding to or detracting from the *Annual* motion, should either leave behinde, or cast forward, the loose waters incumbent on the Earth, (and thereby cause a Tide, or accumulation of Waters) and most of all at the Full Moon and New-moon, where those Accelerations or Retardations are greatest.

Now this *Menstrual* motion, if nothing else were superadded to the *Annual*, would give us two Tides in a moneth, and no more; (the one upon the Acceleration, the other on the Retardation;) at New moon and Full-moon; and two Ebbs, at the two Quarters; and in the Intervals, Rising and Falling water.

But the *Diurnal* motion superadded, doth the same to this *Menstrual*, which *Galilæo* supposeth it to do to the *Annual*; that is, doth *Add* to, or *Subtract* from, the *Menstrual* Acceleration or Retardation; and so gives us Tide upon Tide.

For in whatsoever part of its Epicycle, we suppose T to be; yet because, while by its *Menstrual* motion the Center moves in the Circle L T N; each point in its surface, by its diurnal motion mòves in the Circle L M N: whatever effect (accelerative or tardative) the *Menstrual* would give, that effect by the *Diurnal* is increased in the parts L M N (or rather l M n. the Semicircle) and most of all at M: but diminished in the parts N O L (or rather n O l) and most of all at O. So that at M, and O, (that is when the Moon is in the *Meridian* below or above the *Horizon,*) we are to have the Diurnal Tide or High-water, occasioned by the greatest Acceleration or Retardation, which the *Diurnal* Arch gives to that of the *Menstrual*: which seems to be the true cause of the *Daily Tides.* And withall gives an account, not onely why it should be *every* day; but like wise, why at *such a time* of the day; and why this time should in a moneth run through the whole 24 hours; *viz.* because the Moons coming to the *Meridian* above and below the *Horizon,* (or as the Seamen call it, the *Moons Southing,* and *Northing,*) doth so: As likewise of the *Spring tides* and *Neap-tides.* For, when it so happens, that the *Menstrual* and *Diurnal* Accelerations or Retardations, be coincident, (as at New moons and Full-moons they are,) the effect must needs be the greater. And although (which is not to be dissembled) this happen {275} but to one of the two Tides; that is, the Night-tide at the New-moon (when both motions do most of all Accelerate,) and the Day-tide at Full-moon (when both do most Retard the *Annual* motion;) Yet, this tide being thus raised by two concurrent causes; though the next Tide have not the same cause also, the *Impetus* contracted will have influence upon the next Tide; Upon a like reason, as a *Pendulum* let fall from a higher Arch, will (though there be no new cause to occasion it) make the Vibration on the other side (beyond the Perpendicular) to be also greater: Or, of water in a broad Vessel, if it be so jogged, as to be cast forward to a good height above its Levell, will upon its recoyling, by its own gravity, (without any additional cause) mount so much the higher on the hinder part.

But here also we are to take notice, that though all parts of the Earth by its *Diurnal* motion do turn about its Axis, and describe *parallel* Circles; yet not *equal* Circles; but *greater* neer the *Æquinoctial,* and *lesser* near the *Poles,* which may be a cause why the Tides in some parts may be much greater than in others. But this belongs to the *particular* considerations, (of which we are not now giving an Account:) not to the *general* Hypothesis.

Having thus endeavoured to give an account of the *Diurnal* and *Menstrual* Periods of Tides; It remains that I endeavour the like as to the *Annual.* Of which there is, at least, thus much agreed; That, at some times of the year, the Tides are noted to be much higher, than at other times.

But here I have a double task; *First*, to rectify the Observation; and *then*, to give an account of it.

As to the *First*; It having been observed (grosly) that those high Tides have used to happen about the *Spring* and *Autumn*; it hath been generally taken for granted (without any more nice observation) that the *two Æquinoxes* are the proper times, to which these *Annual high Tides* are to be referred; And such causes sought for, as might best sute with such a Supposition.

But it is now, the best part of twenty years, since I have had frequent occasions to converse with some Inhabitants of *Rumney-marsh* in *Kent*; where the Sea being kept out with great Earthen walls, that it do not at high water overflow the Levell; {276}and the Inhabitants livelyhood depending most on grazing, or feeding Sheep; they are (as you may believe they have reason to be) very vigilant and observant, at what times they are most in danger of having their Lands drowned. And I find them generally agreed, by their constant Observations, (and Experience dearly bought) that their times of danger are about the beginning of *February* and of *November*, that is, at those Spring Tides which happen near those times; to which they give the names of *Candlemass-stream* and *Allhallond-stream*; And if they scape those Spring-tides, they apprehend themselves out of Danger for the rest of the year. And as for *March* and *September* (the two *Æquinoxes*) they are as little solicitous of them, as of any other part of the year.

This, I confess, I much wondred at, when I first heard it; and suspected it to be but a mistake of him, that first told me, though he were indeed a person not likely so to be mistaken, in a thing wherein he was so much concerned: But I soon found, that it was not only his, but a general observation of others too; both there, and elsewhere along the Sea coast. And though they did not pretend to know any reason of it, (nor so much as to enquire after it;) Yet none made doubt of it; but would rather laugh at any that should talk of *March* and *September*, as being the dangerous times. And since that time, I have my self very frequently observed (both at *London* and elsewhere, as I have had occasion), that in those months of *February* and *November*, (especially *November*), the Tides have run much higher, than at other times: Though I confess, I have not been so diligent to set down those Observations, as I should have done. Yet this I do particularly very well remember, that in *November* 1660. (the same year that his Majesty returned) having occasion to go by Coach from the *Strand* to *Westminster*, I found the Water so high in the middle of *King-street*, that it came up, not onely to the Boots, but into the Body of the Coach; and the *Pallace-yard* (all save a little place near the *West-End*) overflow'd; as likewise the Market-place; and many other places; and their Cellars generally filled up with Water. And in *November* last, 1665. it may yet be very well remembered, what very high Tides there were, not onely on the Coasts of *England*, (where much hurt was {277}done by it) but much more, in *Holland*, where by reason of those Inundations, many Villages and Towns were overflow'd. And though I cannot so particularly name other years, yet I can very safely say, that I very often observed Tides strangely high about those times of the year.

This Observation did for divers years cause me much to wonder, not only because it is so contrary to the received opinion of the two *Æquinoxes*; but because I could not think of any thing signal at those times of the year: as being neither the two *Æquinoxes*, nor the two *Solstices*, nor the Sun's *Apogæum* and *Perigæum*. (or Earths *Aphelium* and *Perihelium*;) nor indeed, at contrary times of the year, which at least, would seem to be expected. From *Alhollandtide* to *Candlemass* being but three months; and from thence to *Alhollandtide* again nine months.

At length it came into my mind, about four years since, that though there do not about these times happen any *single* signal Accident, which might cast it on these times, yet there is a *compound of two* that may do it; Which is the *Inequality* of the *Natural day* (I mean that of 24. hours, from noon to noon) arising at least from a double cause; either of which singly would cast it upon other times, but both joyntly on those.

It's commonly thought, how unequal soever the length be of the *Artificial* dayes as contradistinguished to nights, yet that the *Natural* Days, reckoning from noon to noon, are all *equal*: But *Astronomers* know well, that even these dayes are *unequal*.

For, this *Natural* Day is measured *not onely* by one intire conversion of the *Æquinoctial*, or 24. *Æquinoctial* hours, (which is indeed taken to be performed in equal times,) *but* increases by so much, as answers to that part of the *Sun's* (or *Earths*,) Annual motion as is performed in that time. For, when that part of the *Æquinoctial*, which (with the *Sun*) was the *Meridian* yesterday at noon, is come thither again to day, it is not yet *Noon* (because the Sun is not now at the place where yesterday he was, but is gone forward about one degree, more or less) but we must stay till that place, where the *Sun* now is, comes to the *Meridian* before it be now *Noon*.

Now this Additament (above the 24 *Æquinoctial* hours, or intire conversion of the *Æquinoctial*) is upon a double account {278} unequal. *First*, because the Sun, by reason of its *Apogæum* and *Perigæum*, doth not at all times of the year dispatch in one day an equal Arch of the *Ecliptick*; but greater Arches neer the *Perigæum*, which is about the middle of *December*; and lesser neer the *Apogæum*, which is about the middle of *June*: As will appear sufficiently by the *Tables* of the Sun's Annual motion. *Secondly*, though the Sun should in the *Ecliptick* move alwaies at the same rate; yet equal Arches of the *Ecliptick* do not in all parts of the *Zodiack* answer to equal Arches of the *Æquinoctial*, by which we are to estimate time: Because some parts of it, as about the two *Solsticial* Points, lie nearer to a *parallel* position to the *Æquinoctial*, than others, as those about the two *Æquinoctial* points, where the *Ecliptick* and *Æquinoctial* do intersect; whereupon an Arch of the *Ecliptick*, neer the *Solsticial* points answers to a greater Arch of the *Æquinoctial*, than an Arch equal thereunto neer the *Æquinoctial* points: As doth sufficiently appear by the *Tables* of the Suns *right Ascension*.

According to the *first* of these causes, we should have the longest *natural* daies in *December*, and the shortest in *June*, which if it did operate alone, would give us at those times two *Annual* High-waters.

According to the *second* cause, if operating singly, we should have the longest daies at the two Solstices in *June* and *December*, and the two shortest at the *Æquinoxes* in *March* and *September*; which would at those times give occasion of four *Annual* High-waters.

But the true *Inequality* of the Natural Days, arising from a *Complication of those two causes*, sometimes crossing and sometimes promoting each each other: though we should find some increases or decreases of the *Natural* daies at all those seasons answerable to the respective causes (and perhaps of Tides proportionably thereunto:) yet the longest and shortest *natural daies* absolutely of the whole year (arising from this complication of Causes) are about those times of *Allhallontide* and *Candlemas*, (or not far from them) about which those *Annual* High-tides are found to be: As will appear by the *Tables of Æquation* of *Natural* daies. And therefore I think, we may with very good reason cast this *Annual* Period upon that cause, or rather {279} complication of causes. For (as we before shewed in the *Menstrual* and *Diurnal*) there will, by this inequality of Natural daies, arise a *Physical* Acceleration and Retardation of the Earths *Mean* motion, and accordingly a casting of the Waters backward or forward; either of which, will cause an Accumulation or High-water.

'Tis true, that these longest and shortest daies, do (according to the *Tables*, some at least) fall rather before, than after *Alhallontide* and *Candlemas* (to wit the ends of *October* and *January*;) but so do also (sometimes) those high Tydes: And it is not yet so well agreed amongst *Astronomers*, what are all the Causes (and in what degrees) of the Inequality of Natural daies; but that there be diversities among them, about the true time: And whether the introducing of this New Motion of the Earth in its *Epicycle* about this Common Center of *Gravity*, ought not therein also to be accounted for, I will not now determine: Having already said enough, if not too much, for the explaining of this general Hypothesis, leaving the particularities of it to be adjusted according to the true measures of the motions; if the General Hypothesis be found fit to be admitted.

Yet this I must add, (that I be not mistaken) that whereas I cast the time of the daily Tydes to be at all places, when the Moon is there in the *Meridian*; it must be understood of *open* Seas, where the water hath such free scope for its motions, as if the whole Globe of Earth were equally covered with water: Well knowing, that in *Bayes* and *In land-Channels*, the position of the Banks and other like causes must needs make the times to be much different from what we suppose in the open Seas: And likewise, that even in the Open Seas, *Islands*, and *Currents*, *Gulfs* and *Shallows*, may have some influence, though not comparable to that of *Bays* and *Channels*. And moreover, though I think, that Seamen do commonly reckon the time of High-water in the *Open Seas*, to be then, when the Moon is there in the *Meridian* (as this Hypothesis would cast it:) Yet I do not take my self to be so well furnished with a *History of Tides*, as to assure my self of it; much less to accommodate it to particular places and cases.

Having thus dispatched the main of what I had to say {280} concerning the Seas Ebbing and Flowing: Had I not been already too tedious, I should now proceed to give a further reason, why I do introduce this consideration of the *Common Center of Gravity* in reference to *Astronomical Accounts*. For indeed, that which may possibly seem at first to be an Objection *against* it, is with me one reason *for* it.

It may be thought perhaps, that if the Earth should thus describe an *Epicycle* about the Common Center of Gravity, it would (by this its change of place) disturbe the *Cælestial* motions; and make the *apparent* places of the Planets, especially some of them, different from what they would otherwise be. For though so small a removal of the Earth, as the *Epicycle* would cause (especially if its *Semidiameter* should not be above 1⅓ of the Earths Semidiameter) would scarce be sensible (if at all) to the remoter Planets; yet as to the nearer it might.

Now though what *Galilæo* answers to a like Objection in his *Hypothesis*; (that its possible there may be some small difference, which *Astronomers* have not yet been so accurate, as to observe) might here perhaps serve the turn; Yet my answer is much otherwise; to wit, that such difference hath been observed and hath very much puzzeled *Astronomers* to give an account of. About which you will find Mr. *Horrocks* (in some of his Letters, whereof I did formerly, upon the Command of the *Royal Society*, make an *Extract*) was very much perplexed; and was fain, for want of other relief, to have recourse to somewhat like *Keplers* amicable *Fibres*, which did according to the several positions of the Moon, accelerate or retard the Moon's motion; which *amicable Fibres* he had no affection to at all (as there appears) if he could any other waies give account of those little inequalities; and would much rather (I doubt not) have embraced this Notion of the Common Center of Gravity, to salve the *Phænomenon*, had it come to his mind, or been suggested to him. And you find, that other *Astronomers* have been seen to bring in (some upon one supposition, some upon another) some kind of *Menstrual Æquation*, to solve the inequalities of the Moon's motion, according to her *Synodical* Revolution, or different Aspects (of New-moon, Full Moon, &c.) beside what concerns her own *Periodical* motion. {281}

For which, this consideration of the *Common Center of Gravity of the Earth and Moon*, is so proper a remedy (especially if it shall be found precisely to answer those *Phænomena*, which I have not Examined, but am very apt to believe) that it is so far from being, with me, an Objection against it, that it is one of the reasons, which make me inclinable to introduce it.

I must before I leave this, add one Consideration more, That if we shall upon these Considerations think it reasonable, thus to consider the *Common Center of Gravity of the Earth and Moon*; it may as well be thought reasonable, that the like Consideration should be had of *Jupiter* and his four *Satellites*, which according to the Complication of their several motions, will somewhat change the position of *Jupiter*, as to that *Common center of Gravity* of all these Bodies; which yet, because of their smallness, may chance to be so little, as that, at this distance, the change of his apparent place may not be discernable. And what is said of *Jupiter*, is in the like manner to be understood of *Saturne* and his *Satelles*, discovered by *Hugenius*. For all these *Satellites* are to their *Principals*, as so many Moons to the Earth. And I do very well remember, in the Letters forecited, Mr. *Horrocks* expresseth some such little inequalities in *Saturnes* motion, of which he could not imagine what account to give, as if (to use his Expression) this crabbed *Old Saturn* had despised his *Youth*. Which, for ought I know, might well enough have been accounted for, if at that time the *Satelles* of *Saturn* had been discovered, and that Mr. *Horrocks* had thought of such a notion as the *Common Center of Gravity* of *Saturn* and his *Companion*, to be considerable, as to the guiding of his motion.

You have now, in obedience to your Commands, an Account of my thoughts, as to this matter, though yet immature and unpolished: What use you will please to make of them, I shall leave to your prudence, &c.

An **APPENDIX,** *written by way of Letter to the* **Publisher***; Being an answer to some Objections, made by several Persons, to the precedent Discourse.*

I Received yours; and am very well contented, that *objections* be made against my*Hypothesis* concerning *Tydes*: being {282}proposed but as a conjecture to be examined; and, upon that Examination, rectified, if there be occasion; or rejected, if it will not hold water.

1. To the first objection of those you mention; *That it appears not how two Bodies, that have no tye, can have one common Center of Gravity:* that is (for so I understand the intendment of the objection) can act or be acted in the same manner, as if they were connected: I shall onely answer, that it is harder to shew *How* they have, than *That* they have it. That the Load-stone and Iron have somewhat equivalent to a Tye; though we see it not, yet by the effects we know. And it would be easy to shew, that two Load-stones, at once applyed, in different positions, to the same Needle, at some convenient distance, will draw it, not to point directly to either of them, but to some point between both; which point is, as to those two, the*common Center of Attraction;* and it is the same, as if some *one* Load-stone were in that point. Yet have these two Load stones no connection or tye, though a *Common Center of Virtue* according to which they joyntly act. And as to the present case, *How* the Earth and Moon are connected; I will not now undertake to shew (nor is it necessary to my purpose;) but, That there is somewhat, that doth connect them, (as much as what connects the Load-stone, and the Iron, which it draws,) is past doubt to those, who allow them to be carried about by the Sun, as one Aggregate or Body, whose parts keep a respective position to one another: Like as *Jupiter* with his *four Satellites,* and *Saturn* with his *one.* Some Tye there is, that makes those *Satellites* attend their *Lords,* and move in a Body; though we do not *See*that Tye; nor *Hear* the Words of Command. And so here.

2. To the second objection; *That, at Chatham and in the Thames, the Annual Spring-tydes, happen about the Æquinoxes; not (as this Hypothesis doth suppose elsewhere to have been observed) about the beginning of February and November.* If their meaning be, that Annual High Tydes, do then happen, and then onely: If this prove true, it will ease me of half my work. For it is then easily answered, that it depends upon the *Obliquity of the Zodiack;* the parts of the Æquinoctial answering to equal parts of the {283} *Zodiack,* being neer the Solstitial points greatest, and near the Æquinoctial points least of all. But beside this *Annual Vicissitude of the Æquinoxes,* not to say, of the 4. Cardinal Points (which my Hypothesis doth allow and assert;) I believe it will be found, that there is *another Annual vicissitude*answering to the Suns *Apogæum* and *Perigæum.* And that the greatest Tydes of all, will be found to be upon a result of these two causes Cooperating: which (as doth the Inequality of Natural dayes, depending on these same causes) will light nearer the times, I mention. To what is said to be observed at *Chatham* and in the *Thames,* contrary to that I allege as observed in *Rumney marsh:* I must at present ἀπέχειν, and refer to a *melius inquirendum.* If those who object this contrary observation, shall, after this notice, find, upon new Observations heedfully taken, that the *Spring-tydes* in *February* and *November,* are not so high, as those in *March* and *September,* I shall then think the objection very considerable. But I do very well remember, that I have seen in *November,* very high Tydes at *London,* as well as in *Rumney Marsh.* And, the time is not yet so far past, but that it may be remembered (by your self or others then in *London*) whether in *November* last when the Tydes were so high at *Dover,* at *Deal,* at *Margate,* and all along the Coast from thence to *Rumney Marsh,* as to do in some of those places much hurt, (and, in *Holland,* much more;) whether, I say, there were not also at the same time, at *London,* (upon the *Thames*) very high Tydes. But a good*Diary* of the Height and time both of High-water, and Low-water, for a year or two together, even at *Chatham,* or *Greenwich,* but rather at some place in the *open* Sea, or at the *Lands end* in *Cornwal,* or on the *West parts of Ireland;* or at

St. *Hellens*, or the *Bermodas*, &c. would do more to the resolving of this point, than any verbal discourse without it.

3. To the third Objection, *That supposing the Earth and Moon to move about a Common center of gravity; if that the highest Tydes be at the New-moon, when the moon being nearest to the Sun, the Earth is farthest from it, and its compound motion at the swiftest; and that the Tydes abate as the Earth approacheth nearer; till it comes into the supposed Circle of her Annual motion: It may be demanded, why do they not still abate as the Earth comes yet nearer to the Sun; and the {284} swiftnesse of its compound motion still slackens? And so, why have we not Spring tides at the New Moon (when the motion is swiftest) and Neap tides at Full Moon (when the motion is slowest) but Spring tides at both?* The answer (if observed) is already given in my *Hypothesis* it self. Because the effect is indifferently to follow, either upon a suddain Acceleration, or a suddain Retardation. (Like as a loose thing, lying on a moving body; if the body be thrust suddainly forward, that loose thing is cast back, or rather left behind, not having yet obtained an equal *impetus* with that of the body, on which it lyes; but if stopped, or notably retarded, that loose incumbent is thrown forward, by its formerly contracted *impetus* not yet qualified or accomodated to the slowness of the Body, on which it lyes.) Now both of these happening, the one at the New Moon, the other at the Full Moon, do cause high Tides at both.

4. To the fourth Objection, *That the highest Tydes are not at all places, about the New Moon and Full Moon; and particularly, that, in some places of the East Indies, the Highest Tydes are at the Quadratures.* I must first answer in *general*, That as to the particular varieties of Tydes in several parts of the World, I cannot pretend to give a satisfactory account, for want of a competent History of Tydes, *&c.* Because (as is intimated in what I wrote in the *general*) the various positions of Chanels, Bays, Promontories, Gulfs, Shallows, Currents, Trade-winds, *&c.* must needs make an innumerable variety of Accidents in particular places, of which no satisfactory account is to be given from the general *Hypothesis* (though never so true) without a due consideration of all those. Which is a task too great for me to undertake, being so ill furnished with materials for it. And then as to the particular instance of some places in the *East Indies*, where the highest Tydes are at the *Quadratures*. I suppose, it may be chiefly intended of those about *Cambaia*, and *Pegu*. At which places, beside that they are situate at the inmost parts of Vast Bayes, or Gulfs (as they are called) they have also vast In-draughts of some hundred Miles within Land; which when the Tydes are out, do lye (in a manner) quite dry: And may therefore very well be supposed to participate the effect of the Menstrual Tydes many dayes after the {285} cause of them happens in the open Sea, upon a like ground as in Straights and narrow Channels the Diurnall Tydes happen some hours later than in the Ocean. And a like account must be given of particular accidents in other places, from the particular situation of those places, as *Bays, Chanels, Currents*, &c.

5. To the 5. Objection, *That the Spring-Tydes happen not, with us, just at the Full and Change, but two or three daies after.* I should with the more confidence attempt an Answer, were I certain, whether it be so in the *Open* Seas, or onely in our Channels. For the Answers will not be the same in both cases. If onely in our Channels, where the Tydes find a large in-draught; but not in the Open Seas: we must seek the reason of it from the particular position of these places. But if it be so generally in the wide Open Seas: We must then seek a reason of it from the general Hypothesis. And, till I know the matter of Fact, I know not well, which to offer at; lest whilst I attempt to salve one, I should fall foul of the other. I know that Marriners use to speak of Spring-Tydes at the New and Full of the Moon; though I have still had a suspition that it might be some daies after, as well in the open Seas, as in our narrower Channels; (and therefore I have chosen to say, in my Papers, *About* the New and Full, rather than *At* the New and Full; and even when I do say *At*, I intend it in that laxer sense in which I suppose the Marriners are to be understood, for *Neer* that time:) Of which suspition you will find some intimations even in my first Papers: But this though I can admit; yet, because I was not sure of it, I durst not build upon it. The truth is, the Flux and Reflux of water in a vessel, by reason of the jogging of it, though it follow thereupon; yet is, for the most part, discernable some time after. For there must, upon that jog, be some time for Motion, before the Accumulation can have made a Tyde. And so I do not know but that we must allow it in all the Periods. For as the *menstrual* High Tyde, is not (at least with us) till some Daies after the Full and Change; so is the *Diurnal* High water, about as many Hours, after the Moons

comming to South; (I mean, At Sea: for in Chanels it varies to all Hours, according as they are neerer or further from the open Sea:) And the *Annual* High-Tydes of *November* and *February*; somewhat later than {286}(what I conjecture to be from the same causes) the greatest Inequalities of the natural Days, happening in *January* and *October*. But this though I can admit, yet (till I am sure of the matter of Fact) I do not build upon. And since it hath hitherto been the custome to speak with that laxness of expression; assigning the times of New-moon, Full-moon, and Quadratures, with the Moons comming to South, for, what is neer those times: I did not think myself obliged in my conjectural Hypothesis (while it is yet but a *Candidate*) to speak more nicely. If the Hypothesis for the maine of it be found Rational; the Niceties of it are to be adjusted, in time, from particular Observation.

Having thus given you some Answers to the Objections you signifie to have been made by several persons to my Hypothesis, and that in the same order your Paper presents them to me; I shall next give you some account of the two *Books*, which you advised me to consult; so far as seems necessary to this business; Which, upon your intimation, I have since perused, though before I had not.

And first, as to that of *Isaac Vossius, De motu Marium & Ventorum*; Though I do not concur with him in his Hypothesis; That all the *Great motions of the Seas*, &c. should arise onely from *so small a warming of the water* as to raise it (where most of all) *not a Foot* in perpendicular, (as in his 12*th* Chapter.) Or that there is no other connexion between the Moons motion, and the Tydes *menstrual* period, than a *casual Synchronism* (which seems to be the doctrine of his 16*th* and 18*th* Chapters;) Beside many other things in his Philosophy, which I cannot allow: Yet I am well enough pleased with what is Historical in it, of the matter of Fact: Especially if I may be secure, that he is therein accurate and candid, not wresting the *Phænomena* to his own purpose. But I find nothing in it, which doth induce me to vary from my Hypothesis. For, granting his Historicals to be all true; the account of the constant Current of the Sea Westward, and of the constant Eastern Blasts, &c. within the *Tropicks*, is much more plausibly, and (I suppose) truly rendered by *Galilæo* long since, from the Earths *Diurnal* motion: (which, neare the *Æquator*, describing a greater Circle, than nearer the {287}*Poles*, makes the Current to be there more conspicuous and swift, and consequently, the Eddy, or recurrent motion, nearer the Poles, where this is, more remiss:) than can easily be rendered by so small a Tumor, as he supposeth. Not to adde; that his account of the Progressive motion, which he fansieth to follow upon this Tumefaction, and by Acceleration to grow to so great a height near the Shoar (as in Chap. 13. and 14.) is a Notion, which seems to me too extravagant to be salved by any laws of *Staticks*. And that of the Moons motion onely Synchronizing with the Tydes, casually, without any *Physical* connexion; I can very hardly assent to. For it can hardly be imagined, that any such constant *Synchronisme* should be in Nature; but where, either the one is the cause of the other, or both depend upon some *Common* cause. And where we see so fair a foundation for a *Physical* connection. I am not prone to ascribe it to an Independent Sychronism. In sum; His History doth well enough agree with my Hypothesis; and I think, the Phænomena are much better salved by mine, than his.

And then as to *Gassendus*, in his discourse *De Æstu Maris*; I find him, after the relating of many other Opinions concerning the Cause of it, inclining to that of *Galilæo*, ascribing it to the Acceleration & Retardation of the Earths motion, compounded of the Annual and Diurnal; And moreover attempting to give an account of the *Menstrual Periods* from the Earths carrying the Moon about it self, as *Jupiter* doth his *Satellites*; which together with them is carryed about by the *Sun*, as one Aggregate; (and that the Earth with its Moon is to be supposed in like manner to be carried about by the Sun, as one Aggregate, cannot be reasonably doubted, by those who entertain the *Copernican Hypothesis*, and do allow the same of *Jupiter* and his *Satellites*.) But though he would thus have the Earth and Moon looked upon as two parts of the same moved Aggregate, yet he doth still suppose (as *Galilæo* had done before him) that the line of the Mean Motion of this Aggregate (or, as he calls, *motus æquabilis et veluti medius*) is described by the *Center* of the *Earth* (about which Center he supposeth both its own revolution to be made, and an Epicycle described by the Moons motion;) not by another Point, distinct from the Centers of both, about which, as the {288} common Center of Gravity, as well that of the Earth, as that of the Moon, are to describe several Epicycles.

And, for that Reason fails of giving any clear account of this *Menstrual* Period. (And in like manner, he proposeth the Consideration as well of the Earths *Aphelium* and *Perihelium* as of the *Æquinoctial* and *Solstitial* Points,   in   order   to   the   finding   a   Reason   of the *Annual* Vicissitudes; but doth not fix upon any thing, in which himself can Acquiesce: And therefore leaves it *in medio* as he found it.)

It had been more agreeable to the Laws of *Staticks*, if he had, (as I do,) so considered the *Earth* and *Moon* as two parts of the same movable, (not so, as he doth, *aliam in Centro et sequentem præcise revolutionem axis, aliam remotius ac velut in circumferentia,* but,) so, as to make neither of them the Center, but both out of it, describing Epicycles about it: Like as, when a long stick thrown in the Air, whose one end is heavyer than the other, is whirled about, so as that the End, which did first fly foremost, becomes hindmost; the proper line of motion of this whole Body is not that, which is described by either End, but that, which is described by a middle point between them; about which point each end, in whirling, describes an Epicycle. And indeed, in the present case, it is not the Epicycle described by the Moon, but that, described by the Earth, which gives the *Menstrual* Vicissitudes of motion to the Water; which would, as to this, be the same, if the Earth so move, whether there were any Moon to move or not; nor would the Moons Motion, supposing the Earth to hold on its own course, any whit concern the motion of the Water.

But now, (after all our Physical, or Statical Considerations) the clearest Evidence for this Hypothesis (if it can be had) will be from Celestial Observations. As for instance; (see *Fig.* 5.) Supposing the Sun at S; the Earths place in its Annual Orb at T; and *Mars* (in opposition to the Sun, or near it) at M: From whence *Mars* should appear in the Zodiack at γ, and will at Full moon be seen there to be; the Moon being at C and the Earth at c; (and the like at the New-moon.) But if the Moon be in the First quarter at A, and the Earth at a: *Mars* will be seen, not at γ, but at α; too slow: And when the Moon is at B, and the Earth at b, *Mars* will be seen at β; yet too slow: till at the {289} Full-moon, the Moon at C, the Earth at c, *Mars* will be seen at γ, its true place, as if the Earth were at T. But then, after the Full, the Moon at D, the Earth at d; *Mars* will be seen, not at γ, but at δ, too forward: and yet more, when the Moon (at the last Quarter) is at E, the Earth at e, and *Mars* seen at ϵ. If therefore *Mars* (when in opposition to the Sun) be found (all other allowances being made) somewhat too backward before the Full moon, and somewhat too forward after the Full-moon, (and most of all, at the Quadratures:) it will be the best confirmation of the Hypothesis. (The like may be fitted to *Mars* in other positions, *mutatis mutandis*; and so for the other Planets.)

But this proof, is of like nature as that of the Parallaxis of the Earths Annual Orb to prove the Copernican Hypothesis. If it can be observed, it proves the Affirmative; but if it cannot be observed, it doth not convince the Negative, but only proves that the Semidiameter of the Earths Epicycle is so small as not to make any discernable Parallax. And indeed, I doubt, that will be the issue. For the Semidiameter of this Epicycle, being little more than the Semidiameter of the Earth it self, or about $1\frac{1}{3}$ thereof (as is conjectured, in the *Hypothesis*, from the Magnitudes and Distances of the Earth and Moon compared;) and there having not as yet been observed any discernable *Parallax* of *Mars*, even in his neerest position to the Earth; it is very suspicious, that here it may prove so too. And whether any of the other Planets will be more favourable in this point, I cannot say.

ANIMADVERSIONS *of Dr.* Wallis, *upon Mr.* Hobs's *late Book,* De Principiis & Ratiocinatione Geometrarum.

These were communicated by way of Letter, written in *Oxford*, July 24. 1666. to an Acquaintance of the *Author*, as follows:

Since I saw you last, I have read over Mr. *Hobs*'s Book *Contra Geometras* (or *De Principiis & Ratiocinatione Geometrarum*) which you then shewed me. A New Book of *Old* matter: Containing but a *Repetition* of what he had before told us, more than once; and which hath been Answered long agoe.

In which, though there be Faults enough to offer ample {290} matter for a large Confutation; yet I am scarce inclined to believe, that any will bestow so much pains upon it. For, if that be true, which (in his *Preface*) he saith of himself, *Aut solus insanio Ego, aut solus non insanio*: it would either be *Needless*, or *to no Purpose*. For, by his own confession, *All others*, if they be not mad themselves, ought to think *Him* so: And therefore, as to *Them* a Confutation would be *needless*; who, its like, are well enough satisfied already: at least out of danger of being seduced. And, as to himself, it would be *to no purpose*. For, if *He* be the Mad man, it is not to be hoped that he will be convinced by Reason: Or, if *All We* be so; we are in no capacity to attempt it.

But there is yet another Reason, why I think it not to need a Confutation. Because what is in it, hath been sufficiently confuted already; (and, so Effectually; as that he professeth himself not to Hope, that *This Age* is like to give sentence for him; what ever *Nondum imbuta Posteritas* may do.) Nor doth there appear any Reason, why he should again Repeat it, unless he can hope, That, what was at first False, may by oft Repeating, become True.

I shall therefore, instead of a large Answer, onely give you a brief Account, *what is in it*; &,*where it hath been already Answered.*

The chief of what he hath to say, in his first 10 Chapters, against *Euclids* Definitions, amounts but to this, That he thinks, *Euclide* ought to have allowed his *Point* some *Bigness*; his *Line*, some *Breadth*; and his *Surface*, some *Thickness*.

But where in his *Dialogues*, pag. 151, 152. he solemnly undertakes to Demonstrate it; (for it is there, his 41th *Proposition*:) his Demonstration amounts to no more but this; That, *unless a Line be allowed some Latitude; it is not possible that his Quadratures can be True*. For finding himself reduced to these inconveniences; 1. That his *Geometrical Constructions*, would not consist with *Arithmetical calculations*, nor with what *Archimedes* and others have long since demonstrated: 2. That the *Arch* of a Circle must be allowed to be sometimes *Shorter* than its *Chord*, and sometimes *longer* than its *Tangent*: 3. That the same Straight Line must be allowed, at one place onely to *Touch*, and at another place to *Cut* the same Circle: (with others of like nature;) He findes it necessary, that these things may not seem Absurd, to allow his *Lines* some *Breadth*, (that so, as he speaks, *While a Straight Line with its Out-side doth at one place* {291} *Touch the Circle, it may with its In-side at another place Cut it*, &c.) But I shou'd sooner take this to be a *Confutation of His Quadratures*, than a *demonstration of the Breadth of a* (Mathematical) *Line*. Of which, see my *Hobbius Heauton-timorumenus*, from *pag.* 114. to *p.* 119.

And what he now Adds, being to this purpose; That though *Euclid*'s Σημεῖον, which we translate, *a Point*, be not indeed *Nomen Quanti*; yet cannot this be actually represented by any thing, but what will have some Magnitude; nor can a *Painter*, no not *Apelles* himself, draw a *Line* so small, but that it will have some Breadth; nor can *Thread* be spun so Fine, but that it will have some Bigness; (*pag.* 2, 3, 19, 21.) is nothing to the Business; For *Euclide* doth not speak either of such *Points*, or of such *Lines*.

He should rather have considered of his own Expedient, *pag.* 11. That, when one of his (*broad*) Lines, passing through one of his (*great*) Points, is supposed to cut another Line proposed, into two equal parts; we are to understand, the *Middle of the breadth* of that Line, passing through the *middle* of that Point, to distinguish the Line given into two equal parts. And he should then have considered further, that *Euclide*, by a *Line*, means no more than what Mr. *Hobs* would call *the middle of the breadth* of his; and *Euclide*'s *Point*, is but the *Middle* of Mr. *Hobs*'s. And then, for the same reason, that Mr. *Hobs*'s *Middle* must be said to have no *Magnitude*; (For else, not the *whole Middle*, but the *Middle of the Middle*, will be *in the Middle*: And, the *Whole* will not be equal to its *Two Halves*; but Bigger than *Both*, by so much as the *Middle* comes to:) *Euclide*'s *Lines* must as well be said to have no Breadth; and his *Points* no Bigness.

In like manner, When *Euclide* and others do make the *Terme* or *End* of a Line, a *Point*: If this *Point* have *Parts* or *Greatness*, then not the *Point*, but the *Outer-Half* of this Point ends the Line, (for, that the *Inner-Half* of that Point is not at the End, is manifest, because the *Outer-Half* is beyond it:) And again, if that *Outer Half* have *Parts* also; not this, but

136

the *Outer* part of it, and again the *Outer part* of that *Outer part*, (and so in *infinitum.*) So that, as long as *Any thing of Line* remains, we are not yet at the *End*: And consequently, if we must have passed the *whole Length*, before we be at the *End*; then that *End* (or *Punctum terminans*) has *nothing of Length*; (for, when the *whole Length* is past, there is nothing of it left.) And if Mr. *Hobs* tells us (as *pag.* 3.) that this {292} *End* is not *Punctum*, but only *Signum* (which he does allow *non esse nomen Quanti*) even *this* will serve our turn well enough. *Euclid*'s Σημεῖον, which some Interpreters render by *Signum*, others have thought fit (with *Tully*) to call *Punctum*: But if Mr. *Hobs* like not that name, we will not contend about it. Let it be *Punctum*, or let it be *Signum* (or, if he please, he may call it *Vexillum.*) But then he is to remember, that this is only a Controversie in *Grammar*, not in *Mathematicks*. And his Book should have been intitled *Contra Grammaticos*, not, *Contra Geometras*. Nor is it *Euclide*, but *Cicero*, that is concern'd, in rendring the Greek Σημεῖον by the Latine *Punctum*, not by Mr. *Hobs*'s *Signum*. The Mathematician is equally content with either word.

What he saith here, *Chap.* 8. & 19. (and in his fifth *Dial. p.* 105. *&c.*) concerning the *Angle of Contact*; amounts but to thus much, That, by the *Angle of Contact*, he doth not mean either what *Euclide* calls an *Angle*, or any thing of that kind; (and therefore says nothing to the purpose of what was in controversie between *Clavius* and *Peletarius*, when he says, that *An Angle of Contact hath some magnitude*:) But, that by the *Angle of Contact*, he understands the *Crookedness of the Arch*; and in saying, the *Angle of Contact hath some magnitude*, his meaning is, that the *Arch of a Circle hath some crookedness*, or, is a *crooked line*: and that, of equal Arches, That is the more crooked, whose chord is shortest: which I think none will deny; (for who ever doubted, but that a *circular Arch is crooked*? or, that, of such Arches, equal in length, *That is the more crooked, whose ends by bowing are brought nearest together*?) But, why the *Crookedness of an Arch*, should be called an *Angle of Contact*, I know no other reason, but, because Mr. *Hobs* loves to call that *Chalk*, which others call *Cheese*. Of this see my *Hobbius Heauton-timorumenus*, from *pag.* 88. to *p.* 100.

What he saith here of *Rations* or *Proportions*, and their *Calculus*, for 8. Chapters together, (*Chap.* 11. *&c.*) is but the same for substance, what he had formerly said in his 4th. Dialogue, and elsewhere. To which you may see a full Answer, in my *Hobbius Heauton-tim.* from *pag.* 49. to *p.* 88. which I need not here repeat.

Onely (as a *Specimen* of Mr. *Hobs*'s Candour, in Falsifications) you may by the way observe, how he deals a Demonstration of Mr. *Rook*'s, in confutation of Mr. *Hobs*'s Duplication of the Cube. Which when he had repeated, *pag.* 43. He doth then (that it might seem absurd) change those words, *æquales* {293} *quatuor cubis* DV; (*pag.* 43. *line* 33.) into these (*p.* 44. *l.* 5.) *æqualia quatuor Lineis, nempe quadruplus Recta* DV: And would thence perswade you, that Mr. *Rook* had assigned a *Solide*, equal to a *Line*. But Mr. *Rook's* Demonstration was clear enough without Mr. *Hobse's* Comment. Nor do I know any Mathematician (unless you take *Mr. Hobs* to be one) who thinks that *a Line multiplyed by a Number will make a Square*, (what ever Mr. *Hobs* is pleased to teach us.) But, That *a Number multiplyed by a Number, may make a Square Number*; and, That *a Line drawn into a Line may make a Square Figure*, Mr. *Hobs* (if he were, what he would be thought to be) might have known before now. Or, (if he had not before known it) he might have learned, (by what I shew him upon a like occasion, in my *Hob. Heaut. pag.* 142. 143. 144.) *How* to understand that language, without an Absurdity.

Just in the same manner he doth, in the next page, deal with *Clavius*, for having given us his words, pag. 45 l. 3. 4. *Dico hanc Lineam Perpendicularem extra circulum cadere* (because neither *intra Circulum*, nor in *Peripherea*;) He doth, when he would shew an errour, first make one, by falsifying his word, *line* 15. where instead of *Lineam Perpendicularem*, he substitutes *Punctum A.* As if *Euclide* or *Clavius* had denyed the *Point A.* (the utmost point of the *Radius*,) to be in the Circumference: Or, as if Mr. *Hobs*, by proving the *Point A.* to be in the Circumference, had thereby proved, that the *Perpendicular Tangent A E* had also lyen in the Circumference of the Circle. But this is a Trade, which Mr. *Hobs* doth drive so often, as if he were as well faulty in his *Morals*, as in his *Mathematicks*.

The *Quadrature of a Circle*, which here he gives us, *Chap.* 20. 21. 23. is one of those *Twelve* of his, which in my *Hobbius Heauton-timorumenus* (from *pag.* 104. to *pag.* 119) are already confuted: And is the *Ninth* in order (as I there rank them) which is particularly considered,*pag*. 106. 107. 108. I call it *One*, because he takes it so to be; though it might as well be called *Two*. For, as there, so here, it consisteth of *Two branches*, which are Both false; and each overthrow the other. For if the *Arch of a Quadrant* be equal to the *Aggregate of the Semidiameter and of the Tangent of 30. Degrees*, (as he would *Here* have it, in *Chap*. 20. and *There*, in the close of *Prop*. 27;) Then is it not equal to *that Line, Whose Square is equal to Ten squares of the Semiradius*, (as, *There*, he would have it, in *Prop*. 28. and, *Here*, in*Chap*. 23.) And if it be equal to *This*, then not to *That*. For *This*, and *That*, are not equal: As I then demonstrated; and need not now repeat it.

The grand Fault of his Demonstration (*Chap*. 20.) wherewith he would now New vamp his old false quadrature, lyes in those Words *Page* 49. *line* 30, 31. *Quod Impossibile est nisi* ba*transeat per* c. which is no impossibility at all. For though he first bid us *draw the Line* R *c*, and afterwards the *Line* R *d*; Yet, Because he hath no where proved (nor is it true) that *these two are the same Line*; (that is, that the point *d* lyes in the *Line* R *c*, or that R *c* passeth through *d*:) His proving that R *d cuts off from* ab *a Line equal to the Sine of* R *c*, doth not prove, that *ab* passeth through *c*: For this it may well do though *ab* lye *under c*. (vid. in case*d* lye beyond the line R *c*. that is, further from *A*:) And therefore, unless he first prove (which he cannot do) that *A c* (a sixth part of *A* D) doth just reach to the line R *c* and no further, he only proves {294}that a sixth part of *ab* is *equal* to the Sine of B *c*. But, whether it *lye above it*, or*below* it, or (as Mr. *Hobs* would have it) just *upon* it; this argument doth not conclude. (And therefore *Hugenius's* assertion, which Mr. *Hobs, Chap*. 21. would have give way to this Demonstration, doth, notwithstanding this, remain safe enough.)

His demonstration of *Chap*. 23. (where he would prove, that *the aggregate of the Radius and of the Tangent of 30. Degrees* is equal to *a Line, whose square is equal to 10 Squares of the Semiradius*;) is confuted not only by me, (in the place forecited, where this is proved to be impossible;) but by himself also, in this same Chap. *pag*. 59. (where he proves sufficiently and doth confesse, that this demonstration, and the 47. *Prop*. of the first of *Euclide*, cannot be both true.) But, (which is worst of all;) whether *Euclid's* Proposition be False or True, his demonstration must needs be False. for he is in this Dilemma: If that Proposition be *True*, his demonstration is *False*, for he grants that they cannot be both True, *page* 59 *line* 21. 22. And again, if that Proposition be False, his Demonstration is so too; for *This* depends upon *That*,*page* 55. *line* 22. and therefore must fall with it.

But the Fault is obvious in *His Demonstration* (not in *Euclid's Proposition*:) the grand Fault of it (though there are more) lyes in those words, *page* 56. *line* 26. *Erit ergo* M O *minus quam* M R Where, instead of *minus*, he should have said *majus*. And when he hath mended that Error, he will find, that the *major* in *page* 56. *line penult*, will very well agree with*majorem* in *page* 57. *line* 4 (where the *Printer* hath already mended the Fault to his hand) and then the *Falsum ergo* will vanish.

His Section of an Angle *in ratione data, Chap*. 22 hath no other foundation, than his supposed *Quadrature* of *Chap*. 20. And therefore, that being false, this must fall with it. It is just the same with that of his 6. Dialogue, *Prop*. 46. which (besides that it wants a foundation) how absurd it is, I have already shewed, in my *Hobbius Heauton-timor. page*119. 120.

His *Appendix*, wherein he undertakes to shew a Method of finding *any number of mean Proportionals, between two Lines given*: Depends upon the supposed Truth of his 22. Chapter; about *Dividing an Arch in any proportion given*: (As himself professeth: and as is evident by the Construction; which supposeth such a Section.) And therefore, that failing, this falls with it.

And yet this is other wise faulty, though *that* should be supposed True. For, In the first Demonstration; *page* 67. *line* 12. *Producta* L *f incidet in* I; is not proved, nor doth it follow from his *Quoniam igitur*.

In the second Demonstration; *page* 68. *line* 34. 35. *Recta* L *f incidit in* x; is not proved; nor doth it follow from his *Quare*.

In his third Demonstration; *page* 71: *line* 7. *Producta* Y P *transibit per* M; is said *gratis*; nor is any proof offered for it. And so this whole structure falls to the ground. And withall, the*Prop*. 47. *El*. 1 doth still stand fast (which he tells us, *page* 59, 61, 78. must have Fallen, if his Demonstrations had stood:) And so, *Geometry* and *Arithmetick* do still agree, which (he tells us, *page* 78: *line* 10.) had otherwise been at odds.

And this (though much more might have been said,) is as much as need to be said against that Piece.

Printed with Licence for *John Martyn*, and *James Allestry*, Printers to the Royal Society. {295}

Num. 17.

PHILOSOPHICAL
TRANSACTIONS.

Munday, Septemb. 9. 1666.

The Contents.

Observations made in several places (at London, Madrid *and* Paris,*) of the late* Eclipse of the Sun, *which hapned* June 22. 1666. *Some Enquiries and Directions, concerning*Tides, *proposed by* Dr. Wallis. *Considerations and Enquiries touching the same Argument, suggested by Sir* Robert Moray. *An Account of several Books lately publish't: Vid. 1.* Johannis Hevelii Descriptio Cometæ, *A. 1665. exorti; una cum*Mantissa Prodromi Cometici. *2.* Isaacus Vossius de Nili & aliorum Fluminum Origine. *3.* Le Discernement du Corps & de l'Ame, *par Monsieur de* Cordemoy.

Observations made in several places, Of the late Eclipse *of the Sun, which hapned on the 22 of* June, *1666.*

The Observations that were made at *London* by Mr. *Willughby*, Dr. *Pope*, Mr. *Hook*, and Mr.*Philips*, are these:

The Eclipse began   t 5h.   3′

	$3/11$			5		
diam.	t 6.	0	dig.		t 7.	6
	4			4		
digits	t 6.	7	dig.		t 7.	3
	5			3		
dig.	t 6.	3	dig.		t 7.	0
	6			2		
dig.	t 6.	1	dig.		t 7.	6
	7			1		
dig.	t 6.	9½	dig.		t 7.	2
	6			0		
dig.	t 6.	7	dig.		t 7.	7

It was darkned,

Its *Duration* hence appears to have been one hour and 54 m. Its *greatest Obscurity*somewhat more than 7. digits. About the middle, between the Perpendicular and Westward Horizontal *Radius* the Sun, viewing it through Mr. *Boyle's* 60. foot-*Telescope*, there was perceived a little of the Limb of the Moon without the Diske of the Sun: which seemed to some of the Observers to come from some shining *Atmosphere* about the Body either of the Sun or Moon.

They affirm to have observ'd the *Figure* of this *Eclipse*, and measured the {296}*Digits*, by casting the *Figure* through a 5 foot *Telescope*, on an extended paper, fix't at a certain distance from the Eye-glasse, and having a round figure; all whose *Diameters* were divided, by 6*Concentrick* Circles, into 12 *Digits*.

The Observations made at *Madrid* by a Noble Member of the *Royal Society*, His Excellence the Earle of *Sandwich*, as they were sent to the Right Honourable, the Lord Vice-Count*Brounker*, are these;

The Eclipse *began* at *Madrid* about 5 of the Clock in the morning, at 5 h. 15', the Suns *Altitude* was 6 deg. 55'.

The *Middle* of it was at 6 h. 2', the Suns *Altitude*, 15. deg. 5'.

The *End* was exactly at 7 h. 5'; the Suns *Altitude*, 25. deg. 24'.

The *Duration*, 2h. 4'.

37. Parts of the Suns diameter remained light.

63. Parts of the same were darkened.

The Observations made at *Paris* by Monsieur *Payen*, assisted by several *Astronomers*, as they were printed in *French*, and addressed to Monsieur de *Montmor*, are these;

The *Eclipse* began there, at 5 h. 44'. 52". *mane*. It ended at 7 h. 43'. 6". So that its *whole Duration* was 1 h. 58'. 14". The *greatest Obscuration* they assign to have been 7. dig. 50. m. but they adde, that it seem'd to have been greater by 3 minuts; which M. *Payen* imputes to a particular motion of *libration* of the Suns Globe, which entertain'd that Luminary in the same *Phasis* for the space of 8. *min.* and some *seconds*, as if it had been stopped in the midst of its Course; rather than to a tremulous Motion of the *Atmosphere*, as *Scheiner* would have it.

They intimate that they took the time of each *Phasis* from half *digit* to half *digit*, as well by a *Pendulum*, as by the *Altitudes* of the *Suns Center* above the *Horizon*, corrected by the *Verticall Paralaxes* and *Æstivall Refractions*, by which they judged, that though the Time by the *Pendulum* may be sufficient for *Mechanicall* Operations, yet 'tis not exact enough for establishing the *Grounds of true Astronomy*.

They further conceive that the apparent *Diameters* were almost equal; seeing that in the *Phasis* of 6. *Digits*, the *Circumference* of the *Moons disk* passed through the *Center* of that of the *Sun*, so as that two Lines drawn through the two *Horns* of the Sun, made with the *Common Semi-diameter* two *Equilateral Triangles*.

Next, they affirm, That there was so great a Variation in the *Parallaxes*, by reason as well of the Refractions of the Air, which environs the Earth, as of the Alteration of the Air, which encompasses the Moon, that the *Horns* of the Sun, there formed by the Shaddow of the Moon, appeared in all kinds of *Figures*; Sometimes inclined to the *Vertical*, sometimes *Perpendicular* to the *Horizon*, and at last *Parallel*; the *Convexe* part respecting the *Heaven*, and the *Concave*, the *Horizon*. By the crossing (*so they go on*) of the {297} *Horns* with the *Angles of Inclination*, it will be easie to those, that have exactly observed them, and that are skill'd in the higher *Astronomical* Calculations, to compute the *true Place* of the *Moon* in her *Orbite*, that so it may be compared with that of the *Tables*, and with that, which has been observ'd in other places, for the more precise determinating of the *Difference of Meridians* (that being the way, esteem'd by *Kepler* the most certain) and for making a good Judgment of the defect or exactnesse of the Celestial *Tables*.

Then they observe, That the *Beginning* and the *Middle* of this *Eclipse* hapned to be in the *North Eastern Hemisphere*, and the *End*, in the *South-Eastern*. The *first Contact* (as 'twere) of the two Disks was observ'd in the *Superior Limb* of the *Suns Disk* in respect to the *Vertical Line*, and in the *Inferior* in respect to the *Ecliptick*: But the *Middle*, and the *End* were seen in the *Superior Limb*, in respect both to the *Vertical* and the *Ecliptick*: And (what to this Author seems extraordinary) both the *Beginning* and the *End* of this *Eclipse* hapned to be in the *Oriental* part of the Suns Disk.

Lastly, they take notice, that by their Observations it appears, that there is but little exactness in all the *Astronomical Tables*, predicting the *Quantity*, *Beginning* and *Duration* of this Eclipse; Those of *Lansbergius* importing, That the Obscuration should be of 10. dig. 48'; those of *Ricciolo*, of 9. dig. 1'; and those of *Kepler*, of 7. dig. 30'. 16": Again, that the *Duration* should be of 2h. 2'. Lastly, The *Beginning* did anticipate the *Ricciolan Tables* by 5 *minuts*, the *End* by 23; and the *Middle*, almost by 11. In the mean time the Author notes, that the *Rudolphin Tables* come nearest to the Truth; and withal assures the *Reader* of the goodnesse of the *Instruments* employed in his *Observations*, and of the singular care, he, together with his skilful Assistants, took in making them.

Some Inquiries and Directions concerning **Tides**, *proposed by Dr.* **Wallis**, *for the proving, or disproving of his lately publish't* **Discourse** *concerning them.*

The Inquisitive Dr. *Wallis*, having in his lately printed *Hypothesis* of Tides intimated, that he had reason to believe, that the *Annual Spring-tides* happen to be rather about the beginnings of *Febr.* and *Nov.* than the two *Æquinoxes*, doth in a late Letter to the *Publisher*, written from *Oxford* in *Aug.* last, desire, that some understanding Persons at *London*, or *Greenwich*, but rather nearer the Sea, or upon the Sea-shore, would make *particular* Observation of all the *Spring-Tides* (*New-Moon* and *Full-Moon*) between this and the End of *November*; and take account of the *Hour*, and of the *Perpendicular height*: that we may see, whether those in *September*, or those of *November* be highest: And it were not amiss, the Low waters were observed too. Which may be easily done by a mark made upon any standing Post in the Water, by any {298}Water-man, or other understanding Person, who dwells by the Water-side.

It would also deserve (thinks he) to be inquired into, whether, when the Tides be highest, the Ebbs be ever lowest, & *contra*; (which is generally affirmed, and almost put out of question) or rather (which sutes best with this *Hypothesis*) whether, when the Tides are highest, both in the *Annual* and *Menstrual* Periods, the Low waters be not also highest; and at Neap Tides, the Ebbes also very low.

He adds, that he should expect, that the Spring Tides now coming, and those at the beginning of *September*, should not be so high, as those at the *middle* of *September*; and then lower again at the *beginning* of *October*, and after that, higher at the *middle* of *October*, and higher yet about the *beginning* of *November* (at the usual times of *Spring-tides* after the *New* and *Full*.)

Considerations and Enquiries concerning **Tides**, *by Sir* **Robert Moray**; *likewise for a further search into Dr.* **Wallis's** *newly publish't* **Hypothesis.**

In regard that the High and Low waters are observed to increase, and decrease regularly at several seasons, according to the Moons age, so as, about the *New* and *Full Moon*, or within two or three daies after, in the Western parts of *Europe*, the *Tides* are at the *highest*, and about the *Quarter-Moons*, at the *lowest*, (the former call'd *Spring-tides*, the other *Neap-tides*,) and that according to the height and excesses of the *Tides*, the *Ebbes* in opposition are answerable to them, the highest Tide having the lowest Ebbe, and the lowest Ebbe, the highest Tide; the Tides from the *Quarter* to the *highest Spring-tide* increasing in a certain proportion; and from the *Spring tide* to the *Quarter-tide* decreasing in like proportion, as is supposed: And also the *Ebbes* rising and falling constantly after the same manner: It is wished, that it may be inquired, in what proportion these Increases and Decreases, Risings and Fallings happen to be in regard of one another?

And 'tis supposed, upon some Observations, made in fit places, by the above-mentioned Gentleman, though, (as himself acknowledges) not thoroughly and exactly performed, that the Increase of the Tides is made in the *Proportion* of *Sines*, the first Increase exceeding the lowest in a small proportion; the next in a greater; the third greater than that; and so on to the mid-most, whereof the excess is greatest, diminishing again from that, to the highest Spring-Tide; so as the proportions, before and after the *Middle*, do greatly answer one another, or seem to do so. And likewise, from the *highest Spring-tide*, to the *lowest Neap-tide*, the *Decreases* seem to keep the like proportions; the *Ebbes* rising and falling in like manner and in like proportions. All which is supposed to fall out, when no Wind or other Accident causes an alteration. {299}

And whereas 'tis observed, that upon the main Sea-shore the Current of the Ebbings and Flowings is sometimes swifter, and sometimes slacker, than at others, so as in the beginning of the Floud the Tide moves faster but in a small degree, increasing its swiftness constantly till towards the *Middle* of the Floud; and then decreasing in velocity again from the *Middle* till to the top of the High water; it is supposed, that in Equal spaces of Time, the Increase and Decrease of velocity, and consequently the degrees of the Risings and Fallings of the same, in Equal spaces of time, are according to the *Proportion* of *Sines*.

But 'tis withall conceived, that the said *Proportion* cannot hold *exactly* and *precisely*, in regard of the *Inequalities*, that fall out in the *Periods* of the *Tides*, which are commonly observed and believed to follow certain *Positions* of the *Moon* in regard of the *Equinox*, which are known not to keep a *precise* and *constant* Course: so that, there not intervening equal portions of Time between one New Moon and another, the Moons return to the same *Meridian*, cannot be alwaies perform'd in the same Time; and consequently there must be a like Variation of the Tides in the Velocity, and in the Risings and Fallings of the Tides, as to equal spaces of time. And the Tides from New-moon to New-moon being not alwaies the same in number, as sometimes but 57, sometimes 58, and sometimes 59, (without any certain order of succession) is another evidence of the difficulty of reducing this to any great exactness. Yet, because 'tis worth while, to learn as much of it, as may be, the *Proposer* and many others do desire, That Observations be constantly made of all these Particulars for some Months, and, if it may be, years together. And because such Observations will be the more easily and exactly made, where the Tides rise highest, it is presumed, that a fit *Apparatus* being made for the purpose, they may be made about *Bristol* or *Cheap-stow*, best of any places in *England*, because the Tides are said thereabout to rise to ten or twelve fathoms; as upon the coast of *Britanny* in *France*, they do to thirteen and fourteen.

In order to which, this following *Apparatus* is proposed to be made use of. In some convenient place upon a Wall, Rock, or Bridge, &c. let there be an *Observatory* standing, as neer as may be to the brink of the Sea, or upon some wall; and if it cannot be well placed just where the Low water is, there may be a Channel cut from the Low water to the bottom of the Wall, Rock, &c. The Observatory is to be raised above the High water 18. or 20. foot; and a Pump, of any reasonable dimension, placed perpendicularly by the Wall, reaching above the High water as high as conveniently may be. Upon the top of the Pump a Pulley is to be fastned, for letting down into the Pump a piece of floating wood, which, as the water comes in, may rise and fall with it. And because the rising and falling of the water amounts to 60. or 70. foot, the Counterpoise of the weight, that goes into the Pump, is to hang upon as many Pulleys, as may serve to make it rise & fall within the space, by which the height of the Pump exceeds the height of the Water. And because by {300} this means the Counterpoise will rise and fall slower; and consequently by less proportions, than the weight it self, the first Pulley may have upon it a Wheele or two, to turn *Indexes* at any proportion required, so as to give the minute parts of the motion, and degrees of risings and fallings. All which is to be observed by *Pendulum-watches*, that have *Minutes* and *Seconds*, with *Checks*, according to Mr. *Hugens's* way.

And because if the Hole, by which the water is let into the Pump, be as large as the Bore of the Pump it self, the weight that is raised by the water, will rise and fall with an Undulalation, according to the inequality of the Sea's Surface, 'twill therefore be fit, that the Hole, by which the water enters, be less than half as bigg as the Bore of the Pump; any inconvenience that may follow thereupon, as to the Periods and Stations of the Floud and Ebb, not being considerable.

And to the end, that it may appear the better; what are the *particular* Observations, desired to be made, near *Bristol* or *Cheap-stow* bridg, it was thought not amiss, to set them down distinctly by themselves.

1. The degrees of the Rising and Falling of the water every quarter of an hour (or as often as conveniently may be) from the Periods of the Tides and Ebbs; to be observed night and day, for 2 or 3 months.

2. The degrees of the velocity of the Motion of the Water every quarter of an hour for some whole Tides together; to be observed by a second *Pendul*-watch: and a logg fastened to a line of some 50 fathoms, wound about a wheel.

3. The exact measures of the Heights of every utmost High-water and Low-water, from one Spring-tide to another, for some Months or rather Years.

4. The exact Heights of Spring-tides and Spring-Ebbs for some Years together.

5. The Position of the Wind at every observation of the Tides; and the times of its Changes; and the degrees of its Strength.

6. The State of the Weather, as to Rain, Hail, Mist, Haziness, &c, and the times of its Changes.

7. At the times of observation of the Tides, the height of the *Thermometer*; the height of the *Baroscope*; the height of the *Hygroscope*; the Age of the Moon, and her *Azimuths*; and her place in all respects; And lastly the *Sun's* place; all these to *minutes*.

And it would be convenient, to keep *Journal Tables*, for all these Observations, each answering to its day of the Month.

For the *Apparatus* of all these observations, there will be particularly necessary.

A good *Pendulum*-watch.

A *Vane* shewing *Azimuths* to minute parts.

An *Intrument* to measure the Strength of the Winde.

A large and good *needle* shewing *Azimuths* to degrees.{301}

Thermometers, Barometers, Hygroscopes.

These Observations being thought very considerable as well as curious, 'tis hoped, that those who have conveniency, will give encouragement and assistance for the making of them; and withall oblige the publick by imparting, what they shall have observed of this kind: The*Publisher* intending, that when ever such observations shall be communicated to him, he will give notice of it to the *publick*, and take care of the improvement thereof to the best use and advantage. A *Pattern* of the *Table*, proposed to be made for observing the *Tides*, is intended to be published the next opportunity, God permitting.

An Account of Several Books lately published

I. *Johannis Hevelii DESCRIPTIO COMETÆ, Anno Æræ Christianæ MDCLXV. exorti; unà cum MANTISSA Prodromi Cometici, Observationes omnes prioris COMETÆ MDCLIV, ex iisque genuinum motum accuratê deductum, cum Notis & Animadversionibus, exhibens.*

This Book (as the Title it self intimates) undertakes two things. *First*, To give an Account of the *Second* of the two late Comets, which appeared, when the *other* was scarce extinct; Concerning which, the Author doth, from the Observations made by himself with a *Sextant*of 6 foot, and divided into *minutes* and *seconds*, assign *both* its true place (as well in respect of the *Ecliptick* as the *Æquator*) *and* its proper motion; Adding a fair Delineation of its Course, together with the genuine Representations of its *Head* and *Train*, in each day of its apparition; and subjoyning a General Description and Discourse of some of the more notable*Phenomena* thereof. It was first seen at *Dantzick* by the Watchmen, the 5th of *April* st. n. 1665. and then observed by the *Author* from *April* 6, about 1½ of the Clock in the morning, till *April* 20 at 3. in the morning. During which time, it went with a reasonable velocity; making 46 deg. in its Orb, *according to the Order of the Signs*, moving from the *Breast* of*Pegasus*, towards the *Head* of *Andromeda*, and the *Left Horn* of *Aries*; having, as 'tis presumed, taken its rise from above *Sagittary*, and run through the *Breast* of *Antinous*, under*Aquila* and the *Dolphin*, to the said *Pegasus*, and so on, as is already expressed.

The *Head* of it is in the Book described of a Colour like that of *Jupiter*, all along much brighter than that of the former Comet, though of a somewhat less magnitude; having in its middle only *one* round, but very bright and big *Kernel* or Speck, resplendent like Gold, and encompassed with another more dilute and seemingly uniform matter: its *Tail* being at first, about 17. deg. and afterwards 20. and sometimes 25 deg. long, and divaricated towards the End.

Next, it is observed, that though this Star did afterwards slacken its pace, yet it retained the vividness of its Colour, both of the *Head* and *Train*; the *Head* especially, keeping at the time as well of the last observations, as of the {302}first, the brightness of its single *kernel*, though the environing more dilute matter were then almost all lost; it being, according to the Author, more and more attenuated, and grown narrow, the nearer the Star approached to the Sun.

Thirdly, 'tis noted, That this *Comet* did very much digress from the *Hypothesis*, delivered by*M. Auzout*, in regard that, whereas according to that *Hypothesis*, this Star should not arrive to the *Ecliptick* till after the space of 3 months, it arrived there the 28 of *April*. And then, that its first Conjunction with the Sun hapned between the 19 and 20 of *April*, and the second, the last of *April*, not (as *M. Auzout*, would have it) the 15 of *May*. So that he concludes, that this Comet never came down to the *Pleiads* and the *Eye of Taurus*, as the Hypothesis of *M. Auzout* requires, but that from *April* 20. it did immediately take its course towards the Ecliptick, deflecting every day more and more from the *Section* of a *Great Circle*, to the*Lucida* of *Aries*, arriving at the *Ecliptick* the last of *April*, about the 8th or 10th deg. of*Taurus*; not in *July* about the 8th of *Gemini*, and the *Eye of Taurus*.

Fourthly, He intimates, that if this Comet had appeared some weeks sooner, it would have confronted the former Comet, being yet in its vigour and of a conspicuous bigness, in the same place, where that was, viz. the *Head of Aries*.

Fifthly, He observes, that this Star in progress of time became *Retrograde*, whence it came to pass, that in the Months of *June* and *July* it did not appear again before the Rising of the Sun, though the Sun left it far behind: whereas, if it had proceeded toward the *Eye of Taurus*, it would have appeared again in the morning.

Sixthly, He maintains, that this Comet was not the same with the former; which he thinks may be demonstrated, onely by a due Delineation of both their Course upon the *Globe*; where he saith it to be evident, that the former could never come to the *Head* of *Pegasus*, as moving already in *February* in a streight Course about the *Head of Aries*; Besides, that the *former* went in the very beginning in a *Retrograde* motion; but *this* perpetually in a direct one: *that*, about the end, very slow, its Head lessning and growing dark; *this* swift enough, with its head conspicuous and bright. To which he adds, that the whole Course of the former was made under a quite different *Angle* of the *Orbite* and *Ecliptick*, and a different Motion of the *Nodes* from the latter: As also that their *Faces* differed very much from one another; the *first* exhibiting all along a matter, which as to its density and rarity, altered from day to day exceedingly, whereas the *second* retained (to the Authors admiration, who affirms, never to have observed the like) all the time he saw it, one and the same round, dense and bright Speck or Kernel.

All which he concludes 1, With an Intimation of his sense concerning two other Comets, pretended to have been lately seen, *One* at *Rome*, about the {303} *Girdle of Andromeda*, in the Months of *February* and *March*, 1664. the other in *Germany* in *Capricorne*, about *Saturne* in the head of *Sagittary*, during the Months of *September* and *October*, 1665. 2ly, With an Advertisement of what he has done in that important Work for the Advancement of *Astronomy*, the due *Restitution of the Fixt Stars, vid.* That he has almost finish't it; himself alone, without trusting to any other mans labour, that was not directed by him.

The *Second* Part of this Book (the *Mantissa* to the *Prodromus Cometicus*) endeavours to justifie the Authors Observations touching the former Comet, excepted against by M. *Auzout*, in several particulars; as 1. That it had not pass'd to the *First*, but *Second* Star in *Aries*, and had mov'd in quite another Line, than He had described. 2. That its *proper motion* about the end of *January* and the beginning of *February*, 1665. had not been rightly assigned. 3. That the *Bigness* of its *Diameter* had not been truly delivered; Nor 4. The *Faces* of its *Head* in due manner represented.

To all which the Author endeavors to answer: 1. By delivering all his Observations of that Comet, thereby to shew, what care and diligence he had used, *particularly* to make out, how great its *Diurnal motion* had been; in what proportion, and how far, it decreased, and where and in what degree it increased again: Which being, as he conceives, duly and exactly deduced, and demonstrated, he esteems it afterwards to be easie for every one, versed in these matters, certainly to collect and to judge, what way the Comet, after it became invisible to the naked Eye, and could be no longer observed with *Sextants* and *Quadrants*, had taken, and what Line it had described. 2, By subjecting all those Observations, with great diligence and labour, to a rigid *Calculus*, thereby to obtain, for every day, the *Longitudes, Latitudes, Right Ascensions, Declinations, Proper motion, Angle* of the *Ecliptick* and the *Æquator*, and the *Nodes* of that Comet; for the construction of an *Ephemerides* of its whole Motion. From all which he pretends to prove, that he has not erred in his Observation of *February* 18, nor been prepossest by any *Hypothesis*, nor deluded by any *Fixt Star*, as M. *Auzout* thinketh; but that near the *First Star* of *Aries* there then appear'd a *Phænomenon*, most like to that Comet, that was seen some dayes before, if compared with the Observations make thereof *Febr.* 12, 13, 14. Though he will not hitherto positively determine, whether that *Phænomenon*, which appear'd to him *February* 18. was {304} indeed that very Comet, which he saw with his naked Eye, and observed with his Geometrical Instruments, the said 12, 13, and 14. dayes of *February*; or whether it was another, and whether he had lost that Comet, which moved towards the *Second Star* in *Aries*. but leaves it to the Learned World, and particularly to the *Royal Society*, after they shall have well examined and considered all his Observations, and the *Calculus* raised therefrom, to judge of this, and the other particulars in controversie.

II. *Isaacus Vossius de NILI et ALIORUM FLUMINUM ORIGINE.* It was *Numb.* 14. of these*Transactions*, that gave an account of the *Cause* of the *Inundation of the Nile*, as it was rendred by Monsieur *de la Chambre*: *This* is to give you another, not only of the *Inundation*, but also of the *Origine* of that, and of *other Rivers*, as it is delivered by Monsieur *Isaac Vossius*, who undertakes in this Book to shew;

1. That those *Subterraneous Channels*, through which several *Philosophers* teach, that the Sea discharges it self into the Rivers, are not only imaginary, but useless, in regard 'tis impossible for the water to rise from the Subterraneous places up to the Mountains, where commonly the Sources of Rivers are.

2. He explicates, why, if a Pipe be put into a Bason full of Water, the water is seen more raised in the Pipe, than in the Bason, and rises higher according as the Pipe is narrower; On the contrary, if the same Pipe be put into a Bason full of Quicksilver, the Quicksilver stayes lower in the Pipe, than in the Bason. The reason, which he renders hereof, is, That as the Water sticks easily to all it touches, it is sustain'd by the sides of the narrow Pipe wherein it is included: And indeed, if the Pipe be quite drawn out of the Water, the Water doth not all fall out, but so much of it remains, as the sides of the Pipe could sustaine: Whence it is, that the Water which is kept up by the Walls of the Tube, weighing no longer upon that which is in the Bason, is thrust upwards, and keeps it self raised above its Levell; but the Quicksilver not adhering so easily, as Water, to Bodies it touches, is not sustained by the sides of the Tube, and so mounts not above its Levell, but rather descends below it, because the Pipe, which is streight, hinders the endeavor that is in the *Mercury* to rise to its Level. He adds, that this Observation makes nothing for the Explication of the *Origine of Rivers*; because, though it be true, that the Water {305}by this means rises above its Levell, yet it does never run out at the top of the Pipe. Having said this, he answers to the other Arguments, commonly alledged to maintain this Opinion.

3. He pretends, that all Rivers proceed from a *Colluvies* or *Rendevous* of Rain-waters, and that, as the Water, that falls upon *Hills*, gathers more easily together, than that which falls in*Plaines*, therefore it is, that Rivers ordinarily take their Source from *Hills*. Thence also comes it (saies he) that there are more *Rivers*, than *Torrents*, in the *Temperate Zones*; and, on the contrary, more *Torrents*, than *Rivers*, in the *Torrid Zone*: For, as in hot Climats the Mountains are far higher, the Water, that descends from them with impetuosity, runs away in a little while, and formes such Collections of Water, as soon dry up, but in cold Climats, the Waters do not run away but slowly, and are renew'd and recruited by Rain, before they are quite dryed up; because the Hills are there lower, and so the Bed of Rivers hath lesse declivity.

Having thus discoursed of *Rivers* in *General*, he treats of the *Nile* in *particular*, and there

1. Observes, That the Order of the Seasons of the Year is quite inverted under the *Torrid Zone*. For, whereas it should be then Summer, when the Sun is near; and Winter, when the Sun is farther off: Under the *Torrid Zone* 'tis never lesse hot, than when the Sun is nearest; nor more hot, than when the Sun is farthest off: So that to the people that live between the*Æquinoctial* and the *Tropicks*, Summer begins about *Christmass*, and their Winter, about St.*Johns* day. The reason whereof is, (*saith he*) that when the Sun is directly over their Heads, it raises abundance of vapors, and draws them so high, that they are presently converted into Water by the coldnesse of the Air; whence it comes to passe, that then it rains continually, which does refresh the Air; but when the Sun is farther off, there falls no more rain, and so the Heat becomes insupportable.

2. He proves by many recent Relations, that the *Sources* of the *Nile* are on this side of the*Æquinoctial* in *Æthiopia*, of which he gives a very accurate *Mappe*, correcting many faults which *Geographers* are wont to commit in the Description of the Kingdom of the *Abyssins*, which they believe to be much greater than indeed it is.{306}

3. This supposed, he easily gives an account, why the *Nile* yearly overflows about the end of*June*: For, as at that time there falls much rain in *Æthiopia*, it must needs be, that the *Nile*, whose source is in that Country, should then overflow, when those rains begin, and subside, when they cease.

There are besides, in this Book, two other *Tracts*. In the *first*, M. *Vossius* endeavours to maintain the Doctrine, he had deliver'd in his Book *De Lumine*, and to shew, that the *Soul* of

Animals is nothing but *Fire*, that there are no invisible Atoms; nor so much as any Pores, even in the Skin of man. Here he treats also of *Refractions*, and alledges the Examples of several persons, who have then seen the Sun by the means of Refraction, when really He was under the *Horizon*.

In the *second*, He discourses of some points of the *Mechanicks*; and relates among other things, that the *Arrows* and *battering Rams (Aries)* of the Antients did as much execution, as our *Muskets* and *Canons*; and then, that the Vehemence of the percussion depends as much upon the Length of the percutient Body, as upon the velocity of the Motion. He adds, that the Length of a Canon ought not to exceed 13 foot, and that a greater length is not onely useless, but hinders also the effect of the Gun, not because the Bullet is thrown out of the Gun, before all the powder is fired (as some believe;) but because the Bullet is then beaten back into the Gun by the Air, re-entring into it with impetuosity, when the flame is extinct.

III. *LE DISCERNEMENT DU CORPS ET DE L'AME*, par M. *de Cordemoy*.

This *French* Treatise (but very lately come to the *Publisher's* hands) examines the different Operations of the Soul and Body, and the Secret of their Union, pretending to discover to every one, what he is, and what is transacting within him. It consists of six Discourses.

1. In the *first*, the Author examines the Notions, we have in *general* of *Bodies* and *Matter*, of *Quantity*; of *Qualities*; of *Place*; of *Rest*; of *Motion*; of *Vacuity*; of *Forms*: to shew what is to be understood by these Terms, which cause all the perplexity that is in the ordinary *Physicks*. He begins with taking notice, that hitherto *Philosophers* have had no *distinct* notions of *Bodies* and *Matter*, from the want whereof he conceives, that almost all the Errors in Common *Physiology* have {307}* It sounds hard, To say, An extended *substance* is indivisible. sprung. To rectify which, he defines *Bodies* to be * *Extended Substances*, and *Matter* an *Aggregate of Bodies*. Whence he inferrs, that *Bodies* are Indivisible and *Matter* divisible; a *Body* being nothing but *one* and the *same* substance, whose different extremities are inseparable, because they are the extremities of one and the same Extension, and, in a word, of one and the same Substance; but *Matter* being nothing but an Association or Collection of Bodies, 'tis evident, *(saith he)* it must be divisible. This doctrine he so much insists upon, that he conceives, Nature cannot subsist, if a Body in the sence he takes it, be divisible; and that *Motion* and *Rest* cannot be explicated without it. As for *Quantity*, he makes that to be nothing but More or Less Bodies; not allowing, that each Body should be a Quantity, though it be a part of Quantity; no more than an *Unite* is a Number, though it make part of a Number: so that *Quantity* and *Extension* are two distinct things with him, the *first* belonging properly to *Matter*, the last to a *Body*. Touching *Vacuity*, he conceives, that the Bodies, which compose a mass, are not every where so near one another, as not to leave some interval in several places. Neither does he think it necessary, that those intervals should be fill'd up; nor unconceivable, that there should be no Body between two Bodies; which touch not one another. And when 'tis said, that those intervals cannot be conceived without Extension, and that consequently there are Bodies that replenish them, he frankly pronounces that not to be true; and affirms, that though it may be said, that between two Bodies, which touch not one another, other Bodies may be placed of so or so many feet, &c: yet ought it not to be inferred, that therefore they *are* there, but onely, that they are thus placed, that there *may* be put between them so many Bodies, as joyned together would compose an Extension of so many feet. So that one conceives onely, that Bodies *may* be placed there, but not that they *are* there: and as we can have an *Idea* of many Bodies, though none of them be in being; so we can conceive, that some Bodies *may* be put between others, where really there are none. And when 'tis alledged, that if all the Bodies, that fill a vessel full, were destroyed, the sides of the vessel would be closed together; He professes, he understands not that ratiocination, nor can conceive, what one Body does to the subsistence of another, more than to sustain themselves mutually, when they are thrust by the neighbouring ones: and therefore sees not, why the sides of the vessel should close, if nothing did thrust them together; but understands clearly, that two Bodies may well subsist so far from one another, that one might place a great many Bodies between them, or none at all, and yet they neither approach to, not recoil from one another. {308}

2. In the *Second*, he examines the *Changes*, which he knows in Matter, and makes it his business to explicate all those that respect *Quantity*, *Qualities* and *Forms*, by *Local Motion*, esteeming that needs no other.

3. In the *third*, he explains the Motion of *Artificial* Engins, and that of *Natural* ones, by one and the same Cause; endeavouring among other things to shew, that the Body of an Animal is moved after the same manner with a Watch. That cause of motion he makes the *Materia Subtilis*; and the finer or subtiler that is, the better and fitter he conceives it to be to preserve Motion.

4. In the *Fourth*, he teaches, that though Experience seems to evince, that the Soul moves the Body, and that one Body moves an other; yet there is nothing but God, that can produce any notion in the World, and all other Agents, which we believe to be the *Cause* of this or that Motion, are no more but the *Occasion* thereof. In doing this, he advances certain *Axioms*, and Conclusions, which are in short,

a. The *Axioms*. That no substance has that of it self, which it can loose, without ceasing to be, what it is: That every body may loose of its motion, till it have no more left, without ceasing to be a Body: That we cannot conceive but two sorts of substances, *vid.* a *Spirit* (or *That which thinketh*) and a *Body*, wherefore they must be considered as the Causes of all, that happens, and what cannot proceed from the one, must necessarily be adscribed to the other: That to *Move*, or to cause motion, is an Action: That an Action cannot be continued but by the Agent, who began it.

b. The *Conclusions*. That no *Body* hath Motion of it self: That the First Mover of Bodies not a Body: That it cannot be but a *Spirit*, that is the First Mover: That it cannot be but the same Spirit, who has begun to move Bodies, that continues to move.

In the *Fifth*, He treats of the Union of the Body and Soul, and the manner, how they act one upon the other; and esteems it not more difficult to conceive the Action of Spirits upon Bodies, and of Bodies upon Spirits, than to conceive the Action of Bodies upon Bodies: the cause of the great difficulty in understanding the two former, arising (according to him) from thence, that we will conceive the one by the other, not considering, that every thing acting according to its own nature, we shall never know the action of one Agent, if we will examine it by the notions we have of another, that is of a quite differing nature. Here he notes, that the Action of Bodies upon Bodies is not {309} more known to us; than that of Spirits upon Bodies, or of Bodies upon Spirits; and yet most men admire nothing but *this*, believing to know the *other*; whereas he Judges, that all things being well examin'd, the Action of Bodies upon Bodies is no more conceivable, than that of Spirits upon Bodies. Mean while the opinion of the Authour touching this subject, is, That the union of Soul and Body consists onely in this, that certain motions of the Body are followed by certain *Cogitations* of the Soul, and, on the contrary, that certain Thoughts of the Soul are follow'd by certain *Motions* of the Body. And, having supposed, that Bodies are said to act upon one another, when they cause some change suitable to Extension; and Spirits to act upon one another, when they cause some change suitable to a Thought; he infers, that when a Body acts upon a Spirit, that cannot be by causing any change of motion, of figure, or parts, as having none of all these; nor when a Spirit acts upon a Body, that cannot be by producing any change of Thought, as having none: But, when this Body, or its motion, or figure, or other thing, depending upon its nature, can be perceived by a Spirit, so as, upon that occasion, this Spirit has thoughts, it had not before, it may be said, that the Body has acted upon this Spirit, for as much as it has caused all the change in it, whereof it was capable according to its nature.

In the *Sixth*, After he hath shew'd, what is to be understood by what we call *Soul*, and by what we call *Body*, he labours to make it out, that we are much more assured of the Existence of the Soul, than of that of the Body, which he conceives he can prove from hence, that we cannot doubt, that we think, because even doubting is thinking; but one may doubt, whether one has a body, for several reasons, which he alledges, and thinks so cogent, that he concludes, it is not evident to him by the light of reason, that he has a Body. But supposing, there be Bodies, he examines, what are the Operations, that belong to the Soul, and what those, that belong to the Body; and lastly, what those, that result from the Union of both: And then explains, how all those operations are perform'd, and particularly, *Sensation*; where he shews, that the Nerves, holding at one end to the Brain, whereof they are but Allongations, and being at the other end extended to the extremities of the Body; when an Object comes to touch those exterior ends of the Nerves, the interior ones in the Brain are presently shaken; and cause different sensations according to the diversitie of Nerves, and the differing manner, in which they are shaken. And to shew, that 'tis this shaking, that causes Sensation, he notes, that if any thing shakes the interior parts of the Nerves, though the object be absent, the Soul has presently the same {310} sensations, as it would have, if it were present. As, if one should knock on's head forcibly against a wall, the shaking, which the blow gives to the Brain, moving the interior extremities of the Nerve, which causes the sensation of Light, the Soul has the same sensation, which it would have, if it saw a thousand Candles: On the contrary, if the interior extremities of the nerves are not shaken, though the object be present, it causes no sensation; whence it comes, that if a strong Ligature be made upon the middle of the Arm, and the hand be then prickt, no pain is felt, because the shaking of the nerves that are pricked, being stopped by the Ligature, cannot reach to the extremities of the Nerves, that are within the Brain.

Advertisement.

The following *Errata*, left by the *Press* in *Num.* 16, the *Reader* is desired thus to correct. Page 269. lin 27. read, *motion of B above the Center; G. is also*, with a *Semi-colon* after the word *Center*. p. 274. l. 13, r. *it to do to the.* p. 277. l. 24. r. *natural days.* p. 281. l. 16. r. *of his.* ib. l. 27. r. *a notion.* p. 293. l. 4. r. *enough without.* ib. l. 43. r. *to the Sine of.* p. 294. l. 1. r. *to the Sine of.*

LONDON,

Printed for *John Martin* and *James Alestry*, Printers to the Royal Society. 1666. {311}

Numb. 18.

PHILOSOPHICAL
TRANSACTIONS.

Munday, *October* 22. 1666.

The Contents.

Patterns *of the* Tables *proposed to be made for* Observing of Tides; *promised in the next foregoing* Transactions. *Other* Inquiries *touching the Sea. Some Considerations touching the* Parenchymous *parts of the Body. Observables concerning* Petrification. *A Relation from* Paris, *of a kind of* Worms, *that eat out Stones. Some promiscuous Observations made in* Somersetshire. *A Problem for finding the Year of the* Julian Period, *by a new and very easie Method. An Account of some Books, not long since publish'd, which are,* 1. Tentamina Physico-Theologica de Deo, *Authore* Samuele Parkero. 2. Honorati Fabri Tractatus duo; Prior, de Plantis et de Generatione Animalium; Posterior, de Homine. 3. Relation du Voyage de l'Evesque de Beryte, par la Turquie, la Perse, les Indes, *&c. per Monsieur de* Bourges.

Patterns *of the* Tables *proposed to be made for* Observing of Tides, *promised in the next foregoing* Transactions; *by Sir* Rob. Moray.

In performance of what was promised in the last of these *Papers* for Observing the *Tides*, here are subjoyned *Patterns* of the *Tables* there mentioned; *One*, for marking the *precise Time* of the High waters and Low-waters during one Month; that is, between *New* and *New* Moon, or *Full* and *Full* Moon. The *other*, for marking the *Degrees* of the Risings and Fallings of the Water in *Equal* spaces of Time, and the *Velocity* of its motion at *several* heights: The *Degrees* of *Heat* and *Cold*, *&c.*

The *Times*, assigned in the *first*, to the High waters and Lowest Ebbs, are taken out of Mr. *Wing*'s Almanack, for this present year 1666, as he calculates them for the Month of *September* for *London Bridge*. Only, whereas he takes notice but of *one* High-water for every day, *Here* are set {312} down the Times of the other, and the two Ebbs intervening, by

148

subdividing the *Differences*, he assignes between two Tides, equally amongst them. In all which, though there may be Errors, that is not to be considered, seeing the Dissein is to Correct and State the *Times* of the *Tides exactly* by *Experiments*, after this method. Mr. *Wing*states the High waters to fall out at *London-Bridge* constantly, when the Moon is 46. deg. 30. min. to the *West-ward* of the *Meridian*. For the Times, he marks for them, are made up by adding every day 3. hours, 6 minutes, to those in his *Table* for knowing the Time of the Moons coming to the South.

The *First Table* consists of *two* Parts, and each part of *four Columns*. The *first* part marks the Tides and Ebbs from the day of the *New*-Moon to its *Full:* The *other*, from the *Full* to the next *New*. The *first Column* in both parts hath the day of the Month and Week; *M.* standing every where for *Morning* and *A.* for *Afternoon*. The *third* column hath the *Character* of the day of the Week prefixt to the Hour and Minute of the High-water, and answering to the day of the Month. The *last* Column hath the same for the time of Low-water, varying the*Character* of the day, as often as the low-water falls out more early than the High-water. In this *Example* between the said *New* Moons there falls out in all just 57. periods of the Tide or Flowing water, and 58. of the Ebb or Low water; which numbers vary according to the Intervals of the Moons changes, but with what constancy and exactness, is to be inquired after: Which whosoever undertakes to do, may keep such a *Table*, as is here proposed, in a Book by it self.

The *other* Table doth in 9. *Columns* comprehend the particular Observations of the *Degrees*of the Rising and falling of the Tides, and the other things specified at the Tops of them: The*first* Column marking the Hour and Minut common to all the several Observations. Each hour is divided in 3. equal Parts, that number of Observations being only pitch't upon by way of *Example*: The numbers may else be varied at pleasure, when other more frequent Observations are thought fit to be made, or when they prove too frequent and laborious; though the most frequent are most desirable, till competent information of all particulars be attained.

The *Rising* of the Tide from Low-water to the highest pitcht of the full Sea, is here supposed to be 60. foot: And the Degrees of its rising every 20. Minuts, to be in the *Proportion* of*Sines*, The whole time of Flowing supposed to be 6. hours. But this *Example* will serve for marking the *Spaces* of the Increasing or Rising, as well as of the falling of the water, in order to the investigation of their *Proportions* to one another, when the *Duration* of the Tide exceeds 6. hours by any number of *minuts*, as well as for just 6. hours; seeing they may be easily collected from any Number of Observations; their precise Time and that of the Duration of the waters Rising and Falling (that is, the just interval between the High-Water and Low-water) being known: This Calculation by *Sines*, being only set down as a*Conjecture*, flowing from Observations of the Motion of the water in its Rising and Falling, {313}which seems to observe this or some such like Proportion; which is supposed still to hold in*all* Tides, be the *Duration* what it will; the Increase still continuing proportionably till the very middle of the Hight and Duration, and Decreasing afterwards in the same manner: Which whether it be so indeed or not, is that, which is desired to be known.

There is the like Proportion here supposed to be in the *different degrees* of the *Velocity* of the Current of the Water after *Equal* spaces of Times, as in its Rising and Falling: And so it is markt in the *Third* Column. But because the *true Velocity* of the Current of the Water, raised above the Levell $^{456}/_{1000}$ of a foot, is unknown, it is by way of Supposition set at Ten feet in one Minute of an Hour, which being once stated, the rest distant from each other by the space of 20. Minutes of an Hour, are set down according to the same *Proportions* of *Sines*before suggested. It being supposed, that of the *Velocity* of the Current of the Tide, after it hath flowed 20 minuts of an hour, be such, as a Log of Wood placed in the Water will move 10 foot in the space of one minute of time, at the middle of the Tide it will in the like space of Time move 114 f. $^{276}/_{1000}$, and so proportionably at other times: Which, howsoever these Proportions shall be found by Experiments to fall out, may be not unworthy of the pains and charges requisite to acquire the knowledge of it. For, besides the satisfaction it may afford upon other accounts, it may possibly be of no small use to those, who need an exact reckoning of their Ships running, when the Velocity of the

Current of the Tide may be necessary to be known; lest through the defect of the knowledge of that, especially when it is reckoned less than indeed it is, the Ship be thrown in the night upon Shores, Rocks or Sands, when they reckon themselves to be far from them.

The Numbers in the 4, 5, 6, 7, and 8. *Columns* are set down at random, only for *Examples*sake; there being no difficulty in the apprehension of it, and imitating of it in setting down the true Hights and Variations of the *Thermometer, Baroscope,* &c. The Use whereof is so vulgarly known, that there needs no further Direction concerning them. But if any person who would make these Experiments, do not know the fabrick or use of any of the Instruments requisite for some of these Observations, nor where to have them, he may address himself to Mr. *Shortgrave*, one of the *Operators* of the *Royal Society*, lodged in*Gresham Colledge*, from whom he will receive full satisfaction about these things.

But the labour employed in the Observations of the Heat, Cold, &c. required to be taken notice of in order to the Ends proposed in the former *Tract*, and others that may be of no less delight than advantage, will be much retrenched, when Dr. *Christopher Wren* puts in practice, what he some years ago proposed to the *Royal Society* concerning an *Engine* with a*Clockwork*, which may perform these Observations in the last enumerate *Columns*, without being toucht or lookt after but once or twice a day.

The Tables themselves follow,

{314}

A Perpendicular Line divided into **Signes,** *supposed to be the* **Periods** *of the Risings and Fallings of the Tides, as is in the other Table represented.*

1 666. Sept.	Age of the ho.mi.	Time of High water. Day. Hour. Min.		Time of Low water. Day. Hour. Min.	
· ·	New	2 . 57.	Morn.	9 . 8.	Morn.
	8 .38'.	3 . 19.	Aftern.	9 . 30.	Aftern.
· ·		3 . 41.	M	9 . 51½	M
		4 . 2.	A	1 0. 12½	A
· ·		4 . 23.	M	1 0. 33¼	M
		4 . 43½	A	1 0. 53¾	A
· ·		5 . 4.	M	1 1. 14½	M
		5 . 25.	A	1 1. 35½	A
· ·		5 . 46.	M	1 1. 56½	M
		6 . 7.	A	0 . 17½	M
· ·		6 . 28.	M	0 . 39½	A
		6 . 51.	A	1 . 2½	M
· ·		7 . 14.	M	1 . 23½	A
		7 .	A	1 .	M

		. 37.	8	M	. 48¼	2	A
. 0.		. 0.	8	A	. 13.	2	M
		. 26.	8	M	. 39.	3	A
. 1.	1 . Qu.	. 52.	9	A	. 5.	3	M
	1 0 A.	. 18.	9	M	. 31.	3	A
. 2.		. 44.	1	A	57¾	4	M
		0. 11½	1	M	25¼	4	A
. 3.		0. 39.	1	A	. 53.	5	M
		1. 7.	1	M	. 21.	5	A
. 4.		1. 35.	0	M	. 49.	6	M
. 5.		. 3.	0	A	. 17.	6	A
		. 31.	0	M	. 45.	7	M
. 6.		. 59.	1	A	. 13.	7	A
		. 27.	1	M	. 41.	8	M
. 7.		. 55.	2	A	. 9.	8	A
		. 23.	2	M	36¾	9	M
. 8.	F *ull.*	. 50½	3	A	4¼	9	A
	1 1.10'.	. 19.	3	M	31¼	9	M
. 9.		. 45.	4	A	58½	1	A
		. 11.	4	M	0. 25½	1	M
. 0.		. 39.	5	A	0. 52½	1	A
		. 6.	5	M	1. 20.	1	M
. 1.		. 34.	6	A	1. 48.	0	A
		. 2.	6	M	. 16.	0	A
. 2.		. 30.	6	A	. 44.	1	M

1666. Sept. 3. Hour. M.	R Rising, and fall of Tides Foot 1000	V Velocity of the Current Foot 1000	T Thermo- metre Inch 10	B Baro- scope Inch 10	H Hygro- scope Inch 10	Azimuth. Force of the Wind deg. deg.	Weather.
		0, 00 .					
	. 58.		.	.	. 12½	.	
		7	M	.	1	A	
. 3.		. 27.	.		. 41½	.	
		7	A		2	M	
	. 36.		.	.	10¼	.	
		8	M		2	A	
. 4.		. 24½	.		38¾	.	
		8	A		3	M	
	. 53.		.	.	6¾	.	
		9	M		3	A	
. 5.		. 20½	.		34¼	.	
		9	A		4	M	
	. 48.		.	.	1¾	.	
	1	1	M		4	A	
. 6.	ast Q	0. 15½	.		29¼	.	
	3	1	A		4	M	
	.11'	0. 43.	.	.	56½	.	
		1	M		5	A	
. 7.		1. 10.	.		23½	.	
		1	A		5	M	
		1. 37.	.	.	48.	.	
		1	M		6	A	
. 8.		1. 59.	.		10.	.	
		0	M		6	M	
. 9.		. 21.	.	.	32.	.	
		0	A		6	A	
		. 43.	.		54.	.	
		1	M		7	M	
. 0.		. 5.	.	.	16.	.	
O		1	A		7	A	
ctob.		. 27.	.		38.	.	
		1	M		7	M	
. .		. 49.	.	.	59.	.	
		2	A		8	A	
		. 9.	.		19.	.	
		2	M		8	M	
. .		. 29.	.	.	39.	.	
	N	2	A		8	A	
	ew.	. 49.	.		59.	.	
	1	3	M		9	M	
. .	.38'	. 9.	.	.	19.	.	

152

		,	00.						. t o W			
II.	0.			0,	00.	.	.	8.	.	.	. t o W	0.	.	*ain great*	Ⱶ
		,	56.						. t o W .			
	0.			0,	00.	.	.	8.	.	.	. t o W .	7.	.	*ain great*	Ⱶ
		,	53.						. t o W .			
	0.			6,	50.	.	.	8.	.	.	. t o W .	0.	.	*ain small*	Ⱶ
		,	11.									
.	0.			8,	87.	.	.	8.	.	.	. W .	5.	.	*ain small*	Ⱶ
		,	00.									
	0.			6,	58.	.	.	8.	.	.	. W .	0.	.	*ain very small*	Ⱶ
		,	96.									
	0.			1,	53.	.	.	8.	.	.	. W .	6.	.	*air but cloudy*	Ⱶ
		,	84.									
I.	0.			3,	89	.	.	8.	.	.	.	9.	.	*air*	Ⱶ

				.					W .		*and warm*
	0.	,	40.	03,	89.	.	.	8.	.	.	.	W .	2.	.	*arm and cloudy*
	0.	,	49.	10,	24.	.	.	8.	.	.	.	W .	9.	.	*unshine*
II.	0.	,	11.	14,	76.	.	.	8.	.	.	.	W .	0.	.	*unshine and clear*
	0.	,	11.	10,	24.	.	.	8.	.	.	.	W .	3.	.	*un clouded*
	0.	,	49.	03,	89.	.	.	8.	.	.	.	W .	0.	.	*loudy*
III	0.	,	40.	3,	89.	.	.	8.	.	.	.	W .	0.	.	*azy about the Horiz.*
	0.	,	84.	1,	53.	.	.	8.	.	.	.	W .	7.	.	*isty*

										Λ
	, 96									
0.	6, 58	.	.	8.	.	.	.	W 0.	.	isty
	00									(
. 0.	8, 87	.	.	8.	.	.	.	W 9.	.	learing up
	11									(
0.	6, 50	.	.	8.	.	.	.	W 0.	.	lear
	53									S
0.	0, 00	.	.	8.	.	.	.	W 0.	.	unshine
	56									S
I. 0.	0, 00	.	.	8.	.	.	.	W 0.	.	unshine
	, 00									

{315}

Other Inquiries Concerning the Sea.

* *This last Clause containing difficult*Quaere *and that may seem something odd, Mr.* Boyl *thinks fit to note, That having recommended this matter, among others, to a learned Physician, that was sailing into* America, *and furnished him with a small*Hydrostaticall*Instrument, to observe from time to time the Differences of Gravity he might meet with; This account was returned him, That he found by the Glass, the Sea-water to increase in weight, the nearer he came to the* Line, *till he arrived at a certain Degree of*Latitude*; as he remembers, it was about the 30th; after which, the Water seemed to retain the same specifick gravity, till he came to the* Barbadoes, *or*Jamaica.

The *Publisher* of these *Tracts*, knowing that the Honorable *Robert Boyle* had not left unconsidered the Natural History of the *Sea*, of which Subject the late, and these present Papers, have entertained the *Reader*as to the Observables of its *Flux* and *Reflux*; He was on this occasion instant, with that Gentleman to impart to him, for publication, these Heads of Inquiries, he had drawn up, touching that Subject: Which having obtained (though the *Author* desires, they may be lookt upon as unfinisht) he thus subjoyns.

What is the Proportion of Salt, that is in the Water of differing Seas; And whether in the same Sea it be always the same? And if it be not, how much it differs?

What is the Gravity of Sea-waters in reference to Fresh Waters and to one another: Whether it vary not in Summer and Winter, and on other Scores? And whether in the same Season its Gravity proceed *only* from the greater or lesser Proportion of Salt, that is in it, and not sometimes from other Causes? And what are the differing Gravities of the Sea-water, according to the Climats. *

What are the Odors, Colours and Tasts, observable in Sea-water?

What is the depth of the sea in several places, and the Order of its increase and Decrements? And whether the Bottom of the Sea does always rise towards the Shore, unless accidentally interrupted?

Of the Bottom of the Sea, and how it differs from the Surface of the Earth, in reference to the Soyl, and evenness or Roughness of the Superficies, And the Stones, Minerals and Vegetables to be found there?

What the Figuration of the Seas from North to South, and from East to West, and in the several Hemispheres and Climats?

What communication there is of Seas by Streights and Subterraneal Conveyances?

Of the Motion of the Sea by Winds, and how far Storms reach downwards towards the Bottom of the Sea?

The particulars whereof (saith the Author) are here omitted; Sir Robert Moray and Dr. Wallishaving by there more accurate inquiries about Tides made them needless.

Of the grand Motions of the Bulk or Body of the Sea; especially of the Tides *; Their History as to their Nature and Differences.

{316}

What power the Sea hath to produce or hasten Putrefaction in some Bodies, and to preserve others; as Wood, Cables, and others that are sunk under it?

Of the Power ascribed to the Sea to eject Dead Bodies, *Succinum,Ambergris*?

Of the shining of the Sea in the night?

What are the Medical vertues of the Sea, especially against *Hydrophobia*?

What is its vertue to Manure Land? And what are the Plants, that thrive best with Sea-water.

Some Considerations concerning the Parenchymous *parts of the Body.*

These were communicated by the inquisitive M. *Edmund King* at the Instance of the*Publisher*, as follows;

The *Parenchymous* parts of the Body, are by *Anatomists* generally supposed to be in very many places wholly *void of Vessels*, designed chiefly to fill up Cavities and interstices between the Vessels, and to boulster up the same, and to convey them through the parts.

But having many years endeavoured to excarnate several parts of the Body, *viz.* the Liver, Lungs, Spleen, Kidneys, &c. (not to name the *Placenta Uteri*, which seems to be*Parenchymous* too;) and being very desirous to make a *Scheme* of the Vessels of any of these, what ever they were, I fixt upon; I found, notwithstanding all my care to preserve the Vessels, when I was freeing them, as heedfully as I could, from the supposed *Parenchyma*, that in every breach, I made, either with my fingers or otherwise, all my endeavors were destructive to my purpose: and that, upon examination of those bits, much of which is called*Parenchyma*, I met in them more Vessels, than I had preserved in the parts whence they came: And though the portion were never so small, yet my bare eye could make this discovery; much more could I, when assisted by a *Microscope*, perceive, I had destroyed more Vessels than preserved, in despite of the exactest care, I was capable to use. And being not a little concern'd, that I should undertake to preserve the Vessels by such a Cause, as I saw plainly to be their definition (were the part never so big, or never so small) I was both confounded and tired. For I saw (and so must any, that will attempt this work) in my endeavouring to preserve one Vessel of a traceable magnitude, I spoiled an infinite number of others less discernable, which were as truly Vessels, as the other, differing only in size and figure (as to appearance.) Then reviewing what mischief I had done in every place, quite through the whole Tract of my Fingers, Knife, &c. I begin to think with my self, That it was not impossible for these parts to consist wholly of Vessels curiously wrought and interwoven (probably for more Uses, than is yet known;) And the {317} consideration, which came into my mind, of a piece of fine Cloth (which consists of so many several minute Hairs, call'd *Wool*) was no discouragement to this opinion. Yet I durst not be presumptuous as to indulge my self too much in it; much less to venter presently to speak of such a thing, which seem'd to contradict so many Learned Men's belief. But being restless, till I might receive more satisfaction in the thing, I iterated experiments over and over; some of which prov'd so successful to my apprehension, that I was encouraged in the year 1663. and 1664 to discourse of it to several very worthy Persons, as Mr. *Boyl*, Sir *William Petty*, Dr. *Williams*, Dr. *Lenthal*, Dr. *Jaspar Needham*, Dr. *Samson*, (who afterwards sent me a Letter from*France*, intimating the acquaintance he had made with the learned *Steno*, who hath since published something of the same Discovery) Mr. *Daniel Cox*, and Dr. *Samuel Parker*, &c, who doubtless cannot but remember, that then I related to them, I found much cause to believe, that that substance commonly called *Parenchyma*, was in most, if not in all its*Parenchymous* parts, full of Vessels; however it had been imagin'd by all, I could ever meet with, to consist in great part of a substance, in many places void of Vessels, designed for such uses, as are above mentioned.

Against which I have now further to alledge, 1. That I observe in a piece of *Musculous* flesh (so call'd) either raw, rosted, or boiled, *&c.* that if I so far extend it as to make it to be seen through, I can (assisting my Eye) perceive it full of Vessels placed as thick as is possible to be imagin'd, (the fat if there be any, being first removed) there appearing then nothing but vessels, yet so as with a *Microscope* may be seen through, when they are extended. 2. That, if any one, as he is at dinner, take a piece of flesh, and begin either at the head or tail of a*Muscle*, he may divide it *in infinitum* all along from head to tail, without breaking any thing of that, called Flesh, only these transverse *Fibres*, that seem to stitch them together, and (as I am apt to think) pass through the very Bodies of the smallest of them, and quite through the whole Muscle up the Cutaneous porosities; so that there is not one of these small *ducts*, that run *per longitudinem*, but 'tis furnisht with a sufficient number of outlets, when need requires, though too minute to suffer any *alimentary* juice to pass transversly (in a living Body) or any other liquor, when the Body is dead and cold. But to wave their use at present, and to return to what I was saying. Compress between the fingers this bit of flesh, and you shall find the Juice, especially if the Meat be Hot, to go before your fingers toward either end you please; but if you compress both ends, you shall see it swell into the middle; and again, if you press the middle, it will run out at both ends. But further, suppose a piece of flesh, called *Parenchyma*, as big, or as little as you please, in any part of the Body, and let me prick it with a Needle, where you shall appoint; if you feel it, I presume you will acknowledge, a *Nerve*, or a *Fibrilla*, related to it, is touch'd; If you feel it not, I am sure some liquor either sanguineous or other, will follow the Needle; And from whence can that come, but out of Vessels? unless {318}accidentally, as by a *Contusion*, &c., it be extravased, in which case my Argument will not be injured, because the part is depraved, whereas I speak of the parts, as they are in their natural State.

To confirm and illustrate all which, I desire, that the following *familiar* Observations may be considered:

1. If a Horse, fat and fair to look on, without a hollow to be seen between his Muscles, be rid extreme hard, and into a great sweat, and then kept one day without water or moist meat, you shall see him took so thin in many places as in the *musculous* parts, that you will hardly believe it to be the same Horse, especially if he be (as the Phrase is among Horse-masters) a*Nash* or *Wash-Horse*. The cause of which thinness will easily be granted to be only an exhaustion of Juice, expended out of the Blood, which did stuff out these Vessels. And whoever, that is used to ride hard, shall observe, how thick this foul Horse breaths, and at what a rate he will reek and sweat, will not much wonder at the alteration. But if the Horse be a hardy one, and used to be hard ridden, then you will see, that one days rest, and his belly full of good meat and drink, will in one day or two almost restore him to his former plight, the food being within that short space of time so distributed, that all the Vessels will be replenish'd again, as before. And the cleaner the Horse is, the sooner recruited, and the less sign of hard riding will appear. This seems to shew the facility, with which the Juice,

called Blood, passeth; Which surely, if there were such a thing as a *Parenchyma* might by several accidents (not difficult to mention) be so deprav'd in several parts of it, that it might lose its receptive faculty; than which it may be thought to have none of greater use, being supposed to be without Vessels.

2. Discoursing sometimes with *Grasiers* in the Country, about the Pasture of Cattle, I have been informed by them, that, if they buy any Old Beasts, Oxen, or Cows to feed, they choose rather those that are as poor as can be, so they be sound; because that, if they are pretty well in flesh, what they then add to them by a good pasture, though it make them both look and sell well, yet it will not make them eat so well, their flesh proving hard and very tough: Which some may suppose to be the age of *Parenchyma*; and so it is of that so called. But if those Beasts be old and extremely poor, then they feed very kindly, and will be not only very fat but spend well, like young ones, and eat very tender.

Of which I take the reason (excluding a *Parenchyma* now) to be this. When an Oxe or a Cow is grown old, and in an indifferent plight as to his *flesh* (for so it is called) all those Vessels having been kept at that size for the most part, have contracted a tenseness and firmness, and their *fibers* less extensive, nor so fitted for the reception of more unctuous particles to relaxe them; and that additional unctuous matter, which occasions fatness, is forced to seek new quarter any where (often remote from Muscles) where it can be with least difficulty received; sometimes to one place, sometimes to {319}another, as may be seen in Shambles. Whereas, if there were such a thing as a *Parenchyma*, that certainly would, like a hungry Sponge, immediately swell up in several parts, (which without much difficulty might be discover'd in the dissection) and more eminently, where it should find the pores most potent: And in the dissection of such Muscles it would be very strange, not to find some, if not many, pieces of them in various shapes, to the great inconvenience of the parts, in which they are seated: Which yet I confess I could never find in any Muscle unless it were where there had been a *Contusion*, or an *Impostume*, or the like. But according to my opinion of the*Parenchymous* parts, the reason, why the Flesh of a very lean Ox or Cow, that hath got new Flesh in a good pasture, eats tenderer, seems to be this: That in a very lean Beast the Vessels designed for admitting and distributing the nourishing Juice, are so near contracted, and lye so close together; that, when once they are relax'd; by fresh and unctuous nourishment, they extend every way in all *extensive* parts, until in a short time the whole Creature is, as it were, created a new, having got new flesh upon old bones. And the necessity of extreme extension makes all those parts, that are, as has been said, for the admission of nourishment, so thin and fine, that it will make the lean Beast, put into a rich pasture, eat young and tender: Whereas one of the same Age, that never was very poor, fed in the same pasture, shall eat hard and tough.

3. It has been observed, that Corpulent Persons in some Diseases, that seize on them, do fall away to wonder, not only in the Wast, but in the Arms, Legs, and Thighs; and the very Calves of the Legs have been observed so flaccid and loose, that one might wrap the skin about the bones. The reason whereof, according to the opinion deliver'd, may be easily rendred to be, A great Consumption of the Stock of Liquors, that in Health kept the Vessels turgid; Which Vessels I suppose to make up those Muscles. But when the Pores are obstructed, that the nourishment is hindred (which then also uses to be but sparingly administred) and sweats, either spontaneous, or forced, are large, there must needs be a great expence of those Liquors, the supply being but inconsiderable: which cannot but contract all these ducts of all sorts nearer together, and make them much less in themselves, meerly from Exhaustion: Or, if there should be no sweats, the internal Heat spends the spirits, and dries up the Liquors; the consequence whereof may reasonably be presumed to be this Flaccidity of parts, and great and sudden Change, made in them; not that there is need of any*Parenchyma* to fill up these Muscles considering what hath been said. Mean while, I humbly conceive, that if it be in any part of a Muscle, their Ingenuity, that plead for it, will put them upon some experiments, to bring it to Ocular Demonstration, either in Living or Dead Muscle, any kind of flesh, raw, rosted, boyl'd, or in what they can best make it out. And when I shall be convinc'd of an Errour in what I have discoursed, I shall beg pardon for giving the Occasion of the trouble of that Experiment, which shall prove a {320}*Parenchyma* in any Muscle; and think my time well spent in receiving a full satisfaction

of the ungroundedness of my opinion; and readily submit to the Author, with a grateful acknowledgement of my Obligation to any one that shall rectifie me in my mistake, if it be one.

Observables touching Petrification.

Though much hath been already said and written of *Petrification*, yet 'tis conceived, that all that comes so far short of a competent stock for the composing of a perfect *History of Petrification*, that the incompleatness thereof ought to awaken the more diligent attention of the Curious, and to call in their aid for Additions, thereby so to encrease and to complete the *Materials* for that work, that it may the better serve to clear and make out the Cause of that Transmutation. And that the rather, because if it lay in the power of humane Skill (by the knowledge of *Nature*'s works) to raise *Petrification*, or to allay, or prevent it, or to order and direct it (which perchance in time might be attained the said way) much use might be made of this Art; especially if it could be made applicable to hinder the Generation of the Stone and Gravel in humane Bodies, or to dissolve the Stone, where 'tis formed; besides other valuable Uses, that might be excogitated.

Upon this Consideration, care is, and further *will be* taken in these Papers, to record, among other Observables of Nature, what shall be communicated of this kind of *Change*.

In *Num.* 1. 2. and 5. several Relations have been made belonging to this Argument. Much of it, together with considerable Reflections may be seen in Mr. *Boyle*'s *Essay of Firmness.* In *Helmont de Lithiase*, where, among other remarques, is recited the Testimony of *Paræus* of a *Petrified Child* seen at *Paris*, and by the Owner used for a *Whetstone*: In *Densingius*'s Historia *Infantis in Abdomine inventi, & in duritiem lapideam conversi*: In Mr. *Hook*'s *Micrography*, and in others. To omit now, what has been related (but perhaps not well enough attested) by Authors, concerning the stupendious Petrifications of whole Companies of Men, and Troops of Cattle; by *Aventinus*, lib. 7. *Annal. Bojorum*; by *Purchas* in his *Pilgrimage* p. 416. in fol. printed at *London* 1614, and, (of a Troop of *Spanish* Horsemen) by *Jos. Acosta* lib. 3. c. 9.

To all which, the curious Dr. *Beale* now adds a Narrative of a Stone, not long since taken out of the Womb of a Woman of his neighbourhood neer *Trent* in *Somersetshire*, by incision, and afterwards perfectly cured, though she had born the Stone with extreme torments for. 8. or 9. years. The operation he relates to have been made in *Easter* last; after which time, he affirms to have seen the Stone, and weigh'd it in Gold Scales, where it wanted somewhat of four Ounces, but had lost of the weight, it formerly had, {321} being very light for a Stone of that Bulk. He further describes to be of a whitish colour, lighter than Ash-colour; perchance (*saith he*) not unlike to that recited out of *Scaliger* by Mr. *Boyle* in his *Essay of Firmness* pag. 238. *qui aëris contactis postea in gypseam tum speciem tum firmitatem concreverat.* It had no deep asperities, and had somewhat of an Oval figure, but less at one end, than a Hen-Egge, and bigger and blunter at the other end, than a Goose egge.

This Stone, (so he concludes) is intended for the *Royal Society*, with the Testimony of the *Chirurgion*, that perform'd the Operation, and other Witnesses of special credit; where also will be annexed the *manner* of Operation.

It appears by this last clause (to add that on this occasion) that this Well-wisher to the Improvement of all usefull knowledge, has taken notice of that considerable *Collection of Curiosities*, lately presented to the lately nam'd Society for their *Repository*, by the Publick-minded Gentleman Mr. *Daniel Colwall*, a very worthy and useful Member of that Body: To which Repository whatsoever is presented as rare and curious, will be with great care, together with the *Donors names* and their *Beneficence* recorded, and the things preserved for After-ages, (probably much better and safer, than in their own private Cabinets;) and in progress of Time will be employed for considerable Philosophical and Usefull purposes; of which perhaps more largely in another place.

A Relation of a kind of Worms *that eat out* Stones.

This is taken out of a Letter, written by one *M. de la Voye* to *M. Auzout*, to be found in the 32. *Journal des Scavans*, as follows.

In a great and very ancient Wall of Free-Stone in the *Benedictins Abby* at *Caen* in*Normandy*, facing Southward, there are to be found many Stones so eaten by Worms, that one may run his hand into most of the Cavities which are variously fashion'd, like the Stones, which I have seen wrought with so much Art in the *Louvre*: In these cavities there is abundance of live-Worms, their excrement, and of that Stone-dust, they eat. Between many of the Cavities there remain but leaves, as it were, of Stone, very thin, which part them. I have taken some of these living Worms, which I found in the eaten Stone, and put them into a Box with several bits of the Stone; leaving them there together for the space of eight days; and then opening the Box, the Stone seem'd to me eaten so sensibly, that I could no longer doubt of it, I send you the Box and the Stones in it, together with the living Worms: and to satisfie your Curiosity, I shall relate to you, what I have observed of them both *with* and*without* a *Microscope*. {322}

These Worms are inclosed in a Shell, which is grayish and of the bigness of a Barlycorn, sharper at one end, than the other. By the means of an excellent *Microscope* I have observ'd, that 'tis all overspread with little Stones and little greenish Eggs; and that there is at the sharpest end a little hole by which these Creatures cast out their excrement, and at the other end, a somewhat bigger hole, through which they put out their heads and fasten themselves to the Stones, they gnaw. They are not so shut up, but that sometimes they come out, and walk abroad. They are all black, about two *Lines* of an inch long and three quarters of a *Line*large. Their Body is distinguish't into several plyes, and near their head they have three feet on each side, which have but two Joynts resembling those of a Lowse. When they move, their Body is commonly upwards, with their mouth against the Stone. They have a big head, somewhat flat, and even, of the colour of a Tortoise-Shell, braunish, with some small white hair. Their mouth is also big; where may be seen four kinds of Jaw-bones, lying crossewise, which they move continually, opening and shutting them like a pair of *Compasses*, with four branches. The Jaws on both sides of the mouth are all black, the nether Jaw hath a point like the Sting of a Bee, but uniform. They draw threds out of their mouth with their fore-feet, using that point to range them, and to form their Shells of them. They have Ten Eyes, very black and round, which appear to be bigger than a Pins head. There are five of them on each side of the head, standing after this manner,

But besides these Worms, I have found, that *Mortar* is eaten by an infinite number of small Creatures, of the bigness of Chees-Mites. These have but two Eyes, and are blackish. They have four feet on each side pretty long. The point of their Muzzle is very sharp, as that of a Spider. I send you but one of them, though I had abundance, but they are dead and lost. It may be, you'l find some at *Paris*, seeing that in the old Mortar betwixt Stones, that is found in Walls made with rubbish, there is great store of them, together with great plenty of their little Eggs. I have not yet examined, whether these be those, that in the surfaces of all the Stones, where they are met with, make little round holes, and small traces and impressions, which make them look like *Worm-eaten Wood*. But 'tis probable, they are such. It should be observed, whether these Worms do not take Wings, and all the other appearances of Caterpillars; and whether they are not to be found in plaister that is full of holes, in Bricks, in Greety Stones, and in Rocks.

You may observe more of them in Walls exposed to the *South*, than in others; and that the Worms, that eat the Stone, live longer, then those, {323} that eat the Mortar, which keep not above eight days alive. I have observed all their parts with a very good *Microscope*, without which, and a great deal of attention, 'tis difficult to see them well.

I have seen other very old Walls altogether eaten, as those of the *Temple* at *Paris*, where I could find no Worms, but the Cavities were full of Shells of various kinds, diversly figur'd and turn'd: all which I believe to be little Animals petrified.

Some promiscuous Observations, made in Somerset shire*, and imparted by the above-mentioned Dr.* Beale.

His words are these, in a Letter to the *Publisher*, of the 24. *Septemb.* 1666 at *Yeovill* in*Somersetshire*;

I have two or three remarks, perhaps not unworthy to be recorded for further application in like cases of time and place

1. In the Moores from hence towards *Bridgewater*, in the extreme drought, we have endured this Summer, some lengths of pasture grew much sooner whithered and parched, than the other pasture. And this Parched part seem'd to bear the length and shape (in gross) of Trees. They digg'd, and found, in the place, *Oakes* indeed, as black as Ebony. And hence they have been instructed to find and take up many hundreds of Oakes, as a neighbour of good credit assures me. This advertisement may be instructive for other parts, as *Kent*, *Essex*, *Lincoln*, &c.

* This had somewhat of a Vitriolate taste. But the Experiment being made with greater quantities of this water, which questionless will be done, the nature and kind of it may be better known.

2. My Cosen *Philips* of *Montague* has in his pastures of *Socke*, about three miles off, a large Pool, to which Pigeons resort; but the Cattle will not drink of it, no not in the extream want of water in this drought. To the taste it is not only brackish, but hath other loathsome tasts. In a Venice-glass it looked greenish and clear, just like the most greenish Cider as soon as it is perfectly clarified. I boyl'd a Pint of it in a Posnet of Bell-Mettall (commonly used to preserve Sweatmeats:) suddenly it yeilded a thick froth, whence I scumm'd half a score Spoonfulls; of which the inclosed is a part, * Suffering the water to be boyl'd all away, it left much of the same on the sides and bottom of the Posnet.

3. From *Lamport*, towards *Bridge water*, Eeles are so cheap in the frosts of Winter, that they vend them for little. Their abundance is from hence, that as the people walk, in the frosty Mornings, on the banks of river, they discern, towards the edges of the banks, some parts *not hoar*, as the rest, but *green*; where searching the holes of the banks they find heaps of Eeles.

{324}

A Problem for finding the Year of the Julian Period *by a new and very easie* Method.

This occurs in the *Journal des Scavans* n°. 96. as it had been proposed communicated to the Learned *Jesuit DE BILLY.* viz.

Multiply the *Solar* Cycle by 4845. and the *Lunar*, by 4200. and that of the *Indiction*, by 6916. Then divide the Sum of the Products by 7980. which is the *Julian Period*: The *Remainder* of the Division, without having regard to the *Quotient*, shall be the year required after.

E. g. Let the Cycle of the *Sun* be 3; of the *Moon* 4; and of the *Indiction*, 5. Multiply 3. by 4845, and you have 14535; and 4. by 4200. comes 16800; and 5. by 6916. comes 34580. The Sum of the products is 65915, which being divided by 7980. gives 8. for the *Quotient*, and the number 2075. which remains, is the Year of the *Julian Period*.

Some learned Mathematicians of *Paris*, to whom the said *P. de Billy*, did propose this *Problem*, have found the Demonstration thereof; as the same *Journal* intimates.

An Account of some Books, not long since published.

I. TENTAMINA PHYSICO-THEOLOGICA DE DEO, *Sive* THEOLOGIA SCHOLASTICA, *ad Normam Novæ & Reformatæ Philosophiæ concinnata, & duobus libris comprehensa. Quorum altero, de Dei existentia adversus Atheos & Epicureos ex ipsorummet Principiis disputatur; altero, de ejusdem Essentia & Attributis; primò secundum Theologiam Ethnicam, ubi explicatur, Quantum hactenus Alii in Gentilium sententiis, de summi Numinis Natura eruendis, hallucinati fuerint; deinde secundum Theologiam Christianam: Et quid de Divina Essentia ac Attributis statuendum sit, diceretur. Quibus postremò accedit specialis Dissertatio de Primo Numinis Attributo, ÆTERNITATE.* Authore *Samule Parkero,* A. M.

This Treatise, published the last year, would sooner have been taken notice of in these *Tracts*, had it not escaped the *Publishers* view till of late, when he, upon serious perusal, found it very worthy the recommending it to all sorts of persons; and particularly to those who either please themselves with that fond opinion, *That Philosophy is the Apprentiship of Atheisme*; or hearken to the aspersions, that are generally laid upon the *Reformation* of *Philosophy*.

This excellent piece removes both these; and being joyned and compared with the truly Noble Mr. *Boyle*'s Considerations in his *First part* of the {325} *Usefulness of Experimental-Natural Philosophy*, will strongly evince, How Much that Philosophy, which searches out the real Productions of Nature (the true Works of God) does manifest the Divine Glory more, than the Notionals of the Gentiles.

This Author (now a Fellow of the *Royal Society*) delivers his Matter in two Books.

Lib. 1. Cap. 1. Atheists are disappointed of the Authority of *Epicurus*, and of other Antient Philosophers, for their gross Atheisme.

Cap. 2. The beautiful Frame of the World evinceth the Architectonical Author and Governor.

Cap. 3. The admirable Contrivance in the Structure of Mankind, and of Animals, does more conspicuously shew the Deity.

Cap. 4. The Atheist caught in his own Net, or convinced by the true force of his own Arguments.

Cap. 5. The Arguments devised against Atheists by *Des Cartes*, and drawn from the *Idea's* of our Mind, examin'd and found imperfect and invalid.

Lib. 2. Cap. 1. The opinions of the Gentiles concerning God, unduly applied to the *Deity*, which we worship: but properly to be understood by them of the *Sun*, or of the *Soul of the World*.

Cap. 2. More expresly proved, that the Antient Philosophers conceived, the *Soul of the World* to be God.

Cap. 3. The Historical Theology of the Gentiles for the most part is unduly applyed or accommodated to the Holy Scriptures.

Cap. 4. The Divine Substance, Immensity, Incomprehensibility, Invisibility, explicated, as far as our weak reason does teach.

Cap. 5. The Divine Perfections, and other Attributes and Affections, how far explicable.

Cap. 6. The Eternity of God, how apprehended.

These are in short the Heads of the Book, which is yet but in Latin. It were to be wisht, the Author would make it speak his own lively *English*.

II. HONORATI FABRI *Soc. Jesu Theologi, Tractatus duo; quorum Prior est de Plantis & de Generatione Animalium; Posterior de Homine.*

As the Matter of this Book is considerable, so is the order and dependence of all its parts excellent; in regard that all the Propositions are ranged according to a Geometrical method, and so well disposed, that the latter do always suppose the former, and seem to depend all of them upon certain evident principles, whence they flow by a natural consequence.

This *Volume* contains two Treatises.

The *First* is divided into 5. Books. In the *four first*, he treats of *Plants*, and distributes them into three *Classes*; some growing *in the Earth*, as *Trees*; others, growing upon *Plants*, as *Mosse*; and a third sort growing upon *Animals*, as *Hair*, *Horns*, and *Feathers*. He examins and considers the {326} Parts of all these Plants and their Use, the manner, how they are produced, and nourished; and their different Qualities. He discourses also of Bread, Wine, Oyle, and the other Mixtures, that are made of Plants.

In the *Fifth Book*, he treats of the *Generation of Animals*, where he delivers many curious matters, explicating in a very easie and familiar way that Argument, which hath always been lookt upon, as one of the obscurest in Natural Philosophy.

The *Second* Treatise consists of 7. Books; wherein the Author considers, what appertains to *Man*. He discourses *first*, of Digestion, of the Circulation of the Bloud, and of the Use of the principal parts of the Humane Body. *Next*, he treats of the Senses, External and Internal; of all the Motions of the Body, both Natural and Voluntary, of the sensitive Appetite, and the Passions; *Thence* he proceeds to the Temperaments, Habits, Instinct, Sleep, Sickness, &c. *Lastly*, passing to the *Rational Soul*, he endeavours to demonstrate the Immortality thereof, and to explain also the Manner, how it worketh upon the Body, and is united with the Body; where he omits not to reason of all the Powers of the Soul, of Liberty, and of the Operations of the Understanding and Will.

In *general*, the Author makes it his study, for the explicating of the most perplext Difficulties, to shew, that Nature works not but by very simple and easie wayes.

In *particular* he intersperses several curious remarks. *E.g.* He teaches how to make*Perspectives*, that magnifie Objects, without Glass; telling us, that when an Object is look't upon through a small hole, it appears much greater than it is; and that therefore, if instead of Glasses one did cast before ones eyes two *Plates* having little holes in them, it would furnish us with a new kind of *Perspectives*, more commodious than those of Glasses, which spoil the Sight by reason of the refraction of the Rayes, caused thereby. *Again*, He renders the cause of that common, but surprising, effect of Painters, drawing certain Pourtraictures, which seem to look directly upon all their Beholders, on what side soever they place themselves: *Videl.* That in those Pictures, the Nose it a little turned to one side, and the eyes to the other. Whence it comes, that such pictures seem to look to the right side, because the Eyes are indeed turned that way; but they appear also to look to the left, because the point of the Nose is turned that way, and the Table, whereon the Picture is drawn, being flat the Looker on perceives not, that the Eyes are turned th'other way; which he would do, if the Eyes of the Pourtrait were convex: Whence it comes, that no Figure can be made embossed, which looks every way.

The art, which he teaches of making *Parsley* shoot out of the ground in a few hours, is this. Infuse the seed of it in Vinegar; and having sown it in good ground cast on it a good quantity of the Ashes of Bean-Cods, and sprinkle it with Spirit of Wine, and then cover it with some linnen. He mentions also; that if you calcine Earth, and then water it well, it will {327}produce a great variety of different Herbs, and that the Ashes of Corn burnt, being sown, have sometimes produced other Corn.

To add that by the by, this Author is not so addicted to *Aristotle*, as to be on his side, when he thinks Truth is not. He hath emancipated himself considerably from the *Scholastick* way of Philosophing. He dares maintain, that the Vegetative and Sensitive Souls are not*Substantial* Forms; and that it is with Plants and Animals, as with Artificial things, the Form whereof results from the Union and Disposition of the parts. According to this *Hypothesis* he explicates all the Operations of Plants and Animals, without having any recourse to the Soul. He avers also, that there are no *Species Intentionales*, and no Habitudes, and that the Animal Spirits, which Philosophers commonly believe to be necessary for all the Operations of Life, are useless.

It might also be observed out of this Author, what he discourses of the Generation of Animals by Putrefaction; of the Cause of intermittent *Feavers*, and of the Animal Instinct, and of many other particulars; were it not better to refer the curious to the Book it self.

III. *RELATION DU VOYAGE de l' Evesque de Beryte, par la Turquie, la Perse, les Indes,*&c. *jusques au Royaume de Siam, & autres lieux*; par M. *de Bourges, Prestre* &c.

This Author imploying his Pen chiefly, according to his design, to give an Accompt of the Success, the Undertakers of this Voyage had, in propagating the Christian Faith in the remoter parts of the World, and relating on that occasion, What number of Churches they have founded in *Cochin, China*, and the Kingdom of *Tonquin*, (in which latter alone he affirms, that there are more than three hundred thousand Christians;) being I say principally intent upon that Subject, he seems not to have made many Philosophical observations in those places. Mean while he does good service to those that have occasion to travel into the*East-Indies* mostly by Land, by describing the passage, they took thither; which was, That they embarqued at *Marseilles*, in *September*, the most convenient and favourable season for that Voyage; whence Ships do ordinarily pass every Month from *Syria*, reckoning one Month for the time of Sayling, to *Alexandretta*. Thence to *Aleppo*, counting one Month more for the Stay, to be made there to meet the *Caravane* for *Babylon*, and six weeks more for the march from *Aleppo* to *Babylon*, where a fortnight will pass before an opportunity happen to embarque upon the *Tyger* for *Balsora*; which Journey will require a fortnight more: And about this time it will be about the end of *January*. Thence is always conveniency to pass from *Congo*, 4 days Journey from *Comoron* or *Gombroun*, to which latter part there is also frequent occasion to pass by Sea from *Balsora*, which will take up some 15 or 16. days Sail. There (vid. at *Comoron*) you will every year meet with *English, Portugal, Dutch*, and*Moorish* Vessels, from *Surat*, from *October* till the end of *April*, for they are obliged to be at*Surate*, before the end of *May*, because all the ports of those {328}*Indies* are shut the 4. ensuing months, by reason of the danger of that *Sea*.

But besides this Direction, the Book is not quite destitute of *Natural* Observations. It relates, 1. How Diamonds are found and separated in *Golconda*; They take of the Earth, held to be proper to form them, which is reddish, and distinguish'd with white veins, and full of flints and hard lumps. Then they put near the places, which they will digge, a close and even Earth; and to it they carry those Earths, they have digg'd out of the Mine, and gently spread it abroad, and leave it exposed to the Sun for two days. Then being dryed enough they beat it, and sifting this Earth, they find the Diamonds in ashes of Flints, in which Nature hath set them. Here he adds, that the King of that Country farms out these Diamond-Mines for 600000. Crowns *per annum*, reserving to himself the right of all the Diamonds, that exceed ten *Carats* in weight. There are Diamonds, that mount to 35. and 40. *Carats*. And this is the great Treasure of that Prince.

2. That the most esteemed fruit in those parts; the *Durion* (of the bigness and shape of an ordinary *Melon*) has a very unpleasing and uneven untollerable smell, like to that of a rotten*Apple*.

3. That *Rice* prospers most in waterish grounds; and that the fields, where it grows best, resembles rather to Marshes, than to any ploughed Soyle: Yea, that that Grain has the force, though 6. or 7. foot water stand over it, to shoot its Stalk above it; and that the Stem, which bears it, rises and grows proportionably to the height of the water, that drowns the field.

4. That the way of keeping ones self harmless from a wild *Elephant*, when he runs directly upon one, is, to hold something to him; as a Hat, a Coat, a piece of Linnen, which he seises on with his Trunk; and playes with it, as if he were pleased with this apparent homage, done to him; and so passes on. If he be in a rage, that then the only remedy is, to turn incessantly behind him to the left side, in regard that naturally (*saith this Author*) he never turns himself that way, but to the right: And the time, there is to turn, because of the Beasts unweildiness, affords leisure enough to climbe up some high Tree, or to mount some steep ground: all which if it fail, by holding always his tail, and turning with him, the Animal will be tired, and give opportunity to escape.

London, Printed by *T. R.* for *John Martin*, Printer to the *Royal Society*, and are to be sold at the *Bell* a little without *Temple-Bar.*
{329}

**PHILOSOPHICAL
TRANSACTIONS.**

Munday, November 19. 1666.

The Contents.

An Addition to the Instances of Petrification, enumerated in the last of these*Papers.*

164

This Instance *was some while since communicated to the* Royal Society *by that Ingenious Gentleman Mr.* Philip Packer, *a worthy Member of that Body; in these words;*

On a Bank in a Close of Mr. *Purefoy*, neer his house, call'd *Wadley*, a mile from *Farrington*in *Berks*, there grows an *Elme*, which hath now lost the top, and is grown hollow, containing neer a Tun of Timber. From the But of the same Tree, one of the spreading Clawes having been formerly cut off with an Axe, that part of the But, from whence the same was sever'd, being about 1½ foot above ground, and inward within the trunk {330}of the Tree, hath contracted a petrfied Crust, about the thickness of a *shilling*, all over the woody part within the Bark; the Marks of the Axe also remaining very conspicuous, with this petrified crust upon it. By what means it should thus happen, cannot well be conceived, in regard there is no water neer it; the part, above the ground and out of the weather; the Tree yet growing: unless being cut at some season, when the sap was flowing, the owsing of the sap might become petrified by the Air, and the Tree grow rotten and hollow inward since that time; which how long since, is not known.

A piece of that part cut, was presented, together with this Account, to the said *Society*, for their *Repository*.

Articles of Inquiries touching Mines.

What the Honourable *Robert Boyle* gave the Reader cause to hope for, in *Numb*. 11. when he was pleased to impart those *General Heads* for a Natural History of a Country, *there*publish'd; He is not un-mindful to perform, by enlarging them as occasion serves, with*Particular* and *Subordinate* Inquiries. Here he gratifies the Curious with a considerable Set of Inquiries about *Mines*: which though unfinish'd, yet the *Publisher*, was instant to obtain their present Publication, to the end, that he might the more conveniently recommend them to several Forreigners of his Acquaintance, now ready to return to their several Countryes, which he understands to abound in Mines; and from the Curious Inhabitants whereof, he expects to receive a good Accompt upon some at least of these Inquiries; which also by several of them have been earnestly desired, as Instructions, to direct them, what Particulars to inquire after upon this Subject.

These Quæries are reduced by the *Author* to six Heads:

The *first*, The neighbouring Country about the Mines.

The *second*, The Soyl where the Mines are.

The *third*, The Signs of Mines.

The *fourth*, The Structure and other particulars belonging to the Mines themselves.

The *fifth*, The Nature and Circumstances of the Ore.

The *sixth*, the Reduction of the Ore into Metal.{331}

QUÆRIES
About the first Title.

1. Whether the Country be Mountainous, Plain, or distinguish'd with Vales? And in case it be mountainous, what kind of Hills they are; whether high, or low, or indifferently elevated? Whether almost equal or very un-equal in height? Whether fruitful or barren; cold or temperate; rocky or not; hollow or solid? Whether they run in ridges, or seem confusedly placed; and, if the former, what way the ridges run, North and South, *&c*. And whether they run any thing parallel to one another?

2. Whether the Country be barren or fruitful? And, if any way fruitful, what it produces, and what it most abounds with?

3. What Cattle it nourishes, and whether they have any such thing peculiar in point of bigness, colour, shape, longævity, fitness or unfitness to make good meat, *&c*. as may be rather adscribed to the peculiar nature of the place, than to the barrenness of the Soyl, or other manifest causes?

4. Whether the Natives, and other Inhabitants, live longer or shorter than ordinary? Whether they live more or less healthy? Whether they be subject to any *Epidemical* Diseases, that may very probably be imputed to the Mines; and what these Diseases are; and what Remedies are found successful?

5. Whether the Country be, or be not furnish'd with Rivers, Brooks, Springs, and other Waters; and how these waters are conditioned?

6. Whether the Air be dry or moist; hot or cold; clear or foggy; thick or thin; heavy or light; and especially, whether the Weather be more or less variable than ordinarily; or whether it be subject to great and sudden changes, that may probably be imputed to the Mineral and Subterraneous Steams; and what they are? {332}

About the second Title.

7. Whether the *Soyle* that is neer the Surface of the Earth, be Stony; and, if it be, what kind of Stones it abounds with? Whether it be Clayie, Marley, Chalkye, *&c.* And, if it be of several kinds, how many they are; and by what properties they are distinguish'd?

About the third Title.

8. By what *Signs* they know or guess, that there is a Mine in such a place?

9. These Signs are *either* upon the Surface of the Earth, *or beneath* it.

To the *former* belong these *Quæries*.

10. Whether the Ground be made barren by Metalline or Mineral Effluviums?

11. Whether it be observed, that Trees and other greater Plants seem to have their tops burnt, or other leaves or outsides discoloured? or whether there be any Plants, that do affect to grow over such Mines; and whether it have been tryed, that other Plants, that would prosper in the adjacent places, will not be made to grow and thrive there?

12. Whether the Stones and Pebles, that are wash'd by the Brooks, Springs, or other Waters, have any colour'd substance left upon them; and if they have, of what colour, weight, *&c.* these adherences are?

13. Whether the Waters of the place proposed, do by their tast, smell, ponderousness, *&c.* disclose themselves to contain Minerals? And, if they do, what Minerals they or their residences, when they are evapourated away, do appear to abound with, or to participate of?

14. Whether *Snow* will not lye, or *Frost* continue so long, or *Dew* be generated or stay upon the ground in the place proposed, as on other neighbouring grounds?

15. Whether the *Dew* that falls on that ground, will discolour white Linnen or Woollen-Cloths, spred overnight on the {333} surface of the ground, and employed to collect the Dew? And whether the *Rain* that falls there, and may be supposed to come thither from elsewhere, will discolour such Clothes, or afford any residence of a Mineral Nature?

16. Whether the Place be more than ordinarily subject to Thunder and Lightning, and to sudden Storms or Earthquakes; as likewise to Nocturnal Lights and fiery Meteors.

17. Whether Mists use to rise from Grounds stored with Minerals? What is observable in them, and what Minerals they signify, and may be supposed to be produced by?

18. Whether the *Virgula Divinatoria* be used to find out the Veins of proposed Mines; and, if it be, with what success?

19. What other Signs above ground afford probability of Mines, or Direction for following a Vein over Hills, Valleys, Lakes, Rivers, *&c.*

The *second* sort of *Signs* belonging to these *Quæries*, are such as follow.

20. Whether there be any Clayes, Marles, or other Mineral Earths, yellow or liquid matters, that usually give notice of the Ore? And if there be more than one, how and at what depths they are wont to lye respectively? Of what thickness and consistence they are; and in what Order the Diggers meet with them?

21. Whether there be any Stones or *Marchasites* to be found neer, or not very far from the surface of the ground, by which one may have ground to expect a Mine? As is often observed in the Tin-Mines of *Cornwall,* over which such kind of Stones are divers times found lying above ground?

22. Whether all Stones of that kind do equally signify that Mine? And, if not, how the significant Stones are to be known, as by Colour, Bigness, Shape, Weight, Depth under ground, *&c.*

23. Whether there be any Earths of peculiar kinds, as to Colour, Consistence, *&c.* that indicate a Mine beneath or near them; and, if there be, what they are, and what is their consecution, if they have any?

166

24. Whether Heat or Damps give any assurance or a probability of finding a Mine?{334}

25. Whether Water of any kind, met with in Digging, especially at this or that depth, do betoken a Mine?

26. Whether there be any Signs of the neerness of the Mine, and what they are?

27. Whether there be any Signs of ones having miss'd the Mine, either by being past above, or beneath, or having left it on either hand; and what they are?

28. Whether there be any Signs not only of the distinct and determinate kind of Metals or Minerals; but of the Plenty and Goodness of the Vein; and what they are?

29. Whether there be any Signs of the depth of the Vein beneath the surface of the Earth; and what they are?

30. Whether there be any proper or peculiar Signs, that show it to be hopeless, or at least unlikely, to find a Vein in the place where it is digg'd for; and what those are?

About the fourth Title.

31. What is the depth of the Shaft or Groove (which though named in the *singular* Number; the Questions about it are *generally* applicable) till you come at the Vein or Ore?

32. Whether the Vein run or lye Horizontal, or dippe? And if it dippe, what *inclination* it hath, how deep the lowest part lies; and consequently how much deeper than the uppermost? As also, what it's Flexures, if it have any, are? And whether it runs directly *North* or *South,East* or *West*; or seem rather to have a Casual tendency, than any determinate one by Nature? and how far it reaches in all?

33. What is the Wideness of the Groove at the Top, and elsewhere? Whether the Groove be perpendicular or crooked; and if crooked, after what manner, and with what distance it winds?

34. How the Groove is supported? What are the kinds, length, bigness, and way of placing the Timber, Poles, &c. that are employed to support it? And how long the Wood will last, without being spoyled with the subterraneous fumes and waters? and what wood lasts longest?{335}

35. What Air-shaft belongs to the Mine? Whether it be *single*, or more than One? Of what breadth the Air-shaft is at the Orifice? Whether it be convenient enough, or not? How neer it is placed to the Groove; and in what position? And if there be *several* Air-shafts, what their Distances and scituation are in reference to the Groove, and to each other? Or how Air is supplied, if there be no Air-shafts?

36. Whether they meet with any Waters in the Mine? And, if they do, how copious they are; at what depths they occur; how they are qualified; and what way they Spring, &c.

37. Whether they are constant or temporary? whether they increase or diminish notably in Summer or Winter, or at any other time of the year; and if they do, at what season that is; how long it is wont to last; and the proportions of Increase and Decrease?

38. What Expedients and Engines are employed to free the Mines from Water? The materials, the parts, the bigness, the shapes, the coaptation; and, in short, the whole structure, number, and way of applying the Instruments, that are made use off to free the Mines from Water?

39. What are the Conditions, Number, &c. of the *Adits*?

40. Whether the Mine be troubled with *Damps*, and of what kind they are? whether they come often or seldom at any set time, or altogether irregularly? what Signs fore-run them? what mischief they do? what remedies are the most successfully imployed against them, aswell in reference to the Cleering of the Mine, as to the Preservation and Recovery of the Workmen?

41. What Methods the Mine-men use in following the Vein, and tracing their passages under ground (which they call *Plumming* and *Dyalling*) according to the several exigencies? And whether they employ the Instruments, made with the help of the Load-stone, the same way that is usual; and if not, wherein they differ in the use of the same Instruments; or what Instruments they substitute in their place?

42. What ways they take to secure themselves from the uncertainty, incident to the guidance of *Magnetick* Needles from the *Iron-Stone* or Ore, that they may meet with under

ground?{336}(of which yet perhaps there is not so great danger, as one may imagine; as far as I could find by a Trial, I purposely made in a Groove, where I was sure, there wanted not Iron-Ore.) And what other wayes may be used to direct Miners without the help of a Load-stone?

43. How the Miners deal with the Rocks and Sparrs, they often meet with, before they come at the Ore? Whether they use Fire to soften, calcine, or crack them? How they employ it, and with what measure of success?

44. What wayes and cautions they use, to free the Mine and secure the Work-men from the inconveniencies and danger accruing from the use of much fire in it?

45. What Instruments they use to break the Rock &c? And how those Instruments are conducive; and how long they last?

46. How the Mine-men work; whether naked or cloathed? And what Lights they use to work by; what materials they are made of, what measure of light they give; how long they last; and by what wayes they are kept burning in that thick and foggy air?

47. How Veins are follow'd, lost, and recover'd? And how several Miners work on the same Vein? And what is the best way of getting all the Ore in a Vein, and most conveniently?

48. How they convey out their Ore, and other things, that are to be carried out of the Mine? Whether they do it in Baskets drawn up by Ropes, or upon Mens backs; and if this last-named way; what kind of Vessels they use for matter, shape, and capacity? And whether the Work-men deliver them one to another; or the same Work-men carry them all the way? And whether the Diggers descend and ascend by Ladders of Wood, or of Ropes, &c.

About the Fifth Title.

49. Whether the Ore runs in a Vein; or lie dispers'd in scatter'd pieces; or be divided partly into a Vein, and partly into loose masses; or like a Wall between two Rocks, as it were in a Cleft; or be interspers'd in the firm Rock, like speckled Marble? Or be found in *Grains* like *Sand* or *Gravel*, as store {337}of excellent *Tin* is said to be found in some parts of *Cornwall* at the Sides and in the Channels of running Waters, which they call ...; or whether the Ore be of a softer consistence, like *Earth* or *Lome*, as there is Lead-ore in *Ireland* holding store of Silver, and Iron-ore in the North parts of *Scotland* and elsewhere? And what is observable in it as to Weight, Colour, Mixture, &c?

50. Whether any part of the Metal be found in the Mine perfect and complete? (As I have had presented me good valuable *Copper*, and pieces of perfect *Lead*, that were taken up, the one at *Jamaica*, and the other by an acquaintance of mine, that took them out of the ground himself in *New England*.)

51. Whether the Mine affords any parcels of Metal, that seem to grow like *Plants* (as I have sometimes seen Silver growing, as it seemed, out of Stone, or *Sparre* almost like blades of Grass; as also great Grains of a Metal, which appear'd to me, and which those, that tryed some of it, affirmed to be Gold, abounding in a stony lump, that seem'd to consist chiefly of a peculiar kind of *Sparre*.)

52. Whether the Vein lie near, or much beneath the surface of the Earth, and at what depth?

53. Whether the Vein have or have not any particular Concomitants, or Coats (if I may so call them;) and, if any, what they are, and in what order they lie? (As the Veins of *Lead-ore*, with us, have frequently annnext to them a Substance call'd *Sparre*, and next to that another, call'd *Caulk*.)

54. Whether (besides these Coats) the Vein have belonging to it any other *Heterogeneous* substance? (As in *Tin-mines* we often find that yellow substance, which they call *Mundick*.)

55. What are the principal Qualities of these Extraneous substances? (As that *Sparre* is white, but transparent, almost like course Crystall, heavy, brile, easily divisible into flakes, &c. *Caulk* is of a different texture, white, opacous, and like a Stone, but much more ponderous. *Mundick* I have had of a fine golden colour; but, though it be affirm'd to hold no Metal; yet I found it in weight, and otherwise, to differ from *Marchasites*, and the Mine-men think it of a poisonous nature.){338}

56. Whether the Vein be inclosed every way in its Coats; or whether it only lye between them?

57. Whether the Vein be every way of an uniform breadth, and thickness; and, if it be, what these Dimensions are; and if not, in what places it varies, and in what measures? (The like Questions are to be made concerning the *sparre*, *Caulk*, and other Teguments or mixtures of the Ore?)

58. Whether the Vein be un-interrupted, or in some places broken off; and whether it be abruptly, or not; and whether it be by Vales, Brooks, Gullets, *&c?*

59. How wide the Interruptions are? what Signs, whereby to find the Vein again? whether the ulteriour part or division of the Vein be of the same Nature, and hold on in the same Course, as to its tendency upwards or downwards, or Horizontally, Norward, Southward, *&c.* with the Vein, from which it is cut off?

60. Whether, in case the last end of the Vein be found, it terminate abruptly, or else end in some peculiar kind of Rock or Earth, which does, as it were, close or Seal it up, without leaving any crack or cranny, or otherwise? And whether the terminating part of the Vein tend upwards, downwards, or neither? And whether in the places, where the Vein is interrupted, there be any peculiar Stone or Earth, that does, as it were, seal up the Extremity of it?

61. Whether it be observed; that the Ore in Tract of time may be brought to afford any Silver or Gold, which it doth not afford, or more than it would afford, if it were not so ripe? And whether it have been found, that the Metalline part of the Vein grows so, that some part of the Mine will afford Ore or Metal in tract of time, that did not so before? And whether to this Maturation of the Mine, the being exposed to the free Air be necessary; or, whether at least it conduce to the Acceleration of it; or otherwise?

62. Whether all the Ore, contained in the Mine, be of the self-same nature and goodness; and, if not, what are the differing kinds; and how to be discriminated and estimated?

63. What is the fineness and goodness of the Ore, by which the Mine is wont to be estimated? And what are the marks and {339} characters, that distinguish one sort from another?

64. What proportion of Metal it affords? (As in our *Iron-mines* 'tis observed, that about three Tuns of Iron-stone will afford one Tun of Metal: And I have had *Lead-Ore*, which an Ingenious man, to whom I recommended such Tryals, affirm'd to me to afford three parts in four of good Lead.)

65. Whether the Ore be pure in its kind from other Metals, and, if not, of what Metals it participates; and in what proportion? Which is especially to be Inquired into, in case the Mine be of a *base* metal, that holds a *noble* metal: (As I have known it observ'd, that *Lead-Ore*, that is poor in its own metal; affords more Silver, than other; and I remember, that the *Ore* lately mention'd, being rich in Lead, scarce afforded us upon the *Cuppel*, an Atome of Silver. And *Matthesius* informs us, that a little Gold is not unfrequently found in *Iron-Ore.* And I have by me some Gold, that never endur'd the Fire, taken out of a Lump of Tin-Ore.)

About the sixth Title.

66. What are the mechanick and prævious Operations, as Beating, Grinding, Washing, *&c.* that are used to separate the Ore from the Heterogeneous Bodies, and prepare it for the Fire? Or whether the Ore requires no such preparation? (as it often happens in Lead, and sometimes in Iron, *&c.*)

67. Whether *Mercury* be made use off, to extract the nobler from the baser metals? (as is their practice in *Peru*, and other parts of the *West-Indies.*)

68. Whether the leaving the Ore expos'd to the open Air and Rain for a good while, be used as a Præparative? (as I have seen done in *Iron-stone.*)

69. Whether the Burning and Beating of the Ore be used to prepare it for the Furnace? (as is practised in *Iron*, and almost always in *Copper.*) And, in case they use it more than once, how often they do it; (for, *Copper-Ore* is in some places washed 8. or 10. times, and in others, 12. or 14.) and with what circumstances; as, how long the Ignition lasts at a time, whether the Ore be suffer'd to cool of it self, or be quench'd? whether it be washed betwixt each Ignition?

70. What Flux-powders, and other ways they have to try {340}and examine the goodness of the Ore in small quantities?

71. Whether, when they work in *great*, they use to melt the Ore with any Flux or Additaments, or only by the force of the Fire, or in any way between both? (As throwing in of Charcoals when they melt Iron-stone does not only serve to feed the Fire, but perhaps by the *Alchaly* of its Ashes to promote the fusior: so Lime-stone, &c.)

72. What kind of Furnaces they use, to melt the Ore in? Whether they be all of one sort and bigness, or of differing?

73. What are, the Situation, Materials, Dimensions, Shape, Bigness, and in short what is the whole structure and Contrivance of the Furnace? If there be any thing peculiar and remarkable? What Tools are used in Smelting, their Figures, use, &c. And the whole manner of working?

74. What kinds of Fewel, and what quantities of it, are wont to be employed in the Furnace, within the compass of a day, or week? How much is put in at a time? How often it is renewed? And how much Ore in a determinate time, as a week or a day, is wont to be reduced to Metal?

75. In case an Additament be employed, what that is, and in what proportion it is added? Whether it be mingled with the Ore, before that be put into the Fire, or cast in afterwards; and, if so, at what time, &c?

78. Whether the Ore be melted by a Wind, excited by the Fire it self; as in Wind-ovens? Ore by the course of Waters? Or acuated by the blast of Bellows; and, if so, whether these Bellows be mov'd by a Wheel, turn'd by Water running under it, or falling on it? And what are, the Dimensions, Situation, &c. of the Bellows?

79. What contrivance they have, to let or take out the Metal, that is in fusion; and cast it into Barrs, Sows, Pigs, &c?

80. What Clay, Sand, or Mould they let it run or pour it through? And after what manner they refrigerate it?

81. Whether or no they do, either to facilitate the fusion, or to obtain the more or better Metal, mingle differing sorts or degrees of Ore of the same metal? (As in some places 'tis usual, to mingle poor and rich Ore; and at *Mendip* they mix two or more of these differing kinds of *Lead-ore* that they call *Frim-ore, Steel-ore, Potern-ore,* &c.) {341}

82. Whether or no, having once brought the Ore to fusion, they melt all the Metal it self, to have it the more pure? And, if they do, with what circumstances they make the fusion?

83. Whether they have any Signs, whereby to know whether the Fusion have been well or ill perform'd; and the Metal have obtain'd the perfection, to be expected from such Ore, melted in such a Furnace?

84. Whether they observe any great difference in the goodness of the Metal, that first melts, from that of the rest of the Metal which comes afterwards in the same or another operation? And whether the Rule holds constantly? (For, though they observe in *Tin-Mines*, the best Metal comes first, yet in the works of an Industrious friend of mine, he informs me, that the best Metal comes last.)

85. Whether the produced Metal be all of the same goodness? And if it be, how good it is in reference to the Metal of other Mines, or other parts of the same Mine or Vein? And if it be not, what differences are observ'd between the produced portions of Metal; and what disparity that amounts to in the price?

86. What are the Wayes of distinguishing them, and estimating their goodness?

87. Whether they do any thing to the Metal, after it is once brought to Fusion, and, if need be, melt it over again, to give it a melioration? (As when *Iron* is refined, and turn'd into Steel;) And what distinct Furnaces, and peculiar Ways of ordering the Metals are employ'd to effect this improvement? With a full description of them and the Tools in all Circumstances, observ'd in the refining of Metals.

88. Whether in those places, where the Metal is melted, there be not elevated some Corpuscles, that stick to the upper parts of the Furnace, or Building? And, if there be, whether they be barely fuliginous and recrementitious exhalations, or, at least in part, Metallin Flowers? (As in the *Cornish* Tin-mines, after some years they usually destroy the

thatch'd Houses, where the Ore hath been melted, to get the stuff, that adhears to the insides of the Roofs, out of which they melt store of excellent Tin.)

89. Whether the Metal, being brought to fusion, affords {342} any Recrements? (As *Iron-stone* affords store of a dark Glass or Slagg) And, if it do, what those Recrements are? How they are separated from the Metal; and to what Uses they are employed?

90. Whether, after the Metal has been once melted, the remaining part of the Ore being exposed to the Air, will in tract of time be impregnated, or ripen'd, so as to afford more Metal? (For, this is affirm'd to me of the *Cornish* Tin-Ore; and what remained after the fusion of *Iron-ore* in the *Forest of Dean*, is so rich in Metal, that a Tenant of mine in *Ireland*, though he had on the Land, he held from me, an Iron-Mine, found it less profit to work it, than to send cross the Sea to the *Forest of Dean* for this already us'd Ore, which having lain for some ages, since it was thrown aside in great heaps expos'd to the Air, he affirm'd to yield as well great great store of Iron, as very good: though I somewhat doubt, whether this be *totally* to be ascribed to the Aire, and length of time; or to the leaving of Metal in the Slaggs in old times, before great Furnaces were in use.)

Promiscuous Inquiries about Mines, from the same Author.

1. Whether the Territorie, that bears the Mine, abounds with no other Kind of Mineral in some distinct part of it? (As in *Kent* near *Tunbridge*, one part of the Country which is Hilly, abounds all along with *Iron-Mines*; the other, which is also Hilly, and divided from it but by a small Valley, abounds exceedingly (as the Diggers and Inhabitants told me upon the place) in *Quarry's*, which the Metallin-Country wants, but is quite destitute of Iron-stone. And so at *Mendip*, in one part of the Hill, I saw store of *Lead-Mines*, containing several Kinds of Ore of that Metal; another part of the Hill I found to be full of *Cole-pits*, which had some *Marchasites*, but no Metal; and in another place, *Iron-ore*, and mixt Ores, which yet they did not think fit to work.)

2. Whether the Air appear to be really cold in Summer, {343} and hot in Winter at the bottom of the Mines, by surer proofs than the Testimony of our Touch?

3. Whether they ever meet with places and Stones actually very hot, as *Matthesius* relates? And whether that spring not from the quenching of *Marchasites*?

4. Whether they find in the Mines any Mineral Gelly, such as the *German* Naturalists call *Ghur*? And whether in process of time it will harden into a metal, or Mineral Concretion?

5. What are the Laws, Constitutions, and Customs, *Oeconomical, Political, Ethical*, that are receiv'd and practis'd among the Mine-men?

6. Whether the Diggers do ever really meet with any subterraneous *Demons*; and if they do, in what shape and manner they appear; what they portend; and what they do, *&c*?

7. Whether they observe in the Trees and other Plants, growing over or neer the Mine, not only, (as hath been already intimated) that the Leaves are any whit gilded or silver'd by the ascending Mineral Exhalations, but also, that the Trees or other Plants are more solid and ponderous? And if they have not also some discernable Metalline or Mineral Concretes, to be met within the small Cavities and Pores of their substance?

8. Whether there be not Springs, and also greater Streams of Water neer the Mine, that rise, and run their whole course under ground, without ever appearing above it?

9. Whether the Subterraneous Springs do rise with any wind or determinate change of weather?

10. How much heavier the *Atmosphere* is at the bottom of the Mine, than at the top? And whether Damps considerably increase the weight of it?

11. Whether they find any strange substances in the Mines, as Vessels, Anchors, Fishes inclos'd in Sparr or Metal, *&c*.? {344}

Promiscuous Inquiries, *chiefly about* Cold, *formerly sent and recommended to* Monsieur Heuelius; *together with his Answer return'd to some of them.*

A considerable piece of the grand Design of the Modern *Experimental* Philosophers being, to procure and accumulate Materials for a good Natural History, whence to raise in progress of time a solid Structure of Philosophy; all possible Endevours are used in *England*, to send abroad and recommend to as many of Forreign parts, as there is opportunity, *Directions* for searching into the Operations of Nature, and for observing what occurs therein, aswell as in Mechanical operations and practices.

Several Heads of that kind have been already publish'd for this purpose in several of the former Tracts; to which, as we have added, in this, the *Quæries* about *Mines*, so we shall subjoyn those, that were not long since committed to the care of that Excellent Promoter of Astronomy and Philosophy, Monsieur *Heuelius*, Consul of *Dantzick*; who demonstrates so much zeal for the advancement of real knowledge, that he not only improves and promotes it by his own Studies, but labours also to incite others to do the like; having already warmed many of the Northern Climate, particularly *Poland, Prusse, Livonia, Sweden* and *Denmark*, into a disposition to be studious and active in inquiring after such particulars concerning Philosophy, as are recommended from hence, and rendred them, very willing to employ themselves in things of that nature.

The Inquiries sent to Dantzick, are these;

1. What Signior *Burattini* (an *Italian* Gentleman, Master of the Mint to the King of *Poland*, and reputed a great Master in the *Mechanicks*) hath perform'd in *Diopticks?* Whether at present he employs himself, as is related, in grinding a *Telescope* of 120 foot long? And, if so, what way he means to make use {345}of, commodiously to handle a Tube of that length?

2. Whether the same have the Art (as has been written from *Paris*) to make such Glass, as is not at all inferiour to *Venice*-glass, and exceeds any plate of Glass, hitherto made there, twice or thrice in bigness?

3. What is the way of making Pot-ashes in *Poland?*

4. What is to be observed about *Succinum* or Amber? whether it be an Exsudation of the Sea? whether it be seen to float upon the surface of the Sea? whether it be soft, when 'tis first cast on shore? At what season of the year, and in what manner 'tis taken up, *&c?*

5. What is to be observ'd in the Digging of *Sal Gemmæ* in *Poland?* what is the Depth of the Mines, stored with this Salt? what their distance from the Sea, *&c?*

6. What truth there is in that Relation concerning Swallows being found in Winter under waters congealed, and reviving, if they be fish'd and held to the fire?

7. Whether there be in the *Bodnick Bay* a Whirl-pool, as is related to be in the Sea of*Norway*, which is commonly call'd the *Maal-stroom?* And whether there be any Signs, that speak the communication of those Gulphs by subterraneous passages; as the Jesuit *Kircher*affirms in his *Mundus Subterraneus* T. 1. p. 146?

8. To what depth the Cold in those parts peirces the Earth and Water?

9. Whether their Watches go slower by the intense cold?

10. Whether their Oyls in hard frosts are turn'd into true, that is, hard and brile, Ice?

11. Whether they can freeze there a strong Brine of Bay-Salt; and a strong Decoction of *Sal Gemmæ*, or Soot; or a strong Solution of *Salt* of Tartar, or of *Sugar* of *Lead?*

12. Whether they can congeal meer *Blood*, all the serous part thereof being sever'd? Item,*Canary* Wine; the *Lixiviums* of Soap-boylers, and such as are prepared of other Salts; as also, the Spirits extracted out of Salts, as Spirit of *Vitriol, Nitre,* &c?

13. Whether an intense and lasting Frost makes any alteration in *Quick-silver*, exposed very shallow in a flat Vessel.

14. Whether the Purgative virtue of *Catharticks* be increased or lessened, or even totally destroy'd by a strong and continued Cold?{346}

15. Whether Harts-horn thaw'd, and such like substances, using the same method of Distilling, yield the same quantity of Liquor, which they use to yield, when not frozen?

16. What Cold operates in the Fermentation of Liquors?

17. Whether Birds and Wilde Beasts grow white there in Winter, and recover their native colour in Summer?

18. Whether Colours may be concentred by a sharp cold? *E.g.* A strong Decoction of Cocheneel in a fit Glass?

19. Whether the *Electrical* virtue of *Amber*, and the *Attractive* and *Directive* force of the*Magnet*, be changed by a vehement Cold?

20. Whether pieces of Iron and Steel, even thick ones, be made britle by intense frosts; and therefore Smiths are obliged for prevention, to give their Iron and Steel-tools a softer temper?

21. Whether accurate Observations evince, that all Fishes dye in frozen Waters, if the Ice be not broken? Where it is to be diligently inquired into, whether the Cold it self, or the want of changing or ventilating the water, or the privation of Air, be the cause of the death of Fishes?

22. Whether any Physicians or Anatomists have inquired, by freezing to death some Animals (as Rabits, Pullets, Dogs, Cats, &c.) after what manner it is, that Intense Cold kills men? whether they have found any Ice in the Inner parts; and if so, in which of them; Whether in the Ventricles of the Brain and Heart; and in the greater Vessels?

These were the Queries recommended about a Twelve-month ago. Monsieur *Heuelius* in a late Letter of his, accompanied with several papers from others, returns this Accompt.

The Inquiries you proposed to me, I did impart to several of my Learned friends: But hitherto I have attained an Answer but to few particulars. Among the rest you'l find a Letter of the Learned *Johannes Schefferus*, Professor in the *Swedish* University at *Vpsall*, wherein he discourses handsomly of several things, being ready to entertain a Literary Commerce with you about such matters. Touching *Amber*, I am almost of the same mind with him, that it is a kind of *Fossil Pitch* or *Bitumen*, seeing it is not only found on the Shore of the *Borussian* Sea, but also digg'd up in subterraneous places, some *German* miles distant from the {347} and that not only in Sandy, but also in other Hills of firmer Earth; of which I have seen my self pretty big pieces. Concerning *Swallows*, I have frequently heard Fisher-men affirm, that they have here often fish'd them out of the Lakes, in the Winter; but I never have seen it my self. Whilst I am writing this, I receive Letters out of *Denmark*, advertising me, that those two Learned men, *Thomas* and *Erasmus Bartholin*, do intend shortly to answer the same *Quæries*. Next Winter, if God vouchsafe me life and health, I purpose to make a Journey to *Konigsberg*, where I hope to learn many things, especially about *Amber*.

Thus far in answer to those Inquiries for the present.

To this he subjoyns other things, no less fit to be communicated to the Curious, in these words;

The Books you have sent me over sea, I have not yet received: I wish, they were all translated into Latin; for I have not *English* enough, to understand all particulars perfectly. For the rest, you have obliged me, by communicating the Observations of the last *Eclipse* of the *Sun*, aswell those made in *England*, as those of *Paris* and *Madrid*. That I may requite you in some measure, I send you my Observations both of *that*, and the *Moons* last *Eclipse*. In the *Sun's Eclipse*, this is chiefly observable, That the *Semidiameter* of the *Moon* from the very beginning, to about 5. or 6. digits of the increasing *Phasis* was much less than the *Rudolphin* Account imports. For it was then almost equal to the *Semidiameter* of the *Sun*: but, after the greatest Obscuration, when I again contemplated the *Moons Semidiameter*, I found it 8″ or 9″ bigger than that of the *Sun*; so that the *Semidiameter* of the *Moon* was not always, during this Eclipse, constant to it self. It will therefore be worth while, to be hereafter more diligent and curious in this particular, and accurately to observe in the *Phasis* of each *Digit* the *Proportion* of the *Semidiameters* of both Luminaries; to the end, that *first* it may be made manifest, Whether in all the *Eclipses* of the *Sun*, or in some only, that variation happens; *next*, that the Causes of such a *Phænomenon* may be diligently inquired into. Of this Variation, the Excellent *Ismael Bullialdus* hath also observed something at *Paris*. For he has written to me, That in the same Eclipse the *Semidiam.* of the *Sun* to the *Semid.* of the *Moon* was, as 16′. 9″. to 16′. 22″; but that in another {348} *Phasis* of 6 digits, the Semidiameters appear'd equal. These my Observations, if you think them worthy, you may communicate to other Mathematicians. The last year 1665. *July* 27. (*st. n.*) the *Tables* did also indicate an Eclipse of the *Moon*: but though the Sky here was very cleer, yet the Moon was not at all obscured by the *true shadow*, but entred only a little into the *Penumbra*, wherein it continued 50′. The beginning of its touching the *Penumbra* did then almost happen, when *Aquila* was elevated 36° 18′; which is an Example worthy to be noted. I have many Observations of the *Eclipses* of former years by me, which I could not yet make publick, by reason of the multitude of my business, which do almost over-whelm me. The Eclipse of the Moon of this Year 1666. *June* 16. (*st. n.*) was observed from a Hill neer my Garden, to the end, that we might see both together the *Suns setting*, and the *Moon rising*. But I was disappointed of my hopes: For very thick Exhalations, besieging the *Horizon*, where the Moon was to rise, unto 2°. 30′, hindred me from seeing the *Moon rise*, in the Article of the *setting* of the *Sun*. Wherefore the first *Phasis* of 1. *dig.* 45′. did not appear but in the *Moons Altitude* of 2°. 30′; when the greatest Obscuration was already past. The *End* fell out hor. 9. 27′. about 128° from the *Zenith* Westward.

I am very glad to understand, that you have so good *Telescopes*, as to make such considerable Observations in *Jupiter* and *Mars*, as you have lately done in *England*. I have no leasure now, by reason of the Observations of the Fixt Stars, which I now almost constantly am employ'd about, to do any thing in the advancing of *Telescopes*. I am obliged to finish the *Catalogue* of the *Fixt Stars*; having mean while the contentment to find, that many excellent persons labour about the Improvement of *Optick Glasses*. If I could get a good one of those of 60. foot, you mention, at a reasonable rate, you would oblige me in sending me one; perhaps may I be so happy, as to make likewise some good discovery or other, by the help thereof. In the mean time, let me know, I pray, the Dimensions of those Glasses, and how they are to be managed. The ingenious *Burattini* has not yet finisht his *Telescope*; as soon {349}* A Letter, written since from *Paris*, advertises, that some of the Curious there have received one of these Glasses of *Sr. Burattini*, and do esteem it to be good without mentioning the Dimension of it: which yet is look'd for by the next. as he hath, I shall acquaint you with it. * Before I conclude, I must give notice to the Lovers of *Astronomy*, that on the 24. of *September* (st. n) of this year, I have observ'd that *New Star* in *Pectore Cygni* (which from the year 1662. untill this time hath been almost altogether hid) not only with my naked Eye, like a Star of the sixth or seventh Magnitude, but also with a very great *Sextant*. It is still in the very same place of the Heavens, where it was formerly from *A*.1601. to almost 1662. For, its Distance from *Scheat Pegasi* hath been by me found 35′. 20″. and from *Marcab*, 43°. 10′. 50″; which Distances (as I have found in my *Journal*) are altogether equal to those, which I observ'd *A*. 1658. the 1. of *November*. For the Distance from *Scheat* at that time was 35°. 51′. 20″. and from *Marcab*, 43°. 10′. 25″: where that former from *Scheat* exactly answers to the recent; and that from *Marcab*, 'tis true, differs in a very few *Seconds*, but that disparity is of no moment, since it only proceeded from thence, that this *New Star* is not yet so distinctly to be seen, as at that time, when it was of the *third Magnitude*. It is therefore certain, that it is the self same Star, which *Kepler* did first see *A*. 1601. and continued untill *A*. 1662. But whether in time it will grow bigger and bigger, or be lost again, time will shew. He that will observe this Star, must take care, lest he mistake those three more *Southern* ones, of the *Sixth Magnitude*, and now in a manner somewhat brighter (though not extant on the *Globe*) than the *New Star* in *Collo Cygni*. The highest of those three, is distant from *Scheat Pegasi* 36°. 25′. 45″; the middlemost from the same, 37°. 25′. 20″. and the lowest, 38°. 4′. 30″. Farewell, and assure the Most Illustrious *Royal Society* of my humblest Services.

So far Monsieur Heuelius, whose accurate Calcul. of the *Solar Eclipses* Duration, Quantity, *&c.* is intended to be fully represented the next Month, since it could not be conveniently done this time. The *annexed* Papers follow.

One is from Monsieur *Joh. Schefferus*, to this purpose.

1. That he is confident, the *Royal Society* of *England* will do much good for the advancement of usefull Knowledge.

{350}

2. That he conceives *Amber* to be a kind of *Fossil Pitch*, whole Veins lie at the bottom of the Sea; believing that it is hardned in tract of time, and by the motion of the Sea cast on shore: *He adds*, that hitherto it hath been believed, not to be found but in *Borussia*; but he assures, that it is also found in *Sueden*, on the shores of the Isle *Biorköö*, in the Lake *Melero*, whose water is *sweet*. Of this, *he saith*, he hath a fine piece by him, two inches large and thick, presented him by one, that himself with his own hands had gathered it and several other pieces, on the shore of the said Island; affirming withall from the mouth of a Shepherd of that place, that it is thrown out by a strong Wind, bearing upon the shore.

3. That it is most certain, that *Swallows* sink themselves towards Autumne into Lakes, no otherwise than *Frogs*; and that many have assured him of it, who had seen them drawn out with a Net together with Fishes, and put to the fire, and thereby revived.

4. That 'tis also very true, that many *Animals* there grow white in Winter, and recover their own Colour in Summer. That himself hath seen and had *Hares*, which about the beginning of Winter and Spring were half white, and half of their native colour: that in the midst of winter he never saw any but all white. That *Foxes* also are white in Winter; and *Squirrels* grayish, mixt of dark and white colour.

5. That 'tis known there generally, that *Fishes* are killed, by reason of the Ice not being broken: but *first*, in ponds only or narrow Lakes; *next*, in such Lakes only, where the Ice is pretty thick; for, where 'tis thin, they dye not so easily. *Lastly*, that those Fishes that lie in slimy or clayie ground, dye not so soon as others. But, *he adds*, that even in great Lakes, when 'tis a very bitter Frost, Ice is wont to be broken, either by the force of the Waves, or of the Imprisoned Vapors, raised by the agitation of the Water, and then bursting out with an impetuosity; witness the noise made by the rupture of the Ice through the whole length of such Lakes, which *he affirms* to be not less terrible than if many guns went off together. Whereby it falls out, that Fishes are seldom found dead in great Lakes.

6. That neither Oyle, nor a strong Brine of Bay-Salt, is truly {351}congeal'd into Ice, in those parts, *Viz.* at *Upsall* in *Sueden.*

7. That the Frost pierces into the Earth, two Cubits or *Swedish* Ells; and what moisture is found in it, is white, like Ice: That Waters, if standing, freeze to a greater depth, even to three such Ells or more; but those that have a Current, less: That rapid Rivers freeze not at all; nor ever-bubling Springs; and that these latter seem even to be warmer in Winter, than Summer.

So far this Observer; who likewise offers his Services in giving an answer to the remaining*Queries*, and in entertaining a commerce in such other Philosophical matters, as he is conversant in.

Another Paper written by Monsieur *Febre*, chief Secretary to Prince *Ratzivil*, contains these particulars;

1. That the College of the Learned in *Borussia*, finds it not so easie to resolve all those*Queries* sent from *England* to M. *Heuelius:* but yet that they will try what may be done upon it.

2. That as for himself, he can assure from his own Experience concerning the Effects of Cold; *First*, That in the War against the *Muscovites* and *Cosacks, A.* 1655. in *January*, in*White Russia*, at the Siege of *Biskow*, 30. Leagues from *Smolensko*, and three from *Morhilo*, near the River *Boristhenes*, when they had Quarter in a Village call'd *Bikau*, they were seized on with such a Frost, that all their Provisions of *Spanish* Wines or *Petersimen*, and*Beere*, were in one Night frozen upon the Sleds, notwithstanding they were cover'd with Straw; in so much, that when next morning they would have drawn of those Liquors, they found all dry, and were constrain'd to carry them into a Stove, to thaw them; which they could not do in two whole days, and were obliged to break the Vessels, and put pieces of the Icy Wine into Kettles to thaw them over the Fire, for Drink: That they asked not for a Draught, but a *Morsel* of Wine or Beer: That their Horses had no better cheer than themselves, as to matter of Drink; the Pond of the Village being so thoroughly frozen, that there was but very little Water left between the Ice and the bottom of the Pool; whereby the poor Beasts were forced to drink with great reverence, kneeling on the forefeet to thrust their heads into the holes, made for them in the Ice, and to suck thence some drops of Water; and that, if they had not had Snow to eat, there would have dyed a far greater {352}number of them, than there did. Moreover, that he observed, that the *Hungarian Wine*, of which they had a Tun, resisted the Cold better, than the *Peter Simen*; for it was not so much frozen; unless it be, that the Butler had more care of that, than the rest, by transporting it sooner into the Stove, when he found the excess of Cold. Again, that one presenting him in the March with some *Aqua-vitæ*, the Scrue of the Flagon, put to his Mouth, stuck so close to his Lips, that he could not draw it off, without drawing bloud,

In a *third* Paper, I find these particulars from the same M. *Febre.*

1. That a considerable person, one Dr. *Becker*, a great Lover of Curious Inquiries, has given him hopes to entertain this Philosophical Commerce.

2. That he hath seen men dye in *Poland* and *Lithuania* both of *Heat* and *Cold*. And *first*, that *A.* 1653. in *July*, being with this present King of *Poland* in march from *Leopoli* to the Camp of *Glignani*, it was so furiously hot that day of their march, that it caused such an alteration in that Regiment of Foot, which was the Kings Guard, marching most of them bare-foot upon Sands, that more than an hundred of them fell down altogether disabled, whereof a dozen dyed out-right, without any other Sickness. *Secondly*, as to the Cold, that the frost was so bitter, that 3 Souldiers dyed of it, *A.* 1665. the 2. of *January*, in passing a long Ditch: besides, that divers persons lost some of their Lims.

The Success of the Experiment of Transfusing the Bloud of one Animal into another.

This experiment, hitherto look'd upon to be of an almost unsurmountable difficulty, hath been of late very successfully perform'd not only at *Oxford*, by the directions of that expert Anatomist Dr. *Lower*, but also in *London*, by order of the R. *Society*, at their publick meeting in *Gresham Colledge:* the Description of the particulars whereof, and the *Method* of Operation, is referred to the next Opportunity.

Errata to be corrected in Number 18.

Pag. 311. line 18. read *marked*. p. 312. l. 35. r. *Sines*. ib. l. penult. *Sines*. p. 313. l. 13. r. *Sines*. p. 316. l. 26. r. *that* for *if*.

London, Printed for *John Crook* neer the *Blew-Anchor* in *Duck-lane*; and *Mose Pits* at the *White-Hart* in *Little-Britain*.

{353}

Numb. 20.

PHILOSOPHICAL
TRANSACTIONS.

Munday, December 17. 1666.

The Contents.

The Method observed in Transfusing the Bloud out of one live Animal into another: *And how this Experiment is like to be improved. Some Considerations concerning the same. An Accompt of some Sanative Waters in* Herefordshire. *A farther Accompt of the*Vitriolate *Water mention'd* Numb. 18. *together with some other particulars touching Waters. Inquiries for* Turky. *An Observation about Optick Glasses made of Rock-Crystal, communicated from* Italy. *A Relation of the Use of the Grain of* Kermes *for*Coloration, *from* France. *An Accompt of some Books lately publisht*, vid. 1. PINAX *Rerum Naturalium* BRITANNICARUM, *continens VEGETABILIA, ANIMALIA &* Fossilia ANGLIÆ, *inchoatus; Auth.* Christophoro Merret, *M.D.* 2. *PLACITA PHYLOSOPHICA* Guarini. 3. *GUSTUS ORGANUM per* Laurentium Bellini*deprehensum.*

The Method observed in *Transfusing the Bloud of one Animal into another.*

This Method was promised in the last of these Papers. It was first practiced by Dr. *Lower* in*Oxford*, and by him communicated to the Honourable *Robert Boyl*, who imparted it to the*Royal Society*, as follows;

First, Take up the *Carotidal* Artery of the Dog or other Animal, whose Bloud is to be transfused into another of the {354}same or a different kind, and separate it from the Nerve of the*Eighth pair*, and lay it bare above an inch. Then make a strong Ligature on the *upper* part of the Arterie, not to be untied again: but an inch below, *videl.* towards the Heart, make another Ligature of a *running* knot, which may be loosen'd or fastned as there shall be occasion. Having made these two knots, draw two threds under the Artery between the Ligatures; and then open the Artery, and put in a Quil, and tie the Artery upon the Quill very fast by those two threds, and stop the Quill with a stick. After this, make bare the *Jugular* Vein in the other Dog about an inch and a half long; and at each end make a Ligature with a running knot, and in the space betwixt the two running knots drawn under the Vein two threds, as in the other: then make an Incision in the Vein, and put into it two Quills, one into the *descendent* part of the Vein, to receive the bloud from the other Dog and carry it to the Heart; and the other Quill put into the other part of the *Jugular* Vein, which comes from the Head (out of which, the second Dogs own bloud must run into Dishes.) These two Quills being put in and tied fast, stop them with a stick, till there be occasion to open them.

All things being thus prepar'd, the Dogs on their sides towards one another so conveniently, that the Quill may go into each other, (for the Dogs necks cannot be brought so near, but that you must put two or three several Quills more into the first two, to convey the bloud from one to another.) After that unstop the Quill that goes down into the first Dog's *Jugular* Vein, and the other Quill coming out of the other Dog's Artery; and by the help of two or three other Quills, put into each other, according as there shall be occasion, insert them into one another. Then flip the running knots, and immediately the bloud runs through the Quills, as through an Artery, very impetuosly. And immediately, as the bloud runs into the Dog, unstop the other Quill, coming out of the *upper* part of his *Jugular* Vein (a Ligature being first made about his Neck, or else his other *Jugular* Vein being compress'd by ones Finger;) and let his own bloud run out at the same time into Dishes (yet not constantly, but according as you perceive him able to bear it) {355} till the other Dog begin to cry, and faint, and fall into Convulsions, and at last dye by his side.

Then take out both the Quills out of the Dogs *Jugular* Vein, and tye the running knot fast, and cut the Vein asunder, (which you may doe without any harm to the Dog, one *Jugular* Vein being sufficient to convey all the bloud from the Head and upper parts, by reason of a large *Anatomosis*, whereby both the *Jugular* Veins meet about the *Larinx*.) This done, sow up the skin and dis-miss him, and the Dog will leap from the Table and shake himself and run away, as if nothing ailed him.

And this I have tryed several times, before several in the *Universities*, but never yet upon more than one Dog at a time, for want of leisure, and convenient supplyes of several Dogs at once. But when I return, I doubt not but to give you a fuller account, not only by bleeding several Dogs into one, but several other creatures into one another, as you did propose to me, before you left *Oxford*; which will be very easie to perform; and will afford many pleasant and perhaps not unuseful Experiments.

But because there are many Circumstances necessary to be observ'd in the performing of this Experiment, and that you may better direct any one to doe it, without any danger of killing the other Dog, that is to receive the others bloud, I will mention two or three.

First, that you fasten the Dogs at such a convenient distance, that the Vein nor Artery be not stretched; for then, being contracted, they will not admit or convey so much bloud.

Secondly, that you constantly observe the Pulse beyond the Quill in the Dogs *Jugular* Vein (which it acquires from the impulse of the *Arterious* bloud:) For if that fails, then 'tis a sign the Quil is stopt by some congealed bloud, so that you must draw out the *Arterial* Quill from the other, and with a *Probe* open the passage again in both of them, that the bloud may have its free course again. For, this must be expected, when the Dog, that bleeds into the other, hath lost much bloud, his heart will beat very faintly, and then the impulse {356} of bloud being weaker, it will be apt to congeal the sooner, so that at the latter end of the work you must draw out the Quill ofter, and clear the passage; if the Dog be faint-hearted, as many are, though some stout fierce Dogs will bleed freely and uninterruptedly, till they are convuls'd and dye. But to prevent this trouble, and make the experiment certain, you must bleed a great Dog into a little one, or a *Mastive* into a *Curr*, as I once try'd, and the little Dog bled out at least double the quantity of his own bloud, and left the *Mastive* dead upon the Table, and after he was untyed, he ran away and shak'd himself, as if he had been only thrown into water. Or else you may get three or four several Dogs prepared in the same manner; and when one begins to fail and leave off bleeding, administer another, and I am confident one Dog will receive all their bloud, (and perhaps more) as long as it runs freely, till they are left almost dead by turns: provided that you let out the bloud proportionably, as you let it goe into the Dog, that is to live.

Thirdly, I suppose the Dog that is to bleed out into dishes will endure it the better, if the Dogs that are to be administred to supply his bloud, be of near an equal age, and fed alike the day before, that both their blouds may be of a neer strength and temper.

There are many things I have observed upon bleeding Dogs to death, which I have seen since your departure from *Oxford*, whereof I shall give you a relation hereafter; in the mean time since you were pleased to mention it to the *Royal Society*, with a promise to give them an account of this experiment, I could not but take the first opportunity to clear you from that obligation, &c.

So far this Letter; the prescriptions whereof having been carefully observ'd by those who were imployed to make the Experiment, have hitherto been attended with good success; and that not only upon Animals of the same *Species* (as two Dogs first, and then two Sheep) but also upon some of very differing *Species* (as a Sheep and a Dog; the former *Emitting*, the other *Receiving*)

Note only, that instead of a Quill, a small crooked thin {357}Pipe of Silver or Brass, so slender that the one end may enter into a Quill, and having at the other end, that is to enter into the Vein and Arterie, a small knob, for the better fastening them to it with a thread, will be much fitter than a strait Pipe or Quill, for this Operation: for so they are much more easie to be managed.

'Tis intended, that these tryals shall be prosecuted to the utmost variety the subject will bear: As by exchanging the bloud of Old and Young, Sick and Healthy, Hot and Cold, Fierce and Fearful, Lame and Wild Animals, &c., and that not only the same, but also of differing kinds. For which end, and to improve this noble Experiment, either for knowledge, or use, or both, some Ingenious men have already proposed considerable tryals and Inquiries; of which perhaps an account will be given hereafter. For the present we shall only subjoyn some.

Considerations about this kind of Experiments.

1. It may be consider'd in them, that the bloud of the *Emittent* Animal, may after a few minuts of time, by its circulation, mix and run out with that of the *Recipient*. Wherefore to be assured in these Tryals, that all the bloud of the *Recipient* is run out, and none left in him but the adventitious bloud of the *Emittent*, two or three or more Animals (which was also hinted in the *method* above) may be prepared and administred, to bleed them all out into one.

2. It seems not irrational to guess afore hand, that the exchange of bloud will not alter the nature or disposition of the Animals, upon which it shall be practised; though it may be thought worth while for satisfaction and certainty, to determine that point by Experiments. The case of exchanging the bloud of Animals seems not like that of *Graffing*, where the *Cyons* turns the Sap of the *Stock*, graffed upon, into its nature; the *Fibres* of the Cyons so straining the juice, which passes from the stem to it, as thereby to change it into that of the Cyons, whereas in this transfusion there seems to be no such {358}Percolation of the bloud of Animals, whereby that of the one should be changed into the nature of the other.

3. The most probable use of this Experiment may be conjectured to be that one Animal may live with the bloud of another; and consequently, that those Animals, that want bloud, or have corrupt bloud, may be supplyed from other with a sufficient quantity, and of such as is good, provided the Transfusion be often repeated, by reason of the quick expence that is made of the bloud.

Note.

In the last Transactions *was also promised an Accompt by the next, of Monsieur* Hevelius *his accurate Calcul. of the late* Solar Eclipses, *Duration, Quantity, &c. But this being to be accompanyed with* Scheme, *the* Graving *whereof met with a disappointment, it must be still referred to another Opportunity.*

An Accompt of some Sanative-waters in Herefordshire.
This account was communicated by Dr. *B.* in these words.

There are two Springs in *Herefordshire*, whereof one is within a Bolt, or at least Bow-shoot of the top of the near adjoyning loftie Hill of *Malvern*, and at great distance from the Foot of the Hill; and hath had a long and old fame for healing of eyes. When I was for some years molested with Tetters on the back of one and sometimes of both my hands, notwithstanding all endeavors of my very friendly and skilful Physitians I had speedy healing from a neighbouring Spring of far less fame. Yet this Spring healed very old and Ulcerous sores on the Legs of a poor Fellow, which had been poyson'd by Irons in the Gaol, after other Chirurgery had been hopeless. And by many tryals upon my hands, and the Tetters; I was perswaded, that in long droughts, and lasting dry Frosts, those waters were more effectually and more speedily healing, than at other times. And not to omit this circumstance, I did hold this water in my mouth, till it was warm, perchance somewhat intermingled with fasting Spittle, {359}and so dropping it upon the Tetter, I there could see it immediately gather a very thin skin upon the raw flesh, not unlike that which is seen to gather upon Milk over a gentle fire. This skin would have small holes in it, through which a moisture did issue in small drops, which being wip'd away, and the water continued to be dropp'd warm out of the mouth, the holes would diminish, and at last be all quite healed up.

For the *Eye-waters*, I conceived them more strongly tersive, and clearing the Eyes; and they had a rough smartness, as if they carryed Sand or Gravel into the Eye.

I have known and try'd three or four healing Fountains of late discovery, or of no old fame that I could hear of.

I did once put rich *Marle* for some days in a vessel of water, to try whether the water would acquire a healing vertue, but my Experiments were interrupted. I had in my thoughts many other ways of Tryal; which I may resume hereafter.

A farther Accompt of the Vitriolate-water, *mention'd* Num. 18 p. 323. *Together with some other particulars touching waters.*

This comes from the same hand as follows;

I formerly mentioned to you, that, if that Pool of Mr. *Phillip's*, which seems to be of Vitriolate-water, were on my ground, I would drain it, and search the head of the Spring, pursuing the source, till I could well discern, through what lay of Earth or Gravel it does pass. Now I shall tell you, that I have taken order for the further tryal of the said Water, by boiling a greater quantity in a Furnace, &c. But just as we were in readiness for the tryal, a stream of Rain-water fell into the Pool, and so discourag'd us for the present. I have also taken a course to turn the falling Waters aside, and to drain the Pool, that we may see, what the Native Springs (whether one or more) may be. Of which more hereafter.

I wish (*so he goes on*) we had a full Accompt of our *Salt-Springs* at *Droyt-wych* near *Worcester*, and at *Nant-wych* in *Cheshire* (what other Salt-Springs we have in *England*, I know not:) {360}It should be inquired, at what distance they are from the Seas, or from Salt-fluxes, from Hills, and how deep in the Vales? What the weight? Whether in droughts or long Frosts the proportion of Salt or weight increaseth? Whether the Earth near the Springs, or in their passage hath any peculiar ferment, or produceth a blackishness, if it rests, after it is well drained.

Inquiries for Turky.

Though many Relations and Descriptions of *Turky* be extant in Print, yet they leave in many a desire of a fuller information in the following particulars, lately drawn up, for the most part by Mr. *H.* and recommended to an Ingenious Gentleman, bound for that Country; and desired also to be taken notice of by others, that may have occasion to visit the same.

* *Rusma* is a kind of Earth, used in *Turky* to take away hair.

1. In what part of *Turky* the * *Rusma* is to be found; and in what quantity? Whether the *Turks* employ it to any other Uses, besides that of the taking away of Hair? Whether here be differing kinds of it? How it is used to take of hair, and how to get store of it.

2. Whether the *Turks* do not only take *Opium* themselves for strength and courage, but also give it to their Horses, Camels and Dromedaries, for the same purpose, when they find them tired and faint in their travelling? What is the greatest *Dose*, any men are known to have taken of *Opium*? and how prepared?

3. What effects are observed from their use, not only of *Opium* (already mention'd) but also of Coffee, Bathing, shaving their Heads, using Rice; and why they prefer that which grows not unless water'd, before Wheat, &c.

4. How their Damasco steel is made and temper'd?

5. What is their way of dressing and making Leather, which though thin and supple, will hold out water?

6. What method they observe in breeding those excellent Horses, they are so much famed for?

7. Whether they be so skilful in Poysoning, as it is said; and how their Poysons are curable?

{361}

8. How the *Armenians* keep Meat fresh and sweet so long, as 'tis said they do?

9. What Arts or Trades they have worth Learning?

10. Whether there be such a Tree about *Damascus,* call'd *Mouslat,* which every year about the Month of *December* is cut down close by the root, and within four or five Months time shoots up again apace, bringing forth Leaves, Flowers, and Fruit also, and bearing but one Apple (an excellent Fruit) at once?

11. Whether about *Reame* in the Southern part of *Arabia Fælix,* there be Grapes without any grains? And whether the people in that Country live, many of them, to a hundred and twenty years, in good health?

12. Whether in *Candia* there be no poysonous Creatures; and whether those Serpents, that are there, are without poyson?

13. Whether all Fruits, Herbs, Earth, Fountains, are naturally saltish in the Isle of *Cyprus?* And whether those parts of this Isle, which abound in *Cyprus-trees,* are more or less healthful, than others?

14. What store of *Amianthus* there is in *Cyprus,* and how they work it?

15. Whether *Mummies* be found in the sands of *Arabia,* that are the dryed flesh of men buried in those sandy Deserts in travelling? And how they differ in their vertue from the Embalmed ones?

16. Whether the parts about the City of *Constantinople* or *Asia Minor,* be as subject to Earth-quakes now, as they have been formerly? And whether the Eastern Winds do not Plague the said City with Mists, and cause that inconstancy of Weather, it is said to be subject to?

17. Whether the Earth-quakes in *Zant* and *Cephalonia* be so frequent, as now and then to happen nine or ten times a Month? And whether these Isles be not very Cavernous?

18. What is the height of Mount *Caucasus,* its position, temper in its several parts, *&c.*

19. With what declivity the Water runs out of the *Euxine-Sea* into the *Propontis?* With what depth? And if the many Tides and Eddies, so famous by the name of the *Euripi,* have any certain Period? {362}

20. If in the *Euxine-Sea* there can be found any sign of the *Caspian Seas* emptying it self into it by a passage under ground? If there be any different Colour, or Temper as to Heat or Cold; or any Current or Motion in the Water, that may give light to it?

21. By what Inland passages they go to *China;* there being now a passage for *Caravans* throughout those places, that would formerly admit of no Correspondence by reason of the Barbarisme of the Inhabitants?

22. Whether in the Aquæducts, they make, they line the inside with as good Plaister, as the Ancients did? and how theirs is made?

23. To inquire after these excellent works of Antiquity, of which that Country is full, and which by the ignorant are not thought worth notice or preservation? And particularly, what is the bigness and structure of the Aquaeducts, made in several places about *Constantinople* by *Solyman* the Magnificent? *&c.*

An Observation of Optick Glasses made of Rock-Chrystal.

* It may be queried whether those were true Veins, or only Superficial Strictures, and slight scratches.

This is contained in a Letter of *Eustachio Divini*, Printed in *Italian* at *Rome*, as the *39. Journal des Scavans* extracts it, *vid.*

Though it be commonly believed, that *Rock-Christal* is not fit for Optick-Glasses, because there are many Veins in it; yet *Eustachio Divini* made one of it, which *he saith* proved an excellent one, though full of Veins. *

An Accompt of the Use of the Grain of **Kermes** for Coloration.

This was communicated by the Ingenious Dr. *Croon*, as he received it from one Monsieur *Verny*, a *French* Apothecary at *Montpelier*, who having described the Grain of *Kermes*, to be an excrescence growing upon the Wood, and often upon the {363} leaves of a Shrub, plentifull in *Languedock*, and gather'd in the end of *May*, and the beginning of *June*, full of a red Juyce; subjoyns two Uses, which that Grain hath, the one for *Medicine*, the other for *Dying of Wool.* Waving the *first*, notice shall only be taken here of the *latter*, vid. That, for *Dying*, they take the Grain of *Kermes*, when ripe, and spread it upon Linnen: And at first, whilst it abounds most in moisture, 'tis turn'd twice or thrice a day, to prevent its Heating. And when there appears red powder amongst it, they separate it, passing it through a Searce; and then again spread abroad the Grain upon Linnen, untill there be perceived the same redness of the powder; and at the end, this red power appears *about* and *on* the surface of the Grain, which is still to be pass'd through a Searce, till it render no more.

And in the beginning, when the small red Grains are seen to move (as they will do) they are sprinkled over with strong Vinegar, and rubb'd between ones hands: afterwards little balls are form'd thereof, which are expos'd to the Sun to dry.

If this red powder should be let alone, without pouring Vinegar or some other accid liquor upon it, out of every Grain thereof would be form'd a little Fly, which would skip and fly up and down for a day or two, and at last changing its colour, fall down quite dead, deprived of all the bitterness, the Grains, whence they are generated, had before.

The Grain being altogether emptied of its pulp or red powder, 'tis wash'd in Wine, and then expos'd to the Sun Being well dryed, 'tis rubb'd in a Sack to render it bright; and then 'tis put up in small Sacks, putting in the midst, according to the quantity, the Grain has afforded, 10. or 12. pounds (for a *Quintal*) of the dust, which is the red powder, that came out of it. And accordingly, as the Grain affords more or less of the said powder, Dyers buy more or less of it.

'Tis to be noted, That the first red powder, which appears, issues out of the Hole of the Grain, that is on the side, where the Grain adhered to the Plant. And that, which about the end appears sticking on the Grain, hath been alive in the husk, having pierced its covers though the hole, whence it commonly issues, remains close as to the Eye. {364}

An Account of Some Books lately published.

1. *PINAX Rerum Naturalium BRITANNICARUM, continens VEGETABILIA, ANIMALIA & FOSSILIA in hoc Insula reperta, inchoatus, Auth.* Christophoro Merret, *Med. D. & utriusque* Societatis Regiæ *socio.*

The Learned and Inquisitive Author of this Book, hath by his laudable example of collecting together, what Natural things are to be found here in *England*, of all sorts (which he has done upon his own expences) given an invitation to the curious in all parts of the world to attempt the like, thereby to establish the much desired and highly useful commerce among *Naturalists*, and to contribute every where to the composing of a genuine and full *History of Nature.*

In the *Preface* he intimates, that his stock does still encrease dayly; and that therefore the Reader may expect an *Appendix* to this collection.

In the Body of the Book, he enumerates all the *Species*, Alphabetically: And, as to *Vegetables*, he reckons up about 410 sorts; and gives their *Latine* and *English* Names, and the *Places* and *Times* of their growth: reducing them afterwards to certain *Classes*, hitherto used by *Botanick* Writers in their *Histories* of *Plants.* Adding the *Etymology* of their Generick Names, and a compendious *Register* of the Time, *when* and *how long* the *English* Plants do shoot and flourish.

As to *Animals*, he finds of them about 340 kinds in *England*, whereof the *fourfooted* are about 50, *Birds* 170, and *Fishes* 120. *Insects* are innumerable, which yet he endeavours to enumerate, and to reduce to certain *Classes*; into which he also brings the three former kinds.

Concerning *Fossils*, he *first* takes notice of the *Metals* found in *English* Mines; as *Silver, Tin, Copper, Iron, Lead, Antimony*, and some *Gold* extracted out of *Tin*. Next of the *Stones*, of which he finds about 70 sorts; & amongst them, *Bristol Diamonds, Agates, Hyacinths, Emerods, Loadstones, Toad-stones*, (which last yet he affirms to be nothing but the grinding-teeth of the {365} Fish *Lupus*) *Pearls, Corals, Marble, Alablaster, Emery:* To which he adds the various kinds of *Coals*; as also *Bitumens, Turfs* and *Jets*. And *thirdly* of the various kinds of *Allam, Vitriol, Niter, Sea-salt, Pit-salt*. But *fourthly* of the various *Earths*, of which he reckons up 15. peculiar sorts (besides those that serve for *Husbandry*, which are not easily numbred;) and amongst them, *Read-lead, Black-lead* and *Fullers-earth*.

He concludes all with mentioning the several *Meteors* appearing in *England*; and the *Hot springs*, and *Medical Waters*; as also, the *Salin, Petrifying*, and some more unusual Springs: *Item, Subterraneous Trees, Subterraneous Rivers, Ebbings and Flowings of Wells*, &c.

II. *PLACITA PHILOSOPHICA Guarini*. The chief subject of this Treatise is Natural *Philosophy*; upon many important questions whereof it enlargeth, as those of the Motion of the Cœlestial Bodies, of Light, of Meteors, and of the vital and animal functions; leaving sometimes the common opinions, and delighting in the defence of *Paradoxes*.

E. G. That the material substantial Form, is nothing but *mera potentia*, and subsists not by it self: by which means the Author judges, he can free himself from many great difficulties touching *Generation* and *Corruption*, which do perplex the other Philosophers.

He holds *Epicycles* to be impossible, and *Exventricks*, not sufficient to explicate the motion of the Stars; but that all the irregularities of this motion may be salved by the means of certain *Spiral* Lines; largely proving this *Hypothesis*, and particularly explicating the motion of each Planet.

He denies the middle Region of the Air to be cold; and believes that cold is not necessary to condense the vapours into Water.

He admits not that received Axiome, *That the generation of one Body is the corruption of another*; maintaining that there are *Generations*, to which no corruption ever preceded; and that it may happen, that one Animal without dying may be changed into another Animal.

He alledges several reasons to evince, that the Air breathed in, enters not only into the whole capacity of the Chest, but also into the lower belly. {366}

He is of opinion that the Air, which is commonly believed to corrupt easily, is incorruptible; alledging among other reasons, this for one, that experience shews, that if a Bottle be exactly stop'd, there is never any mixt Body form'd in it; wherefore, *saith he*, the Air is not corrupted there.

He maintains, that 'tis not the *Magnet* that draws the Iron, but rather the Iron that attracts the *Magnet*. To explain which he affirms, that the Load-stone spreads abroad out of it self many corpuscles, which the substance of the Iron imbibes, and that, as dry things attract those that are moist, by the same reason Iron drawn the Loadstone.

He rejects the *species intentionales, Vital* and *Animal* Spirits, and holds many other uncommon opinions, touching *Light*, the *Iris*, the *Flux and Reflux of the Sea*, *&c.*

III. *GUSTUS ORGANUM per* Laurentium Bellini *novissimè deprehensum.*

The Author proposing to himself to discover both the principal *Organ* of the *Taste*, and the nature of its *object*, begins with the latter, and examins first, what is *Taste?* He judges that it is caused by nothing but Salts, which being variously figured, affects the tongue variously: alledging this for his chief reason, that the Salt which is extracted by *Chymists* out of any mixt body whatever it be, carries away with it all its taste, and that the rest remains tasteless. He adds that the Teeth in grinding the Food, serve much to extract this Salt: And he notes by the by, that the Teeth are so necessary for preparing the aliment, that certain Animals which seem to have none, have them in their stomach; and that nature has put at the entry of the palat of those that are altogether destitute of them, certain moveable inequalities, which are to them instead of Teeth.

182

But then *secondly*, concerning the *Organ* of Taste, he esteems, that 'tis neither the Flesh, nor the Tongue, nor the Membrans, nor the Nerves found there, nor the Glanduls, called *Amygdalinæ*; but those *little eminences* that are found upon the tongue of all Animals. To obtain which, he observes,

1. That from the middle of the Tongue to the root, as also towards the tip, there are found innumerable *little Risings* {367} called *Papillares*; but that from the tip of the Tongue unto the string there is observed none at all.

2. He hath experimented, that if you put *Sal Armoniack* upon the places of the Tongue, where those *Eminencies* are not, you shall find no Taste; but that you will find it presently assoon as you put any such Salt, where they are to be met with. Ergo, *saith he*, those *Eminencies* are the principal Organ of Taste.

3. He assures, that with a *Microscope*, may be seen in those *Risings* many little holes, at the bottom whereof there are small nerves, terminating there: But *he directs*, to observe this in live and healthy, not in dead or sick Animals.

Having laid down these Observations, he concludes, that the manner, after which Taste is perform'd, is this, That the particles of Salt passing through those pores, which pierce the *Papillary Eminences*, and penetrating as far as to the nerves, that meet them there, do by the means of their small points prick them; which pricking is called the *Taste*.

In the mean time he acknowledges, that before him Signior *Malphigi*, Professor at *Messina*, had made some of these discoveries.

The notice of these two last Books we owe to the *French Journal*.

Correct in Number. 19.

Page, <u>342</u>. line, 33. read *mixt Ores*, in stead of, *mixt with Ores*.

London, Printed for *John Martin*, Printer to the *Royal Society*, and are to be sold at the *Bell* a little without *Temple-Bar*.

{369}

PHILOSOPHICAL
TRANSACTIONS.

Munday, January 21. 1666.

The Contents.

An Account, formerly promised, of Monsieur Hevelius's *Calculation of the late* Solar Eclipse's *Quantity, Duration, &c. The Figure of the Star in the Constellation of* Cygnus, *together with the New Star in it, discovered some years ago, and very lately seen again by the same Mr.* Hevelius. *An Extract of a Letter, written by Mr.* Auzout, *concerning a way of his, for taking the* Diameters *of the Planets, and for knowing the* Parallax *of the* Moon: *Giving also a Reason, why in the* Solar Eclipse *above-mentioned, the* Diameter *of the Moon did increase about the end. A Relation of the loss of the Way to prepare the* Bononian Stone *for shining. A Description of a* Swedish Stone, *affording* Sulphur, Vitriol, Allum, *and* Minium. *A Relation of the Raining of Ashes. An Extract of a Letter from* Rome, *rectifying the Relation of* Salamanders *living in Fire. An Account of several Engagements for* Observing of Tydes. *Some Suggestions for Remedies against Cold. A Relation of an uncommon accident in two Aged Persons. An Account of Two Books,* I. ISMAELIS BULLIALDI ad Astronomos Monita duo: Primum, de Stella Nova, in *Collo Ceti* ante aliquot annos visa. Alterum, de Nebulosa Stella in *Andromedæ* Cinguli parte *Borea*, ante biennium iterum ortâ. II. ENTRETIENS sur les vies & sur les Ouvrages des plus excellens Peintres, antients & modernes, par M. FELIBIEN.

Monsieur* Hevelius*'s Calculation of the late* Solar Eclipse's *Quantity, Duration, &c.

This *Calculus* was not long since communicated by Monsieur *Hevelius* in a Letter to the *Publisher*, as follows, {370}

Eclipsis Solaris.

Observata An. 1666. D. 2. Julii, St. N. Mane, à Johanne Hevelio.

Ordo Phasium	Quantitas Phasium	Tempus æstin. sec. horol. ambulat.	Tempus sec. Sciother.	Altitude	Tempus correct.	Animadvertenda
		H	H	° ′	H	
		5 .51.11	5 .51. 0	7.45	5 .53.12	Quòd Sciatericum cum correcto tempore non omnino convenit,
		5 .57. 5	5 .57. 0	8.37	5 .59.28	non-nisi Lineæ Meridianæ imputandum.
		6 . 0. 0	6 . 0. 0	8.55	6 . 1.28	
	Initium	6 .55.30			6 .57.30	Initium circa 79 gr. à puncto Zenith occasum versùs contigit.
1	0 3/8 dig.	6 .57.30			5 .59.30	
2	0 3/4	7 . 0.23	7 . 0. 0		7 . 2.23	
3	1 1/8	7 . 2.30	7 . 2. 0		7 . 4.30	
4	1 1/2 dig.	7 . 4.50	7 . 5 ferè.		7 . 6.50	
5	1 3/8 ferè.	7 .10.57	7 .10		7 .12.57	
6	3 3/8	7 .14.59	7 .15		7 .16.59	
7	3 3/4	7 .17.50	7 .18 ferè.		7 .19.50	
8	4 3/8 dig.	7 .21.35	7 .21		7 .23.35	
9	4 2/3	7 .23.43	7 .23 ferè.		7 .25.43	Hujusque Semidiameter Lunæ æqualis extitit Solari.
10	5 1/4	7 .27.53	7 .28		7 .29.53	
11	6	7 .31.50	7 .32		7 .33.50	
12	6 3/4	7 .36.55	7 .37		7 .38.55	
13	6 7/8 paul. plus.	7 .38. 5	7 .38		7 .40. 0	
14	7 1/8	7 .39.45	7 .39		7 .41.45	
15	7 1/4 paul.	7 .42.30	7 .42		7 .44.30	

	plus.					
1 6	7 ½	7 .44. 6	7 .44		7 .46. 6	
1 7	7 ⅔	7 .46. 0	7 .46		7 .48. 0	
1 8	8 ferè	7 .48.25	7 .48 ferè		7 .50.25	
1 9	8¹ /5	7 .51.15	7 .51		7 .53.15	
2 0	8 ¼ paul. plus.	7 .53.37	7 .52		7 .55.37	
2 1	8 ¾	7 .55.45	7 .56 ferè		7 .57.45	Maxima obscuratio extitit digit. 8.25′ hora 8.2′.
2 2	8 ¾ paul. min.	7 .59. 5	7 .59		8 . 1. 5	
2 3	8¹ /5	8 . 6.30	8 . 6		8 . 8.30	
{ 371}24	7 ¾	8 .11.25	8 .12		8 .13.25	Hic Semidiameter *Lunæ*a d 8″ vel 9″ major apparuit.* * *See Numb. 19 of the Philosophical Transactions, p. 347.*
2 5	7 ¼ ferè.	8 .17.30	8 .18		8 .19.30	
2 6	7 ferè.	8 .19.41	8 .19		8 .21.41	
2 7	5 ⅞	8 .28. 8	8 .28		8 .30. 8	
2 8	5 ½ ferè.	8 .30.14	8 .30		8 .32.14	
2 9	4 ¾	8 .36.25	8 .36		8 .38.25	
3 0	3 ⅝	8 .43.19	8 .43		8 .45.19	
3 1	3 ¼	8 .46.12	8 .46 ferè.		8 .48.12	
3 2	3	8 .47.32	8 .47		8 .29.32	
3 3	2 ¾	8 .50.57	8 .50		8 .52.57	
3 4	2 ½ ferè	8 .54.15	8 .54		8 .56.15	
3 5	1 ¾	8 .58.24	8 .58		9 . 0.24	
3 6	1 ⅛	8 .59.35	8 .59		9 . 1.35	
3 7	0⁵ /6	9 . 1.38	9 . 1		9 . 3.38	Punctum finis distitit à verticali ad Ortum 143 gr.
3 8	0 ½	9 . 3.20	9 . 3		9 . 5.20	
3 9	Fi nis.	9 . 6.53	9 . 6	A ltit.	9 . 8.53	

9	4	9
.23. 6	7.33	.25 28
9	4	9
.24.16	7.42	.26.45
9	4	9
.28.29	8.10	.30.42
9	4	9
.30.36	8.28	.33.12

This Observation is by the same *Astronomer*, represented also by the *Figures* *AAAAAA*; as that of the *Horizontal Eclipse* of the *Moon*, is, by the *Figures BB*.

{372}

The Figure of the Stars in the Constellation of Cygnus; together with the New Star *in it, discover'd some years since, and very lately seen by* M. Hevelius *again.*

The Relation concerning this *New Star* in the *Brest of Cygnus*, very lately discover'd again at *Dantzick*, by M. *Hevelius*, was publish't *Numb.* 19. *p.* 349. The *Figure* of that *Constellation*, with the *New Star* in it, was thus, hastily drawn, sent over by that Observer.

{373}

An Extract of a Letter written Decemb. 28. 1666. *by M.* Auzout *to the* Publisher, concerning a way of his, for taking the Diameters of the Planets, and for knowing the Parallax of the Moon; as also the Reason, why in the Solar Eclipse above calculated, the Diameter of the Moon did increase about the end.

I did apply my self the last Summer to the taking of the *Diameters* of the Sun, Moon, and the other Planets, by a Method, which one M. *Picard* and my self have, esteem'd by Us the best of all those, that have been practis'd hitherto; since we can take the *Diameters* to *Second Minutes*, being able to divide one foot into 24000. or 30000. parts, scarce failing as much as in one only part, so as we can in a manner be *assur'd*, not to deceive our selves in 3. or 4. *seconds*. I shall not now tell you my Observations, but I may very well assure you, that the *Diameter* of the *Sun* has not been much less in his *Apogee*, than 31. m. 37. or 40. sec. and certainly not lesse than 31. m. 35. sec. and that at present in his *Perigee* it passes not 32. m. 45. sec. and may be lesse by a second or two. That, which is at the present troublesome, is, that the *Vertical* Diameter, which is the most easie to take, is diminisht, even at *Noon*, by 8. or 9. sec., because of the *Refractions*, which are much greater in Winter than Summer at the same height; and that the *Horizontal* Diameter is difficult, because of the swift motion of the Heavens.

As for the *Moon*, I never yet found her Diameter less than 29. m. 44. or 45. sec. and I have not seen it pass 33. m. or if it hath, it was only by a few *seconds*. But I have not yet taken her in all the kinds of situations of the *Apogees* and *Perigees* which happen, with the *Conjunctions* and *Quadratures*. I do not mention all, what can be deduced from thence, but if you have Persons at *London*, that observe these *Diameters*, we may entertain our selves more about this Subject, another time. I shall only tell you, that I have found a Way to know the *Parallax* of the *Moon*, by the means of her *Diameter*. *Vid.* If on a day, when she is to be in her *Apogee* or *Perigee*, and in the most *Boreal* Signes, you take her Diameter towards the *Horizon*, and then towards the *South*, with her *Altitudes* {374} above the Horizon. For, if the Observation of the Diameters be exact; as in these Situations the Moon changes not considerably her Distance from the Earth in 6. or 7. hours, the *Difference* of the Diameters will shew the Proportion there is of her Distance, with the Semi-diameter of the Earth. I do not enlarge, because that as soon as one hath this *Idea*, the rest is easie. The same would yet be practis'd better in the places, where the Moon passes through the *Zenith*, than here, for the greater the difference is of the Heights, the greater is that of the Diameters. I do not note (for it easily appears) that, if one were under the same *Meridian*, or the same *Azimuth* in two very different places, and took at the same time the Diameter of the Moon, one would do the same thing, though this Method goes not to preciseness.

From what has been said, may be collected the reason of the Observation, which M.*Hevelius* made in the last *Eclipse of the Sun*, touching the increase of the Moon's Diameter about the end. I am exceeding glad, that a person, who probably knew not the cause of it, has made the Experiment: but it is strange, that until now no Astronomer has foreseen, that that should happen, nor given any precepts for the Change of the *Moons Diameter* in the *Eclipses of the Sun*, according to the places, where they should happen, and according to the Hour and Height, the Moon should have. For, what hapned in that *Eclipse* of Augmentation, would have faln out contrarily, if it had been in the Evening; for, the Moon, which in that *Eclipse*, that began in the Morning, was higher about the end than at the beginning, was nearer us, and consequently was to appear bigger: But if the *Eclipse* should happen in the Evening, she would be lower at the end, and therefore more distant from us, and consequently appear lesser. So also in two different places, whereof one should have the Eclipse in the Morning, and the other at Noon, the Moon should appear bigger to him that hath it at Noon: And she must likewise appear bigger to those, who shall have a leser *Elevation* of the *Pole* under the same *Meridian*, because the Moon will be nearer them.

I wish, I could satisfie you about the *Optick Glasses* of Signior *Burattini* in *Poland*, which he hath sent hither; but I have not yet seen their performances my self. I only saw once the Glasses, {375}which are perfectly well wrought and well polisht. Those, that have tried them, find them very good; but they are only, the one of 10, the other of 8. foot. A good Astronomer told me, that they would bear a great *Aperture* in respect of their length.

I do not well know, what to say to yours concerning M. *Hevelius*. Mean while, the interest of truth, and the obliging manner, he has treated me with, engage me to answer him, in the matter of the *Comets.* I am perswaded, I shall convince him; but since he hath taken the*Illustrious Royal Society* for Judge, I accept that with all my heart.

A Relation of the loss of the Way to prepare the Bononian Stone *for shining.*

* It is hoped notwithstanding (which also a late Letter from abroad does hint) that some or other of the *Italian*Vertuosi at *Florence*have secured this Secret.

Though several Persons have pretended to know the Art of preparing and calcining the *Bononian* Stone, for keeping a while the Light once imbibed; yet there hath been indeed but one, who had the true secret of performing it. This was an *Ecclesiastick*, who is now dead, without having left that skill of his to any one, as Letters from *Italy* and *France*, some while since, did inform. There is no substance, in Nature, known to us, that hath the effect of this Stone; so that (to the shame of the present Age) this *Phænomenon* is not like to be found any where, but in Books, except some happy *Genius* light upon same or the like skill. *

A Description of a Swedish *Stone, which*
affords Sulphur, Vitriol, Allum*and* Minium.

This was communicated to the R. *Society* by Sir *Gilbert Talbot* Knight, a Worthy Member of that Body, as he had received it in *Denmark*, being his Majesties Extraordinary Envoy there; as follows,

There is a Stone in *Sweden* of a Yellow Colour, intermixed with streaks of white (as if composed of Gold and Silver) and heavy withal. It is found in firm Rocks, and runs in Veins, {376}upon which they lay Wood, and set it on fire. When the Stone is thus heated, they cast Water upon it, to make it rend, and then dig it up with Mattocks. This done, they break it into smaller pieces; and put it into Iron-pots, of the shape represented by*Figure* C; the mouth of the one going into the other. These they place, the*one* in the Oven upon an Iron fork sloping, so that, the Stone being melted, it may run into the *other*, which stands at the mouth of the Oven, supported upon an Iron. The first running of the Stone is *Sulphur.*

The remainder of the burned Stone is carry'd out, and laid upon a high Hill, where it lies exposed to the Sun and Air for the space of two years, and then taketh fire of it self, casting forth a thin blew flame, scarce discernable in the day time. This being consumed, leaveth a blew dust behind it; which the Workmen observe, and mark with woodden pins. This they dig up, and carry into the Work-house, and put it into great Tubs of Water, where it infuseth 24. hours or more. The Water they afterward boyl in Kettles, as we do Saltpeter, and put it into cooling Tubs, wherein they place crosse Sticks, and on them the *Vitriol* fastens, as Sugar-candy doth.

The Water, that remains after the extraction of the *Vitriol*, they mix with an eight part of Urin and the Lees of Wood-ashes, which is again boyled very strong, and being set to cool in Tubbs, crosse Sticks are likewise placed, and thereon the *Allum* fastens.

In the Water, which remains after the *Allum*, is found a Sediment, which being separated from the Water, is put into an Oven, and Wood laid upon it and fired, till it become red, which makes the *Minium*, wherewith they paint their Houses, and make plaister.

So far this Description; Which gave occasion to a curious person to call to mind, That there was a kind of Stone in the *North* of *England*, yielding the same substances, except *Minium*.{377}

A Relation of the Raining of Ashes, in the Archipelago, upon the Eruption of Mount Vesuvius, some years ago.

This came but lately to hand from that knowing person, Mr. *Henry Robinson*, and was thought fit to be now inserted here, that it might not be lost, though it hath hapned above 30 years ago. It was contained in a Letter, (subscribed by Capt. *Will. Badily*) in these words:

* Some of these Ashes were produced by Mr. *John Evelyn*, before the *Royal Society.*

The 6ᵗʰ of *December* 1631, being in the Gulf of *Volo*, riding at Anchor, about ten of the Clock that Night, it began to rain Sand or Ashes, and continued till two of the Clock the next Morning. It was about two inches thick on the Deck, so that we cast it over board with Shovels, as we did Snow the day before: The quantity of a Bushel we brought home, and presented to several Friends *, especially to the Masters of *Trinity House*. There was in our Company, Capt. *John Wilds* Commander of the *Dragon*, and Capt. *Anthony Watts*, Commander of the *Elisabeth* and *Dorcas*. There was no Wind stirring, when these Ashes fell, it did not fall onely in the places, where we were, but likewise in other parts, as Ships were coming from St. *John D'Acre* to our Port; they being at that time a hundred Leagues from us. We compared the Ashes together, and found them both one. If you desire to see the Ashes, let me know.

An Extract Of A Letter not long since written from Rome, rectifying the Relation of Salamanders living in Fire.

This came from that Expert Anatomist M. *Steno*, to Dr. *Croone Videl*. That a Knight called *Corvini*, had assured him, that, having cast a *Salamander*, brought him out of the *Indies*, into the Fire, the Animal thereupon swell'd presently, and then vomited store of thick slimy matter, which did put out the neighbouring Coals, to which the *Salamander* retired immediately, putting them out again in the same manner, as soon as they {378} rekindled, and by this means saving himself from the force of the Fire, for the space of two hours, the Gentleman above-mentioned being then unwilling to hazard the Creature any further: That afterwards it lived nine Months: That he had kept it eleven Months without any other food, but what it took by licking the Earth, on which it moved, and on which it had been brought out of the *Indies*; which at first was covered with a thick moisture, but being dried afterwards, the Urin of the Animal served to moisten the same. After the eleven Months, the Owner having a mind to try, how the Animal would do upon *Italian* Earth, it died three dayes after it had changed the Earth.

An Account of several Engagements for Observing of Tydes.

Since nothing is more important for discovering the Cause of that Grand *Phænomenon* of Nature, the *Flux* and *Reflux of the Sea*, than a true and full *History of the Tydes*; the *Virtuosi* of *England* have of late (especially since the Publication of Dr. *Wallis* his *Theory* touching that *Apparence*) taken care, to direct and recommend in several parts of the World, and particularly in the most proper places of these *Ilands*, such Observations, as may contribute to the elucidating of that Subject.

And as formerly they have sent their *Inquiries* of this Nature to the Isle of St. *Helena*, situated in the open Ocean beyond the *Æquinoctial*, and already received some account thereupon; so they have since dispatcht the like for the *Bermudas*, an *Isle* that hath no less conveniency of situation for that purpose. And they intend (as will more amply appear, God permitting, in a short time) to lodge with such Masters of Ships and Pilots, as shall sayl into remote parts, very particular directions of that kind, to be printed at the *Royal Societies* charges, and to be committed to the care of the Masters of *Trinity House* for disposing of them to that end.

And, as for the Observations, to be made in these Kingdoms; 'tis hoped, that the Masters in the Art of Navigation at *Bristol* (Mr. *Standridge* and Mr. *Iff*) will undertake that business with affection and care: the former of these two having already (as we are informed from a good hand) made a Collection of the Tydes; {379} for some years past, and found them differing from former Observations and Tables; the other promising future diligence in this matter; noting in the mean time, that some Tydes of last Autumn were so far differing from former Observations, that neither he, nor any others there, could make any thing of it.

We must not omit here to mention the readiness, expressed by these worthy Gentlemen, Mr. *Rob. Boyle*, Sir *Rob. Moray*, and Mr. *Henry Powle*, for concurring in this Work; the first, having undertaken to recommend Observations of this nature, to be made, upon the *Western* Coast of *Ireland* *; the second, upon the West of *Scotland*; and the third, in the Isle of *Lundy*; to whom we must adde the inquisitive Mr. *Sam. Colepresse*, for *Plymouth*, and the *Lands-end*. Besides, we hope to engage the curious of *France* in the same undertaking, especially for procuring, besides what is known already concerning that place, a very particular and exact account of the Tydes upon the Coast of *Britany*, where (especially about St. *Malo*) they are found to rise to admiration, even to 60, 70, and sometime 80, feet, at the New and Full Moon.

* The Observations particularly recommended for that Coast, are these;

1. At what hour it is High-water on the day of the New and Full Moon, upon every Cape and Bay of the Western Coast of *Ireland*.

2. How long after the New and Full Moon the highest Spring-tides fall out.

3. What are the perpendicular heights of the Flood, both at the ordinary, and the Spring-tydes.

Some Suggestions for Remedies against Cold.

As there have been Remedies found out against excessive *Heat*, and Means of cooling Meat and Drink; so it was lately, on the occasion of the sharp Season, suggested, That Remedies might be thought on against *Cold*; and that particularly it might be inquired into,

1. What things in Nature, or by Art, or Mechanical contrivance will retain a warming Heat longest, or a melting or scorching Heat?

2. What will continue or maintain Fire longest?

Some that observe common practises and vulgar Trades, take notice, That *Joyners* use *Leaden-Pots* for their Glue, alledging for a Reason, That Lead, being a close Mettal, retains the heat {380} longer than other Mettals. *Cary*'s Warming-stone promised a warmth for six or eight hours; if it performed but for two or three hours, it would be of great use. 'Tis found by sad experience, how hurtful Bright Fires, and especially of Stone-coal are to the Eyes.

To retain Fire long, certain *Black* Earths are useful, as we were newly informed by the Inquisitive Dr. *B.* That a Gentleman in *Sommertsetshire*, called Mr. *Speke*, had bountifully obliged *Ilminster*, and his Neighborhood, by a Black Fat-Earth lately found in his Park. But the same Correspondent adds, That he never saw any parallel to a *Sea-weed*, which he and some of his Fellow-Students had in *Cambridge* in the mouth of a Barrel of good Oysters. It was smaller than Pease-halm, yet cut, it lasted two very great Fires of Sea-coal, burning bright in the midst of the Fire; and by a stroak of the Tongues, it fell into the Hearth, jingling like Mettal.

A Relation of an uncommon Accident in two Aged Persons.

189

This was imparted by the above-mentioned Mr. *Colepresse*, who assures in his Letter, containing this Account, That the matter of fact was thorowly examined by himself, and that he was fully, and in all respects, satisfied of the truth thereof.

The Relation of the one, is in these words.

Joseh Shute Clerk, Parson of *Mary* (nigh *Plymouth*) in the County of *Devon*, aged 81 years, being a temperate man, and of an healthy constitution, having the in-most Grinder loose, and so remaining, perceived, that his mouth, about three Moneths since, was somewhat streightned; and upon inquiry into the cause of it, found, That he had a new Tooth (the third Grinder) being the innermost of the upper Jaw in the Right Cheek, which still remains firm.

The Account of the other follows thus.

Maria Stert of *Benecliffe*, in *Plympton St. Mary* (near *Plymouth*) in *Devon*, aged about 75 years, an healthy person, having had nine children, about the fortieth year of her age lost three of her {381} upper *Incisores* or *Cutters*, the other drawn out, and so remained Toothless, as to them, for about 25 years, when she perceived, that a new Tooth came forth (without any pain) next the *Canini* of the left Cheek: And about two years after, another Tooth grew out likewise without pain, close by the former. The first whereof, never came to above half the length of her former *Cutters*, the latter scarce breaking the skin: Both which yet proved serviceable, till about six weeks since, when she eating (no hard, crusty, or solid) Meat, that Tooth which came out first, fell down into her Mouth, without any loosness before hand perceived, or any pain; which had not a phang like other *Cutters*, but much less, and shorter. The other abides firm, and serviceable.

To the truth of these Relations, not onely the said *Joseph Shute* and *Maria Stert*, have put the one his name, the other her Mark, the third and seventh of *January*, 1666. but also Sir*William Strode*, and Mr. *Colepresse* have subscribed the same, as believing the Relation to be true.

An Account of two Books.

I. ISMAELIS BULLIALDI *ad Astronomos Monita duo: Primum, De Stella Nova, quæ in Collo Ceti ante annos aliquot visa est. Alterum, De Nebulosa in Andromeda Cinguli parte Borea, ante biennium iterum orta.*

The chief end of the *Author* in publishing this Tract, seems to be, To excite Astronomers to a diligent observation, both of that *New Star* in the *Neck* of the *Whale*, to be seen in *February* and *March* next; and of that other, in the Northern part of *Andromeda's Girdle*, to be seen at this very present.

As to the *former* of these Stars, *he affirms*, that, as it hath appeared for many years in the said place, so it will in the beginning of *March* next appear equal to the Stars of the *third Magnitude*, or perhaps bigger; and that about the end of the same Month, if the Crepuscle do not hinder, the greatest *Phasis* of it will appear, if so be, that it keep the same Analogy of Motions and Periods, which it observed from *An.* 1638. to *An.* 1664. Where he takes notice of the Causes, why its two greatest Appearances could not be seen, *An.* 1664, 1665, 1666; and how he {382} comes to know, that in the beginning of *March* next, It will equal, or even exceed the Stars of the *Third Magnitude*; noting, that from the Observations hitherto made of this Star, it is manifest, that the *greatest Phases* thereof do every year anticipate by 32. or 33. dayes; forasmuch as *An.* 1660. its *greatest Appearance* was about the end of *October* and the beginning of *November*; *An.* 1661. about the end of *September*, or the beginning of *October*, *An.* 1662. about the end of *August*, *&c.* so that this year it must be in *March*, if the former Analogy do hold.

He collects also from the Observations, That one *Period* from the *greatest Phasis* to the next, consists of about 333. dayes: but that the interval of the time betwixt the times of its beginning to appear equal to the Stars of the *Sixt Magnitude*, and of its ending to do so, consists of about 120. dayes: And that its *greatest Appearance* lasts about 15. dayes: All which yet he would have understood with some latitude.

This done, he proceeds to the investigation of the Causes of the Vicissitudes in the Emersion and Dis-appearance of this Star, and having discoursed, That the apparent Increase and Decrement of every Lucid Body proceeds *either* from its changed distance from the Eye of the Observer; *or* from its various site and position in respect of him, whereby the angle of Vision is changed; or from the increase or diminution of the bulk of the lucid body it self: and having also demonstrated it impossible, that this Star should move in a *Circle*, or in an*Ellipsis*; and proved it improbable that it should move in a *Strait Line*, he concludes, that there can be no other genuin, or at least, no other more probable cause of its Emersion and Occultation, than this, That the bigger part of that round Body is obscure and inconspicuous to us, and its lesser part lucid, the whole Body turning about its own Center, and one Axe; whereby for one determinate space of time it exhibits its lucid part to the Earth, for another, subducts it: it not being likely, that fires should be kindled in the Body of that Star, and that the matter thereof should at certain times take fire and shine, at other times be extinguisht upon the consumption of that matter.

So far of that Star. As to the other in the *Girdle* of *Andromeda*, seen about the beginning of*An.* 1665; he relates, that, when in the end of 1664. the World beheld the then appearing*Comet*, {383}Astronomers observed also this new *Phænomenon*, which was called by them*Nebulosa in Cingulo Andromedæ.* Concerning which, he notes, that the same had been already seen many years before by *Simon Narius*, vid. *An.* 1612. when with a *Telescope* he search'd for the *Satellits* of *Jupiter*, and observed their motions; alledging for proof hereof, the said *Authors* own words, out of his own Book, *De Mundo Joviali*, publisht *An.* 1614. And farther shews, that it hath formerly appear'd (about 150. years ago) and been taken notice off by an expert, though Anonymous, Astronomer; whose words he cites out of a*Manuscript*, brought out of *Holland* by the Excellent *Jacobus Augustus Thuanus*, returning from his Embassy to *Paris*; wherein also was marked the *Figure* of that *Phænomenon*; represented in print by our Author: who from all this collects, that, whereas this Star hath been seen formerly, and that 150. years since, but yet neither observed by *Hipparchus*, nor any other of the Antients, that we can find; nor also in the former Age by *Tycho Brahe*, nor in our Age, by *Bayerus*; and appear'd also in the Month of *November* last (wherein he wrote this *Tract*) much lessened and obscure, after it had, two years ago, shone very bright; that therefore it must needs appear and dis-appear by turns, like those in the *Necks* of the *Whale*and *Swan*.

II. *ENTRIENS* sur les *Vies et sur les Ouvrages* Des plus excellens Peintres, Anciens et Modernes, par Monsieur *FELIBIEN*.

This Author, having first discoursed of that Royal Pallace the *Louvre*, and the Designs of finishing it; passes on to the Art of *Picturing*, and treats of the three principal things, wherein a good Master of the Art must excel, *vid.* the Composition, Designing, and Laying on of Colours, which done, he ravels into the Origine, and deduces the Progress of Painting, and relates what is most remarkable in the Lives of the Antient Painters: And among many particulars, he observes in the Life of *Andreas de Sarte*, how difficult it is, to judge well of a Picture; relating, that a Duke of *Mantua*, having obtained of *Clement* VII. a Pourtrait of *Leo*X. which had been done by *Raphael Urbin*, and was at *Florence*, those of that Town being unwilling to lose so excellent a {384}piece, caused a Copy thereof to be made by the said *Andreas de Sarte*, which they sent instead of the Original. This *Copy* was so perfect, that *Julio Romano*, who had been bred and taught by *Raphael*, and was one of the best Painters of*Italy*, took it for an *Original*; and would never have been undeceived, if one *Vasari* had not assured him, that it was but a Copy, which himself had seen made, and had not shew'd him certain marks, that were there put to discriminate it from the Original.

In the *Second* Part, the Author has set down all that is requisite to judge and discourse well of Painting. But, to add Examples to Precepts, he discourses of the *Modern* Painters, and making a Description of their best Works, he takes occasion to observe, what is there found most excellent, and to shew, how they have put in practice the Rules of Art. He treats also of the declining of Painting, and affirms, that nothing considerable hath been done in it from the time of *Constantine*, till *An.* 1240. when one, *Cimabue*, began to raise this Art again. After this, he give a List of the Painters, that since have been famous for their Works, preferring before all others, *Raphael Urbin*. The last of all is the above-mention'd *Andrè de Sartes*, who died, *An.* 1530. and whom the liberality of *Francis* I. had drawn into *France*.

The Printing of these Tracts is now return'd to the first Printer thereof, as being somewhat re-setled after the late sad Fire of *London*.
FINIS.

In the *SAVOY*, Printed by *T. N.* for *John Martyn*, Printer to the *Royal Society*, and are to be sold at his Shop a little without Temple-Bar, 1667.

{385}

Numb. 22.

PHILOSOPHICAL
TRANSACTIONS.

Monday, February 11. 1666.

The Contents.

Trials proposed to be made for the Improvement of the Experiment of Transfusing Blood out of one live Animal into another. *A Method for* Observing the Eclipses of the Moon, *free from the Common Inconveniences. An Account of some Celestial Observations lately made at* Madrid. *Extract of a Letter, lately written to the Publisher, containing some observations about* Insects *and their Inoxiousness, &c. An Account of some Books,* vid. I. TOME TROISIEME DES LETTRES DE M. DESCARTES. II. ASTRONOMIA REFORMATA P. RICCIOLI. III. ANATOME MEDULLÆ SPINALIS ET NERVORUM, *inde provenientium,* GERARDI BLASII, *M.D. An Advertisement about the re-printing of* M. Evelyns *Sylva and Pomona. A* Table *of the* Transactions, *printed these two years.*

Tryals proposed by Mr. **Boyle** *to Dr.* **Lower**, *to be made by him, for the Improvement of Tranfusing blood out of one live Animal into another; promised* **Numb. 20. p.** 357.

The following *Queries* and *Tryals* were written long since, and read about a Moneth ago in the R *Society*, and do now come forth against the Authors intention, at the earnest desire of some Learned Persons, and particualrly of the worthy *Doctor*, to whom they were addressed; who thinks, they may excite and assist others in a matter, which, to be well prosecuted, will require many hands. At the reading of them, the *Author* declared, that of divers of them he thought he could fore-see the Events, but {386}yet judged it fit, not to omit them, because the Importance of the *Theories*, they may give light to, may make the Tryals recompence the pains, whether the success favour the *Affirmative* or the *Negative* of the Question, by enabling us to determine the one or the other upon surer grounds, than we could otherwise do. And this Advertisement he desires may be applied to those other Papers of his, that consist of *Quæries* or proposed *Tryals*.
The Quæries *themselves follow.*
1. Whether by this way of Transfusing Blood, the disposition of Individual Animals of the same kind, may not be much altered? (As whether a *fierce* Dog, by being often quite new stocked with the blood of a *cowardly* Dog, may not become more tame; *& vice versa, &c?*)

2. Whether immediately upon the unbinding of a Dog, replenisht with adventitious blood, he will know and fawn upon his Master; and do the like customary things as before? And whether he will do such things better or worse at some time after the Operation?

3. Whether those Dogs, that have *Peculiarities*, will have them either abolisht, or at least much impaired by transfusion of blood? (As whether the blood of a *Mastiff*, being frequently transfused into a *Blood-hound*, or a *Spaniel*, will not prejudice them in point of scent?)

4. Whether acquired Habits will be destroy'd or impair'd by this Experiment? (As whether a Dog, taught to fetch and carry, or to dive after Ducks, or to sett, will after

192

frequent and full recruits of the blood of Dogs unfit for those Exercises, be as good at them, as before?)

5. Whether any considerable change is to be observ'd in the Pulse, Urin, and other Excrements of the *Recipient* Animal, by this Operation, or the quantity of his insensible Transpiration?

6. Whether the *Emittent* Dog, being full fed at such a distance of time before the Operation, that the mass of blood may be suppos'd to abound with *Chyle*, the *Recipient* Dog, being before hungry, will lose his appetite, more than if the *Emittent* Dogs blood had not been so chylous? And how long, upon a {387}Vein opened of a Dog, the admitted blood will be found to retain *Chyle*?

7. Whether a Dog may be kept alive without eating by the frequent Injection of the Chyle of another, taken freshly from the Receptacle, into the Veins of the *Recipient* Dog?

8. Whether a Dog, that is *sick* of some disease chiefly imputable to the mass of blood, may be cured by exchanging it for that of a *sound* Dog? And whether a *sound* Dog may receive such diseases from the blood of a *sick* one, as are not otherwise of an infectious nature?

9. What will be the Operation of frequently stocking (which is feasible enough) an *old* and feeble Dog with the blood of *young* ones, as to liveliness, dulness, drowsiness, squeamishness, &c., *et vice versa*?

10. Whether a *small* young Dog, by being often fresh stockt with the blood of a young Dog of a *larger* kind, will grow bigger, than the ordinary size of his own kind?

11. Whether any Medicated Liquors may be injected together with the blood into the*Recipient* Dog? And in case they may, whether there will be any considerable difference found between the separations made on this occasion, and those, which would be made, in case such Medicated Liquors had been injected with some other Vehicle, or alone, or taken in at the mouth?

12. Whether a Purging Medicine, being given to the *Emittent* Dog a while before the Operation, the *Recipient* Dog will be thereby purged, and how? (which Experiment may be hugely varied.)

13. Whether the Operation may be successfully practis'd, in case the injected blood be that of an Animal of another *Species*, as of a *Calf* into a *Dog*, &c. and of a *Cold* Animal, as of a*Fish*, or *Frog*, or *Tortoise*, into the Vessels of a *Hot* Animal, and *vice versa*?

14. Whether the *Colour* of the Hair or Feathers of the *Recipient* Animal, by the frequent repeating of this Operation, will be changed into that of the *Emittent*?

15. Whether by frequently transfusing into the same Dog, the blood of some Animal of another *Species*, something further, and more tending to some degrees of a change of*Species*, may {388}be effected, at least in Animals near of Kin; (As Spaniels and Setting Dogs, Irish Grey-hounds and ordinary Grey-hounds, &c?)

16. Whether the Transfusion may be practic'd upon pregnant Bitches, at least at certain times of their gravidation? And what effect it will have upon the Whelps?

There were some other *Quæries* proposed by the same *Author*; as, the weighing of the*Emittent* Animal before the Operation, that (making an abatement for the Effluviums, and for the Excrements, if it voids any) it may appear, how much blood it really loses. To which were annext divers others not so fit to be perused but by *Physitians*, and therefore here omitted.

A Method for Observing the Eclipses of the Moon, *free from the Common Inconveniencies, as it was left by the Learned Mr.* Rook, *late* Gresham-*Professor of Geometry.*

Eclipses of the Moon are observed for two principal ends; One *Astronomical*, that by comparing Observations with Calculations, the *Theory* of the *Moons Motion* may be perfected, and the *Tables* thereof reformed: the other, *Geographical*, that by comparing among themselves the Observations of the same *Ecliptick Phases*, made in *divers* places, the*Difference* of *Meridians* or *Longitudes* of those places may be discerned.

The Knowledge of the Eclipse's Quantity and Duration, the Shadows, Curvity, and Inclination, &c. conduce only to the former of these ends. The exact time of the Beginning,

Middle, and End of Eclipses, as also in *Total* ones, the Beginning and End of *Total* darkness, is useful for both of them.

But because in Observations made by the *bare* Eye, these times considerably differ from those with a *Telescope*; and, because the *Beginning* of Eclipses, and the *End* of *Total* darkness, are scarce to be observed exactly, even with Glasses (none being able clearly to distinguish between the *True* Shadow and *Penumbra*, unless he hath seen, for some time before, the Line, separating them, pass along upon the Surface of the Moon;) and lastly, because in small {389}*Partial* Eclipses, the Beginning and End, and in *Total* ones of short continuance in the Shadow, the Beginning and End of *Total* darkness, are unfit for nice Observations, by reason of the slow change of *Apparences*, which the *Oblique* Motion of the Shadow then causeth. For these reasons I shall propound a *Method* peculiarly design'd for the Accomplishment of the *Geographical* end in Observing Lunar Eclipses, free (as far as is possible) from all the mentioned Inconveniences.

For, *First*, It shall not be practicable without a Telescope. *Secondly*, The Observer shall always have opportunity before his principal Observation, to note the Distinction between the *True Shadow* and the *Penumbra*. And, *Thirdly*, It shall be applicable to those Seasons of the Eclipse, when there is the suddenest Alteration in the *Apparences*.

To satisfie all which intents,

Let there be of the Eminentest *Spots*, dispersed over all Quarters of the Moons Surface, a select number generally agreed on, to be constantly made use of, to this purpose, in all parts of the World. As, for Example, those, which *M. Hevelius* calleth,

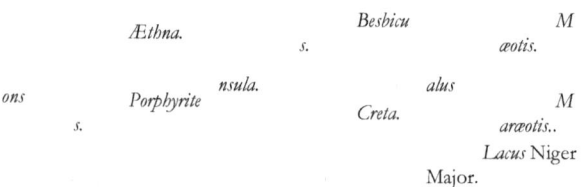

Sinai.

Æthna.   *Besbicu*   M
    s.   *æotis.*

ons   *nsula.*   *alus*
    Porphyrite   *Creta.*   M
    s.   *aræotis..*
    Lacus Niger
    Major.

Serorum.

Let in each *Eclipse*, not all, but (for instance) three of these *Spots*, which then lie nearest to the *Ecliptick*, be exactly observed, when they are first touch'd by the *True* Shadow, and again, when they are just compleatly entred into it, and (if you please) also in the *Decrease* of the Eclipse, when they are first fully clear from the *True* Shadow: For the accurate determinations of which moments of time (that being in this business of main importance) let there be taken *Altitudes* of remarkable *Fixed Stars* on this {390} side of the *Line*, of such, as lie between the *Æquator* and *Tropick* of *Cancer*; but *beyond* the *Line*, of such, as are situate towards the other *Tropick*; and in all places, of such, as at the time of Observation, are about 4. hours distant from the *Meridian*.

An Account of some Observations, lately made in Spain, by His Excellency the Earl of Sandwich.

The Right Honourable the *Earl of Sandwich*, as he appears eminent in discharging the Trust, his Majesty hath reposed in him, of Ambassador Extraordinary to the King of *Spain*; so he forgets not in the midst of that Employment, that he is a Member of the *Royal Society*; but does from time to time, when his weighty State-Negotiations do permit, imploy himself in making considerable Observations of divers kinds, both *Astronomical* and *Physiological*; and communicateth the same to the said *Society*; as for instance, lately, what he has observ'd concerning the *Solar Eclipse* in *June* last, the Suns height in the Solstice, and also the Latitude of *Madrid*, esteeming by the Suns Altitude in the *Solstice*, and by other Meridian Altitudes, the *Latitude* of *Madrid* to be 40 deg. 10 min; which differs considerably from that assigned by others; the General Chart of *Europe* giving to it 41 deg. 30 min. the General Map of *Spain*, 40 deg. 27 min. A large Provincial Map of *Castile*, 40 deg. 38 min.

194

To these particulars, and others formerly imparted, his Excellency is making more of the same nature; and particularly those of the Immersion of the *Satellites* of *Jupiter*.

We must not omit mentioning here, what he hath observed of *Halo*'s about the *Moon*; which he relates in these words;

Decemb. 25. *Old Style*, 1666. In the Evening, here (vid. at *Madrid*) was a great *Halo* about the Moon, the *Semidiameter* whereof was about 23 deg. 30 min. *Aldebaran* was just in the *North-east* part of the *Circle*, and the two Horns of *Aries* just enclosed by the *South-west* of the *Circle*, the Moon being in the *Center*. I note this the rather (*saith he*) because five or six years ago, vid. *Novemb.* 21. *Old Style*, 1661. an hour after Sun-set, I saw a great *Halo* about the Moon of the same *Semidiameter*, {391} at *Tangier*, the Moon being very near the same place, where she was now.

Extract of a Letter, lately written by Mr. Nathaniel Fairfax *to the* Publisher, *containing Observations about some* Insects, *and their Inoxiousness, &c.*

The Ingenious Author of this Letter, as he expresses an extraordinary desire to see the *Store-house* of *Natural Philosophy*, more richly fraughted (a Work begun by the single care and conduct of the Excellent Lord *Verulam*, and prosecuted by the Joynt-undertakings of the *R. Society*) so he very frankly offers his Service in contributing some of his Observations, and begins in this very Letter to perform his Offer. For, Having taken notice of what was publisht in *Numb. 9. p. 161.* out of the *Italian* Philosopher *Redi*, vid. That Creatures, reputed Venomous, are indeed no Poysons, when swallow'd, though they may prove so, when put into Wounds: He, for confirmation thereof, alledges Examples of several Persons well known to him (himself also having been an Eye-witness to some such Experiments) who have frequently swallow'd *Spiders*, even of the rankest kind, without any more harm than happens to Hens, Robin-red-breasts, and other Birds, who make Spiders their daily Commons. And having made mention of some men, that eat even *Toads*, he adds, that though a Toad be not a Poyson to us in the whole; yet it may invenome outwardly, according to some parts so and so stirr'd; an instance whereof he alledges in a Boy, who stumbling on a Toad, and hurling stones at it, some Juyce from the bruised Toad chanced to light upon his Lips, whereupon they swell'd, each to the thickness of about two Thumbs: And he neglecting to use, what might be proper to restore them, they have continued in that mishapen size ever since; the ugliness whereof, when the Relator saw, gave him occasion to inquire after the cause of it, which thereupon he understood to be, as has been recited.

On this occasion, the same Gentleman relates, that once seeing a Spider bruised into a small Glass of Water, and that it tinged {392} it somewhat of a Sky-colour, he was, upon owning his surprise threat, informed, that a dozen of them being put in, they would dye it to almost a full *Azure*. Which is touch't here, that, the Experiment being so easie to make, it may be tried, when the season furnishes those Insects; meantime, it seems not more incredible, that this Creature should yield a Sky-colour, when put in water, than that *Cochineel*, which also is but an Insect, should afford a fine *red*, when steep'd in the same Liquor.

An Account Of Some Books.

I. Le Tome troisieme et dernier des Lettres de *M. DES-CARTES.*

As the two first *Tomes* of M. *Des-Cartes* his Letters, contain Questions, for the most part of a *Moral* and *Physiological* Nature, proposed to, and answer'd by him; so *this* consists of the Contests, he had upon several Subjects with divers Men eminent in his time.

To pass by that sharp Contest, he was engaged in by some Professors of Divinity at *Utrecht*, who endeavoured to discredit his Philosophy, as leading to Libertinisme and Atheisme, notwithstanding he made it so much his business, to assert the Existence of a Deity, and the Immortality of the Soul: We shall take notice of what is more to our purpose, *vid.* the Differences, he had touching his *Dioptricks* and *Geometry*.

As for his *Dioptricks*, though a great part of the Learned World have much esteem'd that Treatise, as leaving little to be said after him upon that Subject; yet there have not been wanting Mathematicians, who have declared their disagreement from his Principles in that Doctrine. The first of them was the Jesuit *Bourdin*, Mathematick Professor in the Colledg of *Clermont* at *Paris*; but this difference was soon at an end. A second was Mr. *Hobbs*, upon whose account he wrote several Letters to *Mersennus*, containing many remarks conducing to the Knowledge of the Nature of *Reflection* and *Refraction*. But the Person, that did most learnedly and resolutely attack the said *Dioptricks*, was Monsieur *Fermat*, {393} writing first about it to *Mersennus*, who soon communicated his Objections to M. *Des-Cartes*, who failed not to return his Answer to them. But *Fermat* replied, and *Des-Cartes* likewise; and after many reciprocations, in which each party pretended to have the advantage, the matter rested; until M. *Fermat* taking occasion to write afresh of it to M. *De la Chambre*, several years after *Des-Cartes*'s death, upon occasion of a Book, written M. *De la Chambre, Of Light*; discoursed with this new *Author* after the same rate, as he had done before with *Des-Cartes* himself, and seemed to invite some-body of his friends, to re-assume the former contest. Whereupon M. *Clerselier* and M. *Rohault* took up the Gantlet, to assert the Doctrine of the deceased Philosopher, exchanging several Letters with M. *Fermat*, all inserted in this *Tome*, and serving fully to instruct the Reader of this Difference, and withal to elucidate many difficult points of the Subject of *Refractions*; especially of this particular, *Whether the Motion of Light is more easily, and with more expedition, perform'd through* dense *Mediums, than* rare.

Besides this, though one would think, Disputes had no place in *Geometry*, since all proofs there, are as many Demonstrations; yet M. *Des-Cartes* hath had several scufles touching that Science. As M. *Fermat* had assaulted his *Dioptricks*, so He reciprocally examined his Treatise *De Maximis & Minimis*, pretending to have met with *Paralogismes* in it. But the Cause of M. *Fermat* was learnedly pleaded for, by some of his Friends, who took their turn to examine the Treatise of *Des-Carte*'s Geometry; whereupon many *Letters* were exchanged, to be found this Book, and deserving to be considered; which doubtless the Curious would easily be induced to do, if Copies of this Book were to be obtain'd here in *England*, besides that one, which the *Publisher* received from his *Parisian* Correspondent, and which affords him the opportunity of giving this, though but Cursory, Account of it.

As to *Physicks*, there occur chiefly two Questions, learnedly treated of in this *Volume*, though not without some heat between M. *Des-Cartes* and M. *Roberval*. The *one* is, touching the Vibrations of Bodies suspended in the Air, and their Center of Agitation: about which, there is also a Letter inserted of {394} M. *Des-Cartes* to that late Noble and Learned English Knight, Sir *Charles Cavendish*. The *other* is, whether Motion can be made without supposing a *Vacuum*: where 'tis represented, That, if one comprehend well the Nature, ascribed to the *Materia subtilis*, and how Motions, called *Circular*, are made, which need not be just *Ovals* or *true* Circles, but are only called Circular, in regard that their Motion ends, where it had begun, whatever irregularity there be in the Middle; and also, that all the Inequalities, that may be in the Magnitude or Figure of the parts, may be compensated by other inequalities, met with in their Swiftness, and by the facility, with which the parts of the *Subtle Matter*, or of the first *Cartesian* Element, which are found every where, happen to be divided, or to accommodate their Figure to the Space, they are to fill up: If these things be well understood and considered, that then no difficulty can remain touching the Motion of the parts of Matter *in pleno*.

Besides all these particulars, treated of in this *Tome*, there occur many pretty Questions concerning *Numbers*, the *Cycloid*, the manner of *Working Glasses for Telescopes*, the way of *Weighing Air*, and many other Curiosities, Mathematical and Physical.

II. ASTRONOMIA REFORMATA, *Auctore* JOHANNE BAPT. RICCIOLI, *Soc. Jesu.*

For the Notice of this Book, and the Account of the Chief Heads contained therein, we are obliged to the *Journal des Scavans*, which informs us,

First, That the Design of this Work is, that, because several *Astronomers*, having had their several *Hypotheses*, there is found so great a diversity of opinions, that it is difficult thence to conclude any thing certain; this Author judged it also necessary, to compare together all the best Observations, and upon examination of what they have most certain in them, to reform upon that measure the Principles of Astronomy.

Secondly, That this *Volume* is divided into two Parts, whereof the *First* is composed of *Ten* Books; in which the Author {395} considers the principal Observations, hitherto made of the Motion of the Planets and the Fixed Stars, of their Magnitude, Figure, and other Accidents; drawing thence several Conclusions, in which he establishes his *Hypothesis*.

The *second* contains his *Astronomical Tables*, made according to the *Hypotheses* of the First Part, together with Instructions teaching the manner of using them.

Thirdly, That Astronomers will find in this Book many very remarkable things, concerning the *Apparent Diameter of the Sun* and the other Stars, the Motion of the *Libration of the Moon*, the *Eclipses, Parallaxes*, and *Refractions*. And that this Author shews, that there is a great difference between *Optical* and *Astronomical* Refraction, which *Tycho* and many others have confounded; undertaking to prove, that, whereas these *Astronomers* have believed, that the remoter any Star is, the less is its Refraction, on the contrary the Refraction is the greater, the more a Star is distant. And among many other things, he ingeniously explicates the two contrary Motions of the Sun, from East to West, and *vice versa*, by one onely Motion upon a *Spiral*, turning about a *Cone*.

Fourthly, That he represents, How uneasie it is to establish sure Principles of this Science, by reason of the difficulties of making exact Observations. So, for example, in the Observation of the *Equinox*, every one is mistaken by so many *Hours*, as he is of *Minutes*, in the Elevation of the *Pole*, or the Diameter of the Sun, or the Refraction, or in any other circumstance. In the Observation of the *Solstice*, the error of one only *Second* causeth a mistake of an *Hour* and an *half*: mean time 'tis almost impossible to avoid the error of a *Second*; and even the sharpest sight will not be able to perceive it, except it be assisted with an Instrument of a prodigious bigness. For to mark *Seconds*, though Lines were drawn as subtil as the single threds of a Silk-worms Clew, (which are the smallest spaces to be discerned by the sharpest Eye) by the Calculation made by this Author there would need an Instrument of 48. feet *Radius*, since Experience shews, that there needs no more at most, than 3600. threds of Silk to cover the space of an *inch*. But, suppose one could have a *Quadrant* of this bigness, who can assure himself, that dividing it into {396}324000. parts (for so many *Seconds* there are in 90. *Degrees*) either in placing it, or in observing, he shall not mistake the thickness of a single thred of Silk? He adds, that Great Instruments have their defects, as the small ones: For in those, that are *Movable*, if the thred, on which the Lead hangs, is any thing big, it cannot exactly mark *Seconds*; if it be very fine, it breaks, because of its great length, and the weight of the Lead: And in the *Fixed* ones, the greater the *Diameter* is, the less the Shadow or the Light is terminated; so that it is painful enough, exactly to discern the extremities thereof. Yet 'tis certain, that the greater the Instruments are, the surer *Astronomers* may be: Whence it is, the some *Astronomers* have made use of *Obelisks* of a vast bigness, to take the *Altitudes*; and Signior *Cassini*, after the example of *Egnatio Dante*, caused a hole to be made on the highest part of a Wall of 95. feet in a Church at *Bononia*, through which the beams of the Sun falling on the Floor, mark as exactly as is possible, the height of that Luminary.

Fifthly, That the Author reasons for the *Immobility of the Earth* after this manner. He supposes for certain, that the swiftness of the Motion of heavy bodies doth still *increase* in their descent; to confirm which principle, he affirms to have experimented, That, if you let fall a Ball into one of the Scales of a Ballance, according to the proportion of the height, it falls from, it raiseth different weights in the other Scale. For example, A Wooden Ball, of 1½ ounce, falling from a height of 35 inches, raiseth a weight of 5. ounces; from the height of 140 inches, a weight of 20 ounces; from that of 315 inches, one of 45 ounces; and from another of 560 inches, one of 80 ounces, &c. From this principle he concludes the Earth to be at Rest; for *saith he*, if it should have a Diurnal Motion upon its Center, Heavy Bodies being carried along with it by its motion, would in descending describe a *Curve Line*, and, as he shews by a *Calculus*, made by him, run equal spaces in equal times; whence it follows, that the Celerity of their Motion would not increase in descending, and that consequently their stroke would not be stronger, after they had fallen thorow a longer space. {397}

III. ANATOME MEDULLAE SPINALIS, ET NERVORUM *inde provenientium*, GERARDI BLASII, *M. D.*

The Author shews in this little *Tract* a way of taking the entire *Medulla Spinalis*, or Marrow of the Back, out of its *Theca* or Bony Receptacle *without Laceration*; which else happens frequently, both of the Nerves proceeding from it, and of the Coats investing it; not to name other parts of the same. This he affirms to have been put into practice by himself, by a fine Saw and Wedge; which are to be dexterously used: and he produceth accordingly in excellent Cuts, the Representations of the Structure of the said *Medulla* thus taken out, and the *Nerves*, thence proceeding; and that of several Animals, Dogs, Swine, Sheep.

He intermixes several Observations, touching the *Singleness* of this *Medulla*, against*Lindanus* and others; its *Original*, vid. Whether it be the Root of the Brain, or the Brain the Root of it: its difference of *Softness* and *Hardness* in several Animals; where he notes, that in.*Swine* it is much softer than in Dogs, &c.

He exhibits also the Arteries, Nerves, and Veins, dispersed through this *Medulla*, and inquires, Whether the *Nerves* proceed from the *Medulla* it self, or its *Meninx*; and discourses also of the *Principle* and *Distribution* of the Nerves; referring for ampler information in this and the other particulars, to that Excellent Book of the Learned Dr. *Willis*, *De Anatome Cerebri*. {398}

Advertisement.

It was thought fit to publish here the following *Advertisement* of *John Evelyn* Esquire, and that, as himself proposed it. *Viz*,

Being much solicited by many worthy Persons, to publish a *Second Edition* of my Discourse and Directions concerning *Timber, &c.* which was printed at the Command and by the Encouragement of the *R. Society*, I do humbly request, that if any Person have any Material, Additions or Reformations, which he thinks necessary either to the Part, which concerns the Improvement of *Forrest-Trees*, or that of *Cider*, he would be pleased to communicate his Notes and Directions to Mr. *H. Oldenburgh*, one of the Secretaries of the said Society, at his House in the *Palmal* of *St. James's Fields Westminster*, with what speed they conveniently can, before our *Lady-day* next, to be inserted into this intended *Edition*.

NOTE,

What was observed, Numb. 20. *p. 364, l. 18, of the Number of* Vegetables, (*vid.* That they are about 410.) *found in* England*; and catalogued by* Dr. Merret *in his* Pinax, *&c. is to be understood only of the different Kinds of Plants, not of the several sorts of several Plants; for, these being comprised, the Number will amount to about 1400.*

{399}

THE
PHILOSOPHICAL TRANSACTIONS
OF
Two Years, 1665 and 1666, beginning *March* 6. 1665.
and ending with *February* 1666; abbreviated in an
ALPHABETICAL TABLE:
And also afterwards Digested into a more
NATURAL METHOD.

In the TABLE, the first *Figure* signifies the *Number* of the *Tracts:* the second, the *Page*, as it is remarked in the same.

A.

Agriculture, Head of Inquiries concerning it. *num.* 5 *pag.* 91.

Air. The weight of it in all changes, by wind, weather, or whatever other influence observable by a standing *Mercurial Balance*, call'd a*Baroscope*, hinted in reference to M. *Hooks* Micrography, *n.* 2. *p.*31.

applied to particulars by Dr *Beale*, 9. 153.

with additions, 10. 163.

described with observables relating to an Earth-quake about *Oxford* by Dr. *Wallis*, 10. 167.

Mr. Boyle's remarks on the same, 11. 181.

The *Wheel-Baroscope* improved and delineated by M. *Hook*, 13. 218.

Another Balance of the Air contrived by M. *Boyle*, and call'd *Statical*, by which the former may be exactly stated and examin'd for many particular applications, 14. 231.

Anatome, see *Flesh, Blood, Animals, Lungs, Petrification, Taste*;
item,*Steno, Graeff, Bellinus, Redi*, in the *Liste of Books.*

Animals, one may live by the blood of another, the whole mass of his own blood being drawn out, and the blood of another infus'd in the mean time, 20. 353. See *Bloods Tranfusion*.

The Generation and Functions of Animals deduced by Mechanical principles, without recourse to *substantial form*, 18. 325. See*Honor. Fabri.* & *n.* 20. *p.* 365. See also *Guarini*.

Artificial Instruments or *Engins*. To weigh *air*, see *Baroscope*, or rather*Air*.

To discern drought or moisture of the Air, see *Hygroscope*. *n.* 2. *p.* 31.

appliable in the observation of *Tydes*, 17. 300.

Thermometers, to measure degrees of heat and cold, 2. 31.

described, 10. 166.

applied in the examination of *Tydes*, 17. 300.

An Instrument for graduating *Thermometers*, to make them *Standards*of heat and cold, 2. 31.

A new Engine for grinding any Optick Glasses of a Sphærical figure, 2.31.

To measure the Refractions of Liquors of all kinds, for establishing the Laws of Refraction, 2. 32.

To break the hardest Rocks in *Mines*, 5. 82.

To try for *fresh* waters at the bottom of the *Seas*, 9. 147.

To find the greatest depths in the Sea, 9. 147.

The *Engin* for fetching up fresh water defended by Explication, 13.228.

Huge *Wheels*, and other Engins for *Mines*, 2. 23.

By the fall of water to blow wind, as with Bellows, 2. 25.

{400}

Astronomical Remarks of a *New Star* seen by *Hevelius* in *Pectore Cygni*, which he supposeth to be the same, which *Kepler* saw A. 1601.and continued until 1602. and was not seen again until 1662. and then almost always hiding it self till 24. *Nov.* 1666. *That*, seen by*Kepler* was of the third magnitude; this now, of the sixth or seventh. Q. Whether it changes place and magnitude, 19. 349.

The *Scheme*, 21. 372.

A *New Star* in *Collo Ceti*, observ'd from 1638, to 1664, 1665, 1666. with its vicissitudes and periods, and causes of change, open'd by *Bullialdus*, who conceives the bigger part of that round body to be obscure, and the whole to turn about its own Center, 21.382.

Another *New Star* call'd *Nebulosa* in *Cingulo Andromedæ*, seen when the Comet appear'd 1665. observ'd by the said *Bullialdus* to appear and disappear by turns, *ibid.* 383.

A method for observing the *Eclipses of the Moon*, free from the common Inconveniences, by M. *Rook*, 22. 387.

B.

Baroscope. See *Air* and *Artificial* Instruments.

Blood. The new Operation of *Transfusing* blood into the veins, out of one Animal into another; with considerations upon it, 20. 353.

The first Rise of this Invention, 7. 208.

The Success, 19. 352.

Proposals and Queries, for the improvement of this Experiment, by M.*Boyle*, 22. 385, 386.

Little Blood-letting in *China*, 14. 249.

Blood found in some mens veins like Milk, or of the colour of Milk, 6.100.

again *p.* 117. 118.

and again 8. 139.

A *Bolus* in *Hungary* good as *Bole Armenick*, 1. 11.

The *Bononian Stone*, see *Light* or *Stone*, 21. 375.

Books abbreviated, or recited:

Laur. *Bellinus* de Gustùs Organo novissimè deprehenso, 20. 366. abbrev.

Gerh. *Blasii* Anatome Medullæ Spinalis & Nervorum inde procedentium, abbrev. 22. 397.

Mr. *Boyle* of Thermometers and History of Cold, abbrev. 1. 8. more 3.46.

—— His *Hydrostatical Paradoxes* abbrev. 8. 145. more largely 10.173.

—— His *Origin of Forms* and *Qualities*, 8. 145. abbreviated 11. 191.

Monsieur *de Bourges* his Relation of the Bishop of *Beryte* his Voyages in *Turky, Persia, India,* abbrev. 18. 324.

Bullialdi Monita duc, abbrev. 21. 381. See sup á *Astronomy.*

Des Cartes his Third Volume of *Letters*, 22. 392.

De la Chambre's Causes of the inundation of the Nile, abbr. 14. 251.

Cordemoy of the difference of Bodies and Souls, or Spirits, and their operation upon one another, abbrev. 17. 306.

Euclidis Elementa Geometrica novo ordine de nonstrata, 15. 261.

Hon. *Fabri* Soc. Jes. Tract. duo 1. de Plantis & Genet. Animalium. 2. de Homine; abbreviated, 18. 325.

Felibien of the most excellent Paintings, 21. 383.

Catalogue of *Fermats* Writings, and his character, 1. 15.

De Graeff, de Succi Pancreatici natura & usu, abbrev. 10. 178.

Guarini Placita Philosophica, abbreviated, 20. 365.

Hevelius's Prodromus Cometicus, abbrev. 6. 104.

His *Descriptio Cometica cum Mantissa*, abbrev. 17. 301.

Hobbes de Principiis & Ratione Geometrarum, described, 14. 193.

Animadverted upon by Dr. *Wallis*, 16. 289.

Hooks Micrographical and Telescopical Observations, Philosophical Instruments and Inventions, abbr. 2. 29.

Kircher's Mundus Subterraneus, abbrev. 6. 109.

Lower's Vindication of Dr. *Willis* de Febribus, 4. 77.

Meret's Pinax Rerum Naturalium Britannicarum, continens Vegetabilis, Animalia & Fossilia, in hac insula reperta, inchoatus; abbr. 20.364.

Parker's Tentamina Physico Theologica, abbrev. 18. 324.

Redi an Italian Philosopher, of Vipers, abbrev. 9. 160.

Ricciolo's Astronomia Reformato, Volumen quartum abbrev. 22. 394.

Smith of K. *Solomon*'s Pourtraicture of Old Age, 14. 254.

{401}

Stetonis de Musculis & Glandulis observatium Specimen; cum duabus Epistolis Anatomicis, abbrev. 10. 176.

Sydenhami Methodus Curandi Febras, abbrev. 12. 210.

Thevenot's Relation of curious Voyages, with a Geographical description of *China*, abbr. 14. 248.

The English *Vineyard* vindicated, 15. 262.

Isaac *Vossius* de Origine Nili, abbreviated, 17. 304.

Vlug-Beig great Grand-child to the famous *Tamerlane*, his Catalogue of fix't Stars, with their Longitudes, Latitudes, and Magnitudes, taken at *Samarcand*, A. 1437. Translated out of a *Persian* M. S. by M. *Hyde*, Keeper of the Bodleian Library, 8. 145.

The *Burning* Concave of *M. de Vilette* in *Lyons*, burning and melting any matter (very few excepted.) What, and How, and at what distance. The proportion; and compared with other rare burning Concaves, 6. 96.

C.

In *China* very ancient Books found of the nature and vertues of Herbs, Trees and Stones, 14. 249.

The Root *there* called *Genseng*, very restorative and cordial, recovering agonizing persons, sold there each pound for three pounds of silver, 14. 249.

China Dishes how made there, *ibid.*

A way found in *Europe* to make *China*-Dishes, 7. 127.

Chymists in *China* pretend to make Gold, and promise Immortality, 14.249.

Cold, see M. *Boyles* History, abbrev. More Inquiries, and some answers touching *Cold*, 19. 344.

How *Cold* may be produced in hottest Summers by *Sal Armoniack*, discovered by M. *Boyle*, 15. 255.

Some suggestions see remedies against *Cold*, by D. *Beale*, 21. 379.

Shining Worms found in Oysters, 12. <u>103</u>.

The Bononian Stone duly prepar'd continues *light* once imbibed above any other substance yet known amongst us, 21. <u>375</u>.

The loss of the way of preparing the same for shining, feared, *ibid.*

Longitudes at Sea, how to be ascertain'd by Pendulum-Watches, 1. <u>13</u>.

Lungs and Windpipes in Sheep and Oxen strangely stopt with Hand-Balls of Grass, 6. <u>100</u>.

M.

Marbles, that a liquor may be made to colour them, piercing into them, 7.<u>125</u>.

Mars, by what steps and degrees of diligence discover'd to be turbinated, both in *England* and *Italy.* Compare *n.* 10. *p.* <u>198</u>. and *n.* 14. <u>239,242</u>. see the Schemes there.

May-dew examin'd by various Experiments, by M. *Henshaw,* 3. <u>33</u>.

Mechanical Principles in a Geometrical method, explicating the nature or operation of Plants, Animals, 8. <u>325</u>.

Medicins in *China* consist for the most part of Simples, Decoctions, Cauteries, Frictions, without the use of Blood-letting, 14. <u>249</u>.

The *Physitians* there, commended for speedy Cures, and easie, *ibid.*

Mediterranean Sea, whether it may be join'd with the Ocean, debated, 3.<u>41</u>.

Micrography epitomized, 2. <u>27</u>.

M. *Auzout*'s Objections to a part of it; vid. the new way of grinding Spherical Glasses by a Turn-lath, 4. <u>57</u>.

M. *Hooks* answer thereunto, 4. <u>64</u>. both at large.

Mercury-Mines in *Friuli,* and the way of getting it out of the earth, 2. <u>21</u>.

Mineral Inquiries, see Directions, Engins, Artificial Instruments.

Mineral at Liege yielding Brimstone and Vitriol; and the way of extracting them, 3. <u>35</u>.

How Adits and *Mines* are wrought at Liege, 5. <u>79</u>.

A Stone in *Sueden* yielding Sulphur, Vitriol, Allum and Minium, and how, 21. <u>375</u>.

See *Kircher*'s Mundus Subterraneus abbr. 6. <u>109</u>.

Monsters, a Calf deform'd, and a great stone found in a Cows womb, *n.* 1.<u>10</u>.

a *Colt* with a double eye in one place, 5. <u>85</u>.

Moons Diameter how to be taken, and why increased in the Solar Eclipse of *Jun.* 22. 1666. *n.* 2. *p.* <u>373</u>.

see *Planets.*

What discoverable in the *Moon,* and what not.

Moons Eclipses how to take without inconvenience, 22. <u>387</u>.

Mulberry-Trees how to be cut low, and easie to be reach'd, for relief of Silk-worms, in *China,* 14. <u>249</u>.

in *Virginia,* 12. <u>202</u>.

see Silk.

N.

Nile's Inundations, the cause attributed to *Niter,* by *Dela Chambre;* opposed by *Vossius.* See both in the *List of Books,* 14. <u>251</u>. and 17.<u>304</u>.

The *North-Countries* of *Poland, Sweden, Denmark,* &c. are warm'd by the influence of the *Royal Society,* 19. <u>344</u>.

{403}

O.

Ocean, what Seas may be joined with it, 3. <u>41</u>.

Opticks, Campani's Glasses do excell Divini's; 'tis easie by them to distinguish people at four Leagues distance, 2. <u>131</u>. and 12. <u>209</u>.

What they discover in *Jupiter* and *Saturn,* 1. <u>1</u>. and <u>2</u>.

The proportions of Apertures in Perspectives reduced to a Table by M.*Auzout,* 4. <u>55</u>.

Animadverted upon by M. *Hook,* 4. <u>69</u>.

How to illuminate Objects to whatsoever proportion, proposed by M.*Auzout,* 4. <u>75</u>.

Hevelius, Hugenius, and some in *England,* endeavour to improve Optick Glasses, 6. <u>98</u>.

Seigneur *Burattini*'s advance in the same inquired after, 19. <u>348</u>.

some answer to it from *Paris,* 22. <u>374</u>.

See a further examination by a severe History of Tydes, Winds, and other circumstances directed, *n.* 17. *n.* 18. *n.* 21.

Trees of Oak how found under-ground in Moors or Marishes, 18. 323.

Thee, in *China* and what; how exchanged there for dried leaves of Sage by the *Dutch,* 14. 249.

W.

Whale-fishing about *Bermudas,* and *New England,* how it is performed, *n.*1. 11. *n.* 8. 132.

Wind, how to be raised by the fall of water, without any Bellows, 2. 25. shewed in a draught.

Worms, that eat holes in stones, feeding on stone, 28. 321.

{405}

The more
NATURAL METHOD.

I. A Natural History of all Countries and Places, is the foundation for solid Philosophy, *See* Directions, Inquiries, and Instructions for a Natural History of a Countrey, *n.* 11. *p.* 186.

See it in part exemplified in the *History of England,* begun by Dr. *Merret*in his *Pinax,* 20. 364.

See the cause of Tydes proposed by D. *Wallis,* 16. 263.

See the further Examination by a severe History of Tydes, Winds, and other Concomitants or Adherents, directed, *n.* 17. *n.* 18, *n.* 21.

See the Inquiries concerning the Seas, and Sea-waters, *n.* 18. 315.

See Directions for Seamen bound for far Voyages, 8. 140.

Kircher's Account of the Subterraneous World, 6. 109.

Mr. *Boyle*'s Directions and Inquires touching Mines, 19. 330.

Philosophical Directions and Inquiries for such as Travel into *Turky, n.*20. 300.

The Relation of M. *de Bourges,* 18. 324.

M. *Thevenots* Relation of divers curious Voyages, &c. more particularly of *China,* 24. 248.

The causes of the inundation of the *Nile,* disputed by *Dela Chambre* and*Vossius.* In the *List of Books.*

See Mr. *Boyle*'s Mechanical Deductions, and Chymical Demonstrations of the *Origine of Forms and Qualities,* 11. 191.

See the Application of these Mechanical Principles more particularly to the Nature, Operation, and Generation of Plants and Animals, and to our humane Contexture, in a Geometrical method, by *Hon. Fabri,* 18. 325.

See Mr. *Boyle*'s History of Cold and Thermometers, *n.* 1. *p.* 8. *n.* 3. *p.* 46.

The History of Winds and Weather, and all changes of the Air (especially in relation to the weight) observable by the Baroscope, *n.* 9. *n.* 10,*n.* 11.

Light, some special search into the causes, and some peculiar Examples.*See* above in *Light.*

Petrification sollicited, see Petrification, Stone.

The Earths Diurnal Rotation, see Earth *suprá.*

Adventurous Essayes in Natural Philosophy, see *Guarini,* 20. 365.

Earthquakes, and their Concomitants observed, *n.* 10. *n.* 11.

The effects of Thunder and Lightning, examin'd, see *Thunder, n.* 13. 222.*n.* 14. 247.

The raining of Ashes and Sand at great distance from the Mount *Vesuvius,* see *Raine,* 21. 377.

Springs, and Waters of peculiar Note, see *Springs.*

Insects in Swarms how begotten; pernicious, and how destroyed, 8. 137.

Monsters, or Irregularities in Nature. The *Calf, Colt,* suprá.

Four Suns at once, and two strange Rainbows, 13. 219.

See the statical position and tendency or gravitation of Liquids, in M.*Boyle*'s *Hydrostatical Paradoxes,* 8. 145.

See in M. *Hooks* Micrography, a History of minute Bodies, or rather of the minute and heretofore unseen parts of Bodies; it being a main part of Philosophy, by an artificial reduction of all gross parts of Nature to a closer inspection.

Medicinals, see Medicine. Physitians, *China.* Friction, Dr. *Sydenham.* Dr.*Lower*, Friction, *suprá. n.* 4. 77. *n.* 12. 206.

Anatome, see *Steno de Musculis & Glandulis.*

How a juyce in the stomack dissolves the shells of Crafishes, *ibid.*

Graeff *de Succo Pancratico*,

that Flesh hath Vessels, *n.* 18. 316.

Blood degenerated to resemble milk, *n.* 6. 117.

The Transfusion of blood, 20. 353.

The organ and nature of *Taste*, 20. 366.

{406}

Salt too much stiffens and destroys the Body, 8. 138.

II. *Singularities* of Nature severely examin'd.

The ordering of *Kermes* for Color. *n.* 20. 362.

How the *Salamander* quencheth Fire, and lives by licking the Earth. *n.* 21.377.

Whether Swallows do lie under water in Winter, and revive in Summer?*n.* 19. 350.

Whether the *Hungarian Bolus* like the *Armenus*? 1. 11.

Rattle-Snakes how kill'd in *Virginia*, 3. 43.

Snakes and Vipers how they differ, see *Snakes* above.

The Qualities and Productions of *May-dew*, 3. 1.

Damps in Mines how they kill, 3. 44.

Teeth growing in aged persons, 21. 380.

Steams and Expirations of the Body how stopp'd; and the stoppage dangerous or mortal, 8. 138.

Shining Worms in Oysters, 12. 203.

III. *Arts*, or Aids for the discovery or use of things Natural. *See* Artificial Instruments in the *Table.*

Agriculture, *see* the Inquiries, 5. 91.

English Vineyards vindicated, see in the *Catalogue of Books.*

Geometry, see *Euclid* methodized for Facility, *Fermat: in the Catalogue of Books.*

Astronomy, see Astronomical

Remarks. *Bullialdus, Hevetius, Comets,Planets, Saturn, Jupiter, Mars, Sun, Moon, Eclipses.*

Opticks *see* that Head in the *Table.*

Picture, *see* that Head in P. and *Felibien* in the *Catalogue of Books.*

How to paint Marbles within, *see* the Head *Marble.*

Pendulum Watches to ascertain *Longitudes* at Sea, 1. 13.

Whale-fishing about *Bermudas*, 1. 11. and 8. 132.

Silk-trade sollicited in *France*, *Virginia*, see *Silk* in the *Table.*

Eeles how to be found in Frosts, 17. 323.

Winds raised to blow by the fall of water without Bellows, 2. 25. shew'd in a *Cutt.*

Elephants enraged, how to escape or subdue, 18. 328.

Seas and vast waters, whether they may be united to the main Ocean, 3.41.

To proportion the distance necessary to burn Bodies by the Sun; and shewing, why the Reflections from the Moon and other Planets do not burn, 4. 69.

The Art of making *Salt-Peeter*, as practised in the *Mogols* Dominions, 6.103.

To make *China*-Dishes, 14. 249.

expected from Seigneur *Septalio* to be made in *Europe*, 7. 127.

To convey blood of one Animal, or other Liquors, into the blood of another Animal, 20. 353.

To preserve Ice and Snow by Chaffe, 8. 138.

To preserve Ships from being Worm eaten, 11. 190.

To preserve Birds taken out of the Eggs, or other small *Fætus*'s, for Anatomical, or other Discoveries, 12. 199.

To allay the heat in hottest Summer, for Diet or Delight, 15. 255.

Remedies against extream Cold suggested, 21. .

Trees of Oak as black as Ebony discover'd, and taken up out of Moors and Marshes in draughty weather, 11. .

Note,

That though in this last Head there is repeated the *Transfusion* of Blood, because the Operation is an Art requiring diligence, and a practised hand to perform it for all advantagious Discoveries, and so to be distinguish'd from the *Anatomical* Account; yet that there is not affected noise and number, may well appear by reviewing and comparing the particulars of *Artificial Instruments* in the {407} *Table,* where sometimes one Engin or Instrument may minister Aid to discover a large branch of Philosophy, as the *Baroscope,* an *Optick Glass,* &c.

And very particularly M. *Rook's* directions for Seamen, which specifies Instruments, may hereunto belong.

And sometimes in one of the Discourses herein mention'd, and abbreviated, there are almost as many Artificial Inventions, as Experiments; as in Mr. *Boyle's* Hydrostatical Experiments: Besides all the Chymical Operations, recited in the *Treatise* of the *Origine of Forms,* &c.

Οὐκ ἐν τῷ μεγάλῳ τὸ εὖ, ἀλλ' ἐν τῷ εὖ τὸ μέγα.

ERRATA.

Pag. 392. lin. 23. blot out, *as.* ibid. lin. 24. read *of the Soul.*

FINIS.